MW01631319

Art of the Himalayas

Art of the Himalayas

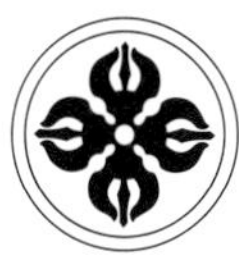

TREASURES FROM NEPAL AND TIBET

by Pratapaditya Pal

with Contributions from Ian Alsop, Heather Stoddard, and Valrae Reynolds

HUDSON HILLS PRESS • NEW YORK
IN ASSOCIATION WITH
THE AMERICAN FEDERATION OF ARTS

First Edition

Published in the United States by Hudson Hills Press, Inc., Suite 1308, 230 Fifth Avenue, New York, NY 10001-7704.

Editor and Publisher:
Paul Anbinder

Copy Editor: Andrea P.A. Belloli

Proofreader: Fronia W. Simpson

Indexer: Gisela S. Knight

Designer: Binns & Lubin/
David Skolkin

Composition: Trufont Typographers

Manufactured in Japan by Toppan Printing Company

Distributed in the United States, its territories and possessions, Canada, Mexico, and Central and South America by Rizzoli International Publications, Inc.
Distributed in the United Kingdom and Eire by Shaunagh Heneage Distribution.
Distributed in Japan by Yohan (Western Publications Distribution Agency).

Library of Congress Cataloguing-in-Publication Data

Pal, Pratapaditya.
Art of the Himalayas : treasures of Nepal and Tibet / by Pratapaditya Pal with Valrae Reynolds. — 1st ed.
p. cm.
Catalogue of an exhibition organized by the American Federation of Arts, presented at the Newark Museum, Portland Art Museum, Helen Clay Frick Foundation, and Virginia Museum of Fine Arts.
Includes bibliographical references and index.
1. Art, Nepali—Exhibitions. 2. Art, Hindu—Nepal—Exhibitions. 3. Art, Buddhist—Nepal—Exhibitions. 4. Art, Tibetan—Exhibitions. 5. Art, Hindu—Tibet—Exhibitions. 6. Art, Buddhist—Tibet—Exhibitions. 7. Zimmerman, Jack—Art collections—Exhibitions. 8. Zimmerman, Muriel—Art collections—Exhibitions. 9. Art—Private collections—United States—Exhibitions. I. Reynolds, Valrae. II. American Federation of Arts. III. Title.
N7310.8.N4P33 1991
709′.5496′07473—dc20
91-71551
CIP

ISBN: 1-55595-066-3 (alk. paper)

This catalogue has been published in conjunction with *Art of the Himalayas: Treasures from Nepal and Tibet*, an exhibition organized and circulated by the American Federation of Arts, with generous support from the National Patrons of the AFA.

EXHIBITION TOUR

Newark Museum, New Jersey
January 5–March 1, 1992

Portland Art Museum, Oregon
March 29–May 24, 1992

Phoenix Art Museum, Arizona
June 21–August 16, 1992

The Helen Clay Frick Foundation, Pittsburgh
September 13–November 8, 1992

Virginia Museum of Fine Arts, Richmond
February 28–April 25, 1993

Pacific Asia Museum, Pasadena
May 22–July 31, 1993

Tampa Museum of Art, Florida
September 5–October 31, 1993

Founded in 1909, the American Federation of Arts is a nonprofit educational organization that serves the visual arts community. Its primary activity is the organization of exhibition and film programs that travel throughout the United States and abroad.

Publication Coordinator:
Michaelyn Mitchell

Contents

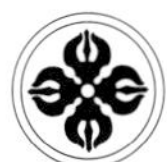

Acknowledgments

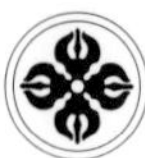

Art of the Himalayas presents an unparalleled group of works attesting to the incredible richness and diversity of both the culture and the art of Nepal and Tibet. Dating from as early as A.D. 1004, the paintings, sculptures, textiles, and drawings in the exhibition, all drawn from the extraordinary Zimmerman Collection, are made available to a national audience for the first time through the American Federation of Arts. We wish to extend our deepest gratitude to the Zimmermans for their generosity in loaning their treasures for the national tour this publication accompanies, and for their gracious cooperation throughout the organization of the project.

Next our appreciation goes to Pratapaditya Pal, Senior Curator, Indian and Southeast Asian Art, Los Angeles County Museum of Art. A most distinguished expert on the art of this region and a great admirer of the Zimmermans' collection, Dr. Pal was the ideal curator for this exhibition, and we were delighted when he agreed to join forces with us. We also want to thank the other contributors to the catalogue: Valrae Reynolds, Curator of Asian Art Collections, the Newark Museum; Ian Alsop, Editor, Classical Newari Lexicon Project; and Heather Stoddard, Head, Tibetan Department, the National Institute of Oriental Languages, Paris.

As usual, the entire AFA staff has participated in the realization of this project with enthusiasm and hard work, and their contribution is recognized with gratitude. A few people, though, should be singled out because their efforts and expertise were central to this exhibition. They include Marie-Thérèse Brincard, Curator; Michaelyn Mitchell, Head of Publications; Carol Farra, Registrar; Deborah Notkin, Publication/Exhibition Assistant; and Julie Min, Exhibition Scheduler. J. David Farmer, Director of Exhibitions; Bob Workman, Assistant Director of Exhibitions; and Jillian W. Slonim, Public Information Director, were also significantly involved in both the exhibition and this publication.

Special recognition for their work on the book is also due Paul Anbinder of Hudson Hills Press, our copublisher; Andrea P.A. Belloli, the editor; and David Skolkin, the designer.

Last, but certainly not least, our deep appreciation goes to the national patrons of the AFA, a loyal group of friends whose contributions made this exhibition possible.

Serena Rattazzi
Director
The American Federation of Arts

Preface

The name Zimmerman is now familiar to all lovers of Himalayan art. For the last two decades, every major exhibition of the arts of either Tibet or Nepal, both in America and Europe, has invariably included outstanding sculptures and paintings from the Zimmerman Collection. In fact, it would not be an exaggeration to say that, as far as the arts of Nepal and Tibet are concerned, the name Zimmerman has become synonymous with quality.

The Zimmermans' initial encounter with Himalayan art occurred at the first international exhibition of Nepali works organized in 1964 for Asia House Galleries, New York, by Stella Kramrisch. Only a few weeks before the show's opening the Zimmermans had heard of Nepal for the first time from a friend who had moved to that country. Walking past the old Asia House on 64th Street, they recognized the name on the exhibition banner and walked into the gallery out of idle curiosity. For Mr. Zimmerman, this was a mesmerizing and memorable experience. This present exhibition is the result of that chance encounter more than twenty-five years ago with the beautiful and powerful works of art seen that day.

Curiously, Mrs. Zimmerman, who was the artist in the family, did not share her husband's instant admiration for what appeared to her as exotic and somewhat bizarre forms. She is an accomplished potter, and her love was ceramics. It took her several years to begin to share her husband's growing obsession and to become accustomed to seeing Himalayan bronzes adorn the shelves with her own creations. By the time I met the Zimmermans in 1969, she had become no less enchanted by the art and is probably even more emotionally attached to the collection today than is her husband.

A glance through Kramrisch's 1964 catalogue demonstrates how unfamiliar Nepali art was to Americans at that time. While a very few museums, such as the Museum of Fine Arts, Boston, had sizable collections, most institutions collecting Asian art had only modest holdings of either Nepali or Tibetan art. This was generally true of private collectors as well. Although the names of a number of private lenders appear in the 1964 catalogue, they could hardly be considered major collectors of Himalayan art. Some, like George P. Bickford of Cleveland, were primarily collectors of Indian art and happened to own a few Himalayan objects, while several of the other lenders were dealers.

As a matter of fact, interest in the arts of both Nepal and Tibet is rather recent. Both countries discouraged foreign visitors, particularly Westerners, until after the Second World War. Nepal opened up only in the early 1950s after the authoritarian Rana regime was overthrown and democracy introduced. Soon thereafter, America rushed in with aid, and Nepali art began to flow out of the country. When I first visited Nepal in 1959, old metal statues were still sold in the bazaars by weight rather than as objects of art.

Tibet was even less well known except as the mysterious Shangri-La made famous by Ronald Colman in the movie *Lost Horizon.* The country continued to remain closed to all foreigners until the 1980s, even though the Tibetan diaspora had begun in the late fifties after the Chinese occupation and flight of Tibet's legitimate ruler, the Dalai Lama. This upheaval led to both the destruction and the abandonment of Tibetan monasteries, and Tibetan art began to reach western art markets. The Chinese Cultural Revolution did further damage, resulting in the dispersal of still more Tibetan art to the voracious markets of Europe and America. After the Chinese opened Tibet up in order to exploit its potential for tourism, more westerners became familiar with the art. As a result, demand grew and prices escalated. While in the sixties America did not allow its citizens to trade with China, Tibetan goods were not contraband. America also surreptitiously supported the Tibetans, particularly the Khampas, in their struggle against the Chinese while accepting China's occupation.

In the late sixties, when I was looking for material for the first Tibetan art exhibition at Asia House Galleries, the number of private collectors of Tibetan art was minuscule. Apart from Stella Kramrisch herself, whose appreciation of Himalayan art went back to the twenties, when she moved from Europe to India, the only other private collections I knew of were in New York. One of them, the Roerich Collection, had been assembled by George Roerich and his family in India in the thirties and forties; it is now at Brandeis University, Boston. Another large collection had been formed by Mme. Jacques Marchais and is still displayed in her original house on Staten Island. A third collection of significant Nepali and Tibetan material was with Alice and Nasli Heeramaneck, the well-known dealers.

Every dealer is a collector at heart (and vice versa), and, more than some others, the Heeramanecks have always been torn between their passion for collecting and their need to earn a living. It was a perspicacious Nasli who recognized the value of a large group of Tibetan *thankas* that were exhibited in the late fifties in a gallery of well-known western art in New York but that failed to sell. The paintings were from the famous collection of the celebrated Italian Tibetologist Giuseppi Tucci and had been published in his monumental *Tibetan Painted Scrolls* (1949). Tucci had formed this collection in Tibet in the course of several trips during the thirties and forties. On the last day of the exhibition, Nasli walked into the gallery and bought the whole lot. When I first met him in New York in 1964, he had not parted with any of them. Subsequently, one group was acquired by the Los Angeles County Museum of Art and another by the Virginia

Museum of Fine Arts, Richmond, but the bulk of the Tucci Collection is now with Robert Ellsworth.

When Nasli Heeramaneck arrived in this country from Bombay, India, in the early thirties, the only museums that were seriously interested in Himalayan art were the Museum of Fine Arts, Boston, and the Newark Museum. The person in charge of the Indian collections (which have traditionally included the arts of Nepal and Tibet) at Boston was the great scholar Ananda K. Coomaraswamy, whose collection the museum had acquired in 1917. It was largely his personal interest in the arts of the Himalayas that gave the museum an early lead in this area. Indeed a bronze Nepali bodhisattva from the Boston collection published in Coomaraswamy's 1929 *History of Indian and Indonesian Art* remained a paradigm of Nepali sculpture until Kramrisch's exhibition in 1964.

The Newark Museum's association with Tibet and its art has been the longest and closest, which is why it is one of the most important repositories of Tibetan art, artifacts, and ethnic material in the world today. This association began with a chance encounter between Dr. Albert L. Shelton and Edward N. Crane on a boat crossing the Pacific Ocean. The former was an American missionary who worked in the mission hospital in the Tibetan city of Batang and the latter a founding trustee of the Newark Museum. Crane arranged for an exhibition of Shelton's collection of Tibetan objects in 1911; this was probably the first display of this kind of material anywhere in the United States. Later the museum acquired the collection. It is particularly appropriate, therefore, that the Zimmerman Collection should begin its national tour some eight decades later at the Newark Museum.

The Zimmerman Collection is rich in the arts of both Nepal and Tibet and includes an extraordinary range of material of high quality. The holdings are particularly strong in Nepali bronzes and paintings, the latter being rather a rare commodity. Even by the early seventies it had become difficult to find outstanding examples of Nepali art, and today, when a few pieces do come onto the market, the prices are usually prohibitive. As the Zimmermans will be the first to admit, for them the golden age of collecting was the late sixties. Mr. Zimmerman still recalls how he bought three paintings literally off the street: "I remember once walking down Madison Avenue and meeting a hippie. He had three Tibetan paintings rolled up under his arm. We unrolled them on the street, I asked the price, and we struck a bargain." This was in the days when America was becoming more deeply involved in the Vietnam War and droves of young Americans were becoming disillusioned with their government's policy. Kathmandu, the capital of Nepal, became the Mecca of the counterculture. By the mid-seventies, however, some of the so-called hippies had become more business minded and had begun asking Madison Avenue prices for objects they had acquired in Nepal. Until Tibet became accessible, Kathmandu was the major center for trade in

Tibetan objects. Moreover, Nepal did not restrict Tibetan art leaving the country. Today, Tibetan art continues to flow into the Western market in a steady stream, principally through Chengdu, China, but Nepali art is a mere trickle. While it would be impossible to assemble a Nepali collection like that of the Zimmermans, forming a similar Tibetan collection would be only a little easier.

Working with the Zimmermans on this project has been a delight. Both have been most cooperative in the selection of objects, which was not an easy task. The primary criterion for inclusion was aesthetic quality rather than art-historical or iconographic significance. Western audiences are so concerned with the religious content of the arts of some of the Asian cultures that they tend to overlook their creative and aesthetic aspects. Awesome as their spiritual power is, the objects are also visually delightful, a sentiment shared by the entire Zimmerman family, which derives both inspiration and pleasure from the collection. Mr. Zimmerman has been particularly helpful in providing much useful information about individual pieces, reading this manuscript, and making helpful comments.

Particularly gratifying has been the cooperation of three distinguished colleagues in writing the present catalogue. Valrae Reynolds, Curator of Asian Art Collections, the Newark Museum, contributed the section on images made with fabrics and threads; Heather Stoddard, Head, Tibetan Department, the National Institute of Oriental Languages, Paris, read and translated the Tibetan inscriptions; and Ian Alsop, Editor, Classical Newari Lexicon Project, along with his colleagues in Nepal, provided similar services for the inscriptions on the Nepali objects. Their contributions, I am sure, will considerably enhance the usefulness of this volume.

In order to avoid confusion for most readers and to be consistent, the names of all deities, as well as technical terms, are given in their Sanskrit forms for both Nepal and Tibet. Where necessary, Tibetan names have been added in both their phonetic and properly transliterated forms. No changes have been made in the system of transliteration followed by the scholars in the two appendices, however.

It is a pleasure to thank several individuals at the American Federation of Arts, New York. The project was initiated by the organization's former director, Myrna Smoot, and has continued to receive support from her successor, Serena Rattazzi. I also deeply appreciate the cheerful cooperation I have received from Marie-Thérèse Brincard, Curator, and Michaelyn Mitchell, Head of Publications.

In California I would like to acknowledge the support of Earl A. Powell, III, Director, Los Angeles County Museum of Art, and of that museum's Board of Trustees. Andrea P.A. Belloli has much improved the text with her judicious editing. I would also like to express my appreciation to my wife for providing me with nourishment for my body while my mind grappled with matters of the spirit.

Pratapaditya Pal
Los Angeles, February 1991

Art of the Himalayas

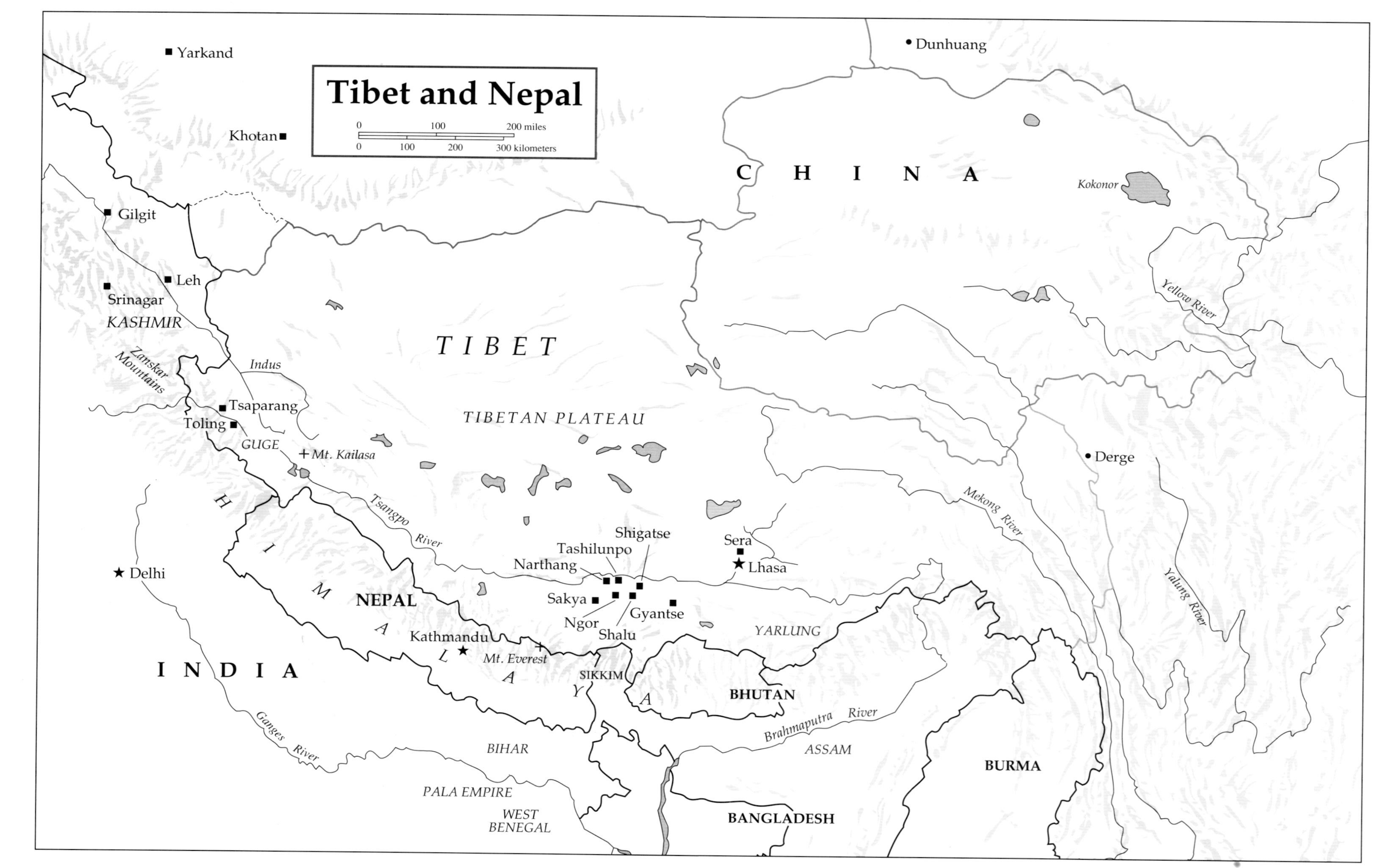

Tibet and Nepal
0 100 200 miles
0 100 200 300 kilometers
Yarkand
Khotan
Dunhuang
C H I N A
Kokonor
Yellow River
Gilgit
Leh
Srinagar
KASHMIR
Zanskar Mountains
Indus
T I B E T
TIBETAN PLATEAU
Tsaparang
Toling
GUGE
Mt. Kailasa
Tsangpo River
Derge
Mekong River
Yalung River
Shigatse
Tashilunpo
Narthang
Sera
Lhasa
Sakya
Ngor
Shalu
Gyantse
YARLUNG
Delhi
H I M A L A Y A
NEPAL
Kathmandu
Mt. Everest
SIKKIM
BHUTAN
I N D I A
Ganges River
BIHAR
Brahmaputra River
ASSAM
BURMA
PALA EMPIRE
WEST BENEGAL
BANGLADESH

Himalayan Art

AN INTRODUCTION

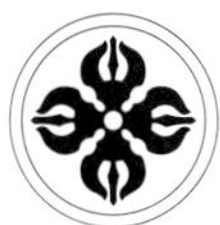

The Deity who assumes innumerable forms,
And has no form, is one and the same
Purusa, and to worship in either way
Leads to the same liberation.

A. K. Coomaraswamy

Neither passion nor absence of passion is found there,
nor yet a middle state. Because of its freedom
from all three the Innate is called perfect enlightenment.

Hevajratantra

The two Himalayan countries whose art is represented in this exhibition and publication are Nepal and Tibet. Though Nepal is a sovereign state, Tibet is now part of China. However, during the period when the art represented in the Zimmerman Collection was created, Tibet too was an independent nation, although the Chinese had exerted some political influence on the country for centuries.

Tibet constitutes a much larger geographical area than Nepal, stretching from Indian Ladakh in the west to the Chinese provinces of Sichuan and Yunnan in the east. In the north too it has a long common border with China and in the south with Nepal, Bhutan, and India. The population of Tibet is much more homogenous than that of Nepal, which is a multiracial society. Tibetan is the principal language in Tibet; it is also spoken in Ladakh and such contiguous areas as Zanskar and Spiti, which have closer cultural ties with Tibet than with India. Indeed the influence of Tibetan civilization extended far beyond her borders, and some of the objects included in this exhibition may have been made in areas outside them.

Nepal is multilingual, and the present-day lingua franca known as Nepali or Gorkhali has little or no significance in relation to its art. Virtually all the Nepali art in this exhibition was created by a minority community known as the

Newars, who were—and still are—concentrated in the small area known as the Kathmandu Valley, almost in the heart of the country. Indeed until fairly recent times the name Nepal applied only to this valley.

The Newars have also played eminent commercial and artistic roles in Tibet. This is only one reason why it is frequently difficult to determine whether an object was made in Nepal by a Newari artist and taken to Tibet or whether it was produced in Tibet itself. In Lhasa, Sakya, Gyantse, Shigatse, and other important Tibetan towns and monastic centers live settled communities of Newari artisans and merchants. Another reason is that Buddhism is the principal religion of the Tibetans as well as the Newars, although some of the latter are Hindus. Today Nepal is regarded as a Hindu state, but the country's artistic heritage indicates that for the greater part of its history Buddhism was no less important or popular.

Both Hinduism and Buddhism originated in India, although Lumbini, the birthplace of the Buddha, is now within Nepal's borders. While it is not known when exactly the two religions established themselves in Nepal, by the fifth century A.D., when the Lichchhavi dynasty had become well entrenched, both faiths were flourishing in the valley. They continued to coexist and prosper until the eighteenth century, when Hinduism began to flex its muscles with the foundation of the present Shah dynasty. This is also when the influence of the Newars began to diminish in Nepali life and culture. Nonetheless both religions have had to exist in close proximity, and there is nothing to indicate that the cohabitation has not been harmonious. Anyone visiting the principal Nepali towns—Kathmandu, Patan, and Bhaktapur—will notice how Hindu temples and Buddhist monasteries rub shoulders with one another.

Tibet has remained predominantly Buddhist. Buddhism was officially introduced from India in the seventh century A.D. After a setback in the ninth century, it was revived through the efforts of several Tibetan scholars and the Indian monk Atīśa Dīpaṅkara Śrījñāna (982–1054), who went to Tibet in 1042 and died there. Some of the older, native Tibetan beliefs and religious practices, strongly influenced by Buddhism, have survived in the religion known as Bon. Buddhism proved to be a much more powerful force in Tibet than in Nepal and came to dominate almost every aspect of Tibetan life, including politics; both political and economic power came to be concentrated in the Buddhist monasteries in Tibet in a way that was unknown in Nepal. Naturally, Buddhism developed along different lines in both countries so their Buddhist arts, despite their commonalities, differ significantly.

Tibet has always had direct relations with China that have resulted in the enrichment of both cultures. Sino-Tibetan contacts were particularly fruitful for the history of Tibetan painting, while from the Mongol period of Chinese history—the thirteenth century—on, Tibetan Buddhism became a strong presence in the imperial court and capital. When the Mongol emperor Kublai Khan (1216–1294) requested the hierarch of the Sakya monks (belonging to the Sa-skya monastery founded in 1073) to send him some qualified artists, the Tibetan lama dispatched eighty artists under the leadership of a young Newari master called Aniko or Anige. Until Buddhism's demise in India in the twelfth century, that country had been the principal source of inspiration for the Tibetans. For a time—probably through the fifteenth century—they turned to Nepal, where Buddhism was still intellectually alive. With the establishment of the three kingdoms of Kathmandu, Patan, and Bhaktapur, with their predominantly Hindu courts, Buddhism began to decline in Nepal. In Tibet, on the other hand, with the reforms of the charismatic monk-teacher Tsongkhapa (1357–1419), Buddhism continued to thrive, as is evident from the expansion of old monasteries, establishment of new ones, vast quantities of surviving art, and enormous compilations of exegetical literature.

Although Hinduism and Buddhism are regarded as two separate faiths in terms of both rituals and arts, they have strong similarities. The form of Hinduism which inspired the art of Nepal is based on two classes of textual authority known as *purāṇa,* or old tradition, and *tantra,* a word difficult to define. A generic term common to both Hindus and Buddhists, *tantra* embodies religious rites and rituals seeking spontaneous liberation, sometimes with an emphasis on apparently unorthodox practices. The puranic literature preserves more ancient and orthodox tradition, while newer beliefs and practices came to be classified under the rubric *tantra*. Most major *purāṇas* had been compiled by the eighth century, even though the tradition is more ancient. The ultimate textual authority of the Hindus is a body of literature known as the *Vedas,* which embodies the spiritual aspirations of the Aryans, the Indo-Europeans who came to India around 1500 B.C. Many of the Hindu gods still worshipped appear first in the *Vedas,* but as far as is known the Vedic Aryans did not use images. They did offer oblations (*homa*) to fire, however, a practice continued in later Hindu worship and adopted by the Buddhists, as is clear from many of the paintings in the Zimmerman Collection (see nos. 33, 34).

Philosophically, Hinduism is a monotheistic religion, but in practice it is pluralistic and polytheistic. Its essence may be summed up in the following Sanskrit sentence: *ekam sad biprā vahudā vadanti* (Truth is one but is called by many names). The Ultimate Being in Hinduism, though formless, can assume an infinite variety of forms. So the Hindus—like the Greeks and Romans, who also were Indo-Europeans—developed a pantheon of numerous gods and goddesses and created a body of mythology to go with them. Once they began installing images of their deities in temples and shrines, the iconographic descriptions of the deities and myths embodied in such texts as the *purāṇas* provided artists with a rich repertoire of subjects.

The principal gods forming a trinity in Hinduism are Brahma, the creator; Vishnu, the preserver; and Siva, the destroyer. Brahma, however, has remained a figurehead, like a constitutional monarch, and is not the focus of popular worship. Vishnu and Siva are the two principal deities in Nepal; the latter, in the form of Paśupatinātha, is the patron deity of the country. Both are represented in art in a number of forms which are particularly favored in Nepal (see nos. 5, 10, 16). The other deities encountered in Nepali art are Kārttikeya or Kumāra (see no. 11) and Gaṇeśa (see no. 17), both sons of Siva and his spouse, Pārvatī.

Pārvatī, known also as Umā and, generically, as Devī, Bhagavatī (simply "the Goddess"), or Śakti (Power or Energy), remains a potent force in Nepali Hinduism. In fact the worship of the Goddess may well be older than that of Siva or Vishnu. In Hindu religion, primarily because of the Sāṃkhya system of philosophy, which advocates a form of dualism, the feminine principle has remained of primary importance. According to Sāṃkhya, the male principle, known as Purusha (Male), remains inert and inactive, and it is Prakṛitī (Nature = Female) that is the active agent and source of creative energy (*śakti*). Although it originated much earlier, Sāṃkhya seems to have become a strong religious force around the middle of the first millennium A.D. This may be one reason why the new genre of literature known as *tantra* had to be created.

Unlike Hinduism, which has no known precise beginning, the origin of Buddhism is traced back to a human teacher called Gautama Buddha (Enlightened One), who lived sometime in the sixth–fifth century B.C. This would make him much older than Aristotle and Plato but slightly younger than Confucius and Lao-Tze. Basically a reformer, the Buddha found that the Vedic religion, with its rigid ritualism dominated by brahman priests, had become complex and meaningless to the masses, and so he advocated a simpler system based on certain fundamental ethical precepts and meditation. His disciples made his teachings the basis for what came to be known as *Buddha dharma,* or Buddhism.

The focal point of Buddhism was—and still is in Buddhist countries—the monastery. For centuries after its foundation, the aniconic, hemispherical structure known as a *stūpa* or *chaitya* in Sanskrit and *chöten* in Tibetan (see nos. 30, 71) remained the most visible material symbol of the faith. By the time of the Maurya emperor Aśoka (third century B.C.), sometimes characterized as the Buddhist Constantine, the religion was already becoming devotion- and ritual-oriented. This was inevitable among a largely illiterate and superstitious population for whom village deities and spirits were more important and relevant than abstract philosophical concepts, no matter how lofty. The modification and expansion of Buddhism were also intended in part to offset the tremendous surge of temple building and image worship by Hindus and Jains (members of a third Indian religion) around the time of the birth of Christ. Thus the Buddhists gradually introduced ideas of multiple buddhas and created a whole new class of beings called bodhisattvas. A bodhisattva is a person who has fulfilled all the requirements to be a Buddha, thereby attaining nirvana, or liberation from the chains of rebirth. He or she chooses to remain behind, however, to help the less fortunate to cross the river of *saṃsāra* (earthly existence). This concept, basic to Mahāyāna (Great Vehicle) Buddhism, enabled the Buddhists to create divine bodhisattvas who are the very embodiment of compassion. Principal among them are Avalokiteshvara (All-Seeing One), Vajrapāṇi (Thunderbolt Bearer), Mañjuśrī (Pleasant-Looking), and Maitreya (Friendly One, also Buddha-to-Be), all of whom are male. Among the female savior deities, the two most important are Tārā (Savioress) and Prajñāpāramitā (Wisdom that Saves). Prajñāpāramitā is also the personification of the most important philosophical text of the Mahāyāna, known as the *Prajñāpāramitā Sūtra of Eight Thousand Verses,* and is generally regarded as the Mother of All the Buddhas. Both in Nepal and Tibet, however, Avalokiteshvara and Tārā have remained the principal bodhisattvas.

Like the Hindus, the Buddhists were influenced by yogic and tantric ideas, which led to the development of the third stage of Buddhism known as Vajrayāna (Diamond or Thunderbolt Vehicle or Path). The word *vajra,* which means both "diamond" and "thunder," also signifies the instrument or emblem called a thunderbolt that was used by the Vedic god Indra and the Greek god Zeus. Like the stūpa in early Buddhism, the thunderbolt became the most potent symbol of Vajrayāna Buddhism. In its meaning as diamond, the word was considered an appropriate epithet to define the adamantine or indestructible character of the new system. Vajrayana Buddhism, also known as Mantrayāna because of its emphasis on *mantra* or incantation, represents the final, the most eclectic development in Buddhism.

Vajrayāna Buddhism basically posits that enlightenment can be achieved through the right combination of compassion (*karuṇā*) and wisdom (*prajñā*). Every male deity is an embodiment of compassion, while the goddesses symbolize wisdom, insight, or knowledge (intuitive rather than discursive). Central to Vajrayāna Buddhist praxis and common also to tantric Hinduism is the belief that personal salvation or enlightenment can be achieved through devotion to a personal tutelary divinity (Sanskrit: *ishṭadevatā*; Tibetan: *yi-dam*) who has his or her own mantra. This mantra can only be received from an appropriate teacher, preceptor, or spiritual counselor known as a guru. Like Hinduism, Vajrayāna Buddhism developed countless ritualistic systems and spiritual empowerments involving a wide variety of mantras, divinities, and mystical diagrams called mandalas to harness cosmic energy, as well as establish a homology between the adept and cosmic forces. The Hindu counterpart of the mandala is called the *yantra* (see no. 23).

There are other similarities between Hinduism and Buddhism that often make it difficult to distinguish between images of the two religions. Similar iconometric principles and theories of proportion are still employed by artists for the deities of both, as is clear from sketchbooks that have survived in Nepal and from the images themselves. In both religions the deities have peaceful and angry forms, although it will be clear to every viewer that there are more of the latter in Buddhism than in Hinduism and in Tibet than in Nepal. Both religions also make imaginative use of multiple limbs to demonstrate the cosmic powers of their deities. This may be the most distinctive difference between the Indic tradition of visualizing divine form and those of all other pantheistic religions.

Some of the other characteristic elements that distinguish deities of the Indic religious traditions, whether Hindu, Buddhist, or Jain, are also significant: The two earthly models for representing divine forms are the yogi and the king. The god, including a Buddha or a bodhisattva, is shown either sparsely dressed—as a meditating ascetic—or attired, bejeweled, crowned, and regally seated on a throne like a monarch. The most appropriate support for a deity, whether seated or standing, is a lotus, which in Indic tradition is the symbol par excellence of purity. It is in fact so ubiquitous that even human teachers, whether apotheosized or not, are shown on lotus supports. The two models, the yogi and the king, are often combined. For example, despite his matted hair, Siva can wear jewelry (see no. 16), and a Buddha may be crowned and ornamented (see no. 62). Apart from their ideal proportions, the deities are also distinguished by certain superhuman body marks, easily noticeable on Buddha images. Short, curly hair is mostly characteristic of buddhas. Another feature of the divinities of both religions is that they usually are envisioned as "immortal adolescents." Rarely is a deity depicted as a senior citizen, and even when a god does sport a beard, he appears not to reveal other evidence of old age.

A comparison of the images in the Zimmerman Collection demonstrates how, apart from employing similar aesthetic theories and iconographical concepts, the two faiths borrowed ideas from each other more directly. Thus while the god of wealth Kubera or Vaiśravaṇa is common to both, the Buddhists created yet another deity of riches called Jambhala. Lakshmī is the Hindu goddess of wealth and prosperity; her Buddhist counterpart is Vasudhārā (see no. 8). Siva's iconography contributed directly to such figures as Samvara and Hevajra, while Mahākāla, the important Vajrayāna protective deity, is in fact Siva as Bhairava in a Buddhist guise. The Vedic goddess of wisdom Sarasvatī has a place in both the Hindu and Buddhist pantheons. Yama, the Vedic and Hindu god of death, and Gaṇeśa, the remover of obstacles (*vighna*) in the Hindu pantheon, have more ambivalent positions in the Buddhist pantheon, however. Both are venerated by the Vajrayāna Buddhists, but both also are symbolized as death and obstacle, respectively. So the Buddhists created such deities as Yamāntaka (destroyer of Yama) and Vighnāntaka (destroyer of the obstacle symbolized by Gaṇeśa), while other divinities trample on Hindu deities as an obvious display of their superiority. Interestingly, after the disintegration of Buddhism on the subcontinent beginning in the twelfth century, many Buddhist deities were adopted into the Hindu pantheon as manifestations of Hindu divinities. The most classic instance is that of Tārā. While in Nepal gods such as Paśupatinātha and Chāṅgu Nārāyaṇa are revered by Buddhists, festivals of Matsyendranātha and Indra are observed by followers of both religions.

An image type encountered more often in Buddhist than in Hindu art consists of male and female divinities in sexual embrace. There are a large number of such forms in the Zimmerman Collection (see no. 19). In Tibetan the expression *yab-yum,* meaning "father-mother," is used to describe such images. Only one tantric Hindu sculpture in the collection (no. 21) shows two Hindu deities locked in such an embrace. The more common way to express the idea of nonduality in Hindu art is to depict them androgynously (no. 26) or as loving couple (no. 16). In Vajrayāna Buddhism, however, the sexual embrace symbolizes the concept of spontaneity *(sahaja)*, which characterizes the state of enlightenment achieved by the combination of wisdom (female) and compassion (male).

Whether Hindu or Buddhist or, for that matter, Bon art in both Nepal and Tibet consists of religious artifacts of various kinds. Principal among these are images of deities in metal, wood, stone, clay, and terra-cotta and paintings on cloth. Only metal and painted images are included in the Zimmerman Collection. Although in both countries there are life-size metal sculptures, the examples in the collection are of easily portable size. Both *cire perdu,* or lost-wax, casting and repoussé, or beaten-metal technique, were used to make metal objects. Tibetan bronzes display a greater variety of styles and of metal alloys than Nepali bronzes. Moreover, Tibetans reveal a greater penchant for brighter surfaces. While gilding was employed in both traditions, only in Tibet were the faces of figures painted with gold. Tibetans also painted their bronze figures more frequently than the Newars did. The most prominent colors were indigo and orange for the hair of benign and angry deities, respectively. In both countries metal images are also inlaid or encrusted with stones—such as opals, garnets, and turquoises—and pearls, but here the Tibetan taste for sumptuousness is much more evident.

Religious paintings of images and mandalas are called *paubhā* in Nepal and *thanka* or *thangka* in Tibet. (The Sanskrit word is *paṭa* or *paṭachitra.*) Although such painted images were used extensively in India by both Hindus and Buddhists, very few of any antiquity have survived. Thus Nepali and Tibetan painted images help us form some idea of how such paintings looked in India. In fact the early Kadampa-style Tibetan paintings from the eleventh through the thirteenth centuries—of which there are several fine examples in the Zimmerman Collection (see nos. 52–54)—are important evidence for determining the form and style of Buddhist paintings executed or hung on the walls of such famous monasteries as Nalanda and Vikramaśīlā in eastern India during the Pāla period (eighth–twelfth centuries). In both Tibet and Nepal the preferred support of painting was cotton or linen, as it was in India, and the medium was opaque watercolor. The Tibetans occasionally painted on silk (see no. 94), the common support for painting in China and Central Asia. Nepali *paubhās* were generally mounted only at the top and bottom on plain blue silk, which may have been the custom in India. Very likely the mode was also preferred in early Tibet, as is known from a few surviving *thankas* that have retained their original mounts. This is further corroborated by later *thankas* from the Sakyapa monasteries, where Nepalese influence has always been predominant. When exactly the Tibetans began using Chinese silks and brocades to mount their *thankas* is not known. Although most surviving examples with similar mounts are from the last three centuries, the practice may have begun earlier, for recent evidence makes it clear that the Tibetan fondness for Chinese materials goes back at least to the Tang period (see below, pp. 106–8). Tibetans also cover their painted images with a piece of soft silk tissue, a practice not familiar in Nepal but known in India. In addition to the *paubhā,* the Newars paint long, narrow, horizontal scrolls known as *bilaṃpau* that depict narrative subjects (see no. 51). A familiar type of painting in India and China, it seems not to have been adopted by the Tibetans with zeal. In Nepal such scrolls are brought out on special occasions to be hung on walls so viewers can follow the story as it is recited.

As with metal sculpture, in painting too Tibetan artists employed a more extensive repertoire and more varied styles than those in Nepal. Of course no Hindu subjects were represented in Tibet, but even if one takes both Hindu and Buddhist paintings of Nepal into consideration, the *thankas* display a greater thematic diversity. The Buddhist repertoire of Nepal is limited to a few major divinities preferred by the small community of Buddhist Newars, but Tibet developed a large number of major orders of Buddhism, each of which has its own systems of theology and rituals with distinct iconographic needs and emphasis. Moreover, the repertoire of Tibetan art was further expanded by the inclusion of a greater variety of local deities and spirits, more prolific use of mandalas or cosmic diagrams, and the inclusion of mortal teachers in the pantheon in a manner unparalleled in other Buddhist countries and certainly not among the Newars. The Tibetans also were much more eclectic in their aesthetic tastes, borrowing freely from both the Indian and Chinese traditions to create new pictorial manners of their own. For instance during the eleventh and twelfth centuries, while the Pāla style of eastern India was dominant in central Tibet, in the western regions of the country the principal artistic source was Kashmir. From the thirteenth century on, the Sakyapas showed a marked preference for Newari artists.

Tibetan art has also benefited from the country's contacts with Central Asia, particularly the ancient kingdom of Khotan. The extent of Central Asian influence on Tibetan culture in general and the visual arts in particular has yet to be properly assessed. While a number of paintings with Tibetan inscriptions have been discovered at Central Asian sites such as Dunhuang, little evidence of Central Asian painting or sculpture has been found in Tibet. An intriguing object in this regard is a small painting on silk in the Zimmerman Collection (no. 79). With its freely drawn figures in muted colors, the distinctive style of this painting is in some ways reminiscent of ninth–tenth-century paintings found in Central Asia. It could have been executed there by a Tibetan artist and brought to Tibet; it could have been drawn in Tibet following a Central Asian model; or it could have been rendered by a monk-artist from Central Asia who had migrated to Tibet.

While there is no doubt regarding the influence of Chinese aesthetics on Tibetan art, it is difficult to determine precisely when Tibetans began borrowing and exactly what they borrowed. Literary evidence is clear about the presence of Chinese artists and objects in the Tibetan capital as early as the seventh century. The earliest monastery in Tibet, founded at Samye in A.D. 775, is said to have been built in the Indian, Tibetan, and Chinese styles. Chinese artists were hired by monasteries to decorate their chapels with murals, Shalu and Gyantse being two of the best-known examples. A number of Chinese embroidered and woven images, some dating from the Song and Yuan periods, have emerged from Tibetan monasteries. However, the idea of depicting figures—particularly idealized representations of apotheosized mystics, teachers, and monks—in landscapes is the most significant contribution of Chinese art to Tibetan painting. These include representations of *arhats* (worthy of veneration, an ideal being in early Buddhism; *lohan* in Chinese), *mahāsiddhas* (great perfected ones, the ideal tantric practitioners), and Tibetan religious hierarchs. In recent years portraits of Tibetan teachers and monks have come to light that may date to as early as the eleventh century. All of these are depicted in the Kadampa style, however, and are strongly figurative. Only from the fourteenth century onward does one encounter portraits of *arhats* and *mahāsiddhas* in landscape settings that derive from the Chinese pictorial tradition. Well into the nineteenth century Tibetan artists continued to depict their teachers, as well as gods, buddhas, and narrative subjects, in brightly colored, highly imaginative landscape settings of pure fantasy whose style, however, has little to do with the original Chinese models.

Apart from painting religious subjects on cloth, artists in both countries developed a tradition of illuminating manuscripts. While Nepal at first adopted the Indian practice of writing on palm leaves, Tibetans had written on paper from the beginning of their historical period. Following the Indian model, they adopted the shape of the palm-leaf folio, but the size of their paper folios is much larger. As in India both the pages of Tibetan books and their wooden covers are embellished. Tibetans preferred to carve the outside of their covers and paint the inside. In Nepal early book covers are painted only on the inside, but later examples are adorned inside and out. The Zimmerman Collection includes a number of Nepali book covers from the seventeenth and eighteenth centuries that are interesting for their unusual and intriguing themes (see nos. 46, 48) and diverse representational styles.

Even more fascinating are the few examples of iconographic sketchbooks included in this exhibition. To date, most such books have come out of Nepal, and they are of considerable art-historical significance. Whenever these books have any text, it is in the Newari language, which means that the artists were all Newars. Some books, however, have notations and text in Tibetan as well, which indicates that the Newari artists worked for both their countrymen and Tibetan patrons. Moreover, the books often contain iconographic elements encountered only in Tibetan paintings. Such sketchbooks seem to have been the joint efforts of the Newari Buddhist priests called *vajrāchāryas,* who wrote the texts, and Newari artists, who made the sketches. Not only do these sketchbooks help us in identifying the complex figures of the Buddhist pantheon; they also demonstrate how artistic ideas and styles were transmitted from Nepal to Tibet.

Apart from cast and painted images, the Zimmerman Collection includes a variety of ritual objects from both countries. Generally, Tibetan ritual objects are more familiar in the West, because more have come out of that country than out of Nepal. Also Tibet seems to have a more diverse and richer repertoire of such objects. As is the case with their sculptures, Tibetans preferred more sumptuous surfaces for their objects, which are often luxuriously encrusted with stones. While some of the ritual objects in the exhibition, such as the priest's crown from Nepal (no. 13) and the bone apron and trident from Tibet (nos. 63, 78), are striking for the complexity of their forms or dramatic effect, others are interesting for their cultural significance. The brass waterpot from Nepal (no. 27) was once the personal property of a king, while the little gilt-copper *stūpa* (no. 30) commemorates the passage from life to death observed only by the Newars today, although at one time it may have been familiar in India.

Finally, a few works of art in the Zimmerman Collection may loosely be compared to European tapestries (see nos. 114–19). This kind of art seems not to have captured the imagination of the Newars, although it was popular in Tibet. As discussed below (see pp. 106–8), there were several different techniques of preparing such "threaded" images. Very likely China was the source for this kind of art, for it appears to have been unknown in India. The fact that no significant evidence of the tradition of woven, stitched, embroidered, or appliquéd images of deities has been found in Nepal, Sri Lanka, Burma, or Thailand further indicates that India had little to contribute to this highly sophisticated and fascinating art form.

Despite the remoteness and harshness of the terrain of the high Himalayas, the arts of Nepal and Tibet did not develop in splendid isolation. On the contrary, in addition to interacting with each other, both countries remained open to ideas from outside that contributed to enriching their artistic traditions. Both the Newars and the Tibetans are receptive and inventive people. The incredible richness and diversity of their artistic heritage as represented in the Zimmerman Collection amply attest to both their fecund imagination and their superb technical skill. It would be futile to try to understand the objects' iconographic complexity, but in this most permissive and eclectic age in art history, few viewers can remain unmoved by the delightfully expressive and dramatically exciting forms created by generations of unknown Himalayan artists.

While the ritual objects have utilitarian functions that often determine their forms, they are also embellished with symbolically significant motifs. Divine images, whether painted or sculpted, are created largely for devotional or meditational purposes. Although we view them today, in an artificial environment, as art, for their creators and patrons they were—and are—ostensible forms, or images, embodying the formless Absolute. They serve as a sort of aide-mémoire to help the devotee in his or her spiritual search. In the cultural and religious milieu in which they were fashioned, such images were more important than their makers, and hence rarely did an artist attach a signature to his work. None of the objects in the Zimmerman Collection, whether from Tibet or Nepal, ever decorated a wall or mantel, and all were primarily esteemed for their spiritual significance rather than their aesthetic allure. In this artistic tradition beauty is not admired for its own sake; the image is viewed by the devotee in a state of grace in which Beauty, Love, and Truth are not inseparable categories but rather three aspects of the Absolute or the spontaneous state of Enlightenment.

Art from Nepal

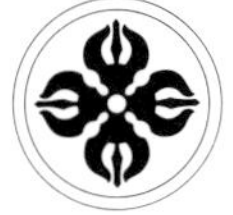

Art from Nepal

INTRODUCTION

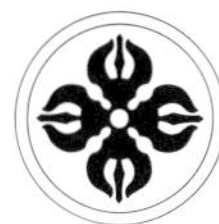

The kingdom of Ni-po-lo . . . is situated in the middle of snowy mountains and, indeed, presents an uninterrupted series of hills and valleys. . . . The inhabitants . . . are gifted with considerable skill in the arts. . . . Buddhist convents and the temples of the Hindu gods touch each other [in the kingdom].

Xuanzang

A wide variety of artworks from Nepal is represented in the Zimmerman Collection, including sculptures and ritual objects in metal, paintings on cloth, iconographic sketchbooks, and book covers in wood. Almost all these objects were made in the Kathmandu Valley by Newari artists between the seventh and nineteenth centuries.

The long history of Nepal may be divided as follows: Lichchhavi period (ca. 400–879/80); Transitional period (879/80–1200); Early Malla period (1200–1482); Later Malla period (1482–1768); and Shah period (1769–present). Some scholars refer to the second period as Ṭhākurī, but no such dynastic name is known from ancient sources. Very likely the kings who ruled from 879/80, when a new era, known as the Newari era, was inaugurated, until 1200 did have some connection with the Lichchhavi dynasty, even though we do not know what it was. From 1200 until 1768 all the kings used the epithet *malla,* meaning "warrior" or "wrestler." Until 1482 the Kathmandu Valley was ruled by one monarchy, but thereafter, until its reunification by the Gorkha invader Pṛithivī Nārāyaṇ Shāh from the west, the valley was divided among three city-states: Bhaktapur, Kathmandu, and Patan. The constant rivalry among the three kingdoms was culturally beneficial for Nepal, for each state tried to outshine the others in artistic and architectural achievements.[1]

Among its oldest inhabitants, the Newars probably settled in the valley in very early times. Apart from being expert craftsmen, they are also the area's principal farmers and traders. Traditionally, they have conducted all of Nepal's trade with Tibet, which was so lucrative that it sustained three kingdoms for almost three centuries. Since Nepal was situated on one of the trade routes between Tibet and India, a great deal of its revenue derived from custom and excise duties.[2] The Newars have always had good relations with the Tibetans. Not only are they predominantly Buddhist, but they are of Mongoloid stock, and their language has affinities with the Tibeto-Burman linguistic group.

No matter what their personal religious beliefs, Newari artists, who were usually Buddhists, worked for both Hindu and Buddhist patrons. This is clear from surviving sketchbooks, which often contain drawings of both Hindu and Buddhist deities, and also from the fact that Hindu and Buddhist objects do not reflect different styles. The same aesthetic norms, iconographic principles, and iconometric theories were applied to the images and themes of both faiths. Over the years each religion influenced the iconographic concepts of the other (see nos. 20, 21). Until the Shah dynasty gained power and the Hindus gained in strength, the two religions existed in relative harmony in a small area. Even today certain festivals such as those of the Buddhist Matsyendranātha and the Hindu Indrayātrā continue to be celebrated as national festivals.

Some of the objects in the Zimmerman Collection have inscriptions written in the Newari script, which is derived from the Indian Brahmi. Only the earliest inscription (no. 10) is in Sanskrit; the others, beginning from the fourteenth century, are all in Newari, although strongly influenced by Sanskrit. The writing in the sketchbooks is mostly in Newari with occasional Tibetan notations. When a date is contained in an inscription, the era used is the Newari one. Apart from giving us a precise date when the object was dedicated, the inscription may contain the name of the ruling monarch, the names of the donor and members of his family, and, occasionally, the name of the officiating priest who performed the dedication ceremony.[3] Seldom is the name of an artist or place mentioned. Most works were commissioned for specific religious ceremonies observed generally by the donors for good fortune, health, and long life. Only one Nepali object in the Zimmerman Collection was a royal commission (no. 27); all other donors were common citizens.

Sculptures and Ritual Objects

The reputation of Newari artists reached the Tang court in China as early as the seventh century, largely due to the observations of Wang Xuanze (Hsüan-tse), who twice visited the Nepali court during the reign of the Lichchhavi monarch Narendradeva (ca. A.D. 645–85). The Tang annals note that houses in Nepal were constructed of wood and the walls adorned with sculpture and painting, as may still be seen in the Kathmandu Valley.[4] These sources also speak of the capital's multistoried palaces in which there were "sculptures to make you marvel." They further note the Newari fondness for decorating sculptures with stones and pearls, a predilection that suited their work to the rich taste of their Tibetan neighbors. These references must be to metal sculptures, for to date no stone or wood figure is known to have been so ornamented. The Chinese ambassador particularly noted Newari artists' skill with metalwork, mentioning the elaborate copper waterspouts and golden *makaras*—mythical aquatic creatures—that adorned the roofs of buildings in Nepal.

Although the Newari artists of the Lichchhavi period followed the same basic iconographic principles and artistic norms that prevailed in northern India during the Gupta period (fourth–seventh centuries), the sculptures they created have a distinctive flavor and ethnic stamp, even if the differences cannot be verbalized easily. For instance, no one would mistake the unique early bronzes in the Zimmerman Collection (nos. 1–4) for work created anywhere else. The smooth, suave quality of the modeling and the expression of whimsy in the posture and attitude of some of the figures are typical local characteristics. The elegant Avalokiteshvara (no. 3), though modeled on a Gupta original from Sarnath, represents a bodhisattva type that became a classic form in Nepal. The Nepali version is different from the model in its figural proportions, details of clothing and ornaments, and facial features and expression.

Simplicity of both form and content are the salient characteristics of early Nepali sculptures in the Zimmerman Collection. And yet the lively variety of the forms and their intriguing iconography make them an exciting group of unconventional figures. Most of the sculptures are of small size, but they are exquisitely crafted. With their sustained quality and playful liveliness, these diminutive statuettes are among the finest examples of early Nepali sculpture.

The Newari penchant for the unusual is also evident in such bronzes of the Transitional period as the beautifully crafted Ratnapāṇi (no. 7) and Vasudhārā (no. 8). Ratnapāṇi is not frequently encountered in Nepali art, and Vasudhārā is presented in an unusual posture. This may also be the earliest known example of the six-armed form of the goddess in Buddhist art. Although this iconography is said to have originated in Kanchipuram in Tamilnadu, only a few Indian examples are known, and they are from eastern India and the twelfth century. In Nepal, Vasudhārā was popular among the Newars from the eleventh century on, but in all later depictions, whether in metal or in paintings, she is shown seated in the more graceful *lalitāsana* posture (see nos. 12, 34).

No less interesting are the two early repoussé objects in the collection (nos. 5, 10). This technique was perfected by the Newars as early as the Lichchhavi period. The architectural embellishments of Nepali buildings so admired by the

Chinese must have been made largely of gilded copper repoussé plaques, panels, spouts, and sheaths that still add so much luster to the valley's traditional architecture. Both repoussé objects display the finesse with which Newari artists produced such plaques. Because of the continued demand for repoussé work during the Later Malla period, as well as in Tibet, the Newari craftsmen's skill with this technique remained creative and vigorous until the present century, as is exemplified by four very different objects in the Zimmerman Collection (nos. 5, 10, 13, 22).

Bronzes of the Malla period show greater complexity and elaborateness in several ways. In contrast to the earlier period, the figures were more frequently gilded. (It is possible that some of the earlier bronzes were also gilded, but that the gilding wore off due to handling or burial in the ground.) However, a large number appear not to have been gilded at all. Very few Lichchhavi-period metal figures are encrusted with stones, but during the Malla period inlay became the norm. Increasingly after the twelfth century, the interest in the modeling of form was replaced by an interest in decorative surfaces. Finally, the iconographic repertoire expanded enormously, especially during the Later Malla period, when tantric cults seem to have become entrenched among both Buddhists and Hindus. There is a greater profusion of iconographically complex forms that required both imagination and technical dexterity.

While some of the earlier forms, such as Vasudhārā (no. 12), the simple bodhisattvas (no. 15), and Umā-Maheśvara (no. 16), remained stock motifs of Nepali art, one also encounters a wide variety of images with multiple limbs which presented artists with new challenges. Here again the Zimmerman Collection includes beautiful examples of familiar and conventional themes, as well as others that depict esoteric deities of the two faiths. These are astonishing as much for their bewilderingly rich iconography as for their ingenious craftsmanship. Indeed, metal representations of divinities belonging to the Hindu tantric pantheon (see nos. 21, 25) are particularly significant in that nothing quite like them is known in Indian Hindu imagery, although they are described in tantric texts originating in India. Often the deities' multiple arms, as well as their varied and dynamic postures, make these sculptures highly energized.

Two of the most charming sculptures in the collection represent mortals rather than immortals. One is of a male (no. 28) and the other of a female (no. 29), but the same basic scheme was employed for both. Each is identified in the dedicatory inscriptions, but it is unlikely that the portraits are realistic, although the woman's face seems more individualistic. Nepali portraiture remained limited to such idealized commemorative representations in metal or stone or to stereotyped depictions on *paubhās*. Nevertheless, these two metal portraits are among the finest known outside Nepal.

In addition to sculptures, the Zimmermans have collected a few interesting ritual objects that are as important for their rarity as for their artistic forms. These include a spectacular, uniquely Nepali Buddhist priest's helmet (no. 13), a rare tantric *yantra* (no. 23) used during worship of the great Hindu Goddess, a brass water pot once used by a king in his personal shrine (no. 27), and a miniature commemorative stūpa related to a rite of passage for the elderly which is still only performed by the Buddhist Newars today (no. 30).

Paintings and Drawings

The principal form of painting in Nepal consists of images of deities known as *paubhās.* Similar to *thankas,* they are in fact much rarer. The Zimmerman Collection includes a large number of *paubhās,* as well as some interesting iconographic sketchbooks, folios from illustrated books, two painted book covers, and a long scroll painting. The *paubhās* date from the fourteenth to the seventeenth centuries, and most are Buddhist. Indeed, compared to Buddhist *paubhās,* few Hindu examples have survived. Those that have are extremely important for the history of Hindu art and religion, since few similar paintings are known in India.

The Zimmerman *paubhās* representing Buddhist themes not only depict all the major forms popular with Newari Buddhists but are of exceptionally fine quality. Several contain dedicatory inscriptions that make it possible to date them precisely. Hence they constitute key documents for the history of Nepali painting. The subject matter usually consists of a group of divinities arranged either in a rectangular composition or in a mandala, a configuration of squares and circles. (It should be noted that simple rectangular arrangements can also be characterized as mandalas [see nos. 31, 37]). Generally, the register at the top of a Buddhist *paubhā* contains images of the five transcendental buddhas with one or two other buddhas, bodhisattvas, or solar and lunar deities. The bottom register is usually divided into three panels. In the two end panels are a scene of worship, in which a priest wearing a crown (see no. 13) offers oblations (*homa*) to the fire; and adoring members of the family. The scene in the middle panel varies. It may include representations of the seven precious jewels of Buddhism (see no. 34), images of protective deities (see no. 36), or other scenes (see no. 33). The portraits of priests and donors are always stereotyped. Indeed the conventionality of such scenes can be gauged from the early Sūryamaṇḍala (no. 33), presumably a Hindu painting though it includes the formulaic representation of a scene of worship with a Buddhist priest. In the top register of this *paubhā* are representations of the principal Hindu deities rather than buddhas.

Like the early Tibetan *thankas,* the Nepali *paubhās* are strongly figurative. When the principal deity is not shown within a mandala, he or she is usually placed within a very elaborate shrine. The shrine consists of ornately designed columns and arches with mythical creatures such as *makaras* or *kinnaras* (half-human, half-avian creatures that inhabit the realm between heaven and earth) and often the half-bird, half-human *garuḍa* at the apex. This kind of distinctive shrine with exquisite, intricate floriate decoration may be regarded as a hallmark of Nepali *paubhās* and is encountered on *thankas* where Nepali influence is predominant. Three of the *paubhās* in the Zimmerman Collection have such luxurious shrines enclosing the figures of the principal deities (nos. 31, 34, 37). Other figures of the family or pantheon are distributed symmetrically around each shrine.

All three Nepali mandalas in the exhibition depict the two principal celestial deities. One represents the sun god (no. 33) and the other two the moon god (nos. 35, 39). Curiously, such mandalas seem to have become popular among Buddhists in the fifteenth century. In fact, only the Sūryamaṇḍala (no. 33) may have been done for a Hindu, on the occasion of the performance of the *Bhīmaratha* rite. All other known examples are Buddhist, and most are of the fifteenth and sixteenth centuries. Why the moon god became so popular with the Buddhist Newars for a limited time remains unexplained. A comparison of the two Chandramaṇḍalas clearly shows how the style had altered in a little over a century. The latter (no. 39) is not only rendered in a more linear technique, but the drawing is more casual. The figures are flatter, having lost their modeled quality. The details are more loosely executed, eschewing the finesse and delicacy of the earlier *paubhā*. There are differences in the physiognomy, clothing, and tonality of the two paintings. Some of these later characteristics appear in sixteenth-century paintings such as the representation of Amoghapāśa Lokeśvara (no. 37).

Apart from the mandalas of the planetary deities, which are typically shown on *paubhās* and not on *thankas,* another theme that was popular only in Nepal consists of myriad *chaityas* (no. 36). Buddhists are not alone in adhering to the view that the larger the number of *chaityas* or images dedicated, the greater the religious merit accumulated. Hindus also believe in earning merit by commissioning a thousand Sivalingas (*sahasralinga*), a Sivalinga being the abstract symbol of the god Siva. Naturally, it is much easier to paint *chaityas* than to have them constructed. By including the image of Ushṇīshavijayā within the central *chaitya,* the dedication and rite ensure a long life for the donor; the goddess is also associated with the *Bhīmaratha* rite (see no. 30).

As far as is known, paintings of myriad *chaityas* were not popular in Tibet, where the idea of the thousand buddhas seems to have been the conceptual substitute. The Zimmerman *paubhā* is not only dated but is a particularly handsome rendition of the theme, revealing the artist's brilliant sense of design. The placement of the *chaityas*—of three different sizes—and of the figural forms creates a pleasing abstract composition. Apart from the fact that the dancing *Dikpālas* (guardians of the directions) are iconographically unusual, one wonders if the artist did not represent them as animated figures in order to contrast them with the rigid shapes of the *chaityas*.

There are only two examples in the Zimmerman Collection of *paubhās* representing angry deities, but both are visually striking for their energized images and strong, contrasting colors (nos. 37, 41). Both subjects were extremely popular with Newari Buddhists. These *paubhās* are particularly appealing for their clear compositions and dramatic imagery. Even more extraordinary is the slightly later and larger painting representing a cosmic manifestation of the Hindu Goddess (no. 42). Iconographically, this is a much more complex composition than either of the Buddhist works, and only a master artist could have handled the theme with such aplomb.

Apart from *paubhās* there are a number of other forms of pictures in the collection that reflect the variety of paintings known in Nepal. The earliest are two illustrated folios from a Buddhist book (no. 32), probably from the early fourteenth century. There is little stylistic distinction between these illuminations and the nearly contemporary *paubhā* (no. 31). Most of the other books or book covers in the collection are from the seventeenth and eighteenth centuries and are rendered in different styles (nos. 43–50). The subjects illustrated in the books and on their covers are either divine images (no. 46) or myths and edificatory tales (nos. 44, 48). A book may consist of pictures only (no. 49) or of texts and illustrations (no. 43).

The folding-book format was very popular in Nepal; the Newari term is *thyāsaphu*. Originally this term was applied to historical chronicles, but subsequently it came to be used to denote all folding books. The seventeenth-century book describing attacks by malignant spirits (no. 43) provides us with an idea of minimalist style generally preferred by Newari artists for narrative subjects from about the fourteenth to the early seventeenth century. Essentially figurative, it allowed only a tree or two and a piece of furniture to be introduced into the composition to provide props. The action always takes place against a monochromatic background, usually red or green, and the representation is flat and pictographic. A second mode, represented by a pair of covers depicting unidentified Hindu myths (no. 44), is much more ornate and florid. The background is exuberant with rich scrolling, and the trees are even more decorative and artificial in appearance. This style, which may have originated in Bhaktapur sometime in the second half of the sixteenth century, probably remained popular for narrative themes for about a century before being replaced by the Newari version of the Rajput style imported from India.

The Zimmerman Collection includes two very distinguished examples of the Newari-Rajput style of painting. The earlier one consists of a pair of book covers depicting legends of the god Krishna (no. 44). The two scenes, painted on the inside, reflect a much more painterly tradition than the earlier Nepali narrative modes and show clear formal and iconographic affinities with late-seventeenth- and early-eighteenth-century paintings from the neighboring Hindu states, now part of India's Himachal Pradesh. More enigmatic, however, are the pure landscapes rendered on the outsides of the two covers. Generally, Nepali book covers are painted only on the inside, and no other example is known where the outsides have been adorned with landscapes lifted unaltered from a Chinese source. Nor can one determine what relevance these landscapes could have had to the subject of the text once protected by the covers. The text must have had something to do with Krishna legends. Sino-Tibetan landscape motifs do appear in Nepali painting in this period, but such outright transference of what appears to be a pure landscape in the Chinese literati tradition to adorn the covers of a religious text is unusual.

A different version of the Newari-Rajput style is discernible in the large, exuberant scroll painting illustrating a story that extolls the Hindu rite known as *Ekādaśīvrata* (no. 51). Here the artist shows a new awareness of nature which is not apparent in earlier narrative paintings. The action now takes place against a uniformly rendered mountainous landscape that serves as a continuous background. Not only are the mountains capped with snow, but the trees appear to be more naturalistic. The same landscape background was also used to set off divine images in religious paintings of the period (see no. 50). The idea of employing a landscape background with snowy mountains may have been inspired by contemporary Tibetan *thankas,* but otherwise India seems to have been the principal source. Displaying their characteristic inventiveness, Newari artists created a vivacious, expressive style that is unmistakably local, differing clearly from both traditions. Despite the addition of landscape elements, there was little attempt to convey a feeling for space, and although the palette is more varied, colors were still applied in well-defined, flat areas.

The Zimmerman Collection also includes a large number of books of drawings and painted sketches of which a few outstanding examples are included in the exhibition.[5] These consist of artists' model books (no. 47), as well as an iconographic manual used by priests (no. 40). Some of the model books have notations in both Newari and Tibetan, clearly indicating that they were used by Newari artists for their Tibetan commissions. The inclusion of specifically Tibetan figures, such as the idealized portrait of a Karmapa hierarch (no. 40), make it evident that the books were employed as iconographic sources for Tibetan art. While the drawings in such books were done by Newari artists, the texts and iconographic information were often supplied by both Newari priests and lamas (Tibetan monks). The sixteenth-century sketchbook (no. 40) was meant for both painter and sculptor, as it contains technical instructions about metal casting.

Apart from images of gods and goddesses, such books also include drawings of architectural and furniture patterns and designs. The quality of the drawing is usually very high. Even though the renderings were meant to serve only as working models and had a practical rather than aesthetic application, they were drawn with great care. Some look like final outlines ready to be filled in with colors. Of course all artists were not equally skilled, so some of the drawings are not as refined as the others. Such books, characteristic of Newari work, remain equally important for the study of Nepali and Tibetan art. No similar model or sketch books from Tibet have come to light.

NOTES

1. For the history and culture of the Kathmandu Valley, see Slusser 1982. For extensive discussions of the arts of Nepal, see Pal 1974; 1978. For metal sculptures, see von Schroeder 1981.
2. The past tense is used because the route is no longer important for Indo-Tibetan trade.
3. See Appendix 1 for the inscriptions and their translations.
4. See Pal 1974, pp. 6–7, for the Chinese statements and sources.
5. For a larger selection and more extensive discussion of such material, see Pal 1985.

SCULPTURES AND RITUAL OBJECTS

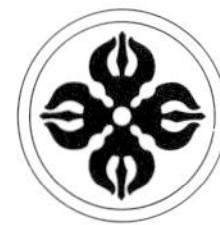

1

Divine Child

SEVENTH CENTURY

COPPER ALLOY WITH TRACES OF GILT

H: 3 IN. (7.6 CM)

Neither the exact function nor the identification of this charming figure is clear. Very likely he was part of a tableau. Apart from his plump torso, his tender age is indicated by his hairstyle. Genuflecting with his body turned toward the object of his attention, he flings his arms forward as if pleading for acceptance. He can be identified as either Krishna or Kumāra, both of whom are depicted in Nepal as lively boys. Considering the early date, however, he is more likely to represent Kumāra, the playful son of Siva and Pārvatī. In Nepal the Bodhisattva Mañjuśrī is also often represented as a boy (see no. 6), but it is unlikely that this figure portrays him.

The figure's spirited modeling, lively and expressive posture, and naturalistically delineated drapery are admirable. If he did not appear to be so well fed, one could imagine him as a mischievous boy with histrionic talent—a feisty Oliver Twist—throwing himself down on one knee and begging for more. Nothing in this figure's form or attitude betrays his divine nature.

Literature Von Schroeder 1981, pp. 304–5, fig. 74D, where the figure is identified as an attendant and dated to the sixth–seventh century.

2

Throne Fragment with Kinnara

SEVENTH–EIGHTH CENTURY

COPPER ALLOY WITH SILVER-GREEN PATINA

H: 4½ IN. (11.4 CM)

Although fragmentary, this object, with its rich, smooth silvery green surface, represents the kind of exquisite metalwork which must have elicited the admiration of the ambassador from the Tang court in the seventh century (see pp. 28–29). For both the modeling of the delightful *kinnara* and the detailing of the throne back, this remains a tour de force of Lichchhavi-period Nepali metal objects. The color of the metal is unusual; the piece almost certainly was buried in the ground for a long time. Very likely it was once a part of a throne for a Buddha. Especially noteworthy is the exuberance of the *kinnara*'s tail feathers. Similarly effusive carving may be seen in small stone stupas of the Lichchhavi period such as those in Chabahil in Deo Patan and at other sites (Slusser 1982, figs. 265–71, 282–86).

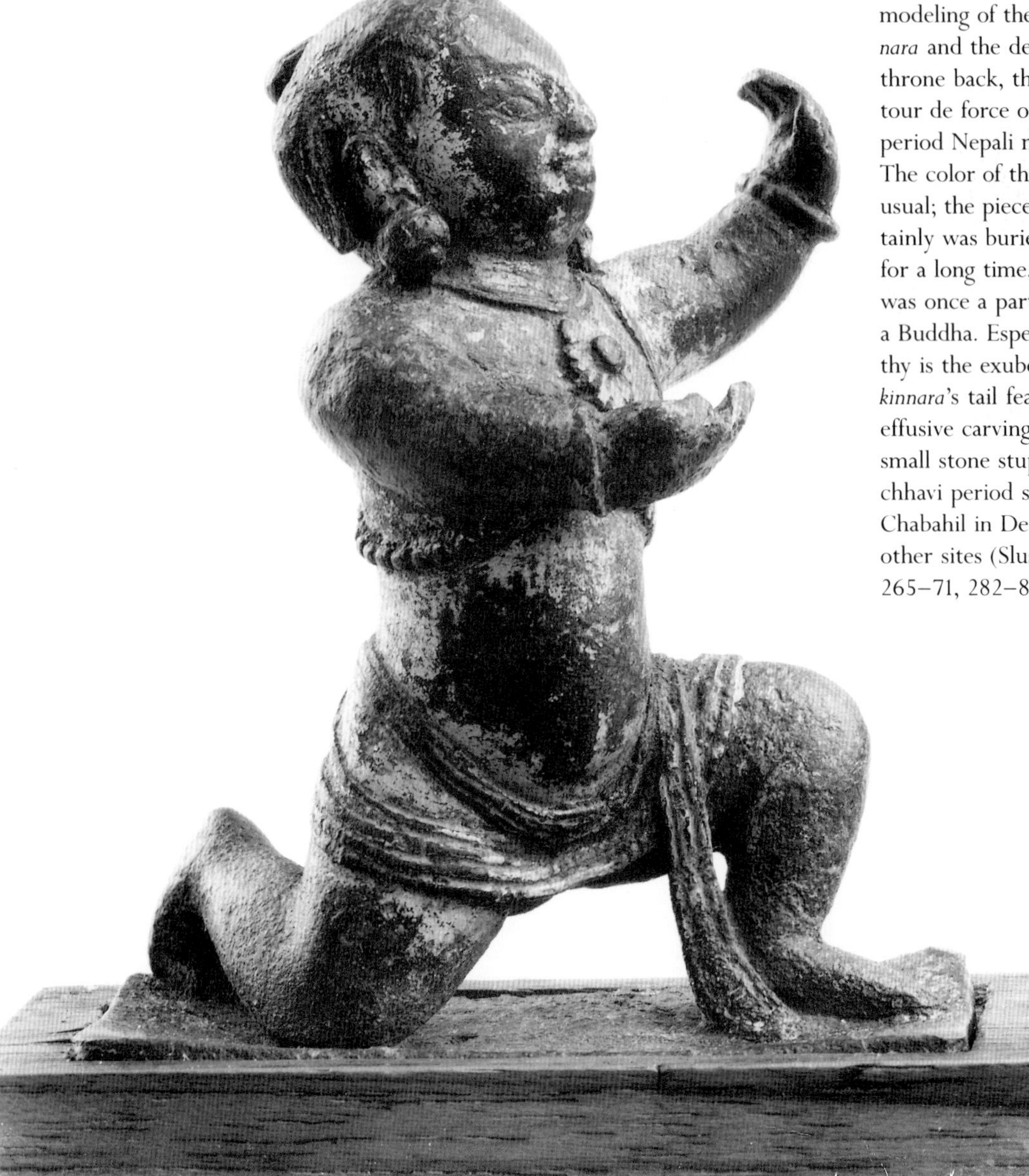

1

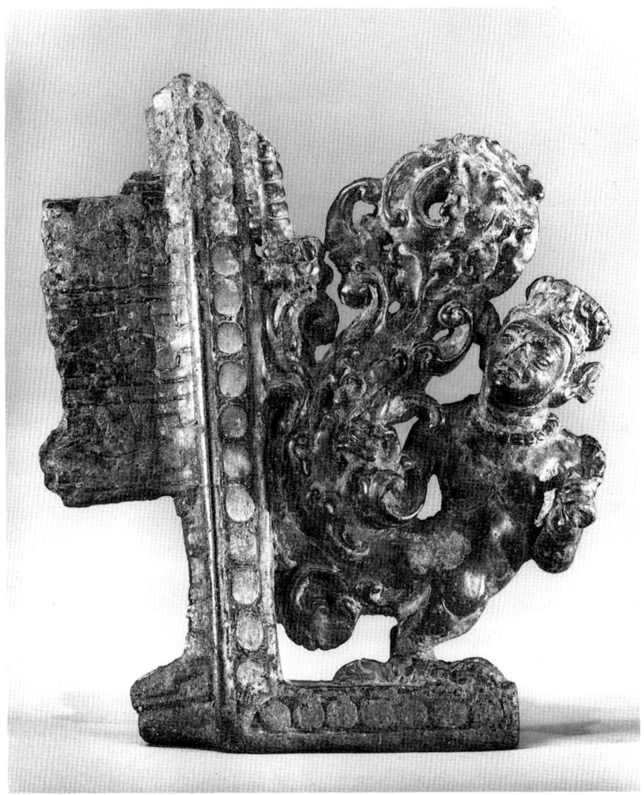

2

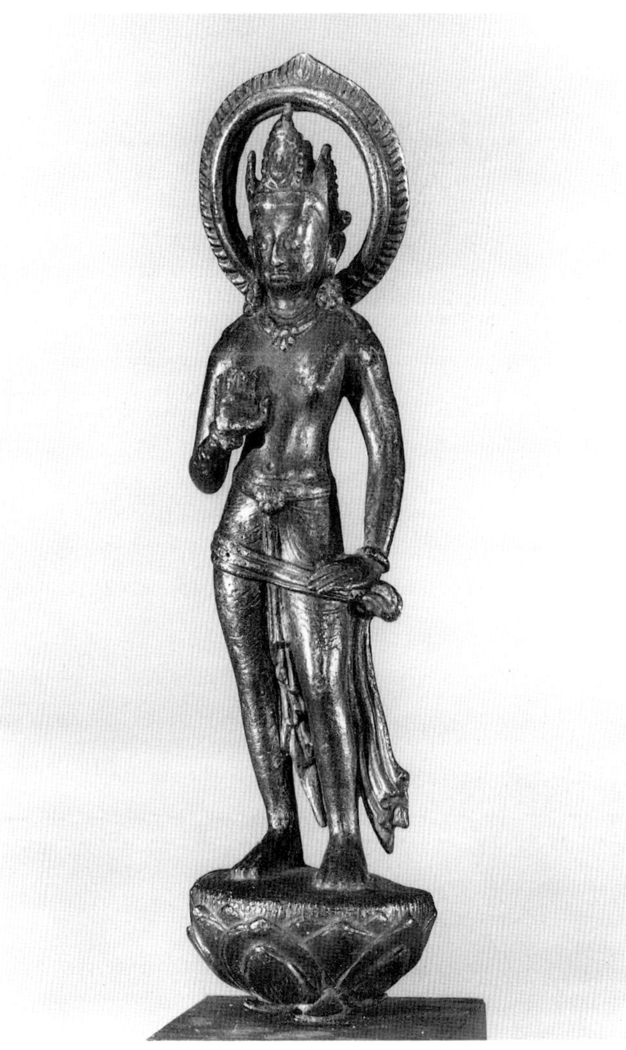

3

3

Bodhisattva Avalokiteshvara

EIGHTH CENTURY

COPPER ALLOY

H: 7¼ IN. (18.4 CM)

Although without any attributes, this figure can be identified with reasonable certainty as the Bodhisattva Avalokiteshvara (One Who Looks on All Sides). A divine figure, he is unquestionably the most popular of all bodhisattvas. Tibetans believe that the Dalai Lama is a mortal emanation of this bodhisattva.

The bodhisattva is represented here in his simplest, most elegant form. He stands gracefully on a lotus, his right hand displaying the gesture of fearlessness. The left rests against his diagonal sash. He wears jewelry and a tiara, and his head is surrounded by a circle of flames attached to his shoulders. The slim proportions; smooth, abstract modeling; half-shut eyes; and hint of a gentle smile are all characteristic of male figures in Nepali sculptures of the Lichchhavi period. Compared to a dated Vishnu image of A.D. 748 (Alsop 1982) and the well-known Dhvakabaha bodhisattva figures of the seventh century (Pal 1974, figs. 13, 14), an eighth-century date for this figure seems appropriate (see Slusser 1982, fig. 466).

Literature Von Schroeder 1981, pp. 308–9, fig. 76D.

4

Thunderbolt Bearer

EIGHTH–NINTH CENTURY

COPPER ALLOY WITH TRACES OF GILT

H: 4 IN. (10.2 CM)

The exact identification and function of this spirited figure remain unclear. His right knee is slightly raised, and his left rests on a rectangular base whose surface suggests a rock formation. The figure looks comfortably poised to strike an adversary. With his chest thrust forward and his crowned head thrown back rather arrogantly, he firmly grasps a thunderbolt in his right hand. The aureole behind him, with a busy scroll-like design that may represent flames, is tilted to follow his posture. Rarely in Nepali sculpture does one encounter such an energized aureole whose flames have been rendered with such exuberance and density. Very likely the motif was adapted from painting.

The thunderbolt is generally the attribute of the Vedic deity Indra—also familiar in Buddhist mythology—and of the Buddhist deity Vajrapāṇi. If this figure represents either, the context remains unclear. He could be an attendant of Māra attacking the Buddha, or a demigod (*asura*) challenging the Goddess Durgā. Images of the combative Durgā, however, are seldom encountered in Nepali art of the Lichchhavi period. Thus this militant figure may have belonged to a tableau representing Śākyamuni's conquest of Māra. Whatever his identification, the diminutive bronze remains a vivacious example of early Nepali sculpture.

Literature Von Schroeder 1981, pp. 306–7, no. 75A, where the figure is identified as Vajrapāṇi and dated to the eighth century.

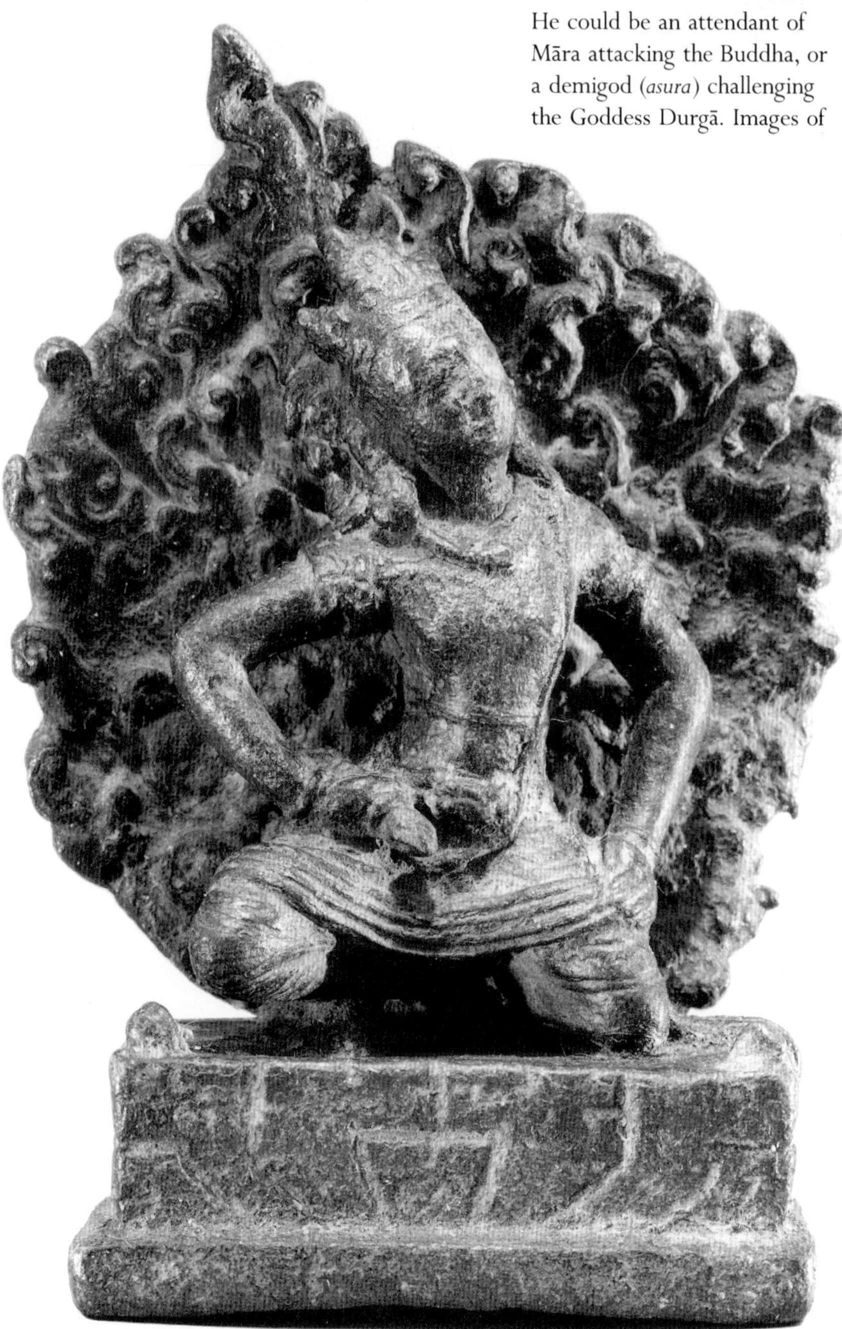

5

Head of Siva

NINTH–TENTH CENTURY

COPPER ALLOY

H: 11 IN. (27.9 CM)

This repoussé object is a metal cover for a face, in this case that of a Sivalinga. The *liṅga* has a phallic connotation, representing procreative powers, but also symbolizes a cosmic pillar. Such covers are called either *kośa* or *kavacha,* the former meaning "cover" and the latter "protective implement." It is possible that such covers were originally used over clay or terra-cotta images to protect them from damage due to daily ablutions. Dedicating such metal covers in a temple is considered especially meritorious, and they often are pledged in return for special favors.

This particular example may well be of the Lichchhavi period; the form and design of the tiara are quite typical of Lichchhavi-period sculptures. Apart from a strand of pearls, Siva is adorned with a snake-necklace. His ears are decorated with ornaments of two different designs, a snake on the right and a ring on the left. The broad face with its scowling expression, perhaps representing the angry aspect of Siva known as *aghora,* is sensitively modeled.

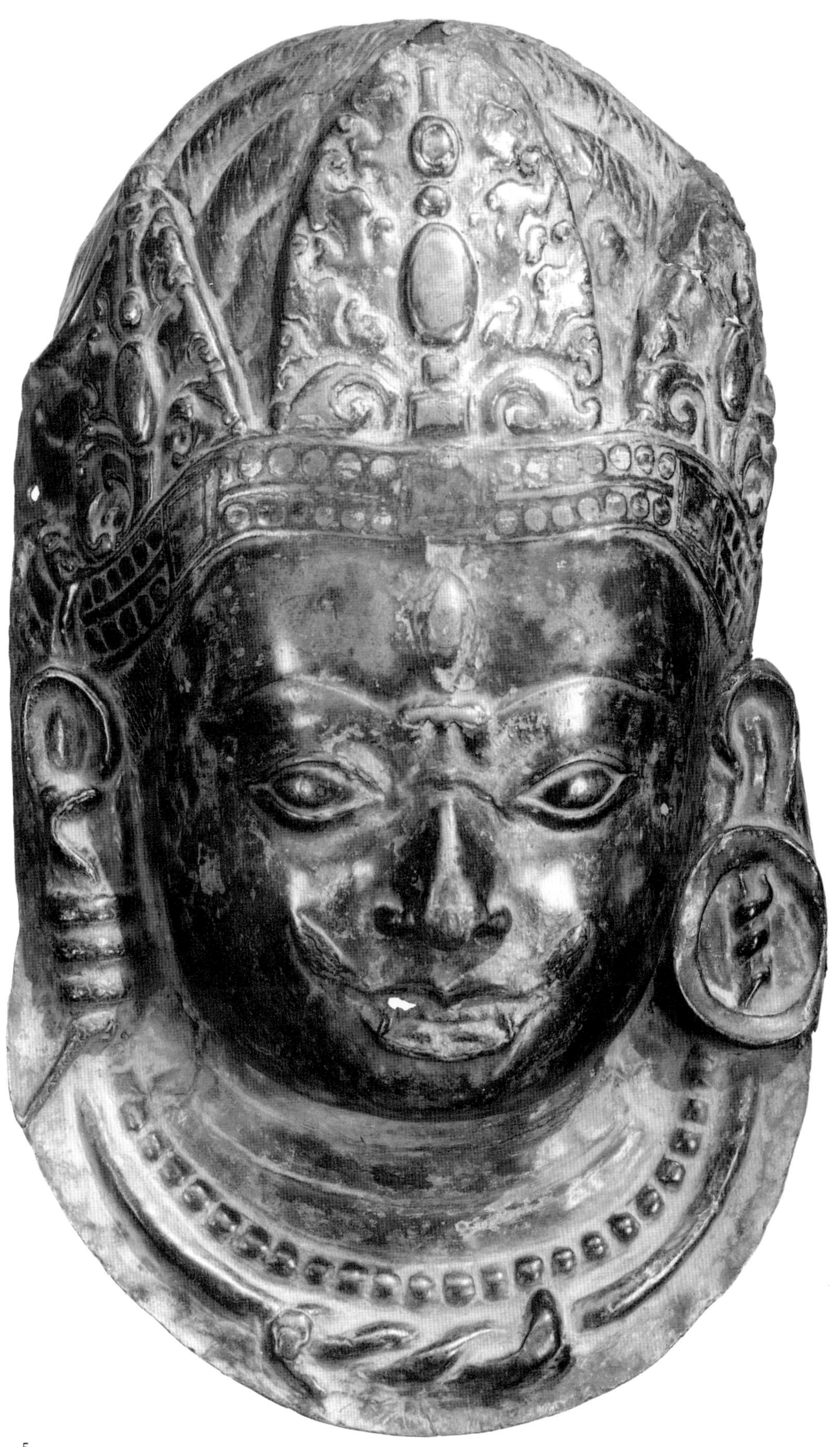

5

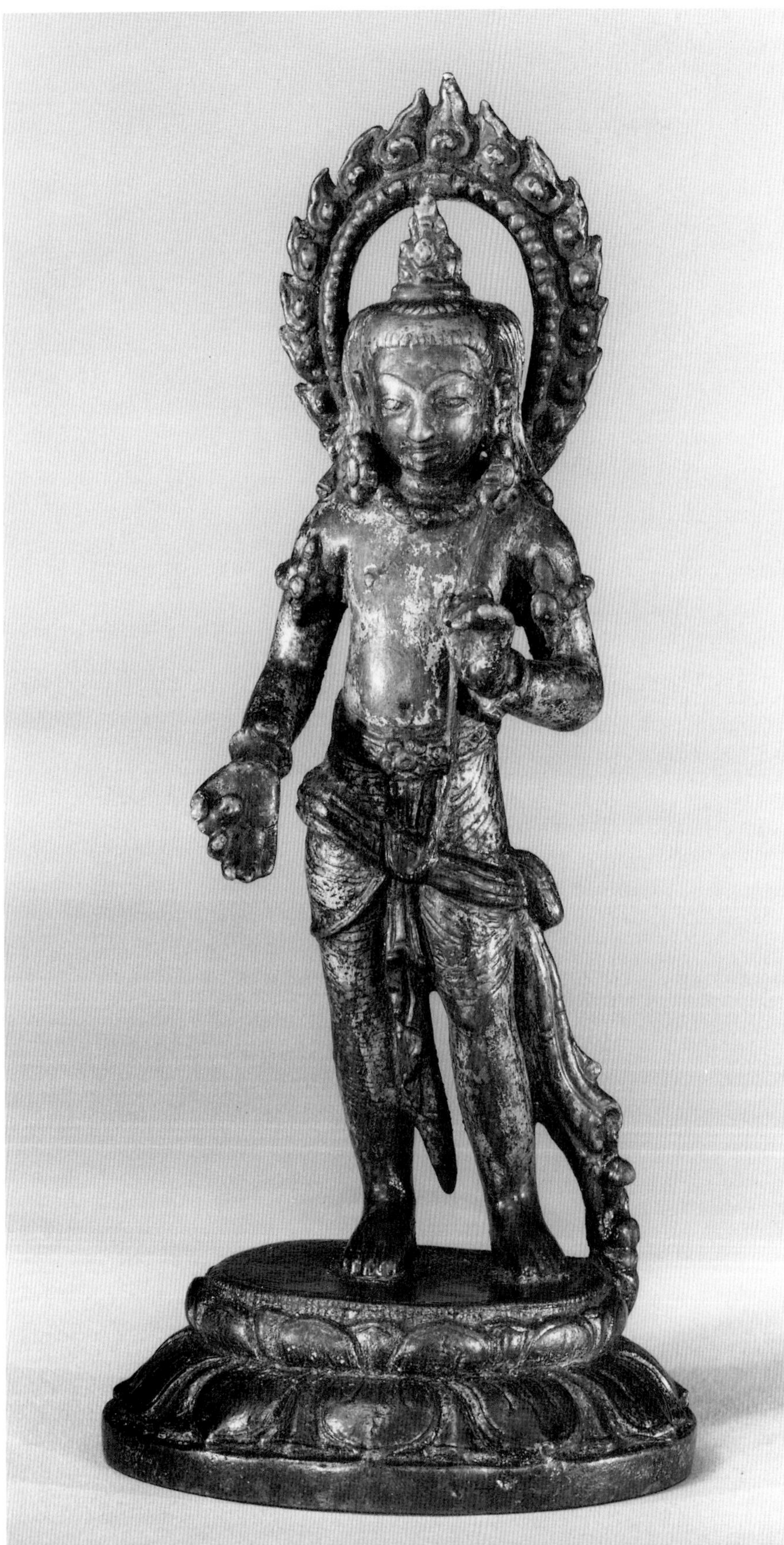

6

6

Bodhisattva Mañjuśrī

NINTH–TENTH CENTURY

COPPER ALLOY WITH TRACES OF GILT

H: 7⅞ IN. (20 CM)

This suavely modeled, boyish figure with a slight paunch indicating his robust health represents the Bodhisattva Mañjuśrī, regarded as the embodiment of wisdom. Although generally addressed as Mañjuśrī, his complete name is Mañjuśrīkumāra, which means "Prince (or Youth) with Pleasant Appearance." This is why he is often represented as a youthful figure, but nowhere is this done more frequently than in Nepal. Apart from the shape of his body and his proportions, this figure's adolescence is clear from his boyish face and the arrangement of his hair, with a small chignon on top and three braids on the sides and back. Otherwise he is dressed and ornamented like an adult bodhisattva.

The divine child (see no. 1) stands gracefully on a lotus base. His head is set off by an oval ring of fire serving as a halo. He stretches his right hand out to bless the devotee. In addition he holds a round object whose significance is not clear. Both Hindu and Buddhist deities often hold such circular objects. They may represent the fruit *myrobalan,* which signifies knowledge (*jñānāmalaka*). The figure's left hand may have held a blue lotus, one of his distinctive emblems. Noteworthy is the sacred thread across his torso, indicating his higher caste. This is worn by other Buddhist deities as well, even though the religion does not recognize the caste system. For a similar Bodhisattva Mañjuśrī attributed

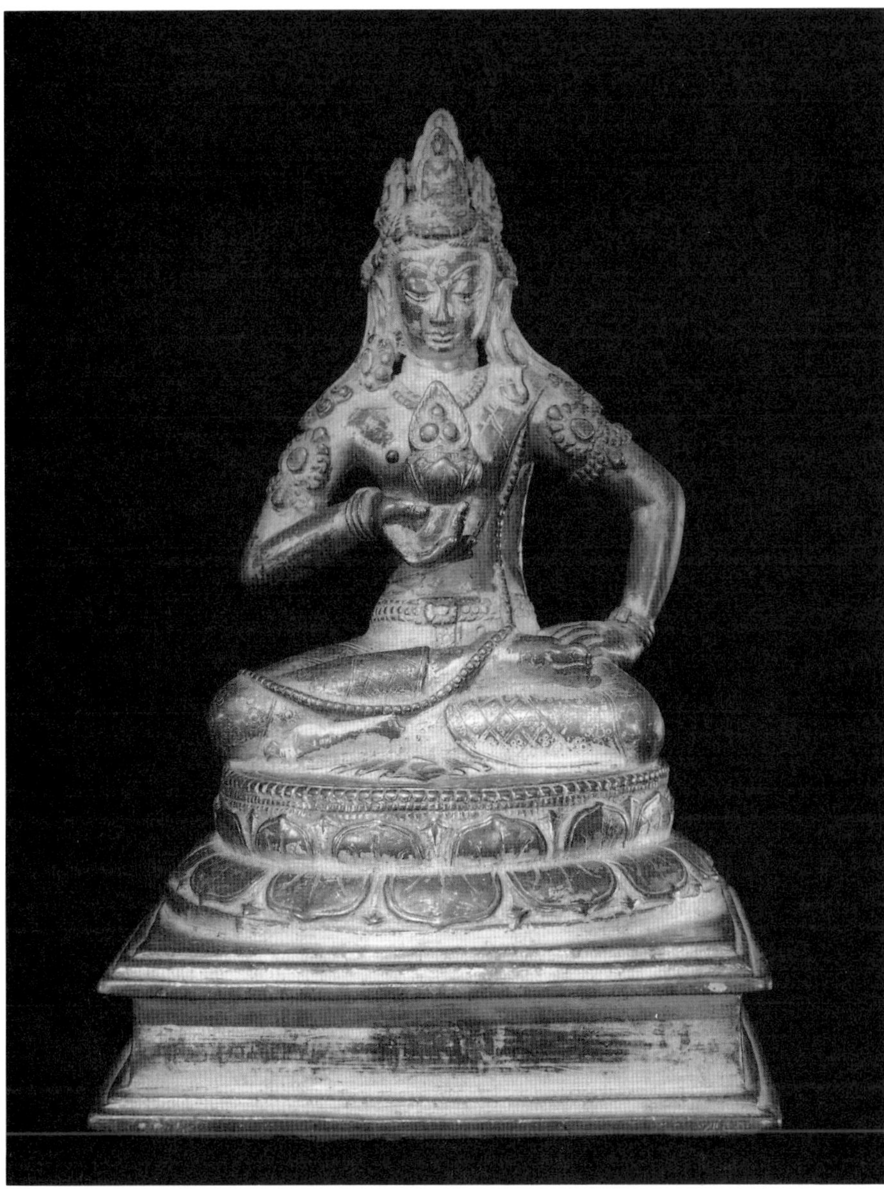

7

to the ninth century, see von Schroeder 1981 (pp. 310–11, fig. 77G).

Literature Reynolds 1986, p. 167, fig. 1.

7

Bodhisattva Ratnapāṇi

TENTH CENTURY
GILT COPPER ALLOY
H: 6½ IN. (16.5 CM)

This elegant bodhisattva's eyes are downcast. He sits in a meditating posture on a lotus atop a square base embellished with simple moldings. Elaborately bejeweled, he wears a sacred thread of pearls and a three-lobed tiara. A tiny image of his parental Buddha is at the front of the central lobe of the tiara. The bodhisattva's left hand rests gently on his left thigh, and his right hand delicately holds a lotus against his chest. On the flower are three gems surrounded by flames. This attribute identifies the figure as the Bodhisattva Ratnapāṇi (Gem or Jewel Bearer), whose parental Buddha is Ratnasambhava (Jewel-Born), one of the five transcendental buddhas of Vajrayāna Buddhism. The three gems (*triratna*) represent the Buddha, the Dharma (Religion), and the Samgha (Monastic Order). The halo is missing. The figure's back is well finished.

Apart from the fact that this is a fine example of a Lichchhavi-period bronze, iconographically it is unusual. Representations of Ratnapāṇi are seldom encountered in Nepali art of any period. There is another image of the bodhisattva in the Norton Simon Museum, Pasadena, which has been misidentified (von Schroeder 1981, pp. 318–19, fig. 81A).

8

Goddess Vasudhārā

TENTH CENTURY
COPPER ALLOY
H: 6¾ IN. (17.2 CM)

Framed by a delicately rendered flame aureole, the goddess in this beautifully designed and crafted bronze is Vasudhārā (Stream of Gems). As her name implies, she is a goddess of wealth and the Buddhist counterpart of the Hindu Sri-Lakshmī. Vasudhārā is particularly popular among Newari Buddhists. Apart from the Buddha and Avalokiteshvara, Vasudhārā is the most frequently portrayed deity in Nepali Buddhist art and is represented in the Zimmerman Collection by several other examples (see nos. 12, 34). On the occasion of her rite it is

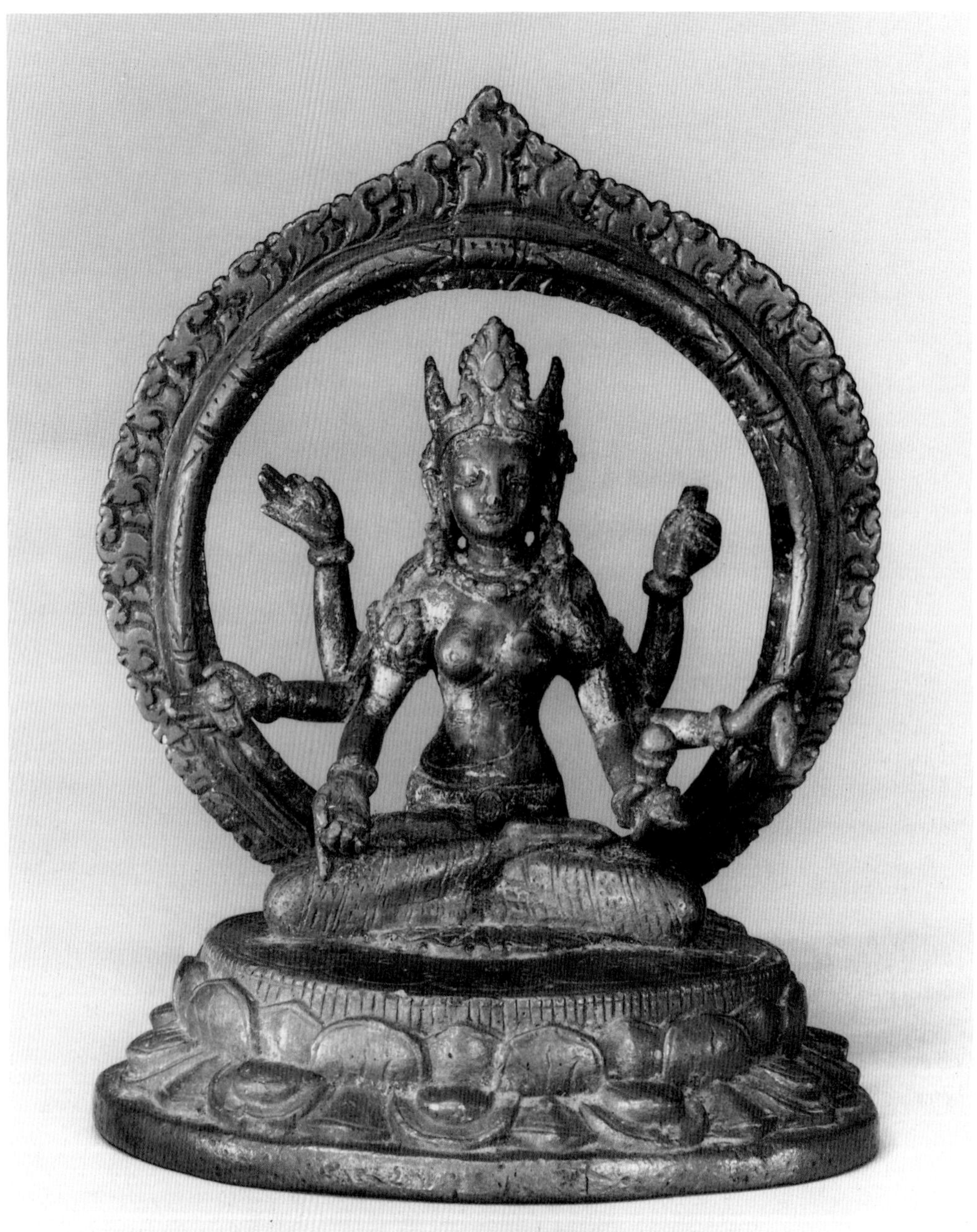

8

customary to commission a painting or bronze, which is why one encounters so many representations of the goddess.

Almost invariably, Nepali Vasudhārā images have six arms. In India, where her form originated, she is rarely depicted with so many. This particular form of Vasudhārā is said to have originated in Kanchipuram in south India (see Pal 1968). With her six arms (clockwise from top left) she displays the following attributes, most of which emphasize her role as a dispenser of material and spiritual wealth: a manuscript, a sheaf of grain, a waterpot, the gesture of munificence, a spray of gems, and the gesture of adoring a Tathāgata (an epithet of the Buddha). Unlike most other known representations is her meditating posture (see nos. 12, 34).

Stylistically, this smoothly modeled, elegant figure is very similar to the Ratnapāṇi in the Zimmerman Collection (no. 7). They may well have been created by the same sculptor or in the same workshop.

9

Bodhisattva Vajrapāṇi

TENTH CENTURY
COPPER ALLOY WITH GILT
H: 8⅜ IN. (21.3 CM)

Portrayed in his fierce form, Vajrapāṇi dances with one leg bent parallel to the ground in the position known in Sanskrit as *ardhaparyaṅka* and the other placed on two corpses lying on a lotus base. He is kept in position by a substantial support rising from the base. Almost everything about him emphasizes his ferocity. His left hand displays the gesture of admonition (*tarjanīmudrā*) even as the right is about to hurl the thunderbolt. Above his dhoti he wears a tiger skin, and his ornaments consist of snakes. His rising hair is like leaping tongues of flame, and his broad face is distinguished by an angry expression enhanced by three rolling eyes and a grinning mouth displaying teeth and fangs. Without multiple arms, he could well represent a masked dancer gyrating on a stage.

Because of the presence of the thunderbolt, the figure can be identified as Vajrapāṇi (Thunderbolt Bearer). One of the oldest bodhisattvas in Buddhist art, he frequently appears in the early Gandharan period as a bodyguard of Buddha Śākyamuni in scenes of his life. In later Buddhist art Vajrapāṇi is portrayed in both placid and angry forms. Normally, in the early art of Nepal he is seen as a placid bodhisattva along with Avalokiteshvara and Maitreya. This spirited and expressive bronze may well be the earliest known representation of his angry manifestation in Himalayan and Indian Buddhist art.

Literature Pal 1975, pp. 43, 77, no. 25; Slusser 1982, fig. 465; Reynolds 1986, pp. 167, fig. 2.

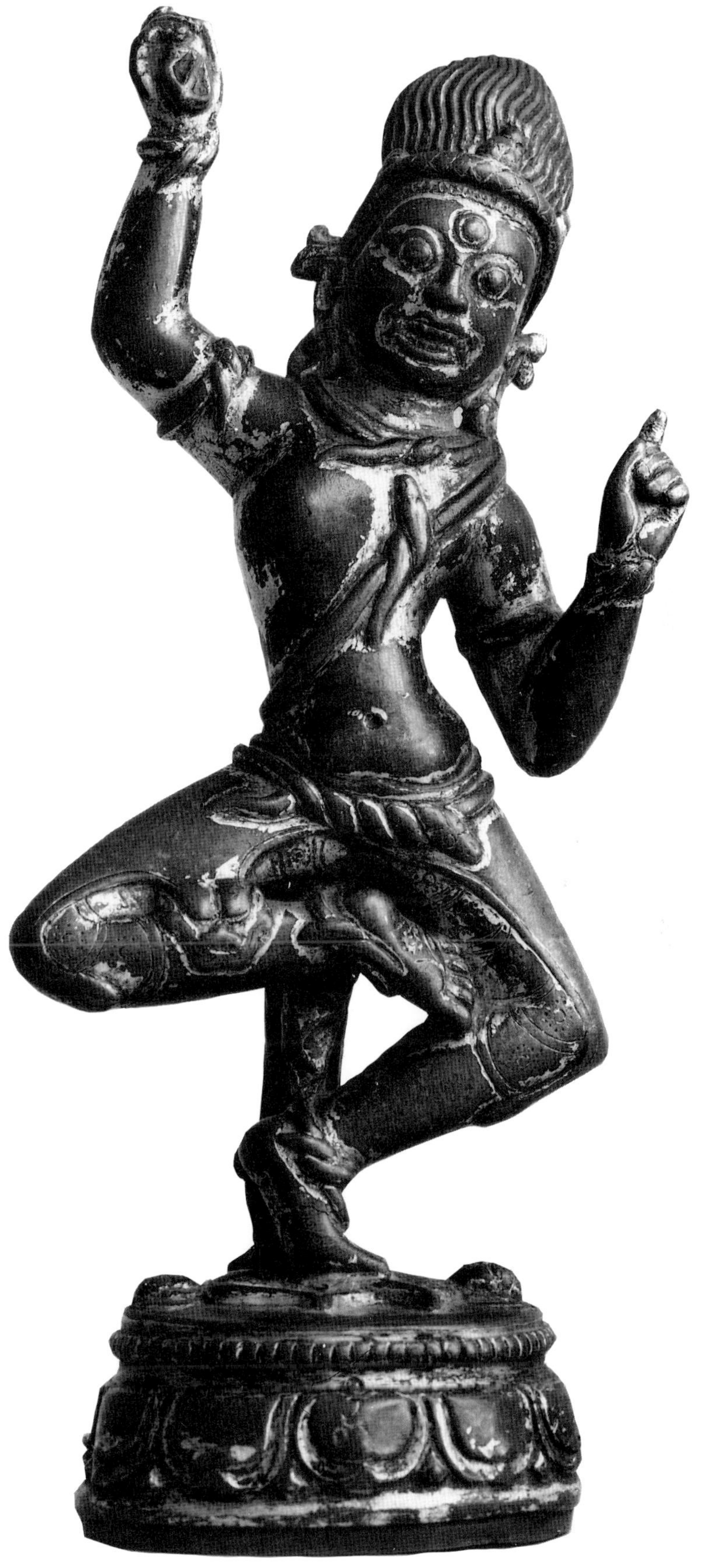

9

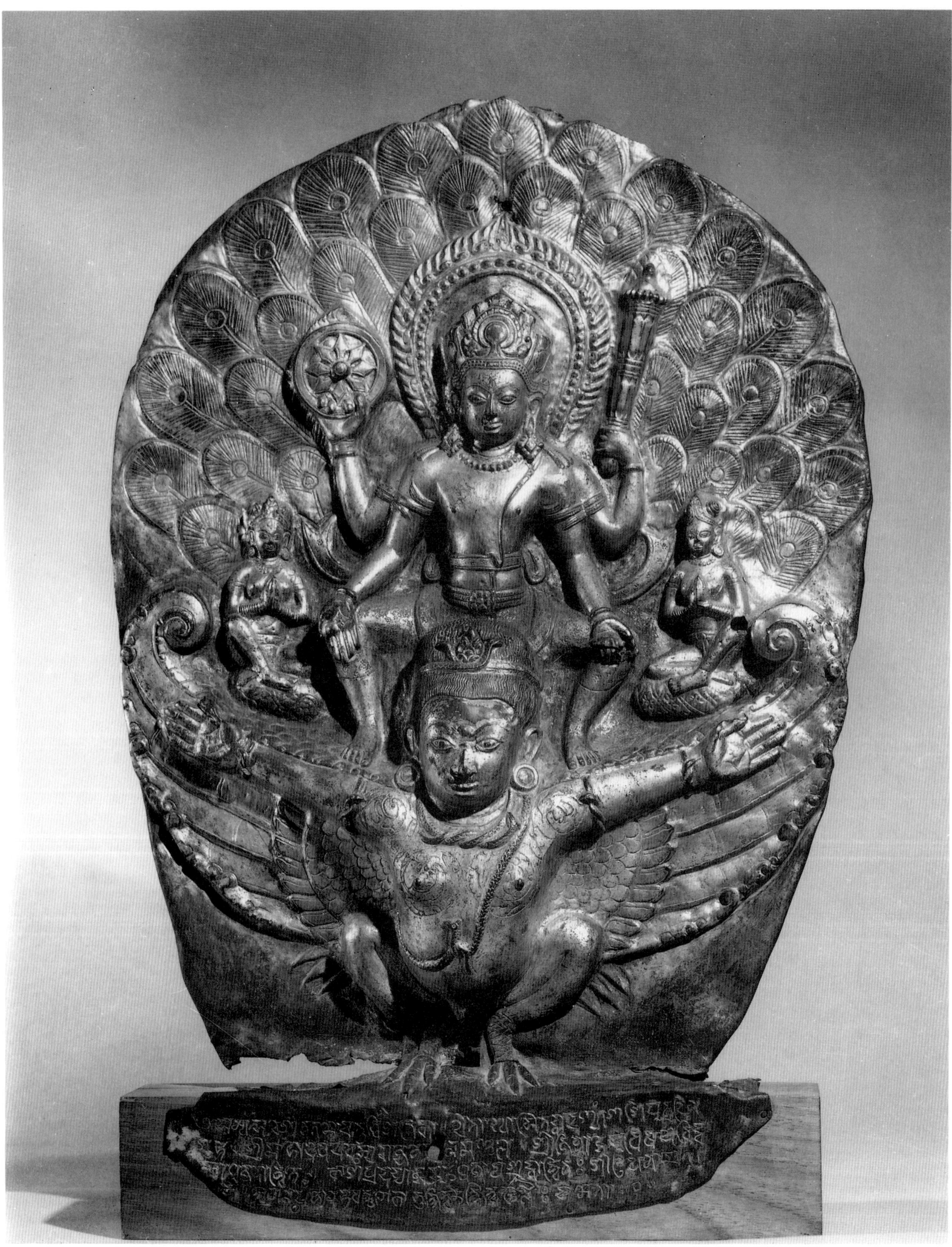

10

10

God Vishnu on Garuḍa

DATED 1004

GILT COPPER REPOUSSÉ

H: 17⅛ IN. (43.5 CM)

Like the cover for a Sivalinga (no. 5), this impressive object also served as a cover for a stone or metal image. Unlike the Sivalinga covers, however, the representation here is livelier and much more elaborate. The god shown is Vishnu, with two spouses who are undifferentiated. All three are seated on the outstretched wings of Garuḍa, Vishnu's half-human, half-avian mount. The elaborately crowned and bejeweled god holds a flaming wheel, a club, a conch shell, and a boss. His head is surrounded by an oval nimbus decorated with pearls and leaping tongues of flame. The two goddesses hold their hands against their breasts in the gesture of adoration (*namaskāramudrā*).

Much more imaginative and interesting is the figure of Garuḍa. The unknown artist has skillfully combined a human body with the features of a bird to create a very credible composite creature. Generously adorned with snakes, the bird-man stretches out his arms along his wings, which are spread like those of an eagle. His legs are like rubbery tubes, but his feet have the talons of a predatory bird. The tail feathers, however, appear to have been modeled on those of a dancing peacock and spread out beautifully to form an aureole for his divine riders.

Known as Garuḍāsana Vishnu, or Vishnu Seated on Garuḍa, this image type symbolizes the god's role as preserver of the universe. Surviving stone examples demonstrate the popularity of this form during the Lichchhavi period, and at least one royal edict begins by invoking the deity (Pal 1970, pp. 69–71). Apart from being a delightful representation of the theme, much loved by Newari artists, this plaque is of great art-historical significance. According to its inscription, it was dedicated in 1004 by a man with an unusual name (see Appendix 1). Interestingly, the word *kośa* is used to denote the object, and instead of the common epithet Garuḍāsana, the god is referred to as Garuḍadhvaja, or One Whose Banner Is Garuḍa.

Literature Pal 1974, p. 33, fig. 30; 1975, pp. 109, 131, no. 79; von Schroeder 1981, pp. 322–23, fig. 83D; Alsop 1986, figs. 3, 16–18; Bangdel 1987, fig. 175.

11

God Kumāra with Peacock

TWELFTH CENTURY

COPPER ALLOY

H: 3¼ IN. (8.3 CM)

This charming little bronze, probably detached from a larger tableau showing the Śaiva Holy Family (see no. 16), portrays the divine child Kumāra playing with his favorite bird and mount, the peacock. Kumāra, known also as

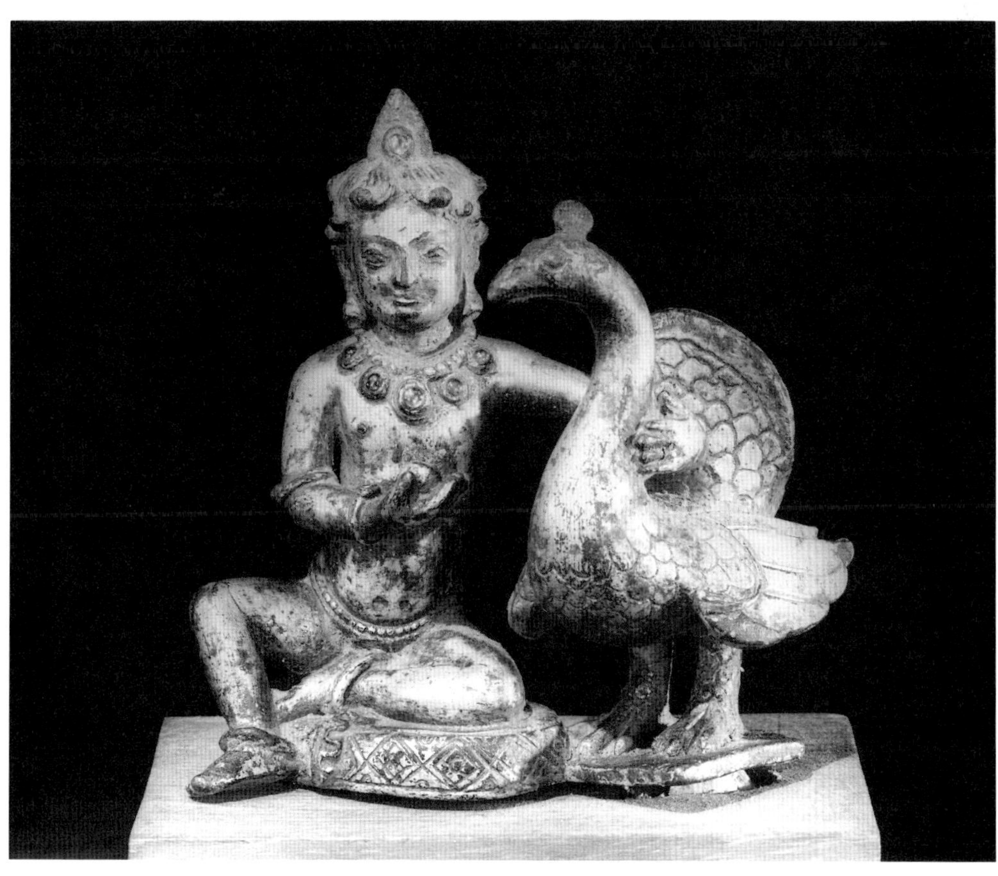

11

Kārttikeya or Skanda, is the son of Siva and Pārvatī and is the war god in Hindu mythology. While he is often portrayed as an adolescent prince, Nepali sculptors preferred to represent him as a playful child, especially on stone reliefs depicting his extended family. It would be no exaggeration to say that in Nepal he seems to have been as popular as the infant Krishna is among Indian Hindus. Indian poets have waxed eloquent about the infant Skanda, and some of that poetic eloquence seems to have rubbed off on Nepali sculptors, as is clear from this exquisitely modeled bronze. Kumāra affectionately puts his left arm around the neck of the peacock; his right hand may hold some food for the bird. The bird reciprocates the sentiment by pecking at his earring. Kumāra's face, however, is expressionless. He looks forward impassively, as if he were posing for a photograph.

12

Goddess Vasudhārā

TWELFTH–THIRTEENTH CENTURY

GILT COPPER ALLOY INLAID WITH GEMSTONES

H: 6½ IN. (16.5 CM)

This golden Vasudhārā figure is more typically Nepali than the earlier representation (no. 8). In most Nepali images, whether sculpted or painted (see no. 34), the goddess sits in this graceful posture, known as *lalitāsana,* on a lotus (missing here). Her pendant right leg is supported by a smaller lotus skillfully attached to the elegantly cascading pleats of her garment. This relaxed posture, as well as the bend of the torso and tilt of the head, enhance the gracefulness of the figure, making it more sensuous than the earlier representation whose rigid posture makes the goddess somewhat remote.

Apart from her posture and the disposition of her head, there are other differences between this figure and the earlier bronze. The proportions, shape, and features of the face have undergone changes. Somewhat square and broad, the face is very much like that of Kumāra (no. 11) and is characteristically Newari. The volume of the garment is no longer indicated by incised geometrical designs, and the goddess appears almost naked. Her tiara and jewels are of more elaborate design and are inlaid with semiprecious stones, mostly turquoise, and rubies.

Literature Pal 1974B, p. 48.

13

Priest's Crown

CA. 1200

GILT COPPER ALLOY INLAID WITH GEMSTONES

H: 12 IN. (30.5 CM)

Crowns such as these are worn by Newari Buddhist priests during esoteric rites. The shape seems to have been unique to Nepal, for nothing similar has been encountered in other Buddhist countries. Even in

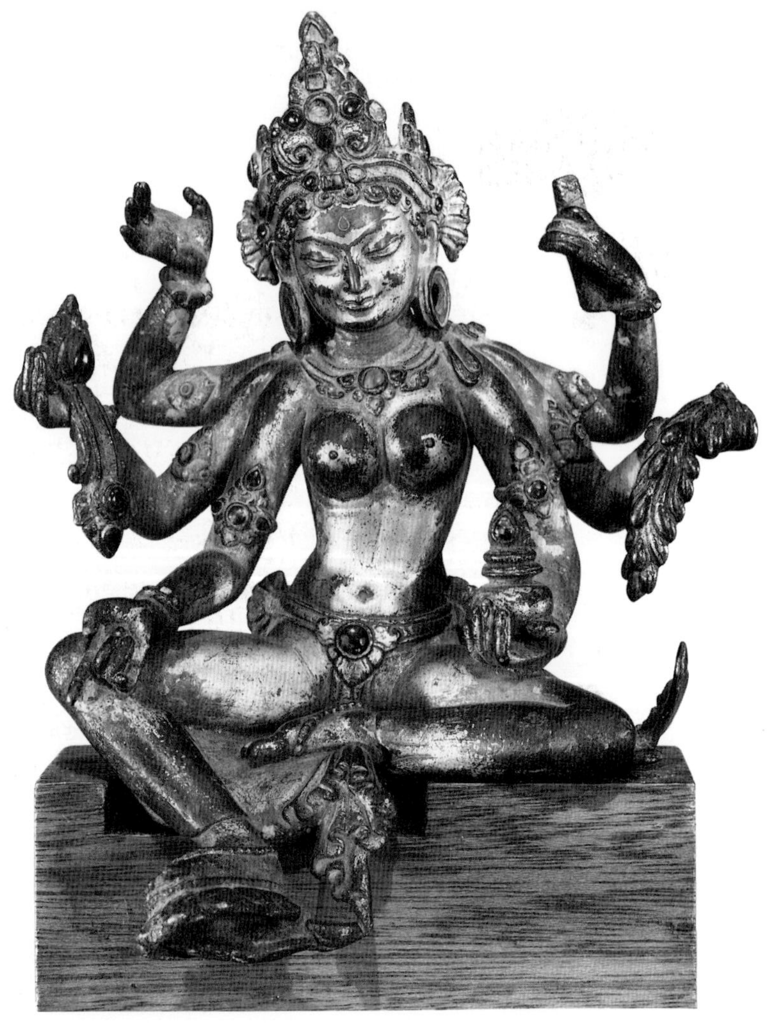

12

neighboring Tibet a different kind of headgear is used. Frequently, such Nepali crowns are adorned with images of the five transcendental buddhas. Their inclusion adds a cosmic dimension to the crown; by wearing it the priest himself becomes homologized with the cosmic principle or divine essence.

The shape of these Newari crowns is always like a conical helmet. At the summit, half a thunderbolt rises from a lotus. To the plain surface of the helmet are attached ornamental bands and several separately cast images of buddhas and deities complete with elaborately designed aureoles. Stones such as lapis lazuli, turquoise, and opal are often used for enhancement, as here.

This particular crown differs from most others in its iconographic program and complexity. Not only are there more figures, but the deities represented are not the usual five transcendental buddhas. Instead they are various emanations of the Bodhisattva Mañjuśrī. Five are peaceful forms and one wrathful. There are also eight smaller figures of goddesses with various offerings, such as a garland and a musical instrument, between the male figures. Thus it would seem that the crown was used in special rites dedicated to Mañjuśrī.

Among published crowns of this type, one in the Musée Guimet, Paris, was dedicated in 1145 (Beguin 1984). This crown was probably made about half a century later and is stylistically similar to two others now in American collections (Pal 1975, p. 68, no. 51; 1985, pp. 106–7, no. S27).

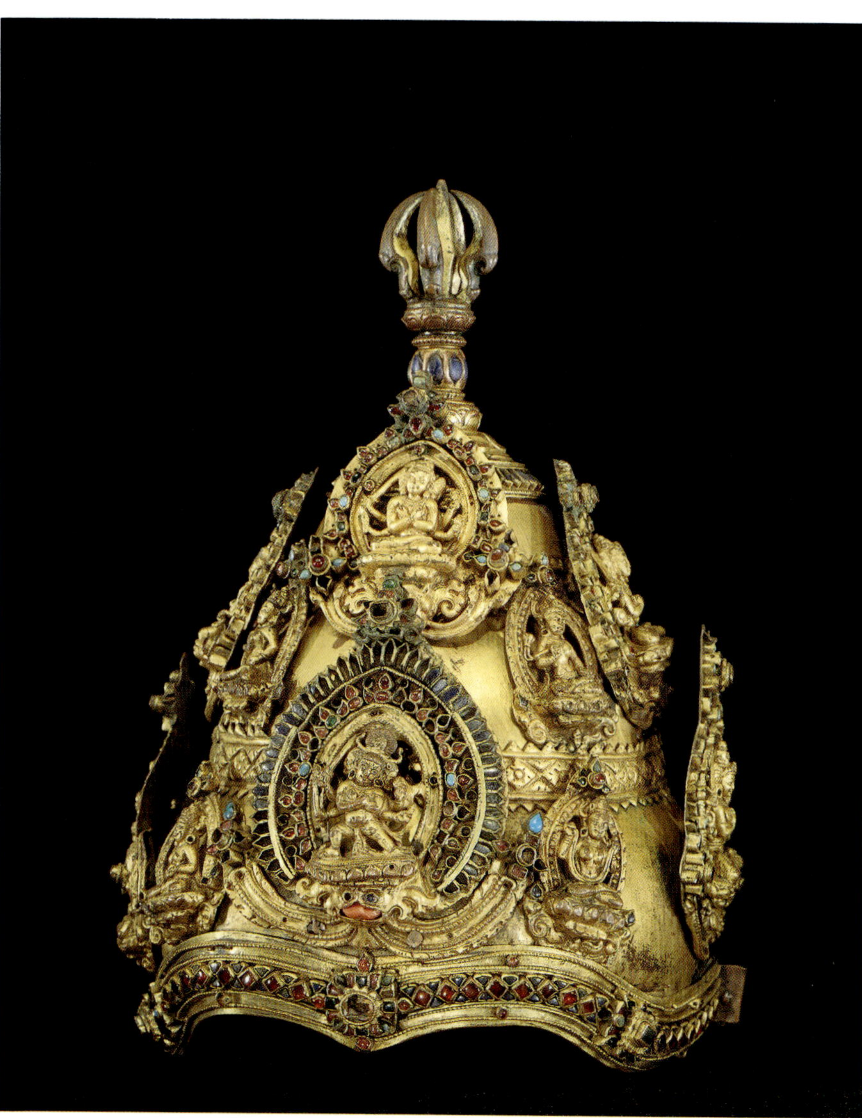

13

14

Goddess

FOURTEENTH CENTURY

GILT COPPER ALLOY INLAID WITH GEMSTONES

H: 13 IN. (33 CM)

Lacking specific attributes other than her hand gestures, this goddess is difficult to identify. She may represent the Hindu Umā, an alternative name of Siva's spouse, Pārvatī (see no. 16), or the Buddhist Tārā (see no. 86). Her outstretched right hand displays the gesture of charity, and her left forms the teaching gesture and may have held a lotus. Both are common gestures for Nepali deities (see no. 6).

Whatever her exact identification, this goddess is an elegant lady with a full, sensuous body whose charms are enhanced by rich jewelry inlaid with semiprecious stones. Originally, she would have sat on a lotus. In her regal poise, she is slightly aloof but approachable. Modeled in the round, the figure is an excellent example of the Newari sculptor's skill in striking an ideal balance between form and complex adornments.

Literature Reynolds 1986, p. 169, fig. 4.

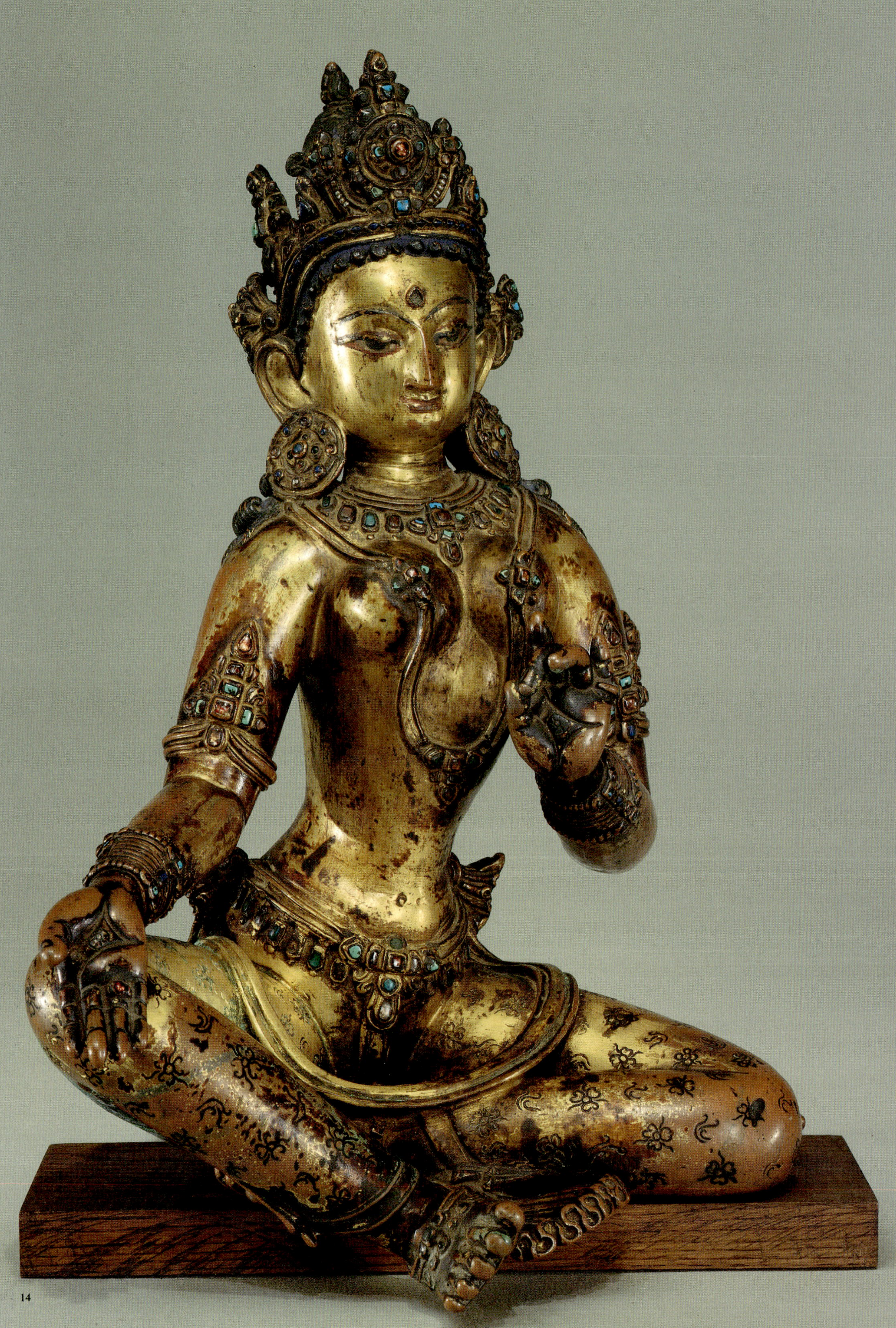

15

Bodhisattva Avalokiteshvara

FOURTEENTH CENTURY

GILT COPPER ALLOY WITH BLACK PAINT AND INLAID WITH SEMI-PRECIOUS STONES

H: 12 IN. (30.5 CM)

Like the much earlier figure (no. 3), this bodhisattva once stood on a lotus base. The iconographic differences between the two figures are minor. Here the right arm is stretched along the bulging right hip, the hand displaying the gesture of charity. Instead of lines, a diamond marks the palm. The left hand would have held the stalk of a lotus, which was attached to the left arm where a bit of foliage remains. The earlier bronze lacks such an attachment, as well as the prominent armbands and sacred thread of two strings of pearls. Although on both sculptures the ends of the sash fall along the left leg, its position across the thighs is different on each figure.

The stylistic differences apparent here are also in the two Vasudhārā images (nos. 8, 12). The tall, slim proportions of the earlier bodhisattva are eschewed here for a heavier figure with more solid limbs. The face is broader with softer features. The hair, painted black, is more prominent, with curls along the edge of the tiara and cascading down the shoulders. The ends of the fillet that ties the tiara behind the head project behind the ears like fan-shaped ornaments. No such fluttering ends appear on the earlier figure. With its gilding and inlaid ornaments, this bodhisattva is more youthful and exuberant than the simpler and more dignified figure of the tenth century.

Literature Pal 1974B, p. 46; Reynolds 1986, p. 170, fig. 6.

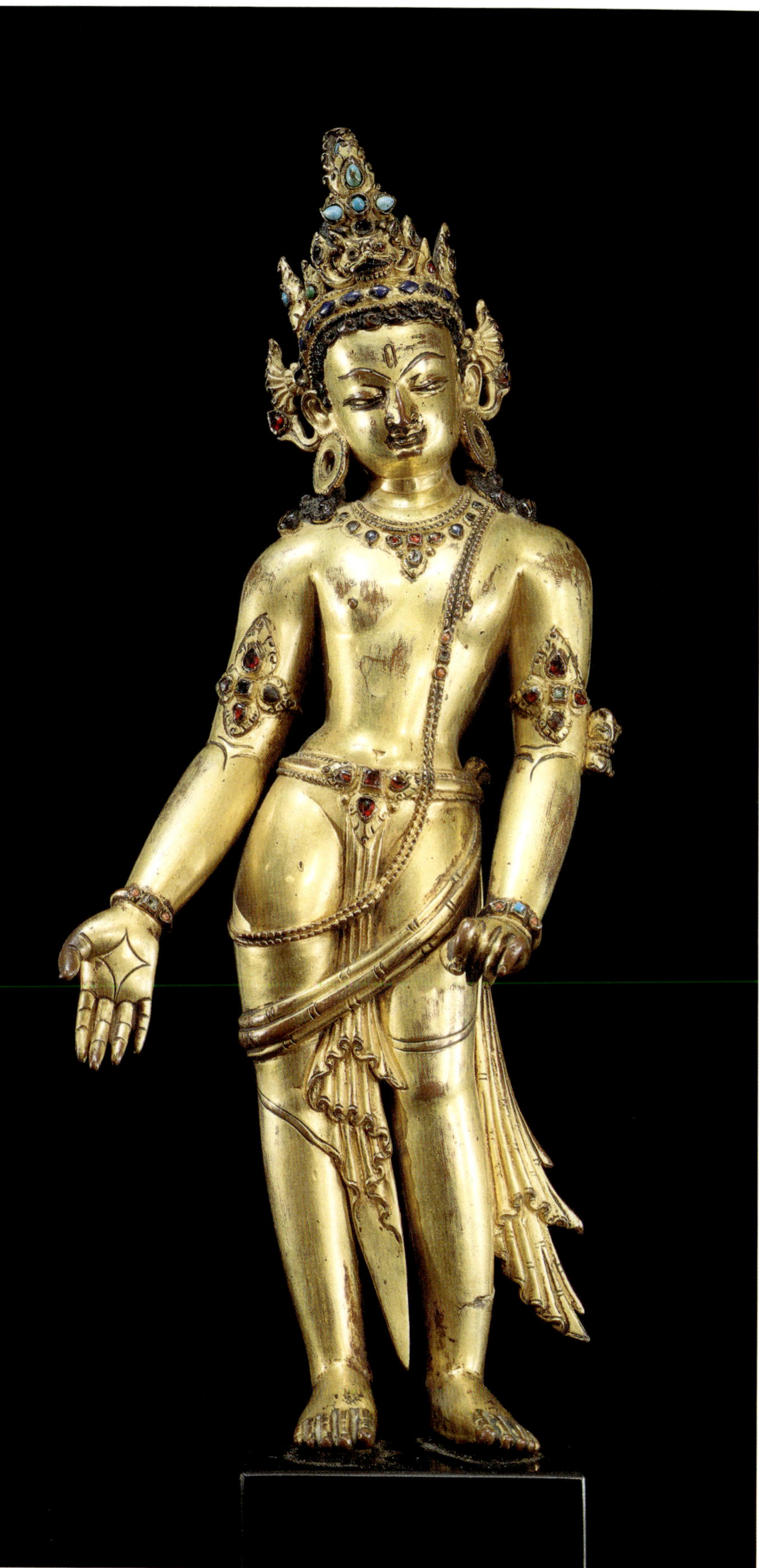

15

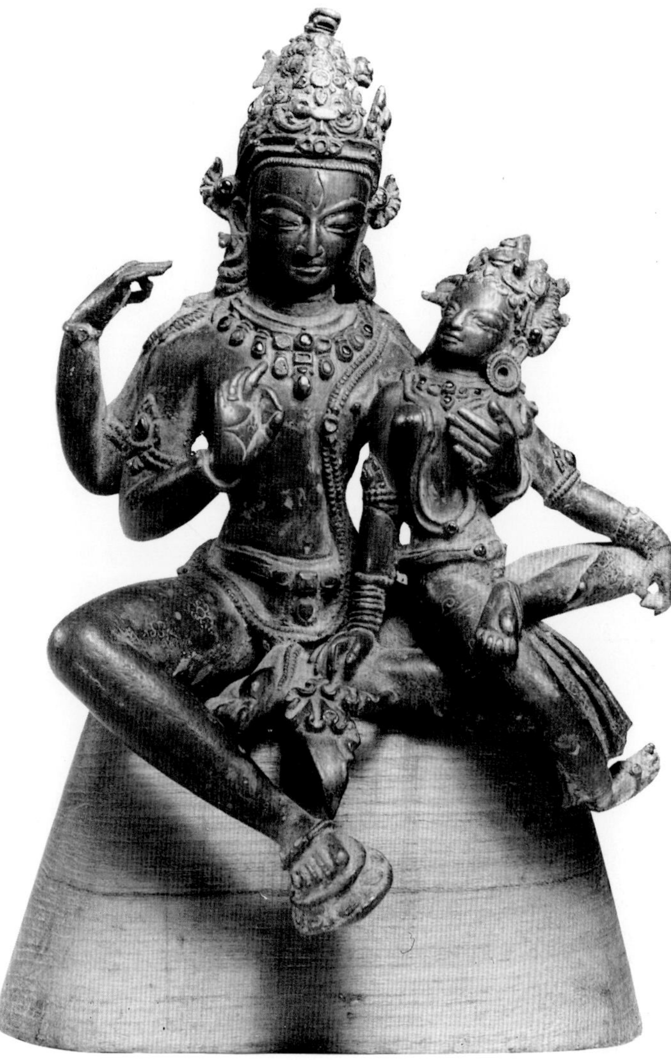

16

16

Divine Couple Umā-Maheśvara

FOURTEENTH CENTURY

COPPER ALLOY

H: 7¾ IN. (19.7 CM)

Only the central couple remains of what may have been a family group. Without additional figures, halos, and aureoles, this appears to be a sculpture in the round showing a princely couple in dalliance. Only the additional arms of the male emphasize that he is a god, in fact the great Hindu god Siva, known as Maheśvara, or Great Lord. The much smaller female seated on his left thigh is his wife, Pārvatī, one of whose epithets is Umā.

In Indian iconography such images of the couple are known as Umā-Maheśvara. With his right leg pendant, Siva is seated in *lalitāsana,* but the lotus seat is missing. A small lotus is attached to his right foot like a sandal.

Although Siva is primarily a wandering ascetic, in such images both he and his wife are represented as regally attired and bejeweled. He is further distinguished by his third eye; she may or may not be given this feature. While he is always depicted with four or more arms, she is, curiously, only shown with two, as if the artists wished to emphasize his divinity and her humanity. In this particular example neither holds any emblems. Both of Siva's right hands display the teaching gesture, even though the upper is turned inward and may originally have held a rosary. One of his left hands is behind Pārvatī, and the other comes around to caress one of her breasts. Her right hand rests on his left leg to support her body, and the other hangs over her left knee. As is usually the case in such Nepali representations, Siva's expressionless face looks with half-shut eyes straight toward the devotee, but Pārvatī has eyes only for him. This particular theme, like that of Vishnu riding Garuḍa (no. 10), was a favorite with Newari artists.

17

Dancing Gaṇeśa

FOURTEENTH CENTURY

COPPER ALLOY WITH TRACES OF GILT

H: 3 IN. (7.6 CM)

As in India, Gaṇeśa is a popular deity in Nepal. His name literally means Lord of the People or Tribe, and he is distinguished by his elephant's head grafted to a rotund human body. In mythology he is one of the two sons of Siva and Pārvatī (see no. 16), the other being Kumāra (see no. 11). In Hindu worship Gaṇeśa is always invoked first, as he is regarded as the remover of all obstacles. The attributes in his hands are a broken tusk, a battle-ax, and a bowl of sweets. The lower right hand is empty. The figure wears a large number of anklets on his legs.

Newari artists were particularly fond of representing Gaṇeśa as a playful child, just as they did Kumāra. In this endearing depiction the boyish god is shown dancing with his favorite animal, a rat. The rat

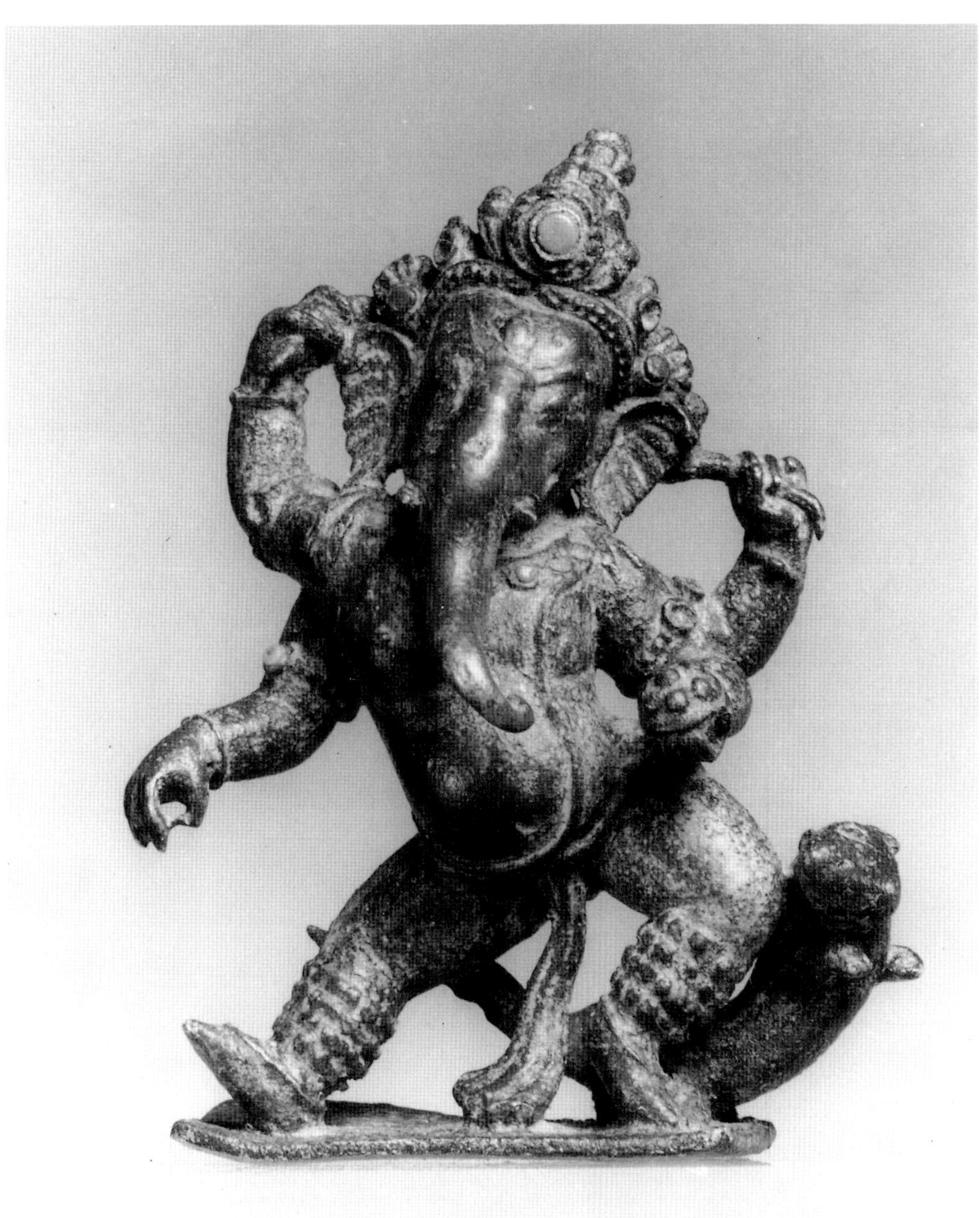

17

emulates his master, looking up at him with admiration. While images of dancing Gaṇeśa are common in Indian art, rarely are they so unaffected and humorous. As if the sight of so plump a boy with four arms and a trunk attempting to dance is not amusing enough, we are also entertained by the nimble-footed rat.

18

Durgā Slaying Mahishāsura

FOURTEENTH CENTURY

COPPER ALLOY

H: 10¾ IN. (27.3 CM)

In her most important manifestation, the Hindu Goddess is known as Durgā. The epithet symbolizes her role either as protectress of the fort (*durga*) or as remover of misfortune (*durgati*). Generally, she is depicted in combat with a demigod called Mahishāsura, which also means "buffalo." The basic iconography is similar to that of the Iranian deity Mithra destroying the bull and symbolizes the triumph of good over evil or truth over falsehood. In Hinduism the sex of the deity has changed, and the bull has been transformed into a buffalo. As in the cult of Mithra, during the autumn festival of Durgā in Nepal buffalo is the principal sacrifice.

While in India the earliest representations of Durgā slaying Mahishāsura go back to the Kushāṇ period (first–third centuries A.D.), in Nepal the image is not encountered much earlier than the tenth century. Thus Durgā's cult seems to have become popular among the Hindus in Nepal rather late, although in other forms the goddess has been worshipped in the valley since prehistoric times. Durgā is represented most frequently in stone and bronze, although painted images are known.

In this spirited bronze tableau, the long-legged goddess attacks her adversary with eight arms and an impressive arsenal. With her right foot placed on the upthrust haunches of her lion and the left on the shoulder of the decapitated buffalo, she stands triumphant, thrusting a trident into the chest of the demon who has emerged from the buffalo's neck. In vain he attempts to unsheath his sword. The horrific sentiment is downplayed, however, and the goddess displays neither anger nor ferocity in her demeanor. While the lion and demon are depicted as combative, she is elegant and serene and performs her task effortlessly. As is customary in such Nepali representations, the lion is conceptually rendered, while the more realistic buffalo reveals the sculptor's familiarity with that animal's form.

Literature Von Schroeder 1981 360–61, fig. 96A, where the sculpture is dated 1350–1450.

19

Hevajra and Nairātmyā in Union

FIFTEENTH CENTURY
GILT COPPER ALLOY
H: 8 IN. (20.3 CM)

The male figure in this embracing couple is Hevajra, the presiding deity of the esoteric Vajrayāna Buddhist ritual described in the *Hevajratantra* (Snellgrove 1959). He is locked in sexual embrace with his

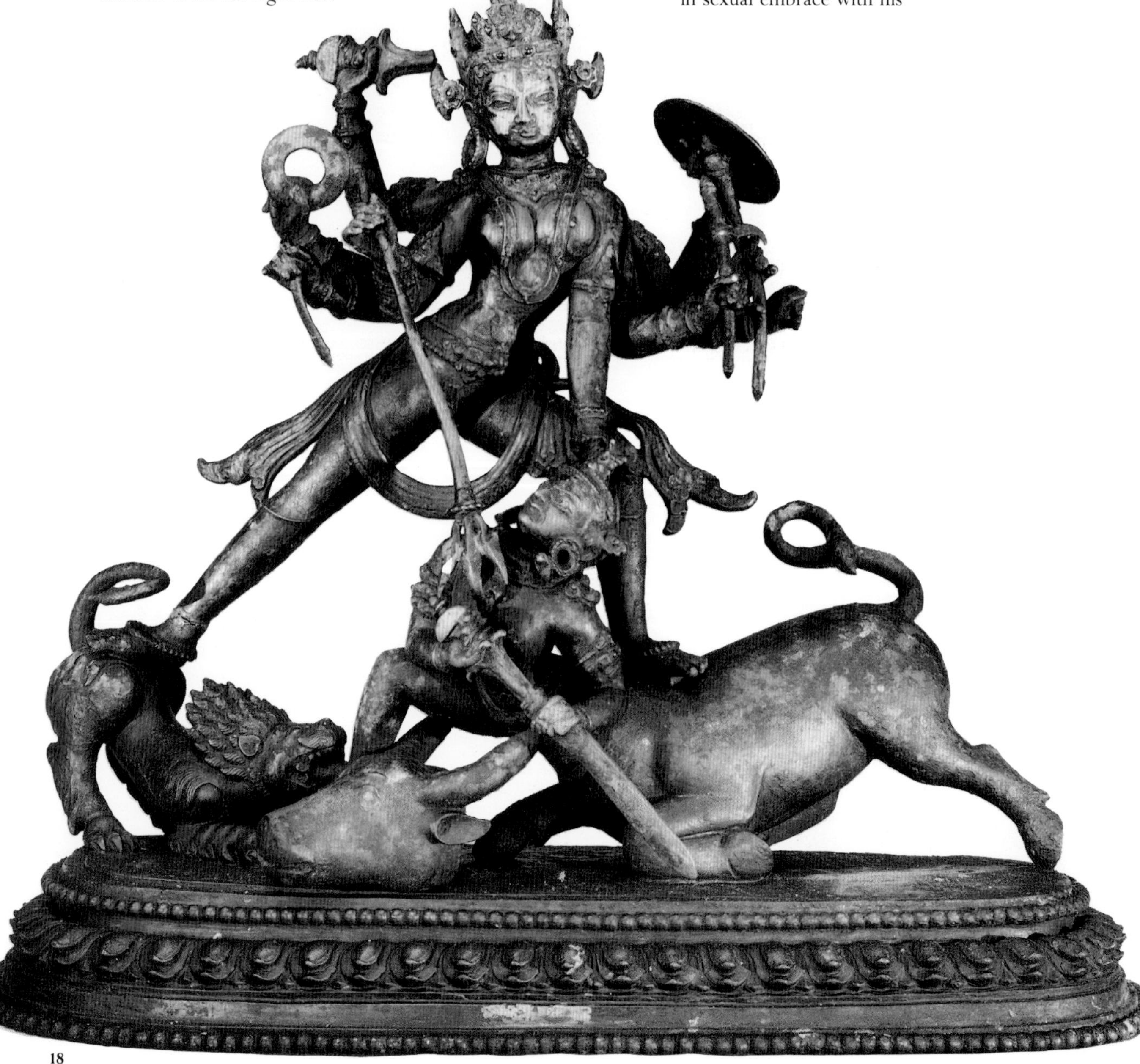

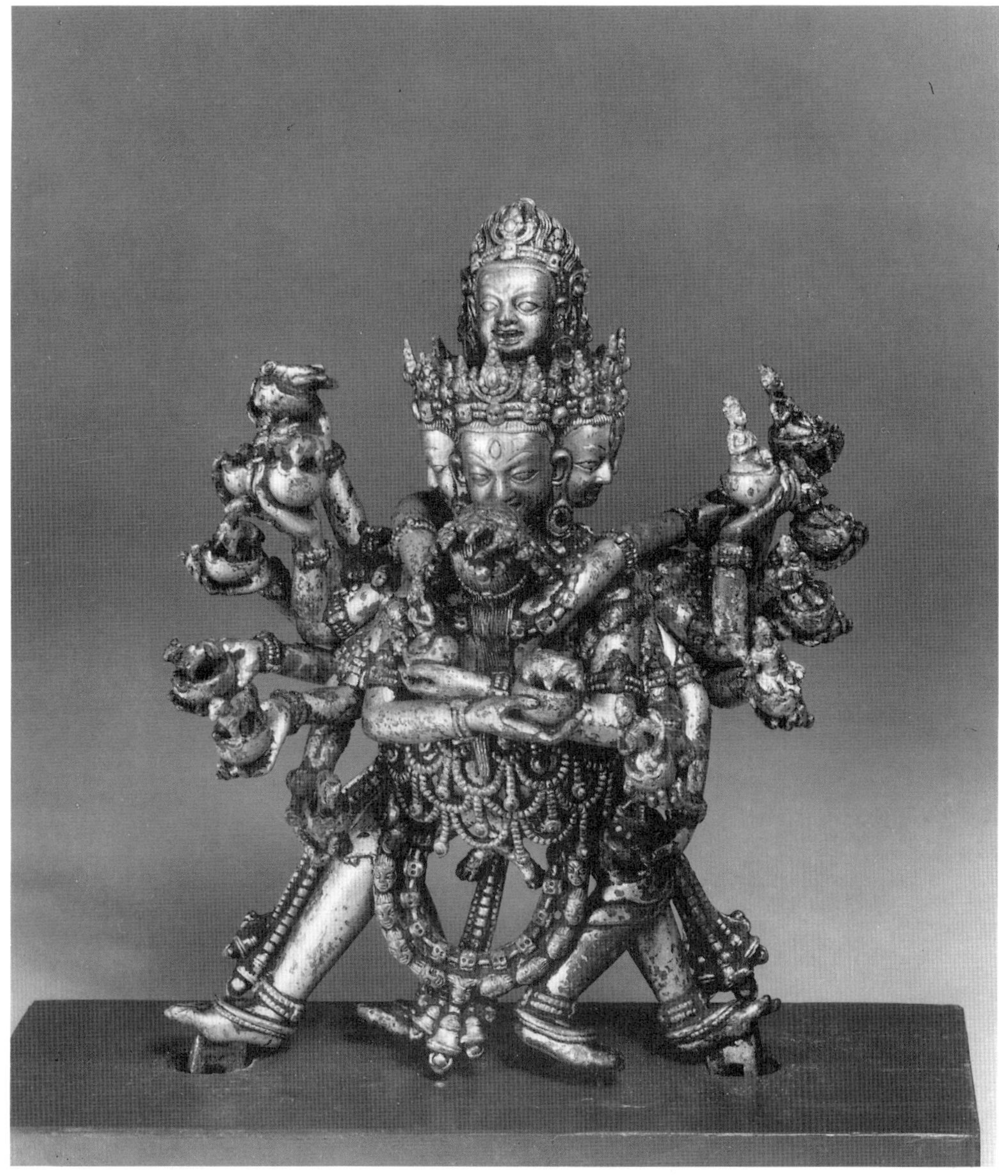

19

female partner, known as Nairātmyā, or No-Soul. The *Hevajratantra,* composed in India sometime before the eighth century, was transmitted to Nepal and Tibet. In Tibet the *tantra* is still popular with both the Kagyupas and the Sakyapas. The text invokes the two deities as follows:

And now the Adamantine One, the mighty King and Lord Hevajra, the giver of all forms, discourses on the maṇḍala. He reposes there in bliss as the essence of all forms, for he is the Lord of the *Maṇḍala* and has emanated from the seed of the Vajra of Mind. He has sixteen arms and eight faces and four legs, and is terrible in appearance with his garland of skulls and he wears the five symbolic adornments. Nairātmyā, clinging round the neck of this hero and god, addresses him. . . .

Then from the sounds of AM and HUM the Lord arises from his trance, spreading his feet upon the ground, and threatening gods and titans. The skulls in his right hands contain these things in this order: an elephant, a horse, an ass, an ox, a camel, a man, a lion, and a cat. Those in the left hands are: Earth, Water, Air, Fire, Moon, Sun, Yama, and Vaiśrvaṇa (Snellgrove 1959, vol. I, pp. 109–11).

It is clear from this enumeration of attributes that the form envisioned and invoked by the adept, who must have been a yogi, displayed the god's cosmic manifestation. In this bronze, however, a different iconographic description appears to have been followed. A human figure kneels in each cup in his left hands, and an animal—including a bird—in each of his right hands. Also, only the head at the summit is terrifying. Otherwise the faces have pleasant, smiling expressions.

Despite the complexity of the composition, it is remarkable how buoyant the figures seem. The legs strike the graceful poses of an expert dancer, and the arms are so skillfully arranged that none obscures the others. Their varied positions create a sense of organic rhythm as if the sculpture has its own dynamic force.

20

Cosmic Samvara and Spouse

FIFTEENTH CENTURY

GILT COPPER ALLOY WITH VERMILLION

H: 6⅝ IN. (16.8 CM)

Much vermillion powder (often thrown at images during worship) still adheres to this sculpture. In places the powder, having been mixed with liquid, has caked. These accretions add to the attractiveness of the gilt bronze.

The multiheaded, multiarmed male figure represents a cosmic form of Samvara, an important esoteric deity of Vajrayāna Buddhism and the presiding deity of a popular tantric system. Generally, he is portrayed with four heads and eight arms, but here his additional limbs symbolize his cosmic nature. Below his feet are the deities Bhairava and Kālarātri; the female he embraces is Vajravārāhī. In contrast to him, she is represented with normal limbs. She holds a chopper and skull cup, while his crossed hands carry a thunderbolt and bell. His heads are arranged like a cone, and his arms fan out on either side to form a circle. As is normally the case, the sculpture was cast in two pieces. The lotus base with the two prostrate figures forms one unit, and the embracing deities constitute the other.

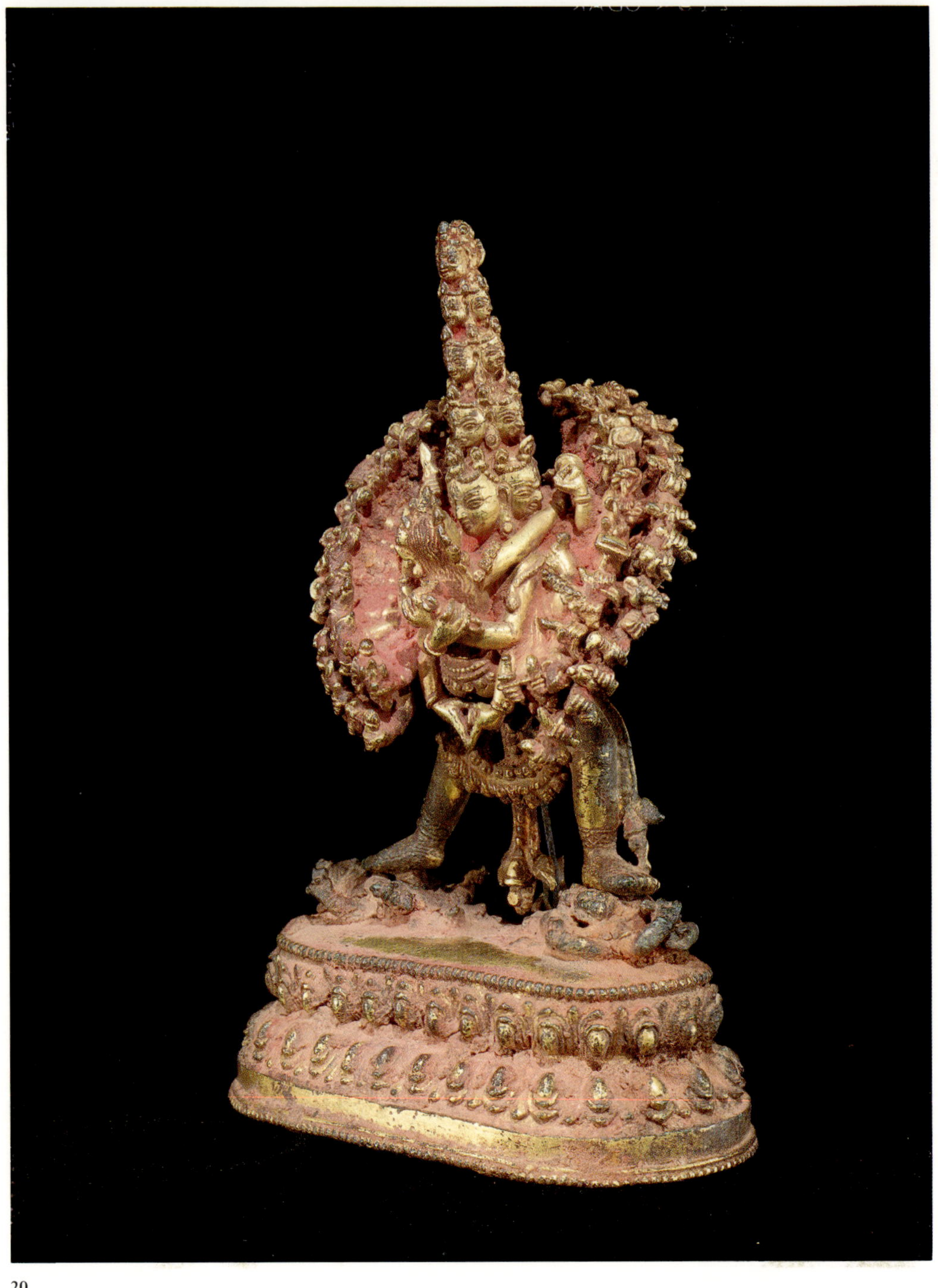

20

21

Cosmic Goddess and Spouse

FIFTEENTH CENTURY

COPPER ALLOY

H: 9 IN. (22.9 CM)

Two multiarmed deities are locked in a sexual embrace on top of a lotus that rises from the navel of a prostrate figure with multiple heads. Very likely he is a form of Bhairava, and the embracing couple represents cosmic forms of Siva and Śakti. It should be noted that unlike Buddhist images (see nos. 19, 20), the figure facing the viewer is the female. Further emphasizing the reversal of roles and demonstrating the supremacy of the feminine force, she is larger and has more limbs than her male partner. Iconographically, she is very close to the painted representation of the cosmic goddess in the Zimmerman Collection (no. 42).

Such images were used in esoteric rituals observed only by the initiated. In India such configurations of two divinities in sexual embrace meant for worship are rarely encountered, but in Nepal they are not uncommon. Both figures hold a large number of emblems in their hands that symbolize their cosmic natures. However, the exact tantric texts in which such images are described remain unknown, so the figures cannot be identified precisely. Such images symbolize the nonduality of Siva and Śakti and express the unitary blissful experience of consciousness. According to Śākta belief, the goddess is not subordinate as in Umā-Maheśvara images (see no. 16). Rather, if Siva is the transcendent aspect, she is the immanent aspect of the Siva-Śakti principle. As a tantric text states unambiguously: "By the union of Siva and Śakti creation comes . . . as all in the universe is both Siva and Śakti (*śivaśaktimaya*), therefore Oh Maheśvara, Thou art in every place and I am in every place. Thou art in all and I am in all" (Woodruffe 1975, p. 249).

Technically, the bronze is a tour de force of exquisite craftsmanship. How effortlessly the artist has organized the complex multiple limbs and forms into a harmonious composition. Strongly modeled, both figures express a sense of cosmic energy with graceful rhythm.

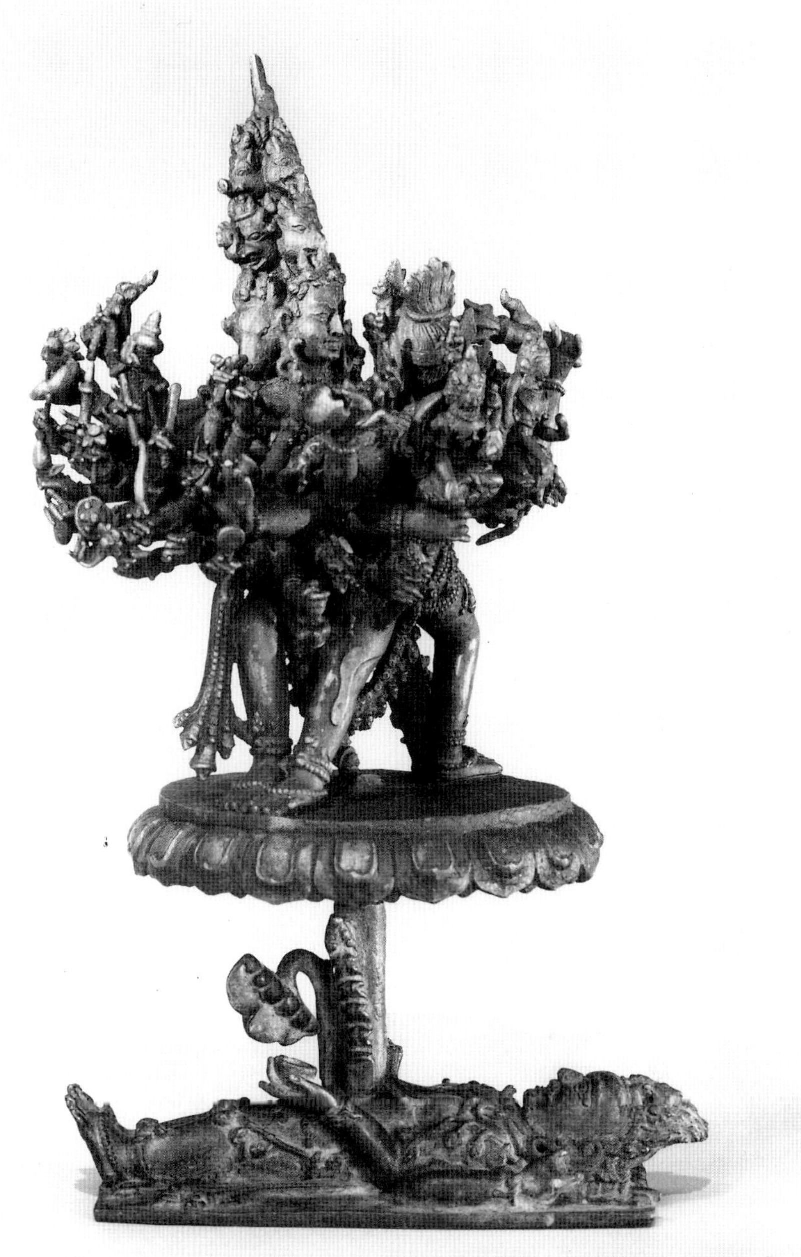

21

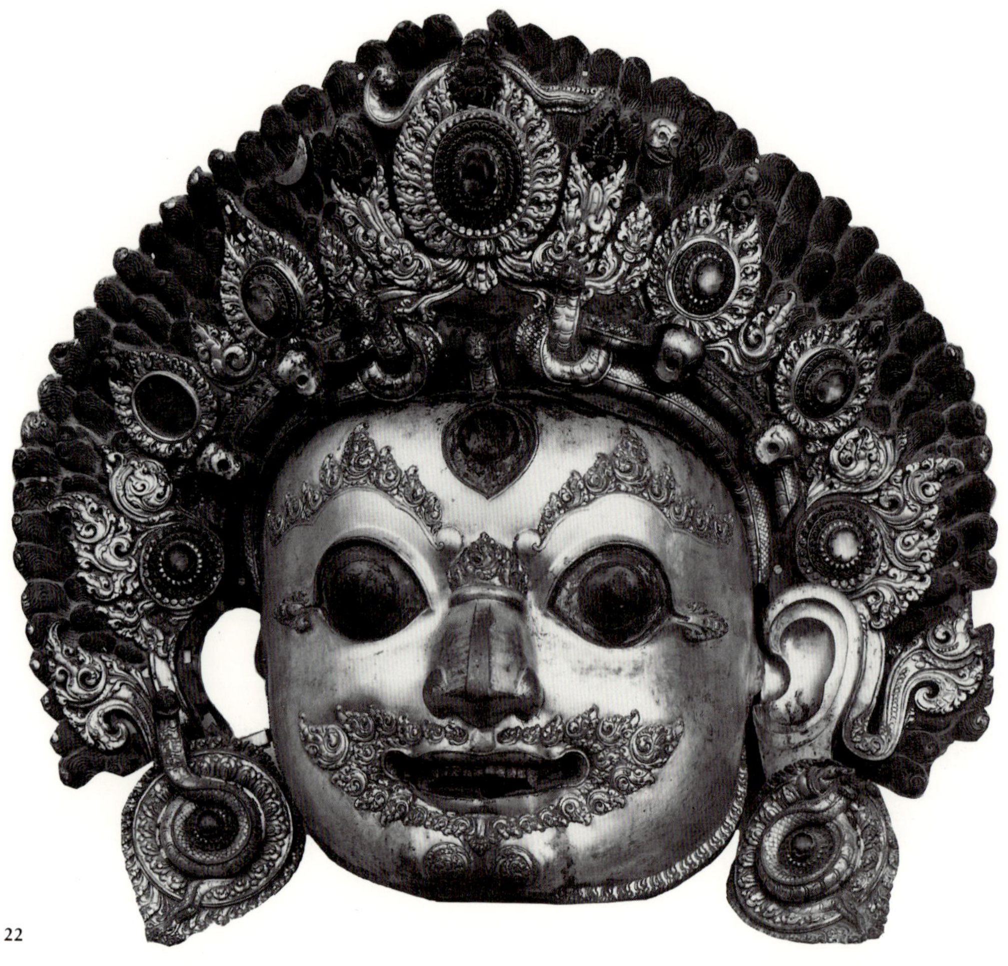

22

22

Head of Bhairava

SIXTEENTH CENTURY OR EARLIER

GILT COPPER WITH GEMSTONES AND PAINT

H: 30 IN. (76.2 CM)

Such masklike sculptures are unique to Nepali culture and art. This is the most impressive metal example outside the country. The deity represented is Bhairava, the angry manifestation of Siva. Such heads, also made of wood and terracotta, are brought out only during the popular annual festival of Indra (*Indrayātrā*) and used in a peculiar fashion. Behind each head is placed a pot filled with home-brewed beer, which is funneled through a pipe emerging from Bhairava's mouth. This consecrated beverage is then consumed with much enthusiasm by devotees (see Slusser 1982). Why Bhairava should have become associated with a festival in honor of the Vedic deity Indra is not known. The custom of drinking as an integral part of the ritual is peculiar to Nepal, where it is a national festival.

A comparison with the much earlier Vajrapāṇi (no. 9) shows the remarkable continuity of artistic conventions in Nepal. This head and its features are similarly conceived, except that the facial hair is more abundant and highly stylized. The hair on the head is arranged in upright curls resembling pinecones and is painted orange. Snakes and skulls are used generously as ornaments. Although essentially decorative, most of these features—along with the discoid eyes—add to the visage's expressive character.

Apart from its size, the head is impressive for its workmanship. In an earlier publication (Pal 1975, p. 67), I suggested an eighteenth-century date for it. However, after a comparison with a dated example of 1560 (Alsop 1986, p. 24, fig. 14), a sixteenth-century date seems more acceptable.

23

Yantra *of the Goddess*

SIXTEENTH CENTURY

COPPER ALLOY

H: 2⅜ IN. (6 CM)

The word *yantra* is used freely in all vernacular languages derived from Sanskrit to denote an instrument or mechanical contrivance. Thus a sitar or a car is a *yantra*. In Vedic Sanskrit, however, the word originally meant an instrument for restraining or holding, a prop or a support. It is in this sense that it has continued to be employed in tantric religious praxis. It connotes a mystical diagram used by priests as a temporary support or abode for the deity being invoked or worshipped. Even if an image is used, a temporary *yantra* is painted with colored powder by the priest. The deity is then persuaded to occupy the *yantra* during performance of the ritual. No Hindu worship can occur without a *yantra*. Usually, *yantras* are painted during worship and then destroyed. In shrines where worship occurs daily, more permanent *yantras* like this example are often made, usually of copper. The Buddhist equivalent of the *yantra* is the mandala.

This is a particularly elaborate example whose precise identification and significance are difficult to interpret except by a tantric follower of the particular form of the Goddess whose *yantra* it is. That she is a form of Durgā is clear from the lion at one of the four gateways of the citadel on its top. The footprints opposite the lion may represent the goddess herself. To the left of the footprints is Gaṇeśa, and to the right a container or cup. In the middle is a lotus, within which is a mystical diagram formed by three intersecting, overlapping triangles, resulting in an eight-pointed star. At the four corners are four more such configurations. One is a sixteen-pointed star, representing the great *Śrīyantra,* and another resembles a Buddhist knot of immutability. On one side of the pedestal is a niche with an image of a seated four-armed god, possibly a guardian of the *yantra*.

Such objects are interesting for their religious rather than aesthetic significance. They were not meant to be seen and admired for their artistic value. After each use they were probably wrapped in pieces of cloth and stored.

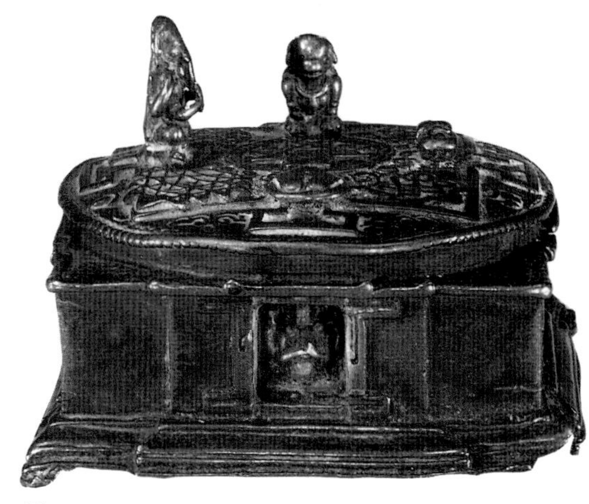

23

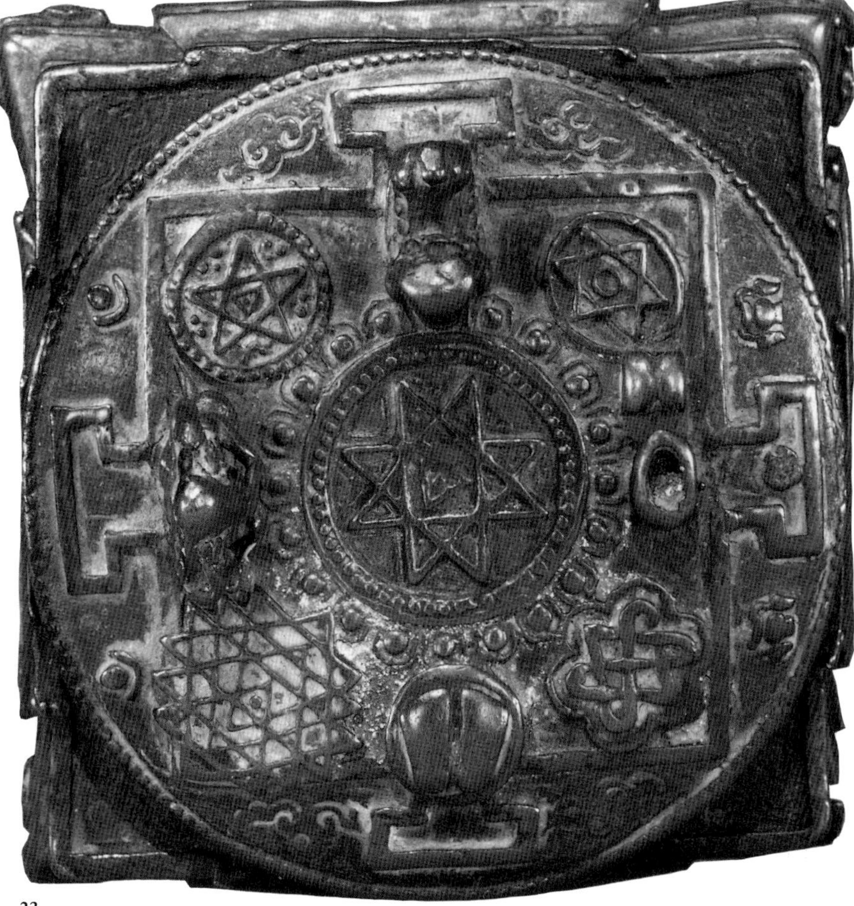

23

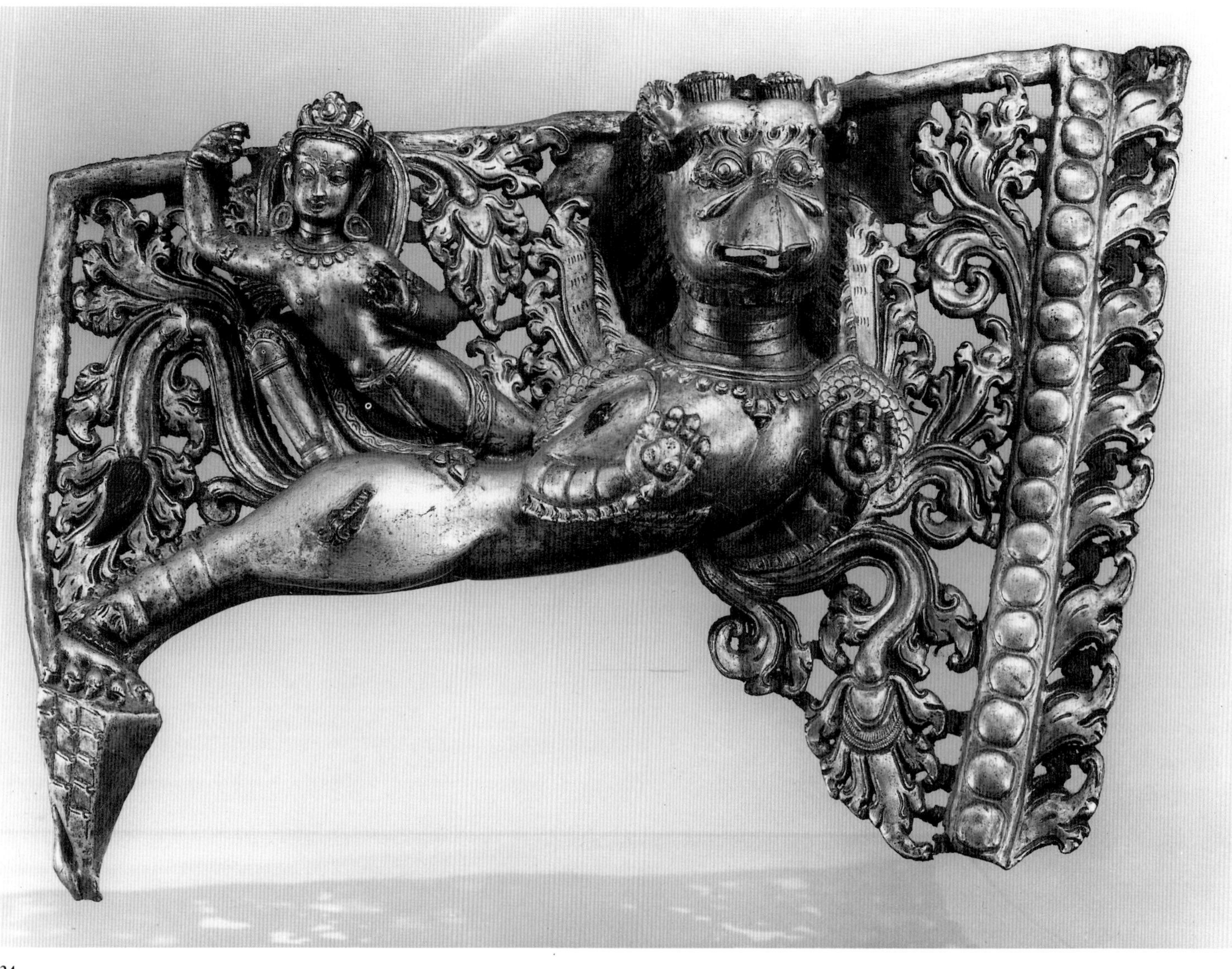

24

24

Ornamental Panel

SIXTEENTH CENTURY

GILT COPPER ALLOY

H: 12½ IN. (31.8 CM)

This repoussé panel once formed part of a throne back or shrine. The design consists of a crowned, bejeweled figure riding a winged mythical creature, very likely a griffin. The griffin has the body of a lion and the head of a *garuḍa*. The combined motif served to protect the throne or shrine from harmful influences, as is clear from the menacing attitude of both griffin and rider.

The representation in such panels is always spirited. Apart from the swift and vigorous movement of the figures, the busy, arabesquelike scrolls enhance the liveliness of the composition. As usual the scroll design is cut away, allowing the forms to achieve clearer relief. This exuberant, rhythmic pattern was much favored in both Nepal and Tibet for architectural decoration.

25

Siva and the Goddess

CA. 1600

GILT COPPER ALLOY

H: 12½ IN. (31.8 CM)

There are three figures in this tableau, two of whom are seated and the third of whom is supine on a shallow base. The supine figure is multiheaded and multiarmed and appears to be a manifestation of Siva himself, very likely the transcendent Sadāśiva. From his belly rises the stem of a lotus. The lotus itself is unusual in that it is shaped like the hourglass or the small drum, called a *ḍamaru,* that the god often holds as an attribute. On this lotus Siva is seated with his personified *śakti* (energy or power), or goddess, on his left thigh. As usual he is the larger figure with four arms, and the goddess has two arms. Each is provided with a halo.

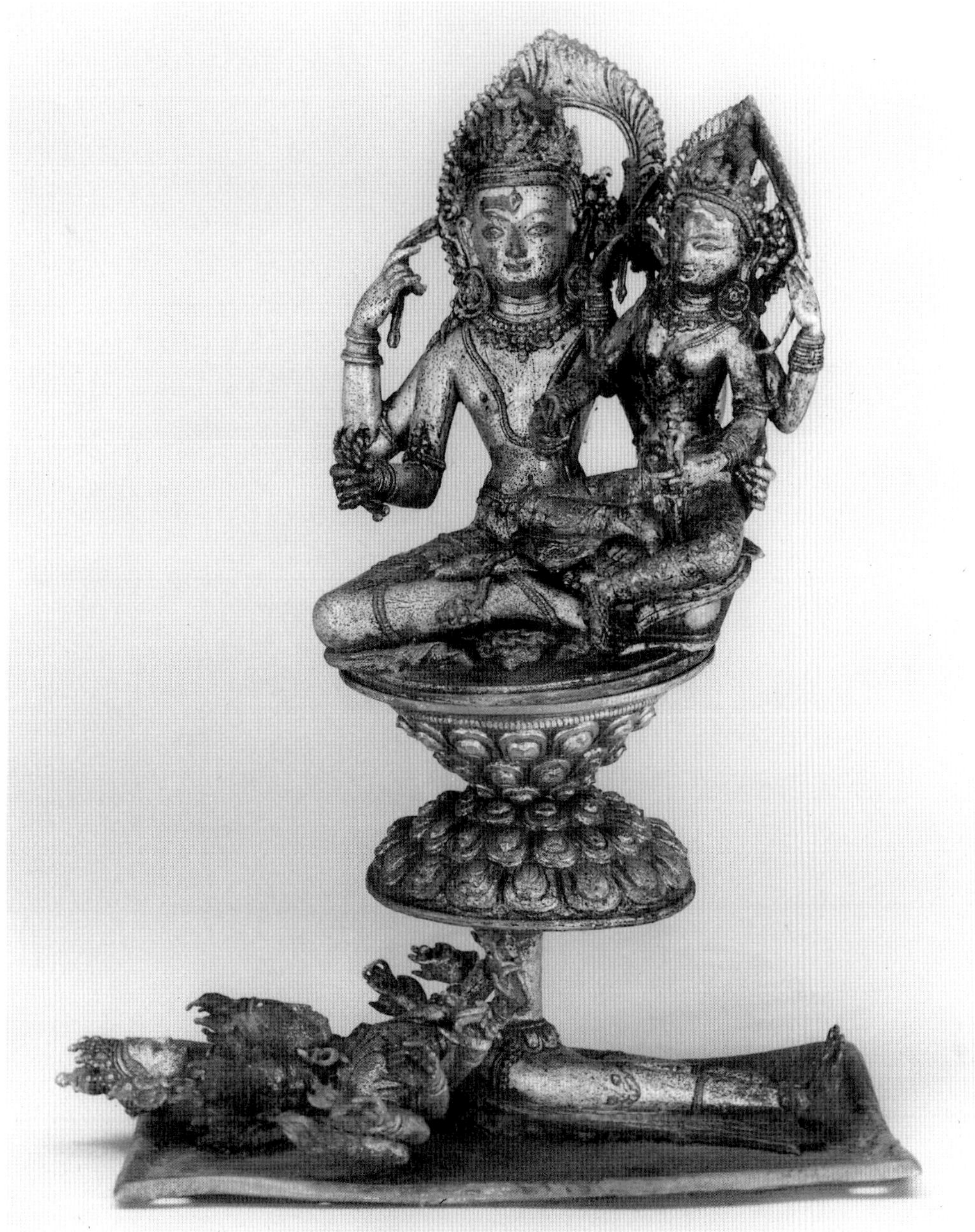

25

That the principal pair of deities is iconographically similar to Siva and the Goddess in Umā-Maheśvara images (see no. 16) is clear. However, while that image represents the family group as described in puranic literature, here the icon has been given a tantric char acter by the inclusion of the prostrate figure.

26

Androgynous Vishnu and Lakshmī

SEVENTEENTH CENTURY

GILT COPPER ALLOY

H: 8⅞ IN. (22.5 CM)

One of the unique features of Hindu theology is its emphasis on the androgynous nature of the supreme being. Just as Siva and Pārvatī are depicted in an androgynous form, so the Vaishṇavas (followers of Vishnu) devised an iconic type in which Vishnu and his wife, Lakshmī, are similarly portrayed. In texts this particular form is known as Vāsudeva-Kamalajā, two of the two deities' many epithets. For unknown reasons, this particular androgynous representation of the Vaishṇava couple appears to have become more popular

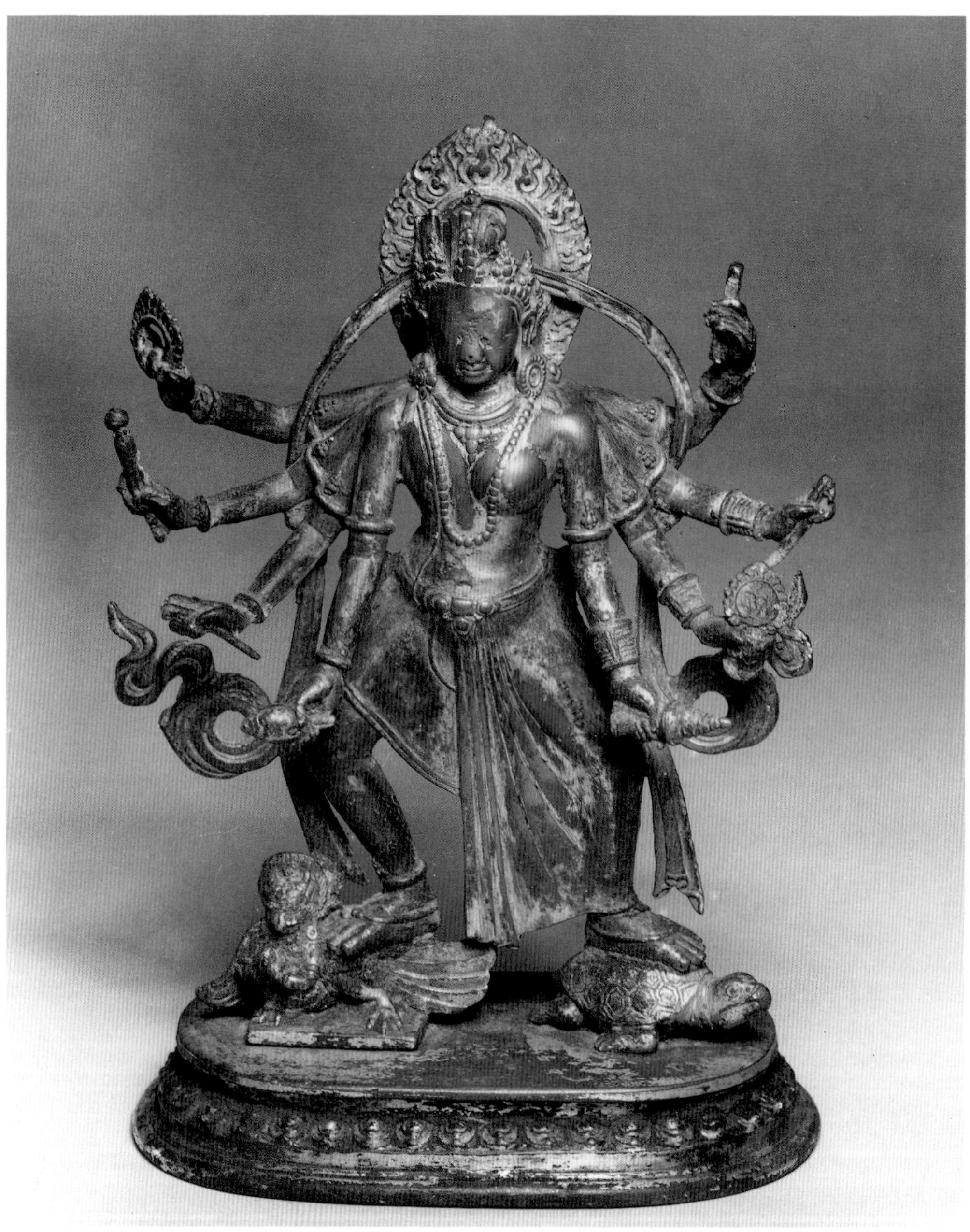

26

in Nepal after the fifteenth century than the Śaiva couple. Generally, they are shown standing erect, but here they strike a somewhat unusual militant posture (*ālīḍha*).

As is characteristic of such images, the right half is male and the left female. The two halves are distinguished here by the prominent breast and the longer attire on the left, different ornaments in the two ears, and the taller crown seen only on the right half of the head. The mounts below the feet and the different attributes in the right hands also distinguish the two halves. Below Vishnu's foot is his mount Garuḍa. Below hers is a tortoise, the usual mount of Sri-Lakshmī in Nepal. His right hands (in descending order) hold a wheel, a club, the stem of a lotus, and a conch. Her hands hold a book, the stem of a lotus, a mirror, and a water pot. In most such images, whether Hindu or Buddhist, the female is given two arms, but here she has four, as if the artist wished to emphasize her equality with the god. The reason for this departure seems to be the importance of the goddess in the theology of certain Vaishṇava schools such as the Pāñcharātra.

Apart from the dynamic pose, the flying arms and billowing scarf with its whirling ends make this an animated representation. A flaming oval halo behind the head further contributes to its liveliness.

Literature Pal 1974B, p. 50.

27

Waterpot

DATED 1675

BRASS

H: 12 IN. (30.5 CM)

A dedicatory inscription (see Appendix 1) informs us that this pot was commissioned by Jaya Jitāmitramalla and his brother Ugramalla on the sixth day of the dark half of Phālguna (February–March) in the Newari era 795 (=A.D. 1675) to please their tutelary deity. Jitāmitramalla was the ruler of Bhaktapur from 1673 until 1696. Presumably, this brass waterpot was dedicated in the royal shrine and can be associated with that city.

The base of the pot is in the form of a lotus. The body and hourglass-shaped neck are fluted. Three bands of floral decoration encircle the shoulder. The slim serpentine spout emerges from the mouth of a *makara*. The pot was made in two pieces and joined. Considering that it was a royal gift, it is rather modest, although the workmanship is fine.

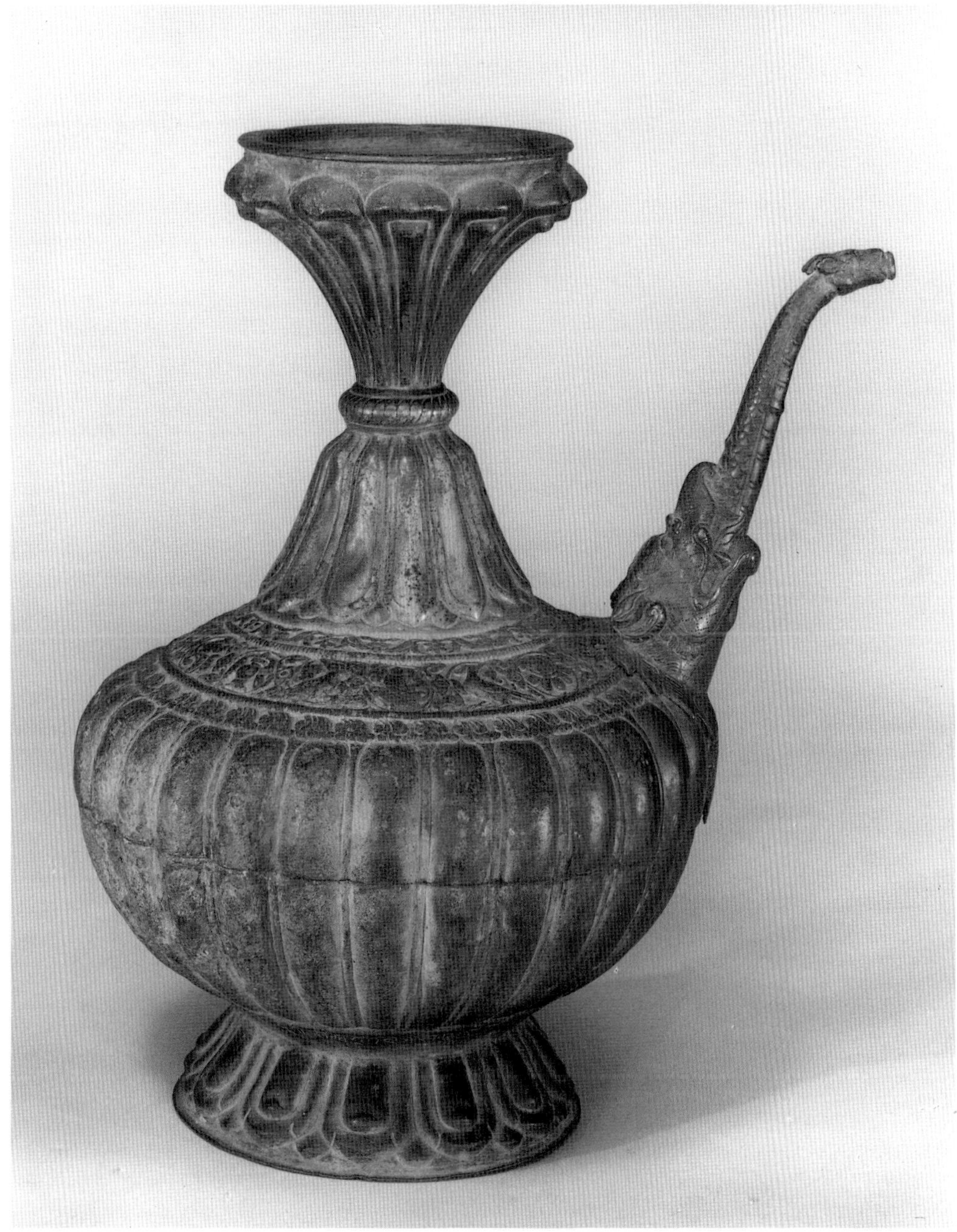

27

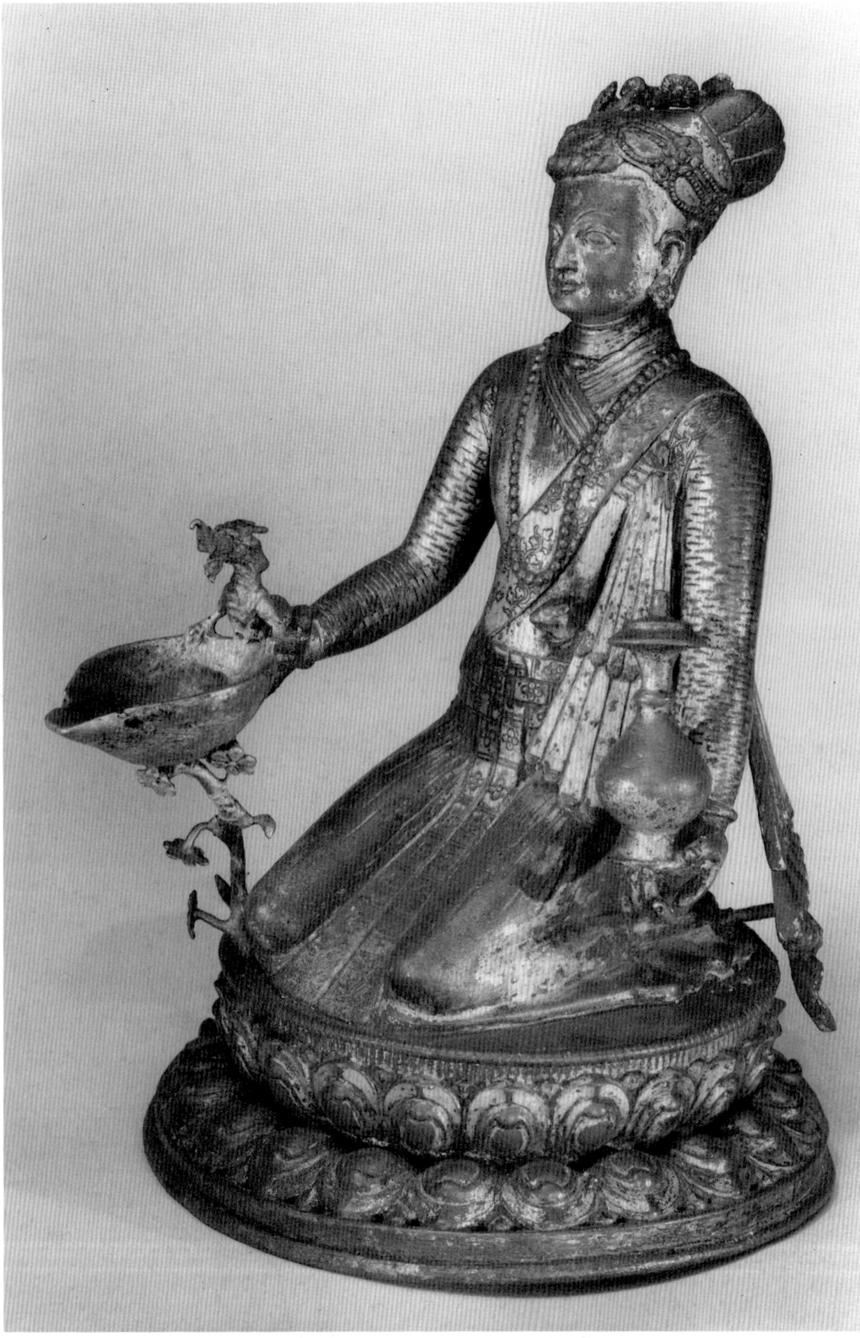

28

28

Idealized Portrait

DATED 1698

GILT COPPER ALLOY

H: 10 IN. (25.4 CM)

Idealized portraiture has an ancient history in Nepal, with some extant examples going as far back as the Lichchhavi period. Visitors to the Kathmandu Valley cannot miss the splendid figures of various monarchs that survey the durbar squares from the tops of pillars in the three major towns. The conceptual representations of donors and priests are frequently encountered on *paubhās,* as may be seen in several examples in the Zimmerman Collection (see nos. 33–35). It was also customary to dedicate small individual portraits in metal, but the depictions were seldom realistic, and no known examples can be dated much earlier than the seventeenth century.

This particular bronze has an inscription around the lotus base that informs us that it was donated in 1698 in honor of Padmapāṇi Lokeśvara in the "name of Śri Muni Vajrāchārya" (see Appendix 1). Although it is not clearly stated, presumably the kneeling figure holding a lamp and a pot represents Muni Vajrāchārya himself. A *vajrāchārya* is a Newari Buddhist priest. In this case, however, the figure is elaborately dressed in princely attire. Although it is true that in most such representations the figure is similarly clothed, in no other example is the attire so elegant. Could the figure represent a king in whose honor the *vajrāchārya* donated the lamp? It is curious that a *vajrāchārya* should be portrayed with a lamp and pot rather than a thunderbolt and bell. However, in paintings of this period *vajrāchāryas* are shown wearing similar dress and offering oblations to the fire. Interestingly, in an eighteenth-century portrait of King Pratāpamalla we see him worshipping with a similar water pot and dragon-handled incense burner (Pal 1978, fig. 194).

Whomever the figure represents, there is little doubt that this is the finest known example of such an object. Both the casting and the chasing are of superior quality. Especially noteworthy are the textures and design of the garments, the elegant turban, the support of the lamp, and its handle rendered in the form of a dragon.

29

Portrait of Bharamayi

DATED 1761

GILT COPPER ALLOY

H: 8⅜ IN. (21.3 CM)

According to the dedicatory inscription on the back of the base, this object was commissioned by the donor herself (see Appendix 1). Since most such donations are posthumous and done in honor of a deceased person, it is most unusual to find a person commissioning a lamp in her lifetime. The inscription seems to take note of this fact when it says that she gave this statue of herself of her own volition. Who the woman was we have no way of knowing. The inscription mentions three lamps, only one of which remains today, supported on the figure's head. The other two were held in her outstretched hands. Very likely the portrait was dedicated to a family shrine, but whether the donor was a Buddhist or Hindu is uncertain.

Elegantly dressed and adorned, with her hair pulled back neatly, the woman sits with her legs folded back. Both her hands are extended forward, so that she is seen proferring the lamps to the deity. The base is not a lotus, as is the case with the earlier portrait statue (no. 28). Perhaps this is because the subject was still alive when the object was made (the lotus is reserved for a god or deceased person). It is doubtful that this is an exact likeness, though the face does betray individualistic features.

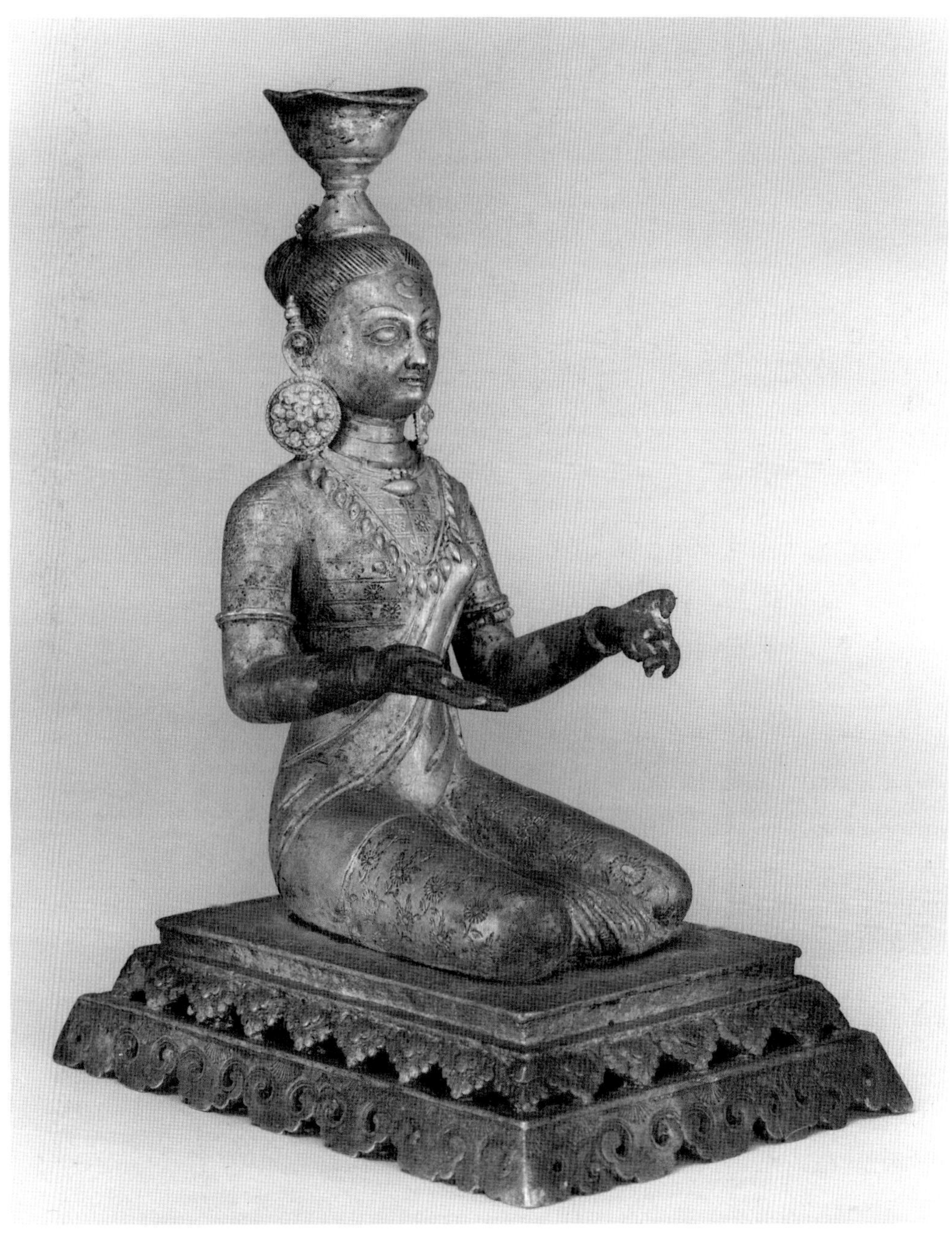

29

30

Commemorative Chaitya

DATED 1882

GILT COPPER

H: 8 IN. (20.3 CM)

The inscription along the base (see Appendix 1) informs us that this *Ushṇīsha chaitya* was dedicated in December 1882 by Sayavasim, Dhana Sumdhara, and others when they performed the *Bhīmaratha* rite in honor of their father, who was still alive, and their deceased mother. It is interesting that this rite was performed for a dead person, since originally it was meant to exonerate the living from the moral consequences of their actions (see no. 33).

It is the inscription that characterizes the object as an *Ushnīsha chaitya*. A *chaitya,* or stūpa, is the most distinguished symbol of Buddhism. It has many different meanings, one of which is funerary. Often a stūpa contains mortal remains and relics of a Buddhist. The word *Ushṇīsha* (generally meaning "turban" and referring in the Buddhist context to the excrescence on a Buddha's head) represents Ushṇīshavijayā (see no. 36), who is invoked for long life and said to reside in the stūpa's womb. Here her image has been attached to its dome. More interesting are the effigies of the couple for whose benefit the rite was performed. They are shown riding a chariot drawn by horses. This is no doubt the literal interpretation of the component *ratha,* meaning "chariot," in the word *Bhīmaratha,* as if the two are ascending to heaven in style. On eighteenth- and nineteenth-century *paubhās* the honorees are frequently shown riding a chariot, which is not attached to the stūpa as in metal representations.

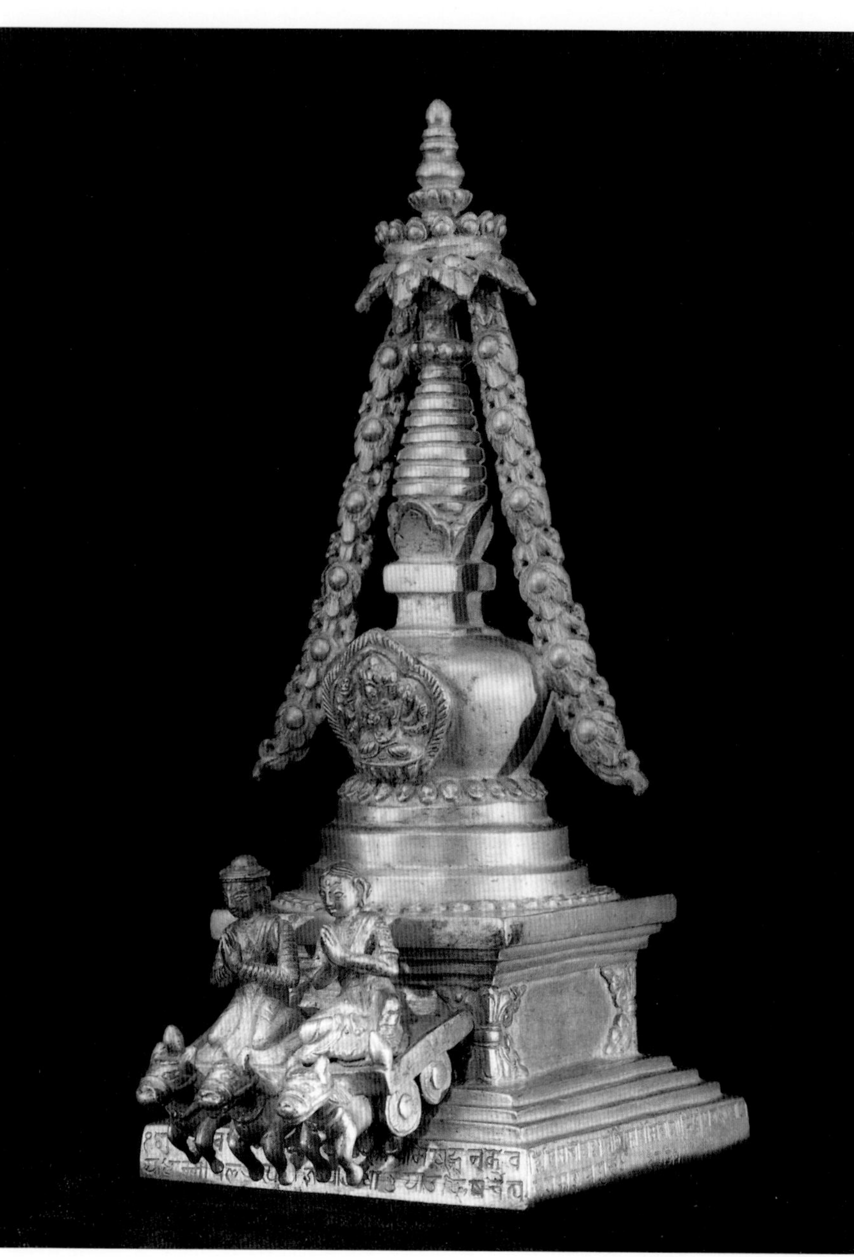

30

PAINTINGS AND DRAWINGS

Irrespective of the support, all paintings were executed in opaque watercolors. Unless otherwise stated, the support is cotton.

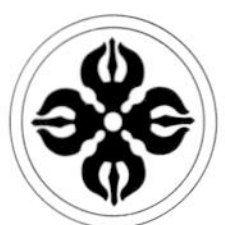

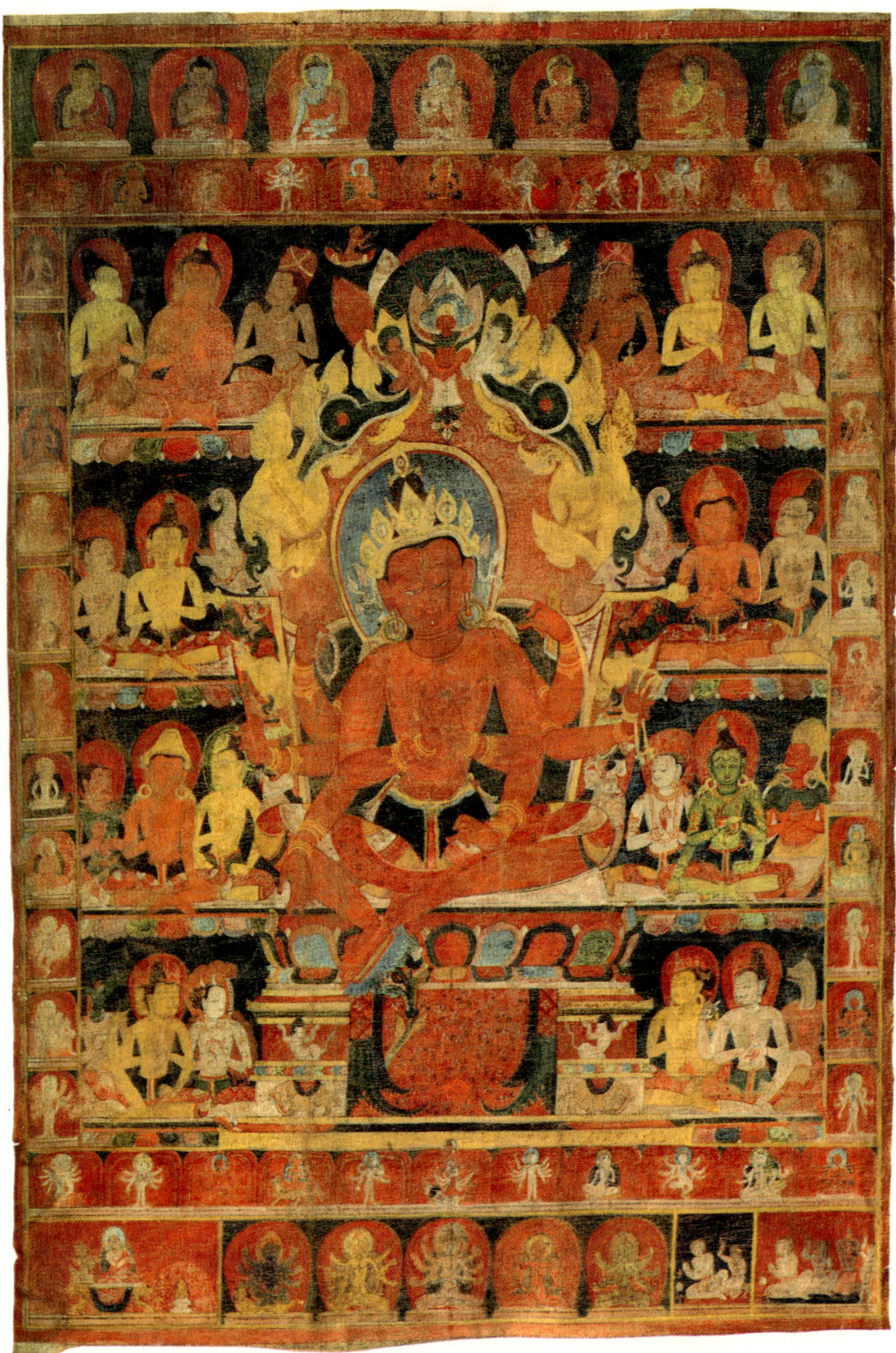

31

31

Bodhisattva and Other Deities

CA. 1300

30¾ × 21¼ IN. (78.1 × 54 CM)

The exact identification of the enshrined central figure is uncertain. Seated in the *lalitāsana* posture, the youthful deity has a red complexion and eight arms. The two principal hands form the gesture of turning the wheel of law. This gesture symbolizes the first sermon of Buddha Śākyamuni at Sarnath and, more generally, all Buddhist teaching. Among the bodhisattvas, the gesture is generally given to Mañjuśrī, whose forte is wisdom or knowledge. The red complexion and other attributes seen here, such as the rosary, the book, and the noose, are shared by Avalokiteshvara also.

However, Amitābha, the parental Buddha of Avalokiteshvara, is not the central figure among the seated buddhas at the top of the painting. Since the face of the central figure appears to be that of an adolescent, he is more likely to represent Mañjuśrī. He is surrounded by a large group of deities and buddhas whose precise identification is not possible unless the exact textual source for the composition can be identified.

Stylistically, the *paubhā* is very likely slightly earlier than the Sūryamaṇḍala of about 1350–1400 (no. 33). The grouping of the larger figures on either side of the central shrine echoes an arrangement seen in earlier paintings in both Nepal and Tibet (Pal 1975, figs. 10, 11). Clearly, the idea is to show the bodhisattva preaching before, and discoursing with, an assembly of gods, buddhas, and other bodhisattvas. The modeling of the larger figures resembles that in earlier manuscript illuminations rather than that in fourteenth-century and later paintings. Noteworthy too is the naturalistic arrangement of these figures and the fact that they seem to interact among themselves and with the enshrined figure. Particularly expressive are the ascetics who flank the buddhas in the upper register of the central section. Finally, the red is not as strong as in later paintings, and blue and yellow are equally prominent.

32

Two Pages from a Buddhist Text

CA. 1350

SILVER, INK, AND COLORS ON PAPER

EACH: 14 × 3¼ IN. (35.6 × 8.3 CM)

A Sanskrit text is written on both sides of each folio in five lines per page. The highly ornate script in silver ink contrasts strongly with the black paper. Paper was introduced into Nepal sometime in the thirteenth century from Tibet, where it had been adopted much earlier from China. Dyeing it black was also a practice adopted from the Tibetans. The shape of each folio continues the earlier tradition of books made of loose palm leaves; this is also clear from the string holes on the folios. However, the size of each folio is wider than that of a palm leaf. The illustrations, placed in the middle of each page, are also larger than those in palm-leaf manuscripts.

The illustration on the lower page represents the Buddha Śākyamuni preaching the text to a congregation of listeners. It is a formulaic representation of the beginning of the sutra, which is always expounded by the Buddha to an assembly consisting of monks, celestial beings, and bodhisattvas, among others. The Buddha, clothed in a red garment, is seated on an elaborate throne with a richly detailed arch. On the upper page a central seated figure of red complexion is seated in meditation. He is

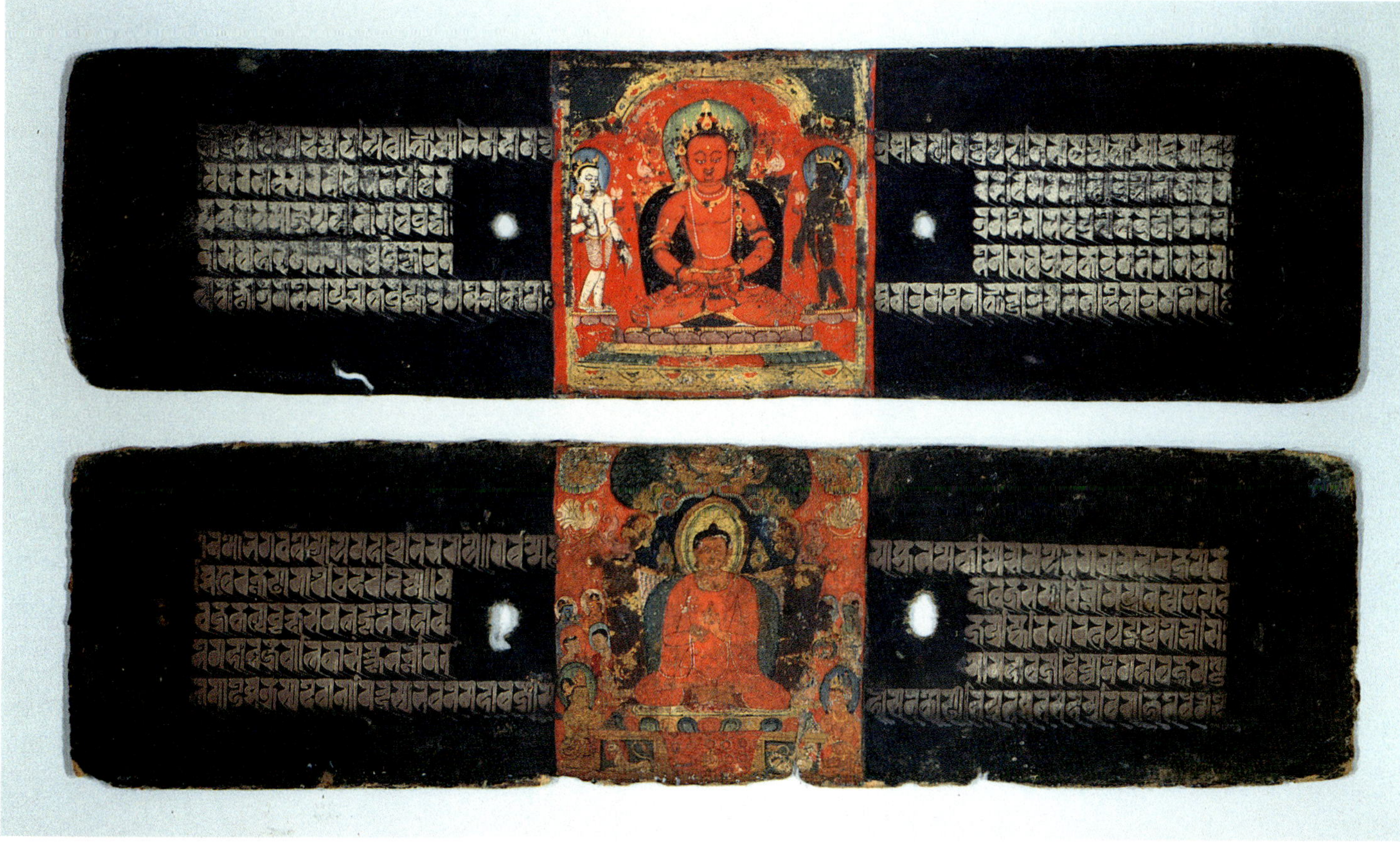

flanked by two bodhisattvas, the white Avalokiteshvara and the dark Vajrapāṇi. Although he is ornamented and crowned, he may represent Amitābha in his resplendent spiritual form or body of bliss (*sambhogakāya*).

Stylistically, these illustrations may be placed somewhere between a mid-thirteenth-century *Pañcharakshā* manuscript and a *Prajñāpāramitā* manuscript dated 1367 (Pal 1978, figs. 27–29). While the figure of the Buddha on the lower page is reminiscent of the elegant forms seen in manuscript illuminations of the thirteenth century, the figures forming his audience and those in the other illustration display greater linearity and diminished plasticity.

33

Mandala of the Sun-God Sūrya

BY KITAHARASA; DATED 1379(?)
36¼ × 21 IN. (92 × 53.3 CM)

The dedicatory inscription on the reverse of this painting is not clearly legible because of the backing (see Appendix 1). However, the first numeral of the year is 4, which gives a date in the fourteenth century. According to my reading when the inscription was more legible, it informs us that the *paubhā* was painted by Kitaharasa to commemorate the occasion when Bhishṇudeveśvara performed the *Bhīmaratha* rite. While it is true that recent evidence indicates that this rite is performed only by Buddhist Newars and that the deity invoked is Ushṇīshavijayā (see no. 30), there is no reason to assume that Hindus did not observe it in the past. It is believed that by observing the rite a person is absolved from the consequences of his or her actions if (s)he becomes senile in old age (Pal 1977). The exact age when the rite is observed is seventy years, seven months, and seven days. In this painting we see the donor in the central panel of the bottom register seated on a lotus like a deity and being entertained by musicians. This is in keeping with modern practice in which the honoree is driven in procession in a chariot to the accompaniment of music. The sun-god who travels across the sky in a chariot would be an appropriate deity to worship on this occasion.

It is not possible to identify all the deities that constitute the mandala. Apart from the sun-god and his acolytes in the center, all the important personalities of the Hindu pantheon are represented. They include such stars as Siva and Pārvatī, Brahma, Vishnu, the *Dikpālas* (guardians of the directions), Grahas (planetary deities), Ādityas (twelve forms of the sun-god), and many lesser deities. The painting should be of particular interest to students of Hindu iconography, since it is the most elaborate Sūrya mandala known and also the earliest. However, no textual description of it has surfaced.

In the center of the mandala, within the pericarp of the lotus, is the principal tableau. Attired in an armored jacket, the red sun-god rides his chariot drawn by seven green steeds. He is accompanied by four wives, two of whom stand gracefully on either side, while the other two are busy shooting shafts of light to dispel darkness. His charioteer is Aruṇa, the ruddy one. Sun worship goes back to very ancient times, and Sūrya is still eulogized by pious Hindus during their daily morning bath. That he rides across the celestial vault in a chariot drawn by seven steeds is also an ancient concept that can be traced back to Vedic literature of around 1500 B.C. (His Greek counterpart is of course Apollo, who also rides a horse-drawn chariot.) Sūrya's attribute, the lotus, is an Indian invention. Apparently, the flower was thought to be appropriate since it opens with the daylight and closes at dusk.

Only one other known Nepali mandala can be placed in the fourteenth century: a mandala of Vasudhārā dated 1367 (Pal 1975, pp. 59–60, no. 43). This Sūryamaṇḍala thus remains the earliest example of a Hindu painting from Nepal. It is characterized as Hindu here because of the absence of any transcendental buddhas along the top. The name of the donor, Bhishṇudeveśvara, is also Hindu. Yet in the scene of worship in the lower register, the priest wears a crown of the Buddhist *vajrāchārya* priest as in another *paubhā* in the collection (no. 13). Possibly the artist was used to painting such subjects only for Buddhists and so used the familiar stock formula for representing Hindu patrons.

Considering the age of the painting, it is remarkably well preserved, and the colors are still radiant. Stylistically, the *paubhā* is close to the Vasudhārāmaṇḍala of 1367. Although nothing is known about the artist Kitaharasa, the fine quality of his draughtsmanship is clear from this rare mandala.

Literature Pal 1978, pp. 75–76, fig. 82.

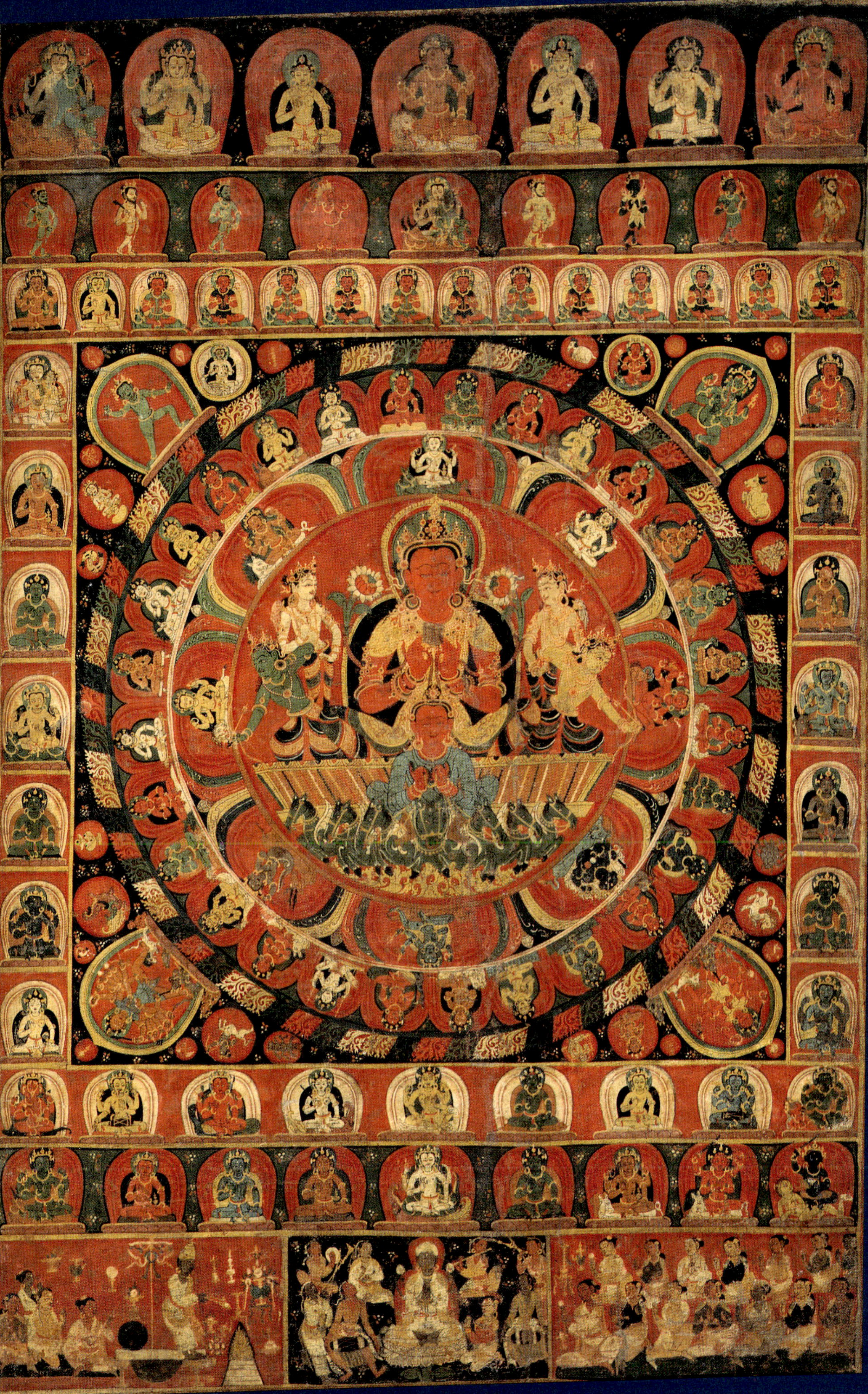

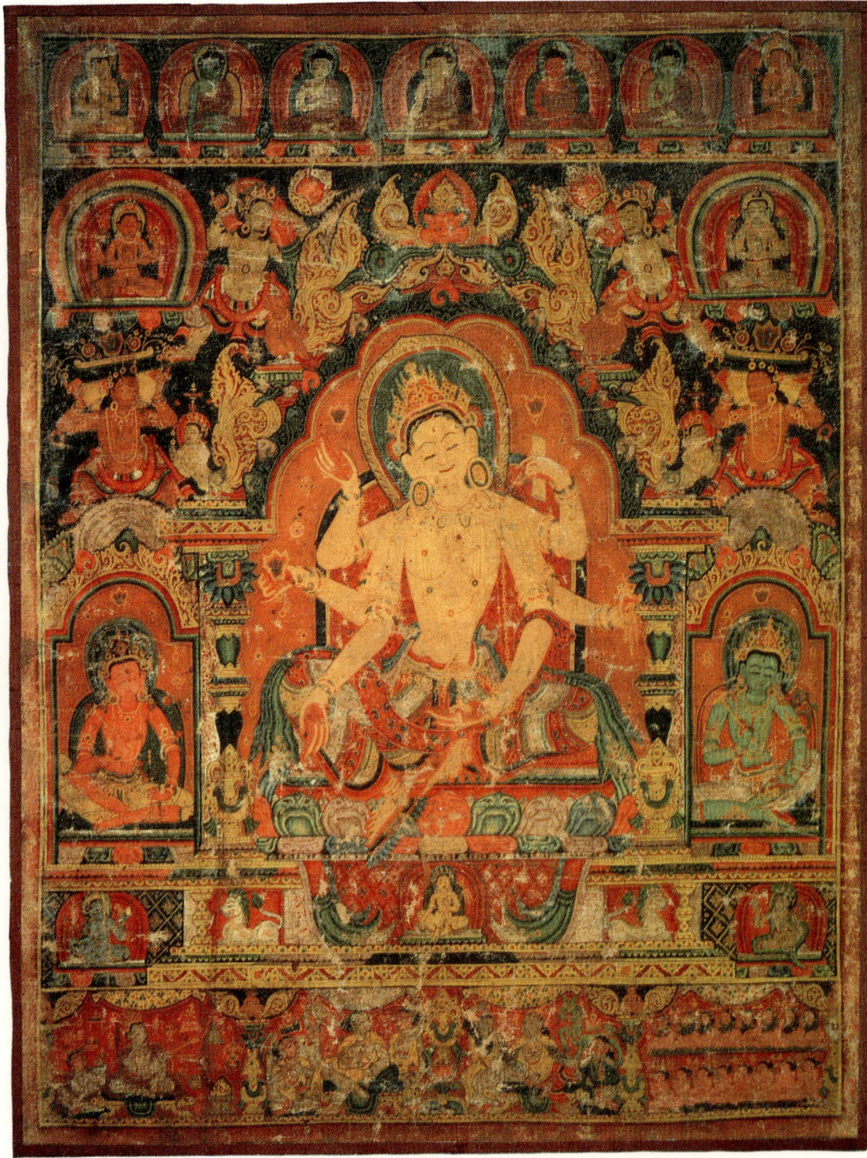

34

34

Goddess Vasudhārā and Companions

DATED 1403

34 × 29 IN. (86.4 × 73.7 CM)

The dedicatory inscription on the back informs us that this painting was consecrated in the year 1403 either by or for Phakomju, about whom nothing is known, however. Very likely he was a Newari Buddhist and a tradesman by profession. According to Alsop's reading of the inscription (see Appendix 1), the *paubhā* was painted earlier than previously suggested (see literature below).

On most *paubhās* the goddess is represented in an elaborate mandala, but here only the central portion of such a mandala has been painted (see Pal 1967). Basically, her iconography is similar to that seen on the two metal images already discussed (nos. 8, 12). Here, however, she has a pleasant smile on her face. She is placed within an elaborate shrine consisting of a base supported by lions and richly carved columns rising from auspicious water pots and supporting a florid arch. The arch consists of *kinnaras* and ganders with ornate tails and has a face of glory (*kīrttīmukha*) at the apex. Four rather ample figures representing *yakshas* (keepers of wealth) bring trays and bags of gems on either side of the arch.

The goddess is flanked by two bodhisattvas, her principal acolytes. The red figure on her left is Avalokiteshvara, and the green one on her right is Vajrapāṇi. The other five deities cannot be identified precisely. Along the top the five transcendental buddhas are flanked at each end by a bodhisattva. In the bottom register a priest offers oblation to the fire in the right panel, and the family of the donor is portrayed at the left. In the central panel are the seven jewels of Buddhism: the king, the queen, the general, the horse, the elephant, the wheel, and the gem.

The painting is rich in details as well as coloring. The colors, mostly yellow, red, blue, and green, have a soft tonality and are harmoniously balanced. Appropriately, yellow predominates; it approximates gold, which represents wealth. The intricate textile patterns, luxuriant decoration of the shrine, and lively figures of the *yakshas* are some of the salient attractions of this *paubhā*.

Literature Pal 1978, pp. 76–77, fig. 85; Reynolds 1986, p. 172, fig. 8.

35

Mandala of the Moon God

CA. 1450

24 × 18 IN. (61 × 45.7 CM)

There is some uncertainty regarding the precise date of this painting because of the indistinct character of the dedicatory inscription at the bottom. When I first published it (Pal 1978, fig. 81), I read the date as 546, while Alsop reads it tentatively as 576 (see Appendix

1). Accepting his reading, the latest date for the *paubhā* would be 1456. However, if his reading of the first letter of the king's name as *su* is correct, there is a complication, for the monarch who ruled Nepal at the time was the great Yakshamalla. In any event a mid-fifteenth-century date is acceptable on stylistic grounds.

The central figure is the moon god Chandra. There can be little doubt that the image and composition were modeled on representations of Sūrya (see no. 33). Except for his complexion, which is greenish gray (usually he is white), he is no different from Sūrya. Like him Chandra holds two lotuses, which are white instead of red. He also rides a chariot driven by a charioteer but pulled by seven geese rather than horses. As in the Sūryamaṇḍala, two women shoot shafts of light against the demons of darkness, although this is not described in the textual tradition (see Pal 1967).

In the first circle around this tableau are the eight planetary deities. The second circle contains sixteen identical figures, the personifications of the lunar half of the months (15 + 1). According to Indian belief the moon has sixteen parts (*kalā*). In the third circle is the group of twenty-eight stars, or *nakshatras*. Outside the mandala are various protective deities including the *Pañcharakshā* goddesses, Mahākāla, and Achala. The twelve signs of the zodiac are represented in the four corners. Along the top are the five transcendental buddhas with two bodhisattvas, and along the bottom are a scene of worship and stereotyped effigies of donors.

Unlike the Sūryamaṇḍala (no. 33), this Chandramaṇḍala was commissioned by a Buddhist. In fact all other known mandalas of the moon god were made for Buddhist rather than Hindu usage. Most are also from the fifteenth and early sixteenth centuries, after which worship of the planetary deities appears to have declined. The sun-god and nine planets, known collectively as Navagraha, have remained important in the lives of both Hindus and Buddhists, but why Chandra should have become popular for a limited period of time, especially with Buddhists in the Kathmandu Valley, remains unexplained.

Apart from their iconography, the mandalas of the sun and moon gods differ structurally and visually. There are also minor variations in the way the two principal deities are shown. Sūrya is represented as a bust, but Chandra's full figure is shown seated in the meditation posture. Chandra is provided with an elaborate shrine that is not given to the sun-god. Sūrya is compensated with two additional wives, who stand by him admiringly, holding fly whisks.

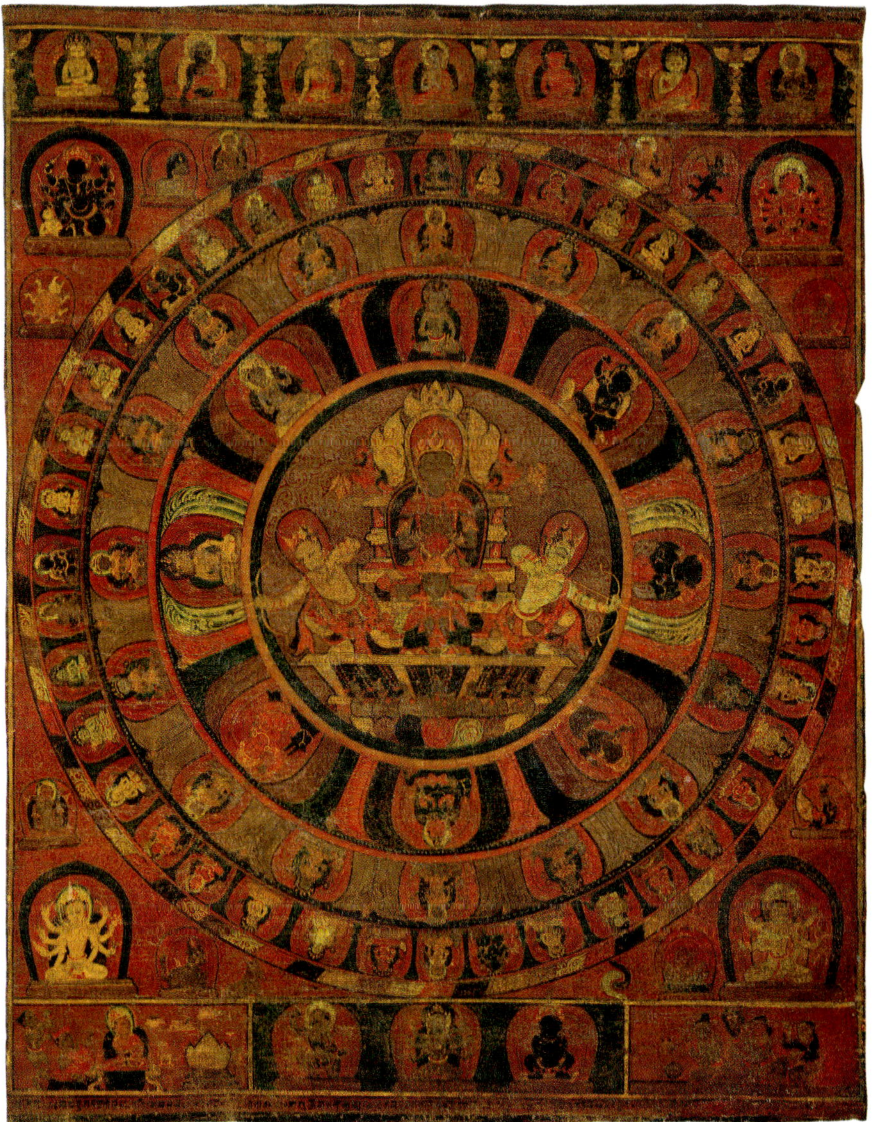

35

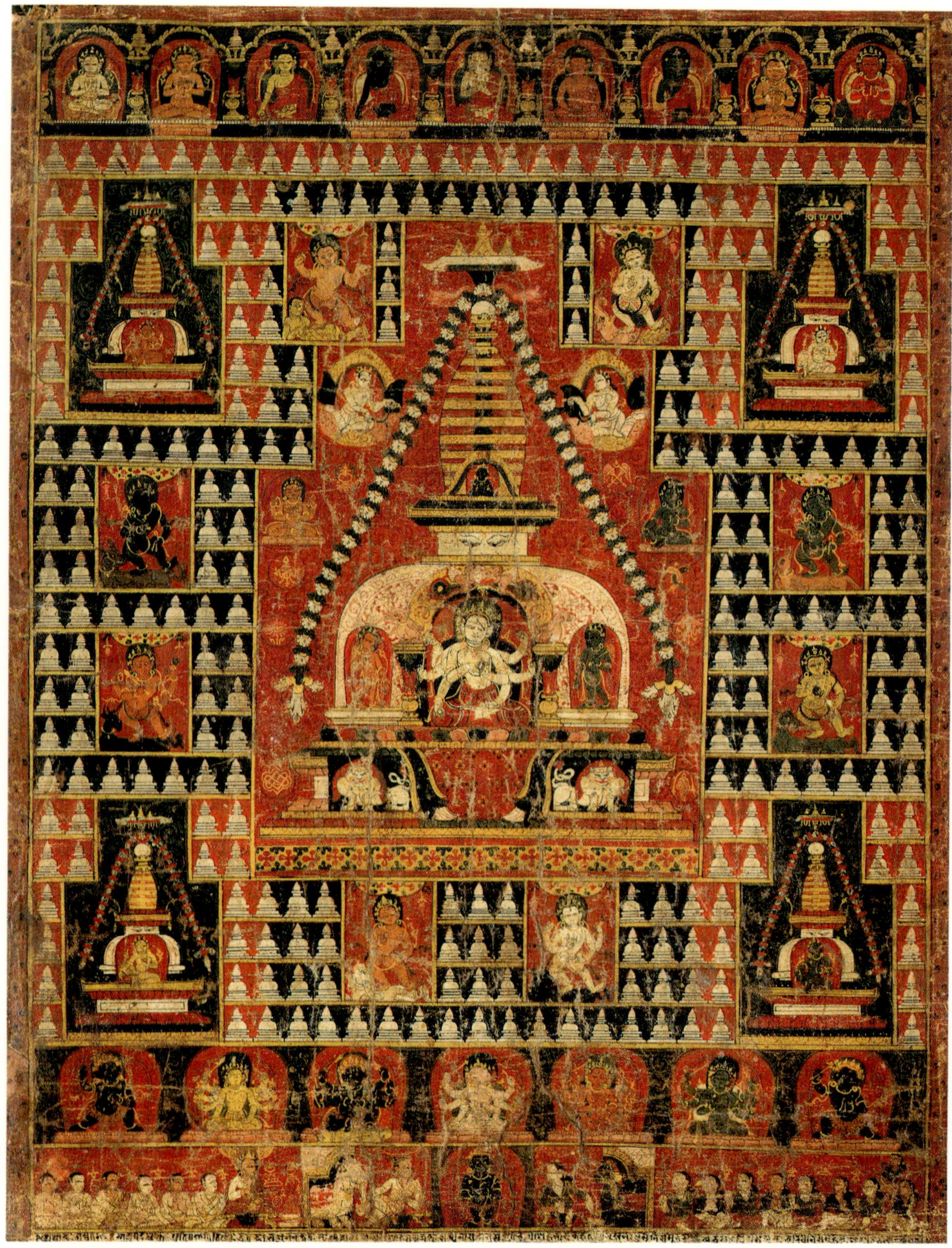

36

36

Myriad Chaityas *with Ushṇīshavijayā*

DATED 1510–19

28½ × 22½ IN. (72.4 × 57.2 CM)

According to the dedicatory inscription along the bottom, this *paubhā* was dedicated in N.S. 63x of the Newari era (=1510–19) by one Jasarāja and members of his family. The large number of *chaityas* very likely indicates that the occasion was the observance of the rite known as *Lakshachaitya*. Buddhists believe that their religious merit increases in proportion to the number of dedications they make; the *Lakshachaitya* rite earns the patron the merit of dedicating a hundred thousand *chaityas*. (In point of fact fewer chaityas are painted on this *paubhā*.) The presiding deity of this rite is the goddess Ushṇīshavijayā, who is said to reside in the womb of a *chaitya*. She is worshipped for long life, so by performing this rite the donor not only ensures a long life but also contributes toward his final freedom from the chain of rebirth.

Flanked by two bodhisattvas, the goddess is represented within a typical Nepali shrine against a characteristically Nepali stūpa. The dome is delicately adorned with lacelike floral designs. The eyes on the entablature over the dome and the elegant conical finial, festooned with floral garlands, are prominent features. The consecrated ground is occupied by two more divinities and symbols, while two celestials float on clouds on either side of the finial.

Although the *chaityas* dominate the composition, interspersed among them are eight directional deities, each dancing elegantly on his mount, and four representations of the goddess Tārā, shown within the womb of a *chaitya* at each corner. In the register at the top, below arches, are the five transcendental buddhas with Vairochana in the middle, flanked by two bodhisattvas and the sun and moon gods at the two ends. In the upper of the two registers at the bottom are the Pañcharakshā flanked by Achala and Vajrapāṇi, two guardian deities. In the lowermost register are conventional scenes of consecration with a priest, the donor and his family, the seven jewels, and an image of Mahākāla, another protector deity.

Since the rite was popular among Newari Buddhists, a number of *Lakshachaitya* paintings have survived. Among them this example is one of the earliest and also particularly attractive. The unknown artist displays a delightful sense of design in integrating the figural forms and *chaitya* motifs into a striking abstract composition.

Literature Pal 1975, no. 47; 1978, pp. 71–72, fig. 79.

37

Amoghapāśa Lokeśvara and Companions

CA. 1525

25¼ × 21 IN. (64.1 × 53.3 CM)

Lokeśvara is an alternative epithet of the Bodhisattva Avalokiteshvara, who has numerous emanations in the Vajrayāna pantheon. In one

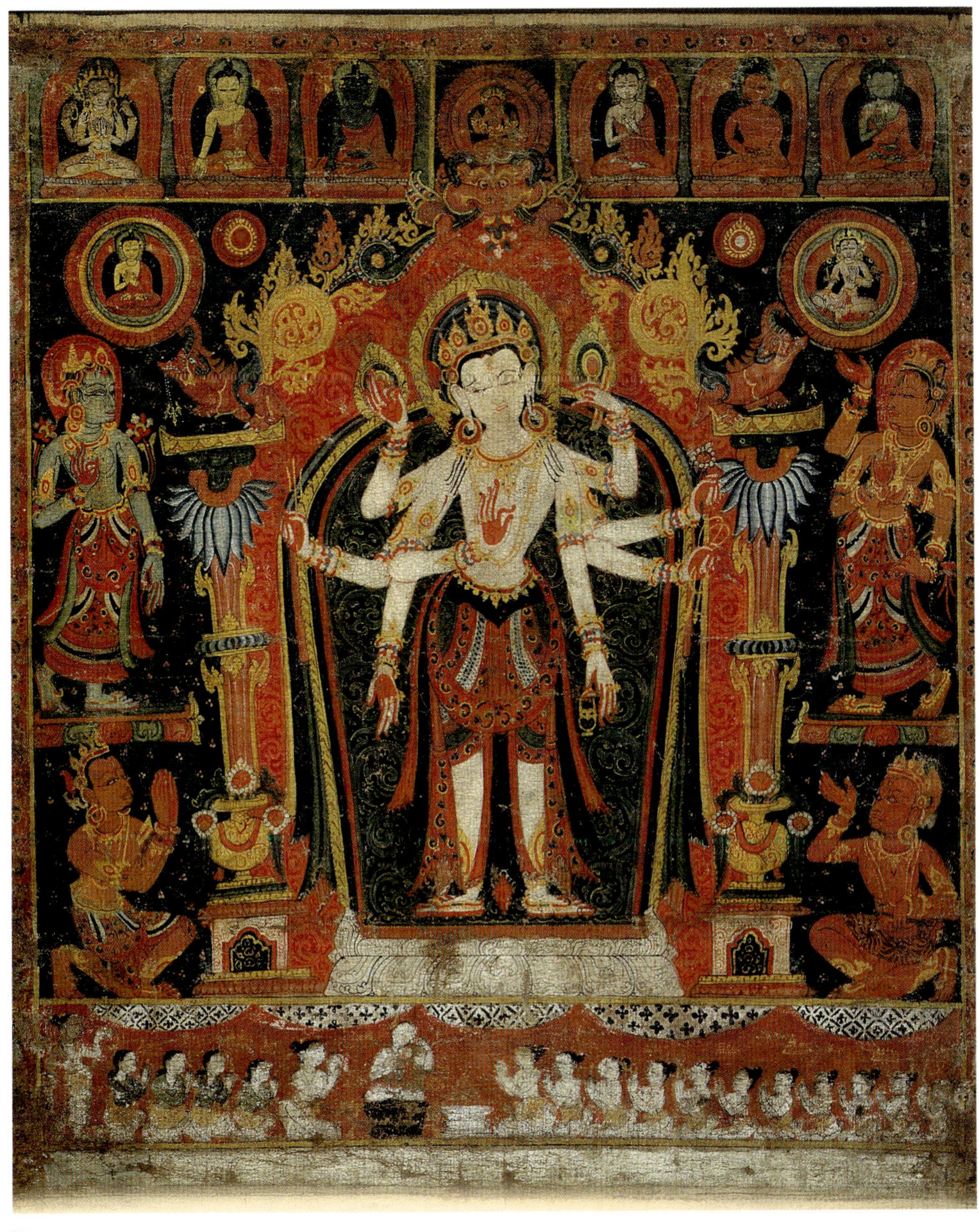

37

of these he is known as Amoghapāśa, or the One with the Unfailing Noose. The noose therefore is an invariable attribute of this form of the bodhisattva and is usually held by the third hand on the left (from the top). The other emblems or gestures are (clockwise from upper left): a book, a lotus, a water pot, the teaching gesture (against the chest), the gesture of charity, the three-pronged staff (*tridaṇḍi*), and the gesture of adoration. Lokeśvara's four companions are the standing goddesses Bhṛikuṭī (with four arms) and Tārā, the gentle Sudhanakumāra with clasped hands, and the ferocious Hayagrīva; the latter two genuflect before Amoghapāśa. The symbols of the sun and moon, various buddhas, and bodhisattvas are included above the ornate shrine. At the bottom a priest offers oblations to the fire as members of the donor's family watch reverently.

The cult of this bodhisattva appears to have been especially popular in Nepal (see Pal 1966). It also seems to have become widespread only from the fifteenth century on, for earlier representations are very rare. He is particularly worshipped on the eighth (*ashṭamī*) day of the lunar fortnight, and the rite is known as *Ashṭamīvrata*. It is customary on that occasion for a patron to commission a painting or sculpture representing Amoghapāśa. It should be noted that his images are extremely rare in Indian Buddhist art, though he was venerated in Java. Only in Nepal, however, have painted representations of the deity survived. This *paubhā* is a characteristic example.

Literature Pal 1975, no. 18.

38

Fierce Achala and Spouse

CA. 1525–50

34 × 25½ IN. (86.4 × 64.8 CM)

Against an oval aureole of stylized flames with leaping tongues are the intertwined figures of Achala and his spouse, Dveshavajrī. Both are painted in two shades of blue. A wrathful emanation of Mañjuśrī, Achala, meaning "Immovable," is also known as Chaṇḍamahāroshaṇa, an epithet implying furious anger. An important deity of esoteric Buddhism, he has an entire tantra, known as the *Chaṇḍamahāroshaṇatantra,* devoted to him. As a protective deity he often appears with Mahākāla in mandalas of other deities (see no. 36).

On *paubhās* Achala is always shown in this characteristic posture as if genuflecting. Both he and his spouse, engaged in a passionate sexual embrace, are generally represented as spirited figures. His aggressiveness is emphasized by the sword he brandishes and the noose held in his left hand. With it he lassoes the ignorant, whom he destroys symbolically with the sword of wisdom. His spouse holds a blood-filled skull cup in her left hand. Except for their delicately rendered ornaments and scarfs, both are naked. Eight other manifestations of Achala are depicted in the flaming aureole, and a host of other esoteric deities, most of whom are violently disposed and engaged in sexual embrace, fills the remaining field. Included also are *mahāsiddhas* and monks, who appear to be wearing Tibetan-style garments, and consecration scenes at the bottom corners.

The central pair is striking against the red background. They appear to be soaring across the surface of the painting. Especially exquisite is the rendering of their ornaments. Delineated mostly in yellow to emulate gold, they offer a strong contrast against the two shades of blue. The entire composition is particularly animated.

Literature Pal 1975, no. 33; 1978, p. 109.

39

Mandala of the Moon God

1550–75

24 × 19 IN. (61 × 48.3 CM)

Painted a little over a century after the earlier Chandramaṇḍala (no. 35), this example is iconographically less elaborate and aesthetically more freely rendered. The row with the sixteen parts of the moon has been dropped and the signs of the zodiac excluded. The five buddhas above are crowned and ornamented, and Achala has been omitted from the central panel below. Instead there is a group of five deities with Mañjuśrī in the center flanked by two standing figures, one red and the other black, representing Avalokiteshvara and Vajrapāṇi, respectively. The two other seated deities of this group are the white Gaṇeśa at the left and the dark Mahākāla at the right. The inclusion of Gaṇeśa perhaps reflects the increasing influence of Hinduism in Nepali society.

A comparison with the fifteenth-century rendering of the same theme shows that this *paubhā* is painted in a different style. Not every detail is drawn precisely, as is clear from the lotus petals, ornaments, and

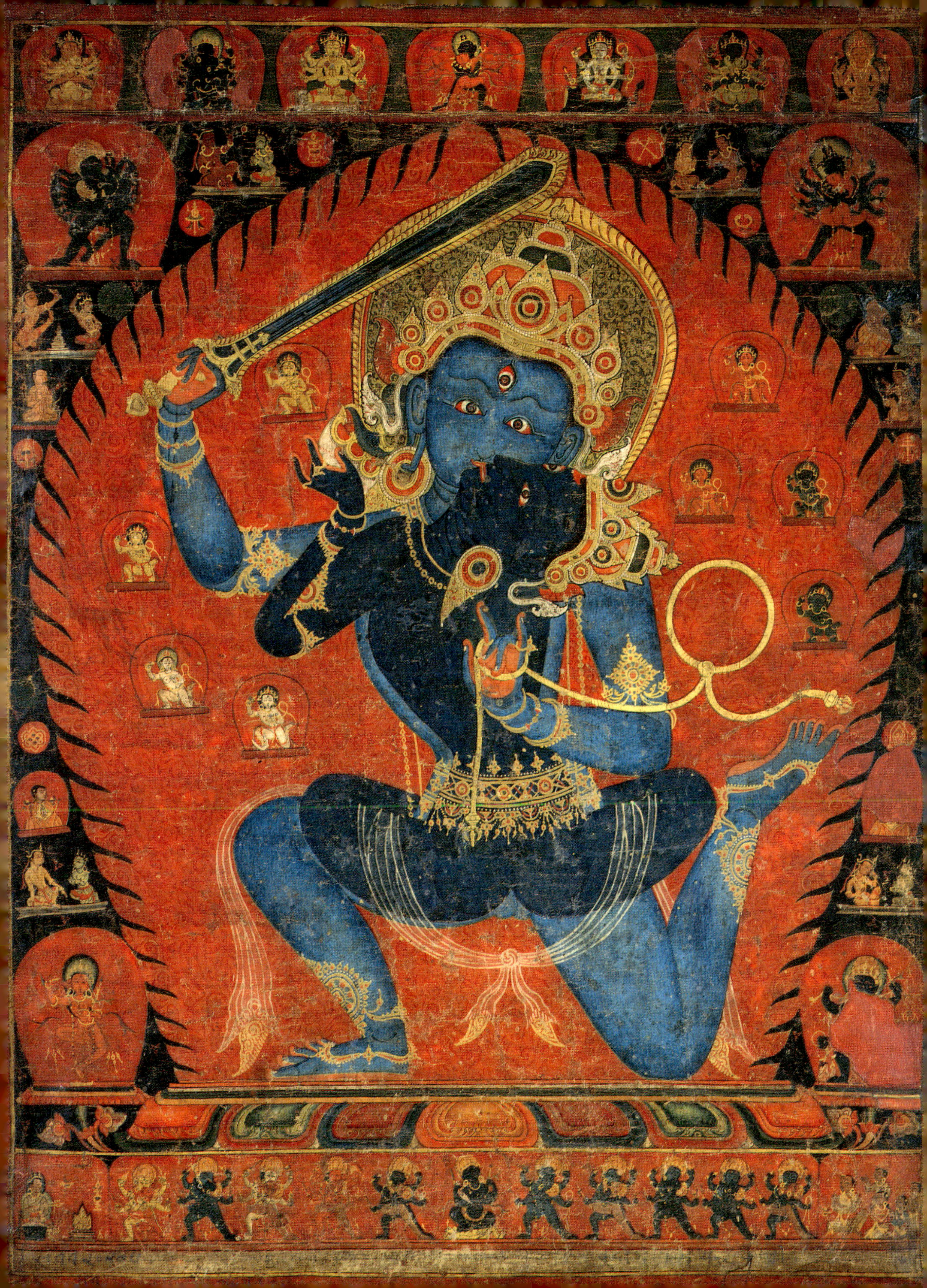

loosely delineated decorative scrollwork outside the mandala. In fact the figures on this *paubhā* are freely drawn with thick outlines and very little modeling. Although there are fewer figures, the composition appears more crowded than in the earlier example.

Literature Pal 1978, fig. 104.

40

Iconographic Sketchbook

SIXTEENTH CENTURY (?)

INK ON PAPER

EACH FOLIO: 10 × 18 IN.
(25.4 × 45.7 CM)

This sketchbook, with drawings of deities on one side and measurements for images of the various divinities on the other, is a rich source of Buddhist iconography. Most of the writing is in Newari, but in one or two instances the deities are identified by their Tibetan names. Very likely the book was used for making images for Newari as well as Tibetan patrons. The text was written by Harshasena Vajrāchārya of Simkomagudi, which may be the present neighborhood of Kathmandu

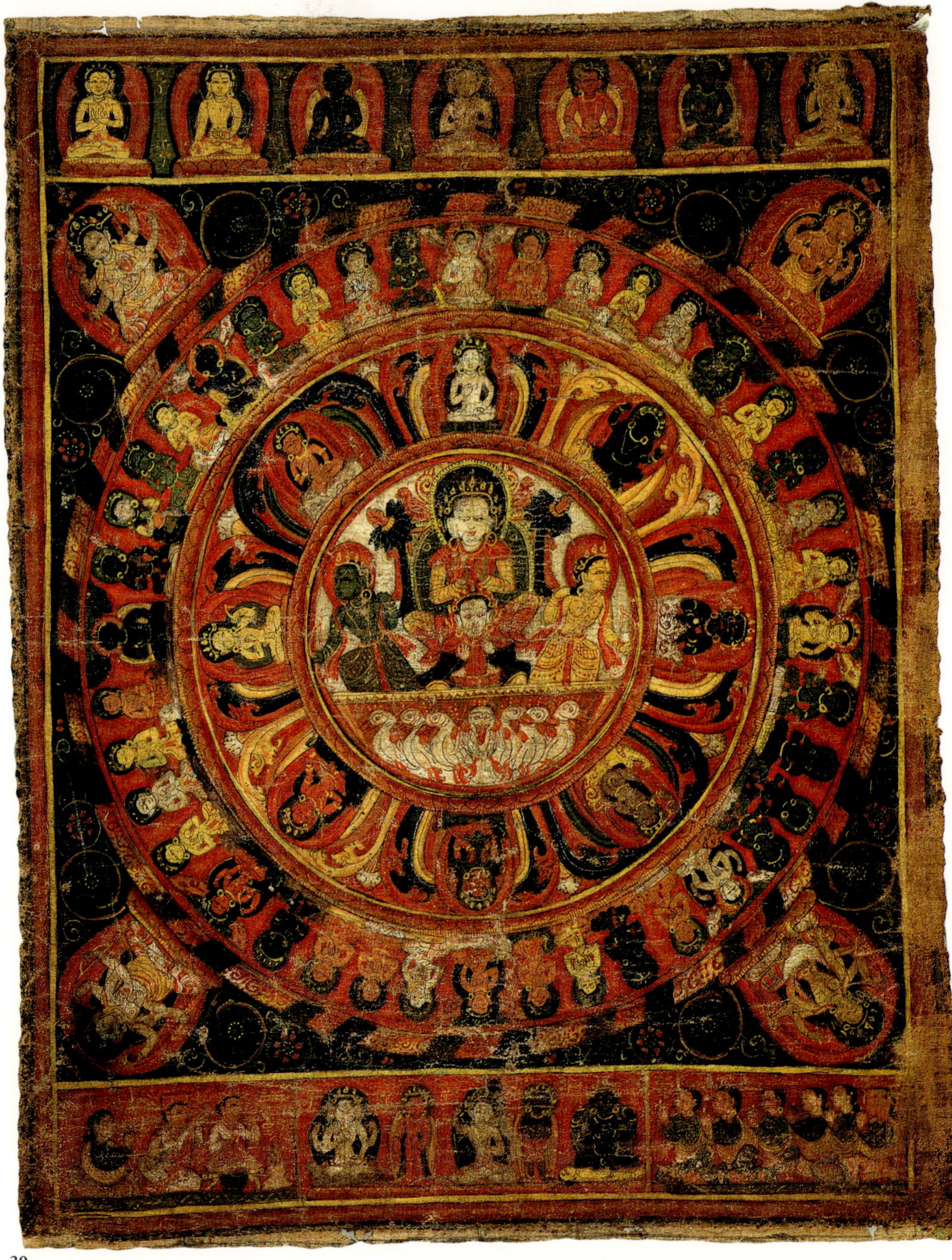

39

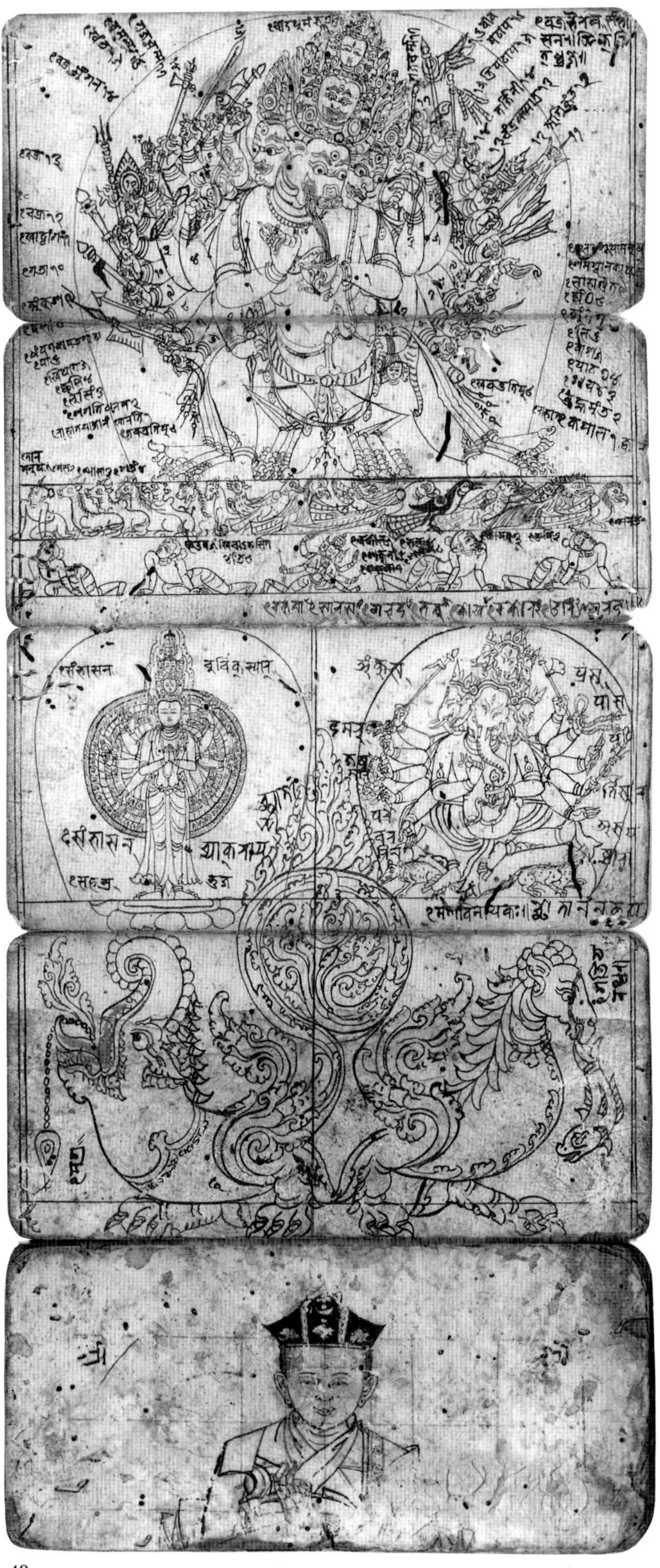

40

known as Sikamugah, as Alsop suggests (see Appendix 1). It was written for Ratnasiṃha, who was very likely the artist. An interesting feature of the text is the inclusion of several recipes for metal alloys, found more commonly in metal casters' handbooks. Ratnasimha was probably a sculptor as well.

Apart from a rich array of Buddhist deities, venerated especially by the Newars and by the Sakyapas in Tibet, the book contains beautiful sketches of ornamental designs used in paintings and metalwork. The deities represented on the folios illustrated here are Vajrabhairava, Thousand-Armed Lokeśvara, and Mahāvināyaka or a cosmic form of Ganeśa. There are also two articulately drawn mythical beings and a bust of a Karmapa, making it clear that the book was used for executing commissions for Tibetan patrons. The quality of the drawing is particularly fine and attests to the excellence of Ratnasimha's draftsmanship. Although undated, the book was probably prepared in the sixteenth century.

41

Chakrasamvara and Vajravarahi

1575–1600

28 × 24 IN. (71.1 × 61 CM)

Trampling the blue Bhairava and the red Kalāratri under their feet, Chakrasamvara and his spouse are locked in a sexual embrace. He is blue with three additional heads in yellow, green, and red and has six pairs of arms. She has a red complexion and a small boar's head attached to her own. Both figures are tall, slim, and highly energized. Against the green ground, four other forms of the god are similarly represented in yellow, red, green, and white. In the upper register are the five transcendental buddhas with two bodhisattvas, but the deities along the bottom are too small to be recognizable.

Samvara (or Sambara) is an important deity of esoteric Buddhism and the presiding deity of the *Chakrasamvaratantra*. He is also identified with both Heruka and Hevajra (see nos. 53, 83); all three are conceptually related, though with divergent iconography. Even a brief glance at Samvara's form reveals how close he is iconographically to the Hindu deity Siva. He is three-eyed, holds a skull cup and trident, and even sports an elephant skin like a trophy, just as Siva did after killing the elephant demon Gajāsura. It should also be noted that while the skull in Siva's hand represents one of Brahma's heads, which he cut off, Samvara holds the other four heads of Brahma in addition to the skull. It would almost seem that while borrowing iconographic elements from the Hindu Siva, the Buddhist theologians wished to display the superiority of their own deities.

The unknown artist responsible for this *paubhā* had a delightful sense of color. This is evident not only in the vibrant coloring of the lotus flower supporting the principal deities but in the harmonization of the green, red, and blue. They complement each other, but also account for the embracing couple's strong silhouette. The fiery aureole has been rendered with particular finesse. The subtle scroll design of the background has the texture of sumptuous muslin. Also interesting is the attempt to model both figures in color, thereby giving their forms greater volume and vitality.

42

Cosmic Form of Kali

1600–50

63½ × 52 IN. (161.3 × 132.1 CM)

One of the largest Nepali *paubhās* known, this is also one of the most complex iconographically. The principal goddess represented is Gūhyakālī, which literally means "Secret or Hidden Kālī." Kālī is of course the black goddess of death who is worshipped by Hindus in innumerable forms all across the subcontinent. As Gūhyakālī she is the spouse of Paśupatinātha, the patron deity of the Hindus

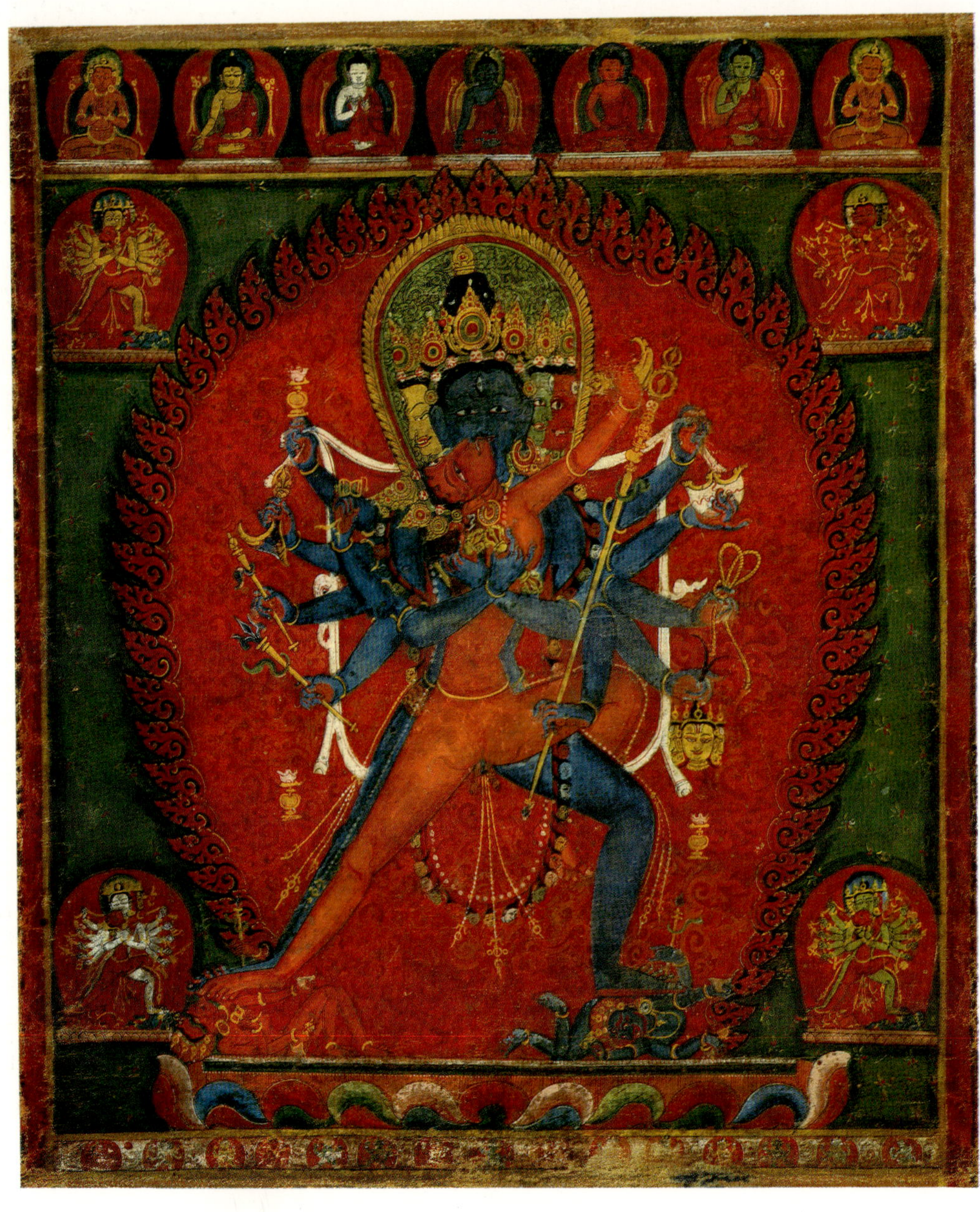

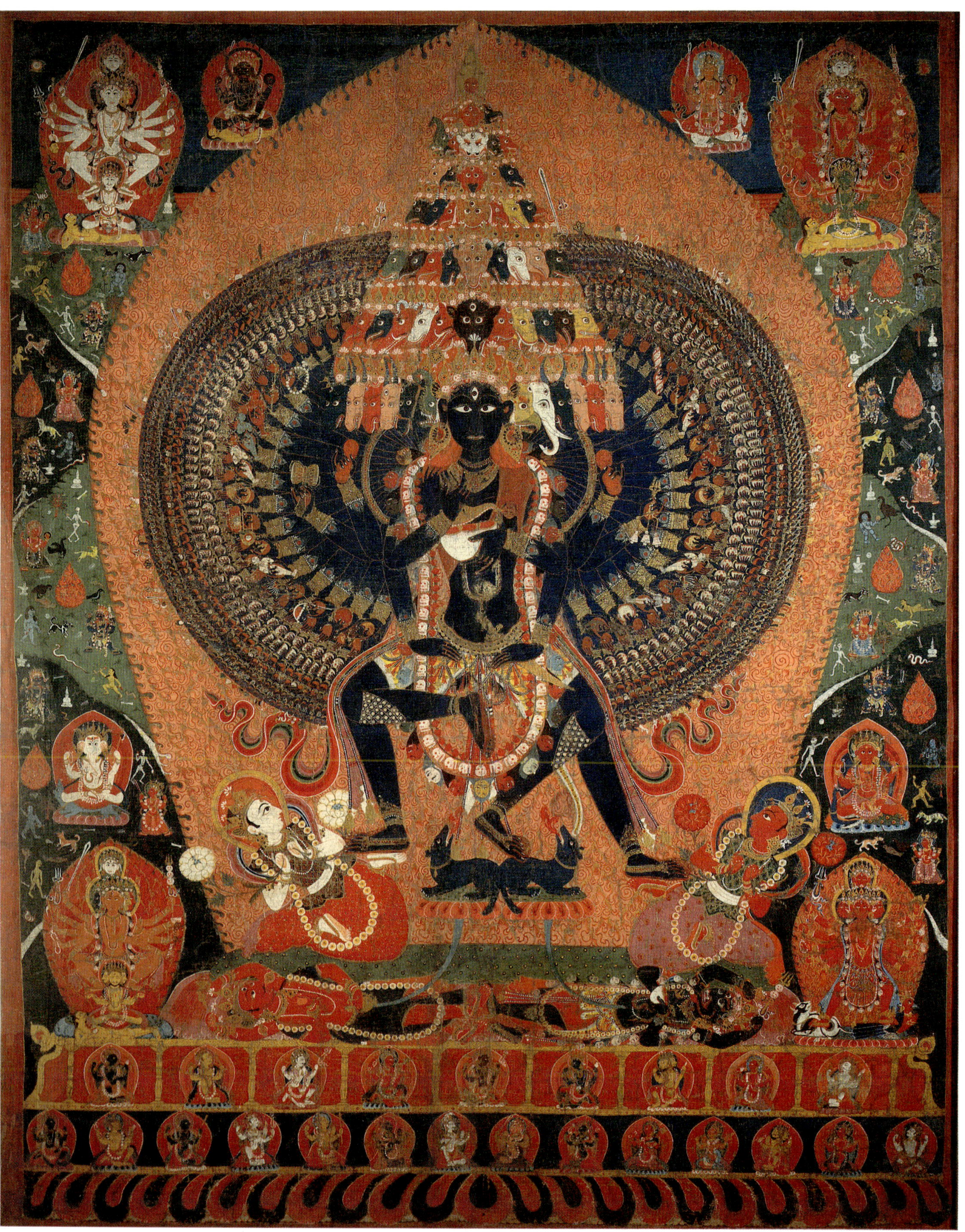

in Nepal. The goddess's temple is across the Bagmati River from Paśupatinātha's. Within the hypaethral shrine a natural stone serves as her symbol. In this impressive painting, however, she is not only represented in an image but shown in her majestic cosmic form.

Twenty-seven different manifestations of Siva and Vishnu as well as Brahma—the trinity of the Hindu pantheon—constitute Kālī's pedestal, thereby clearly demonstrating her superiority over the gods. Above this pedestal lie a benign and an angry form of Siva, above whom are the red sun-god and white moon god, who support two of Kālī's feet. Two more feet strike a dancing posture above two dogs who are black like the goddess. Her thousand arms display a wide variety of attributes including doll-like humans. The two principal hands hold a chopper and skull cup against her chest. Her multiple heads, almost all of which are of birds and animals, both natural and mythical, are arranged in a pyramid, and each has a third eye. Wearing garlands of skulls and severed heads, Kālī is depicted against an aureole of red and orange flames. On either side are four cremation grounds separated by alternating shades of green. Also included in the field are eight other deities; the four smaller figures probably represent forms of Siva, while the four larger figures at the corners represent other cosmic manifestations of the goddess. A precise identification of all the figures in such a mandala is impossible without the correct textual source, which remains unknown.

Although the artist must have followed both verbal and visual models, one cannot but be impressed by his imaginative power and artistic skill. With the exception of the outer circles of the goddess's arms, which have been impressionistically rendered, every detail has been executed with precision. A highly complex and bizarre subject has been made comprehensible with admirable aesthetic sensibility and visual panache.

Literature Pal 1975, pp. 105, 130, fig. 72; 1978, pp. 89, 91, figs. 124, 125.

43

Medico-Astrological Treatise

1600–50

INK AND COLORS ON PAPER

EACH FOLIO: 4 × 8 IN. (10.2 × 20.3 CM)

The title of this text is *Graha Śānti Vidhi,* which literally means "Seizure Peace Procedure" but should be translated as "Procedure to Appease Those Who Seize." The book describes the various forms of seizures which can afflict children and how they can be avoided and remedied. (A description of the book and identification of the various *grahas* are provided in Appendix 1.) As the names indicate, these *grahas* (not to be confused with the planets, who are also called *Grahas*) take the form of a wide variety of creatures, both real and mythical, including humans and animals, ghosts and demons. Among the fauna are the peacock, rooster, horse, tiger, jackal, serpent, etc. The supernatural creatures include *putanā, kumāra, vetāla, bhūta,* and others. It may be recalled that although we encounter Putanā as a particular ogress in

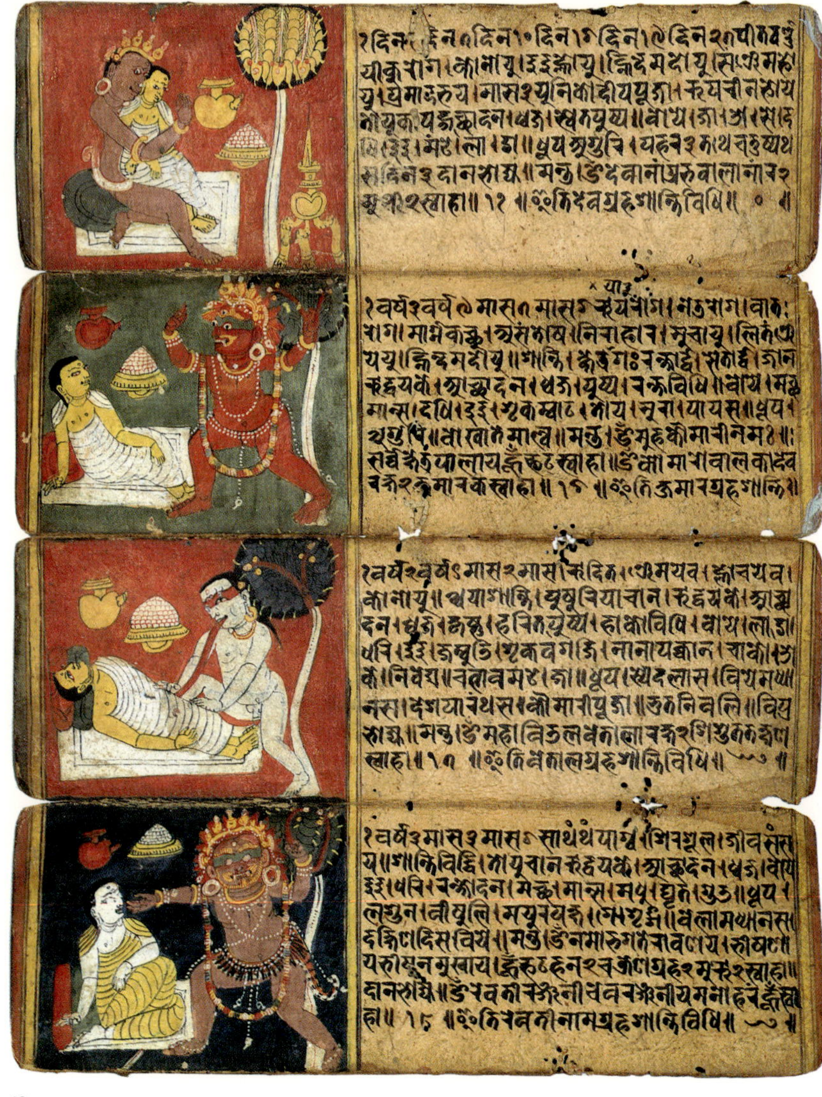

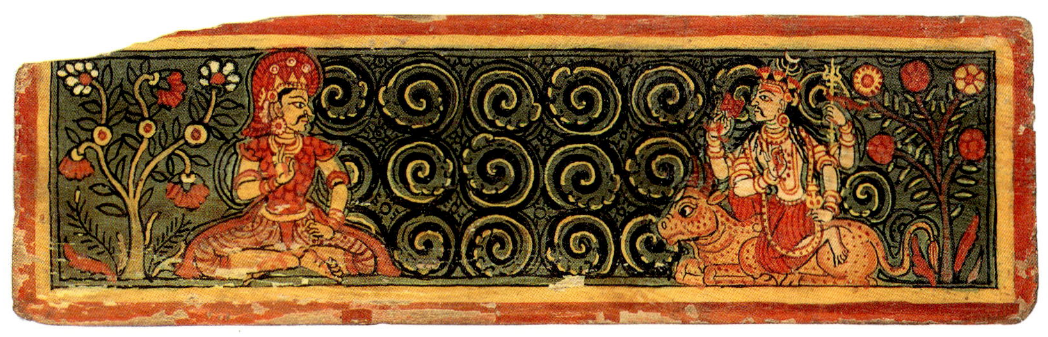

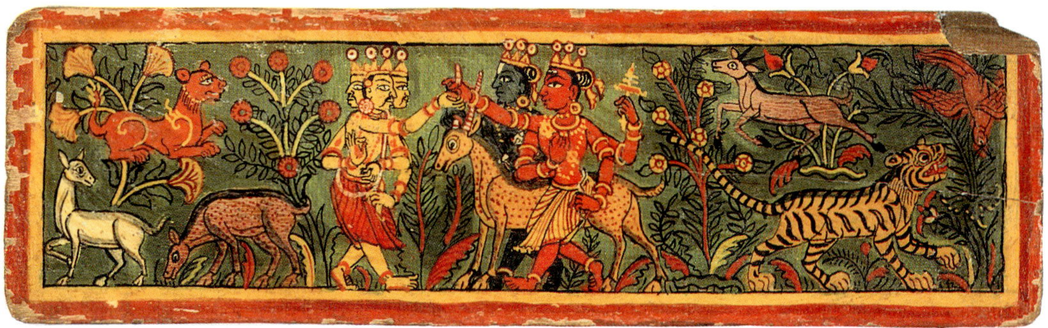

44

the Krishna legends, she really represents a class of malefic beings. Similarly, *kumāras* are personifications of various evil *grahas* who are familiar in early Indian literature and who were propitiated to protect infants. They are in the same class as *śākhas, viśākhas, skandas,* and *ghaṇṭākarṇas*. In later times the general types were particularized and accepted into the Hindu pantheon as the sons of Siva and Pārvatī, becoming known as Kumāra, Skanda, and so on.

Each illustration in this book, accommodated on one end of a page, depicts one of the *grahas*. On one side of the book each page has one illustration, but on the other there is an illustration on every other page. Usually, the *graha,* whose iconography often corresponds to its name, is seen attacking a victim. Sometimes the *graha* catches his victim by his hair, but mostly he is simply shown as approaching the figure seated on a white mat. There is a stylized tree, reminiscent of a palm but with varied foliage, in each composition. Also included are a water pot and what seems to be a plate containing cereal. The victim is either yellow- or white-complexioned, but the *grahas* are a wide assortment of colors. Most look like masked intruders, and the victims appear to be not children but young adults. The backgrounds are painted blue, red, or green. In general the illustrations are lively, showing varied activities and diverse images of the demonic *grahas*.

The *grahas* illustrated here are (from top) Devagraha, Kumāragraha, Vetālagraha, and Revatīgraha. The word *deva* means "god," and in this illustration the victim is seated in Devagraha's lap. Vetāla is a kind of evil spirit, while "Revatī" is both a specific and a generic term. Specifically, it refers to a star, generically to a kind of malevolent celestial creature.

44

Two Covers of a Hindu Manuscript

CA. 1650

COLORS ON WOOD

EACH: 2¾ × 9⅜ IN. (7 × 23.8 CM)

On the top cover Siva, seated on his bull, is engaged in conversation with a titan called *asura* in Sanskrit. That he is a titan can be determined from his headgear, which looks very much like a helmet worn by Greco-Roman soldiers. Sometime in seventeenth-century Nepal this type of headgear was given to the titans in a particular style of narrative painting which seems to have developed in Bhaktapur. Most such pictures are of Hindu mythological stories, and one wonders if the Bhaktapur artists did not adopt a type of headgear worn by Tibetan lamas to distinguish the titans in their pictures. Behind each figure is a flowering tree, and the space in between is filled with an exuberant scrolling pattern in green.

The representation on the bottom cover is even more interesting. In the middle is shown a meeting among a three-headed Siva, Vishnu, and Indra with a large antelope. Vishnu and Indra may have brought the animal for Siva, or it may represent a divinity in disguise. Indra and Siva seem to be shaking hands. The exchange or encounter seems to take place in a forest, for several other animals, including a tiger, a lion(?), a bird, and deer are also present. The forest must be celestial rather than terrestrial, for the trees, like the two on the other cover, are imaginary.

Without a text it is difficult to identify the two scenes. Nevertheless, the representations are colorful and lively. The style, characteristic of the sixteenth and early seventeenth centuries, appears to have been invented in Bhaktapur particularly for narrative themes (see Pal 1978).

45

Two Folios from an Iconographical Sketchbook

SEVENTEENTH CENTURY

BLACK AND RED INK ON YELLOW PAPER

A: 9½ × 8¼ IN. (24.1 × 21.0 CM)
B: 9⅜ × 8¼ IN. (23.8 × 21.0 CM)

These two folios are from an iconographic sketchbook perhaps rendered in Bhaktapur. The figures are deftly drawn in red and black, with notations indicated for colors, as well as for the attributes of the deities. Brief captions identify the figures. The two deities illustrated here are Guru Bhairava and Bagalāmukhī.

Bhairava is a terrifying form of Siva or Rudra and plays an important role in tantric religion. Although there are numerous Bhairavas, a group of eight, representing the eight directions which they also protect, became distinguished. However, none of them is called Guru Bhairava, although one is known as Ruru Bhairava. Perhaps the word *guru* is a mistake for *ruru,* or perhaps it was used as an honorific, for the god is often characterized as a guru, or preceptor. Usually Bhairava's mount is a dog, but here he is seated on a corpse (*śava*). He has nine visible heads and sixteen arms, which hold an array of emblems.

Bagalāmukhī is one of an important group of tantric goddesses known as Mahāvidyā, or Great Knowledge. In point of fact, however, they have little to do with knowledge but are worshipped for all sorts of favors. For instance Bagalāmukhī is propitiated for destroying enemies. There are altogether ten such goddesses, known as the Daśamahāvidyā (see Pal 1981, pp. 57–92). In this animated representation the goddess has four arms. With one she holds the end of a rope to which she has tied her adversary, and with a second she pulls out his tongue. The object in her upper right hand is probably a club, and that in the corresponding left hand is a thunderbolt.

46

Two Covers of a Hindu Manuscript

CA. 1700

COLORS ON WOOD

EACH: 3¼ × 15½ IN. (8.3 × 39.4 CM)

Only the insides of the two covers are adorned with divine figures. On both covers the figures were painted against a bright red background with narrow green borders along

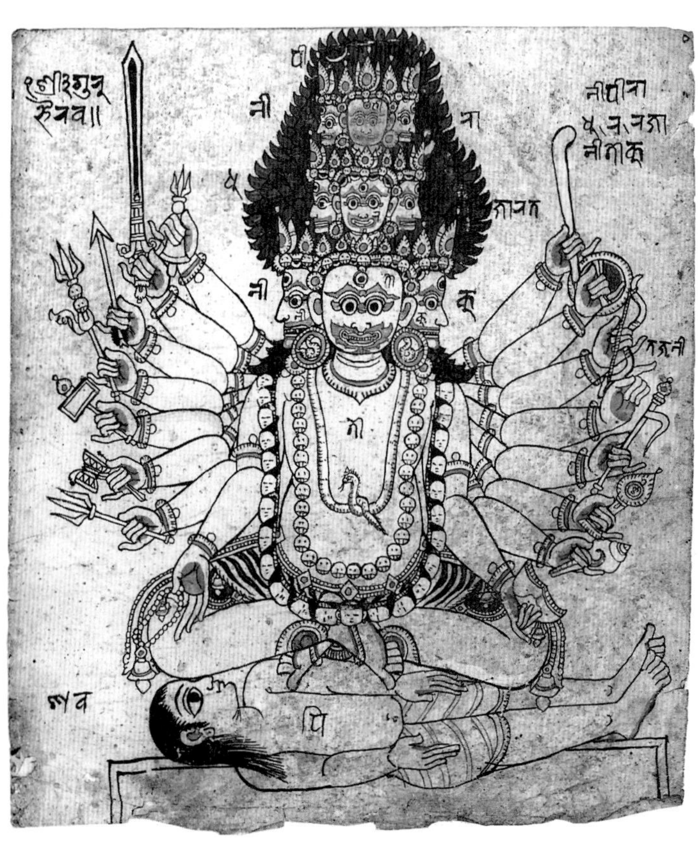

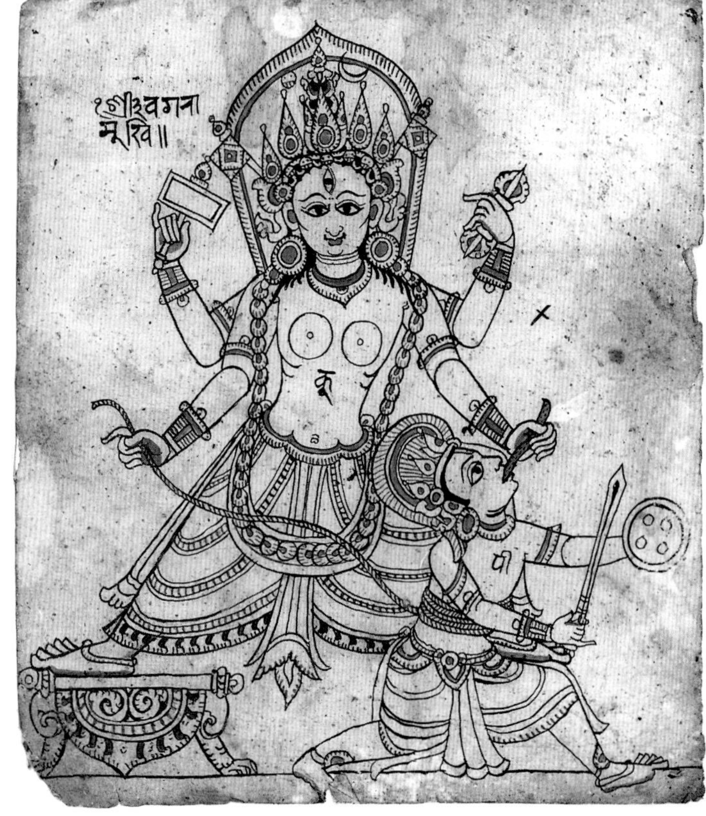

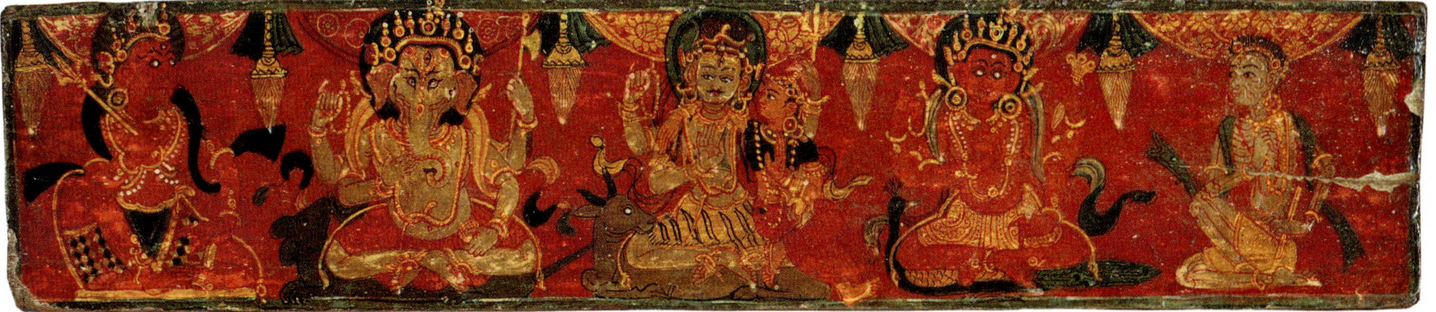

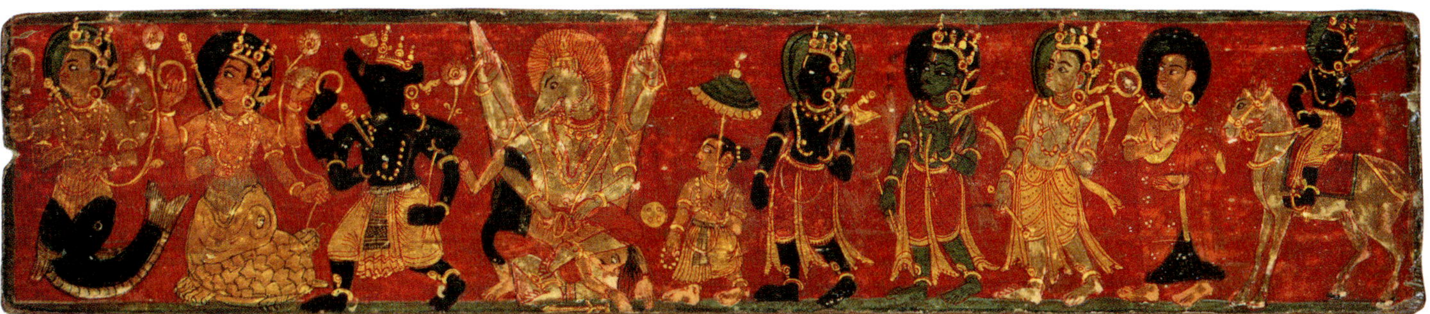

the sides. Otherwise the representations are different.

On one cover are five seated
46 figures, their heads set off
against individual canopies. The figures in the center seated on a bull are Siva and his spouse, Umā. On his immediate right is Gaṇeśa seated on a giant rat and on the left Kumāra on a peacock. All three are represented frontally, while the two remaining figures at the ends, possibly Siva's attendants, are seated with their bodies and heads turned toward the four divinities.

On the other cover are the ten avatars of Vishnu. According to the Hindus, whenever the world is overtaken by evil, Vishnu descends to earth in a suitable form, or avatar, to save the righteous. Ten of these avatars are usually represented as a group. From left to right the avatars are Matsya (Fish), Kūrma (Tortoise), Varāha (Boar), Narasiṃha (Man Lion), Vāmana (Dwarf), Paraśurāma (Rāma with the Battle-Ax), Rāma (the hero of the epic *Rāmāyaṇa*), Balarāma (the elder brother of Krishna), the Buddha, and Kalki, the avatar yet to appear. Except for Kalki, who rides his white horse, all walk in procession from right to left. Varāha and Narasiṃha are composite creatures with animal heads. Interestingly, in the case of Matsya and Kūrma, the god is seen emerging from the mouths of the fish and tortoise.

47

Two Folios from an Artist's Model Book

EIGHTEENTH CENTURY

INK ON PAPER

EACH FOLIO: 5¼ × 8½ IN. (13.3 × 21.6 CM)

These two folios from an artists's model book are the result of collaboration between a Tibetan, probably a lama, and a Newari artist. While a few notations are in Newari, a good deal of the writing is in Tibetan (see Appendix 2). That the book was used primarily to create images for Tibetan patrons is clear from the style and iconography of the figures as well as from such details as cloud patterns, rock formations, water, and draperies, all of which reflect Chinese artistic conventions the Tibetans had adopted. Of particular significance is the fact that the figures are drawn over geometrical grids. For those interested in iconometric theories and rules of proportions, these sketches are invaluable.

The deities represented in the folios illustrated here are two buddhas of the eleven-headed Lukeśvara and two of the four guardians of the cardinal directions. The enthroned Buddha with his hands displaying the gesture of turning the wheel of law is very likely the

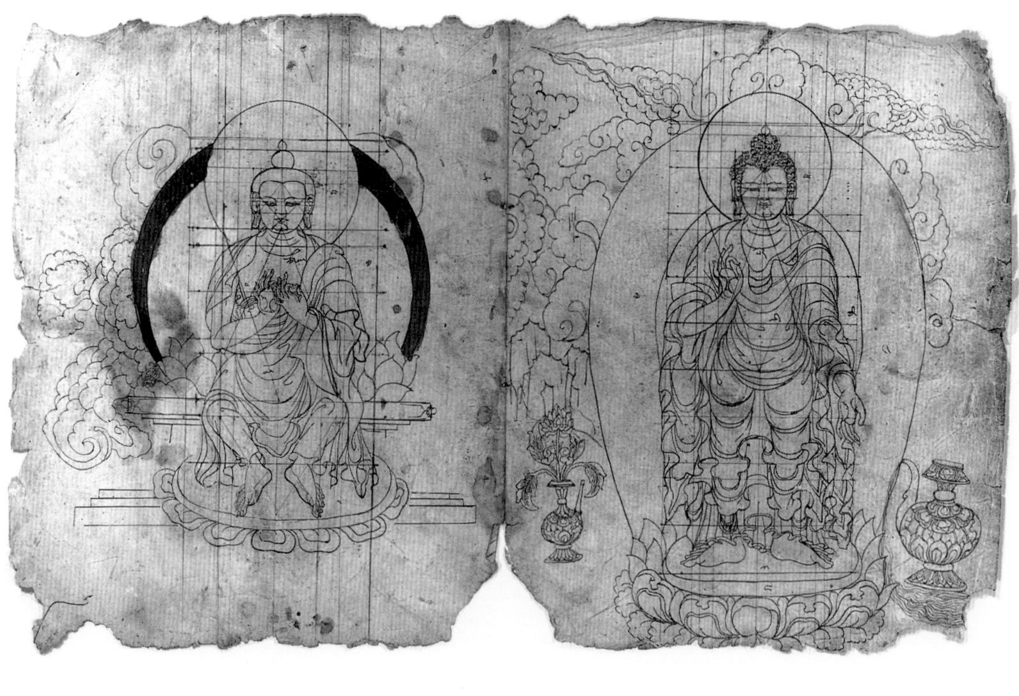

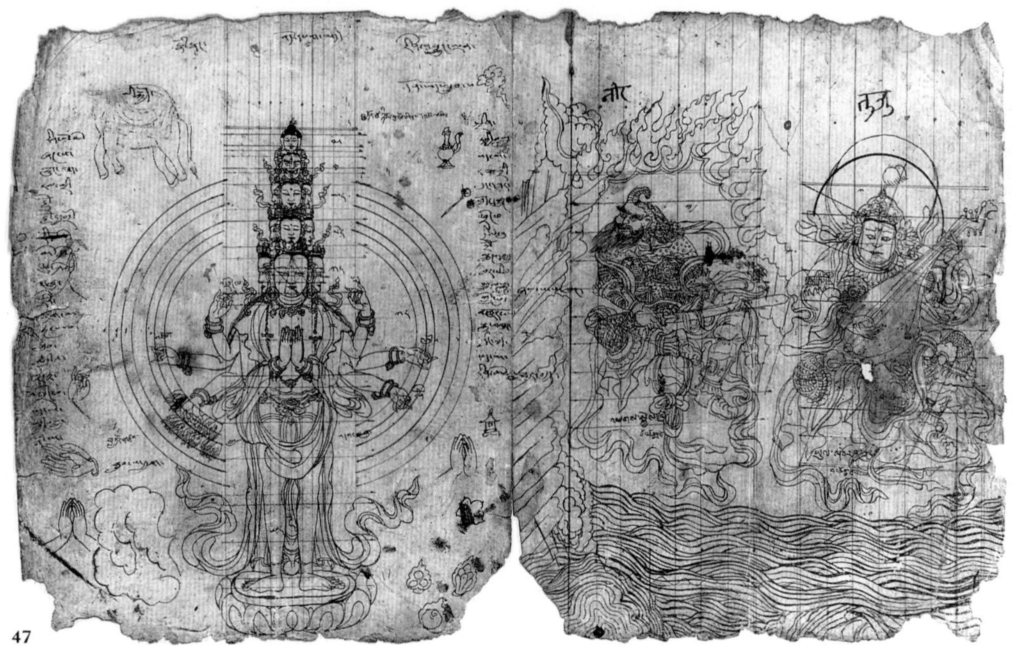

47

future Buddha Maitreya. The Buddha standing on a lotus is Śākyamuni and represents an image that was popular in China and Tibet but not in Nepal. The iconic type, distinguished by the distinctive rippling effect of the garments, is known as the Udayana Buddha.

Of the two guardian kings, the figure with the sword is Viruḍhaka, and the one playing the lute is Dhṛitarāshṭra. Both are dressed in armor and represented in the Central Asian manner.

48

Pair of Book Covers

EIGHTEENTH CENTURY

COLORS ON WOOD

EACH: 7¾ × 12 IN. (19.7 × 30.5 CM)

These two book covers are unusual for several reasons. For one thing they are adorned on both sides, while most Nepali

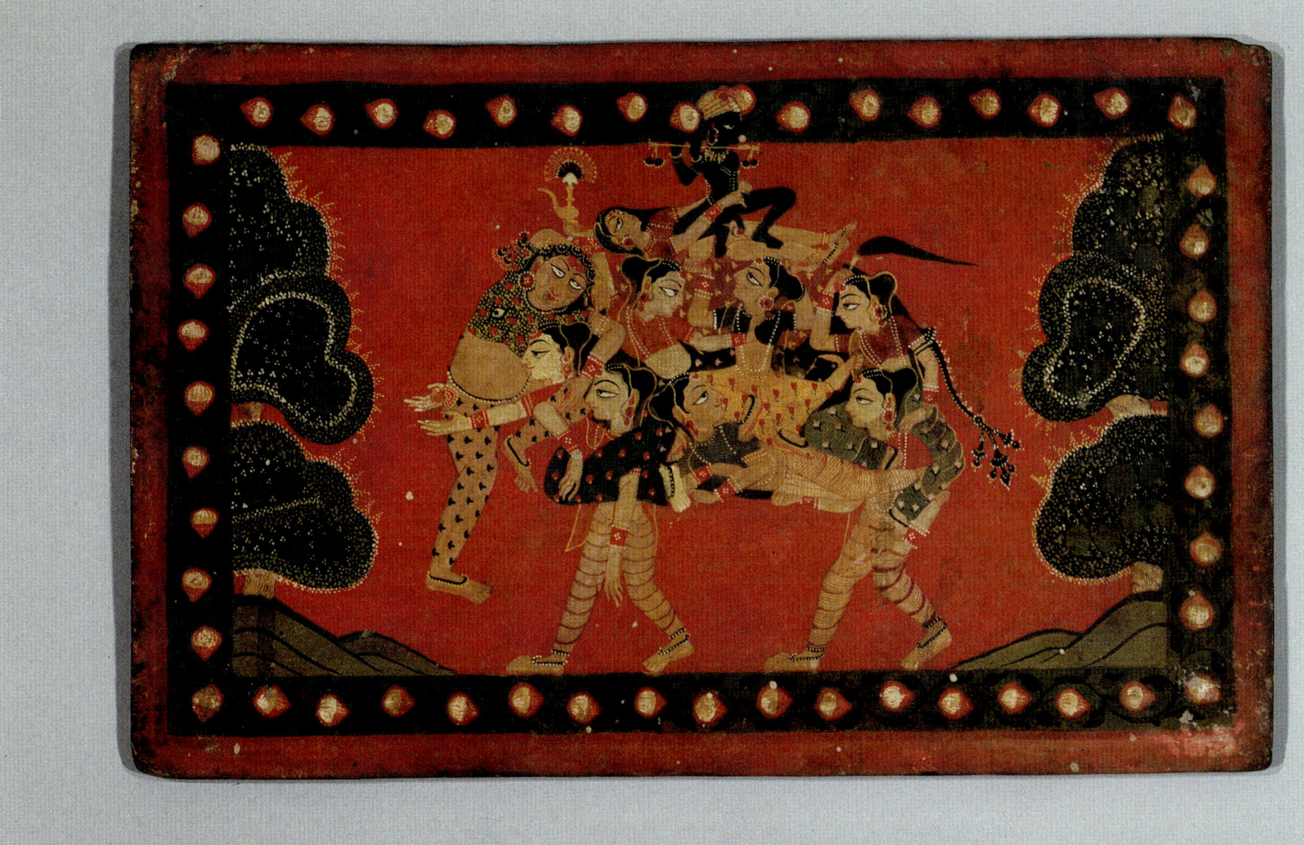

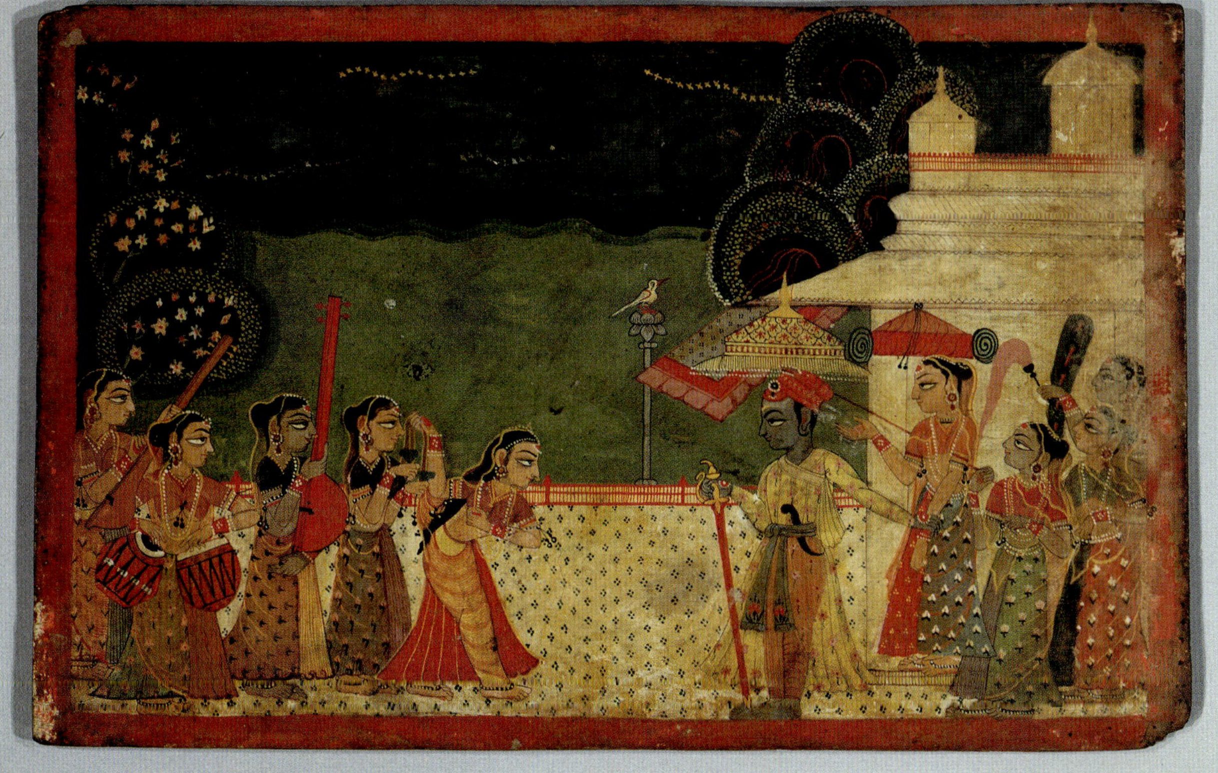

48

book covers are only painted inside. For another, the two sides are painted in two completely different styles. On the insides are two interesting scenes with the amorous Hindu god Krishna and his cowherdess admirers, known as *gopīs,* rendered in a strongly Indian style. On the outside are two different landscapes with buildings in a highly Chinese style. While we do not know whether the text protected by these two covers was Indian or Nepali, what is certain is that it must have had something to do with Krishna legends. Why the outside should be decorated with Chinese-style landscapes without any figures remains a mystery. Nor can we ascertain what the visual source for these landscapes might have been. Could they have been copied from a lacquer tray or box? No other similar examples are known in either Nepali or Tibetan art.

The scenes on the insides are painted in a mode reminiscent of Pahari rather than Rajasthani style. The stylization of the trees is particularly close to that seen in late-seventeenth- and early-eighteenth-century paintings from Basohli or Kulu in Himachal Pradesh in India. On one of the covers is the familiar motif known as *nārīkuñjara* in which an elephant has been cleverly constructed with forms of women. On the back of this elephant a young Krishna appears to be copulating with one of the *gopīs* even as he plays his favorite flute. Strangely shaped foliage and rising grounds in green and black suggest an outdoor scene; otherwise the action takes place against a flat red background. On the second cover a dark prince, presumably Krishna again, stands with female companions and listens to music provided by another group of females. The scene takes place on a terrace with a pavilion to the right, a green middle ground with stylized trees, and a menacing gray sky with flocks of tiny birds, clearly indicating the monsoon season.

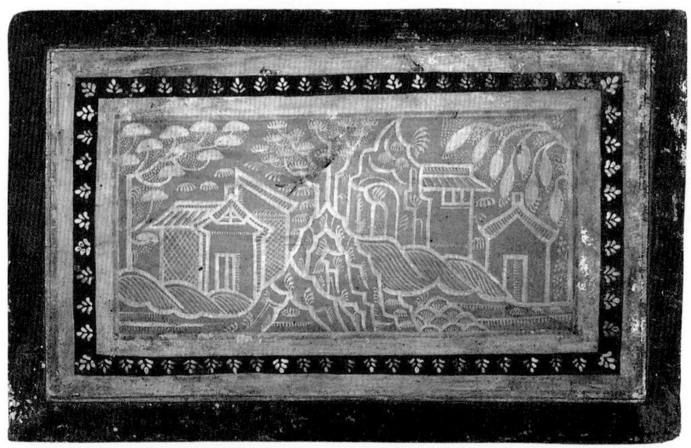

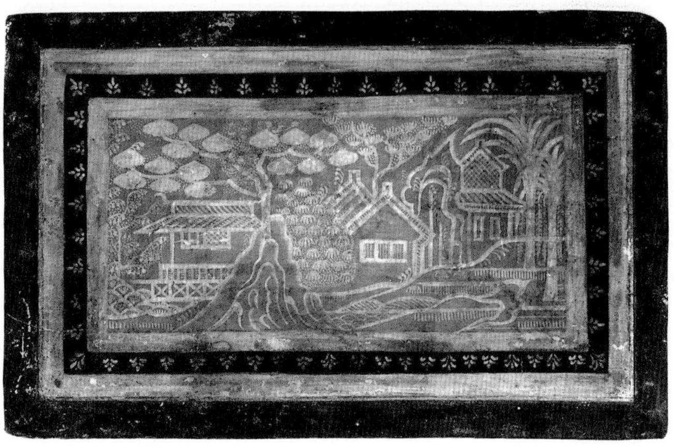

48

49

Book of Yantras *and Deities*

EIGHTEENTH CENTURY

COLORS ON PAPER

OPEN: 9 × 8 IN. (22.9 × 20.3 CM); FOLDED: 9 × 4 IN. (22.9 × 10.2 CM)

Unlike the artist's model book with drawings and sketches (no. 47), in this book the representations are completely colored. Very likely it served as a Hindu priest's manual, for the illustrations are all of Hindu deities and *yantras.* Although there is no difference in the basic geometric forms of a Buddhist mandala and a Hindu *yantra,* the configurations differ from deity to deity. Moreover the *yantras* are not inhabited by images of divinities as mandalas are. As is often the case in such books, two pages are generally given to a representation.

The pages reproduced here illustrate one image of a *yantra* and three of divinities. It is interesting to compare the form of this painted *yantra* with the metal example in the Zimmerman Collection (no. 23). The second illustration from the top represents the angry form of Siva known as Bhairava. The black figure stands on an outstretched corpse. His upper right hand brandishes a sword and, along with the corresponding left hand, holds two corners of an outspread elephant skin. The two principal hands hold a skull cup and chopper against his chest, exactly as the Buddhist Mahākāla does. It should be pointed out that Mahākāla, meaning "Great Time" or "Great Death," is also a common epithet of Siva. Conceptually and iconographically, the Hindu Bhairava and Buddhist Mahākāla are the same deity.

The two other deities shown here are Chhinnamastā (Severed Head) and Dhūmāvatī (One with Smoke), two of the Daśamahāvidyās (see no. 45). Chhinnamastā, holding her own severed head in a cup in her left hand, stands on the copulating Kāma, the god of love, and his spouse, Rati. On such occasions the female lies on top of the male. Interestingly, they are placed on a bed of colorfully painted boulders, perhaps representing the cosmic mountain, Meru. Chhinnamastā is one of the most gruesome though powerful manifestations of the goddess. The symbolic meaning of the image is clearly the primal sacrifice and renewal of creation. Even while the goddess sacrifices herself, her blood sustains both her and her attendants. She is known among Buddhists as Vajrayoginī.

Identified by a label, the naked Dhūmāvatī is painted gray, as is implied by her name. Like Siva her head is adorned with a crescent moon. In textual descriptions she is said to ride in a chariot drawn by ravens, but here she stands on one. More interesting is the fact that while her right hand displays the gesture of charity, her left holds a white head in a white orb rather than the usual winnowing basket. What this represents is difficult to determine, unless it is Siva's. In one late tantric tradition Dhūmāvatī is said to have eaten Siva from hunger (Pal 1981, p. 87). Although not as potent as Chhinnamastā, she is invoked to destroy enemies.

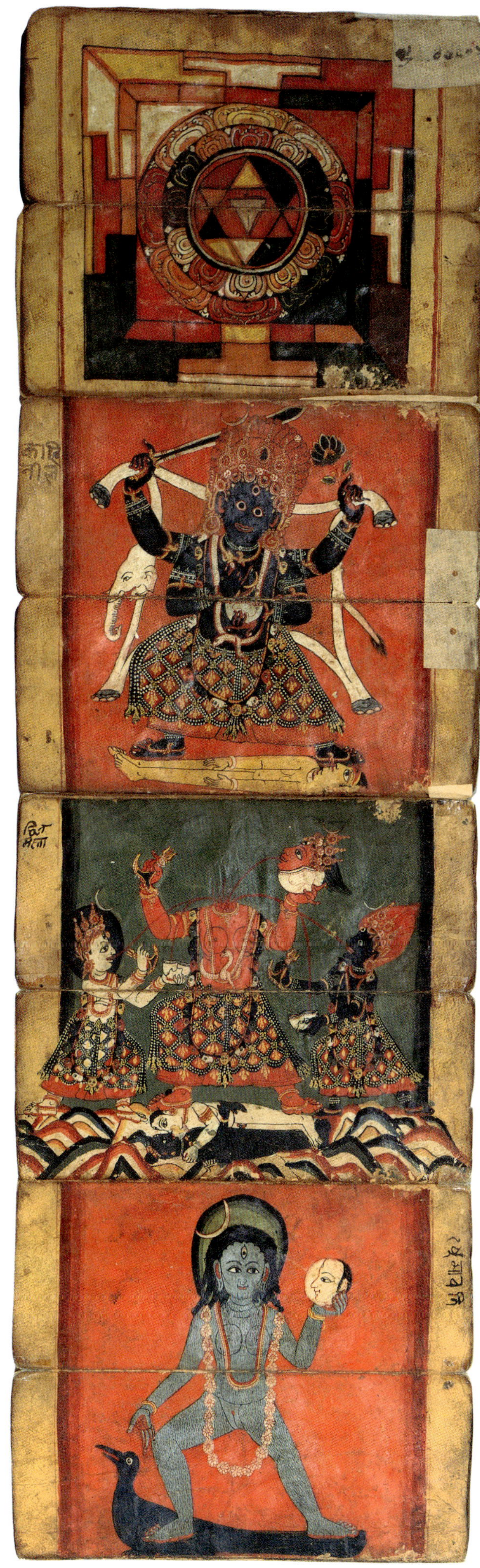

50

Goddesses Chhinnamastā and Chāmuṇḍā

EIGHTEENTH CENTURY

COLORS ON PAPER

EACH: 12¼ × 7¼ IN. (31.1 × 18.4 CM)

These two colorful pictures are from a series depicting the ten Mahāvidyās. The headless goddess on the right is Chhinnamastā (see no. 49). The other figure is the equally terrifying but much older Hindu goddess of death, Chāmuṇḍā, a pan-Indian goddess also commonly known as Kālī. In earlier Hindu art she is included in the group of mother goddesses known as the Mātṛikās. In the tantric pantheon she also became incorporated as a Mahāvidyā.

Both deities are placed in landscape settings as in contemporary Tibetan paintings. The plain green background is now a mountain whose peaks are laced with fluffy white clouds in the center and capped with snow along the sides. Beyond is the indigo-blue sky, which is enlivened in the Chhinnamastā picture with two flying herons or cranes. In the foreground a body of water is suggested by the rising stem and leaves of lotuses on which the deities are placed.

The blue figure of the emaciated Chāmuṇḍā sits on her haunches on a lion rather than on a man, as is more usual. The lion of course is the mount of Durgā, whose hierophant Chāmuṇḍā is. Another similarity with Durgā is that Chāmuṇḍā is represented with ten arms, a common type in Nepal. The flaming aureole of red and gold provides a striking contrast to her blue complexion.

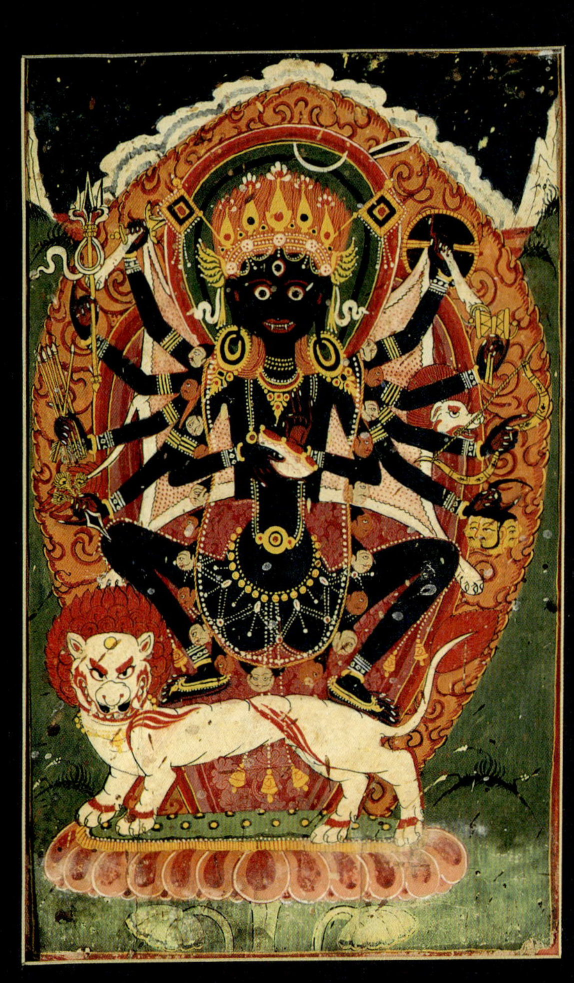

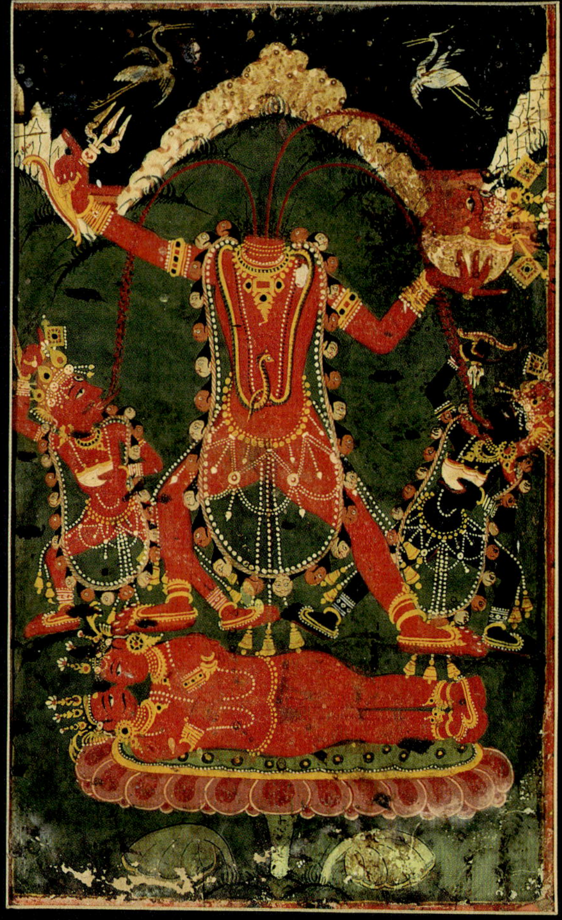

50

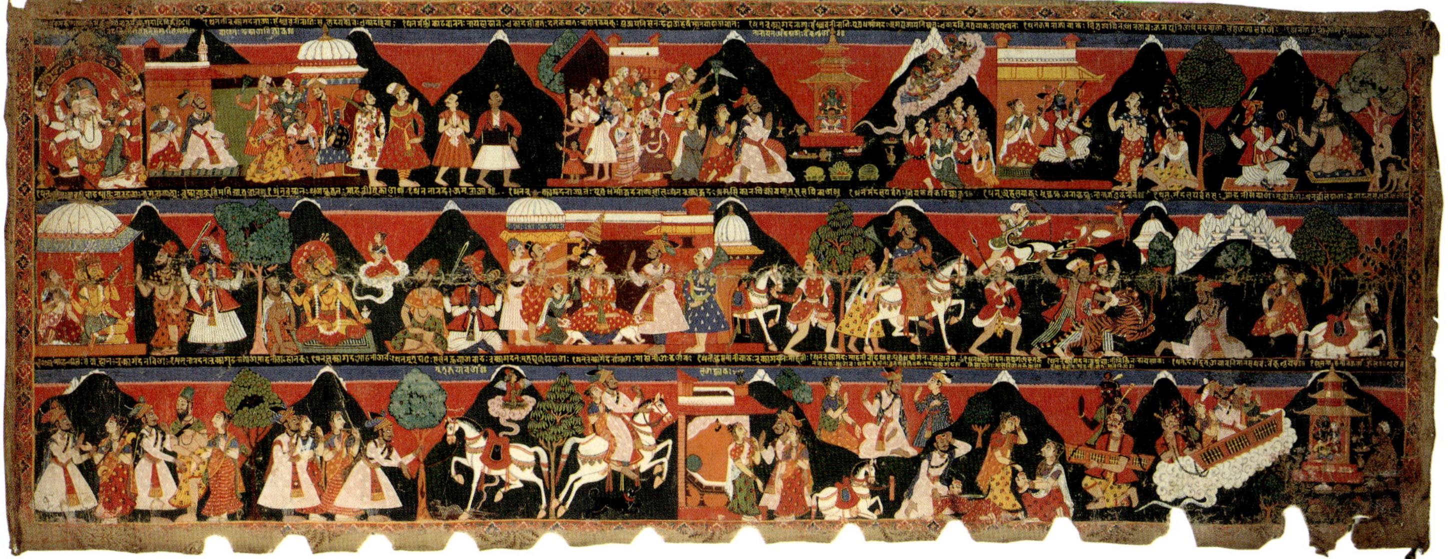

51

51

Narrative Scroll

1750–1800

20 × 52 IN. (50.8 × 132.1 CM)

The story depicted in this well-preserved scroll relates to a Hindu rite known as *Ekādaśīvrata. Ekādaśī* is the eleventh day of each fortnight, and a *vrata* is a rite or religious observance. The rite is obligatory for Hindu householders only on the eleventh day of the bright half of every month, and for all others in both fortnights. Considered one of the most important of all Hindu *vratas*—particularly for Vaishṇavas, since the day is sacred to Vishnu—the rite basically involves fasting and worshipping the god. In order to justify such *vratas,* the brahmans invented various stories of an edificatory nature. One such story extolling *Ekādaśīvrata* occurs at length in the *Padmapurāṇa* (chap. 21). The portion of the story represented here is briefly as follows (see Appendix 1):

A brahman named Rukmāṅgada and his wife Sandhyāvari had a son named Dharmāṅgada. All of them were pious devotees of Vishnu and lived happily in the city of Vidisa. Dharmāṅgada was so generous a man that he did not hesitate to give his head to Mohinī (whom the father had met and married while on a hunt) when she attempted to dissuade the family from performing the rite. Vishnu was so pleased that he brought Dharmāṅgada bodily to his abode, known as Vaikuṇṭha.

This scroll is painted in the Newari-Rajput style, which differs considerably from the earlier mode encountered on a pair of book covers (no. 48). Here the artist has provided local flavor by introducing regional architecture and a backdrop of continuous mountains against which the figures perform. The background is the ubiquitous red, over which is superimposed a conical patch of green capped by snow, representing a mountain. Unlike the Mughal-Rajput tradition, however, no attempt has been made to create any sense of spatial depth, and the various incidents have been presented without any effort to separate the vignettes or compositions. Thus, without reading the text below, it is not easy to determine where one episode ends and another sequence begins. Notwithstanding such constrictions, there is greater interaction among the figures, and some even display greater expressiveness than one encounters in earlier narrative art (see no. 43).

Art from Tibet

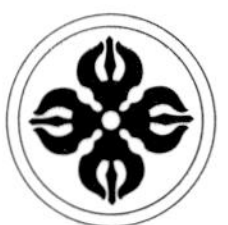

Art from Tibet

INTRODUCTION

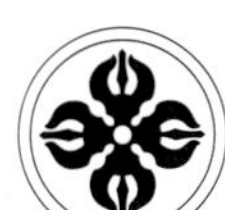

Land so high, made so pure,
Without equal, without peer,
Land indeed! Best of all!
Religion too surpassing all!

From an early Tibetan poem[1]

Introduced in the seventh century, Buddhism has remained the principal religion of Tibet. All the Tibetan objects in the Zimmerman Collection—metal sculptures, *thankas,* ritual objects, and textiles—relate to Buddhism. Tibetan art is not as ancient as that of Nepal—the earliest object in the collection is no older than the tenth–eleventh century. Despite its being related to only one religion, Tibetan art shows greater variation in both type and style than Nepali art.

Unlike Nepal, where all the art was created within the confined area of the Kathmandu Valley, Tibetan art was made in a much wider geographic area with different cultures and peoples susceptible to different artistic influences. For instance, western Tibet and Ladakh are both inhabited by various ethnic types and have remained vulnerable to influences from Central Asia and Kashmir. In the eastern regions of Amdo and Kham, influences from China have been felt more strongly. The larger Tibetan population, with its greater wealth and resources, included zealous patrons of their faith and built more and larger monasteries than the Newars, even today a smaller community. Tibetans could afford to invite artists from Nepal, China, Kashmir, Central Asia, Bihar, and Bengal, all of whom brought their own artistic experiences to enrich the local aesthetic tradition. Although geographically Tibet seems more inaccessible, it was a more open society than Nepal both commercially and culturally. Thus iconographically and stylistically, the history of Tibetan art is far more complex than that of Nepal.

Although introduced a century earlier, Buddhism became securely established during the reign of King Trisong Detsen (b. A.D. 742) of the Yarlung dynasty. Together with the Indian mystic Padmasambhava (see no. 60) and the monk-scholar Śāntarakshita, he founded the first great monastery at Samye around A.D. 779. Before the middle of the following century, however, the imported faith suffered a setback and lost royal patronage. It had not been universally popular with either the nobles or the more humble practitioners of various forms of indigenous religion. Also the Yarlung dynasty ended with the assassination of Langdarma (A.D. 803–842?), characterized as the "apostate king" by later Buddhist tradition.

A period of political uncertainty ensued in the central regions. Doubtless some Buddhist monasteries in central Tibet were neglected, but the faith continued to flourish in the east. *The Blue Annals,* the history of Tibetan Buddhism composed by 'Gos Lotsawa (1392–1481) between 1476 and 1478, mentions how a monk visiting Lha-rtse in the east in the tenth century saw numerous ancient images in a monastic establishment. Throughout the tenth century Tibetan monks continued to visit India, and Indian pundits journeyed to Tibet. Indeed according to *The Blue Annals,* "This was the beginning of the spread of the teaching of Logic which became thus established in the region of dbus and gTsan [in central Tibet]. . . . The great pandit Jnanasri came to Tibet, without being invited. Numerous (other) panditas also came, and made numerous excellent translations (of texts)."[2]

Tibetan monks remained active during the so-called period of persecution. In the east and central regions the most active luminary was Lume (kLu-mes). "During the sixty-four years which preceded Atīśa's [the great Indian scholar] coming to Tibet [in 1042], kLu-mes, teacher and disciple (kLu-mes dpon slob), had erected numerous temples."[3] A second person who was responsible for the renaissance of Buddhism in Tibet before Atīśa's arrival was Rinchen Sangpo (Rin-chen bzang-po). Born in A.D. 958, he welcomed Atīśa in 1042 and died in 1055 secure in the knowledge that the religion had been firmly reestablished. His theater of activity was western Tibet, where his patrons were the royal family of Guge, descendants of the Yarlung dynasty. Apart from traveling three times to Kashmir and at least once to Bihar, Rinchen Sangpo was an indefatigable translator of texts and a munificent patron of the arts. He brought both images and artists from Kashmir to western Tibet and built numerous temples and monasteries, many of which survive today. For its artistic remains, one of the most significant is Tabo in Spiti, in the Indian state of Himachal Pradesh.

Two other eminent Tibetan teachers of the period were Drogmi ('Brog-mi) and Marpa (Mar-pa), both of whom went to India and Nepal to study. To these two are traced the origins of the two major religious orders, known as the Sakya and the Kagyu. Unlike other major orders, that of the Sakyapas takes its name from the region where it originated with the help of the local ruling family. The Kagyu (Transmitted Command) had as one of its early champions the famous Milarepa (see nos. 68, 110), the principal disciple of Marpa. However, the actual founder of the lineage and principal organizer of the order was Gampopa, another one of Milarepa's disciples. In turn, four of Gampopa's disciples founded four suborders of the Kagyu. One of these, initiated by Dusum Kyenpa (1110–1193) in Kham, came to be known as the Karmapas. They not only were significant patrons of the arts but may have inspired the creation of at least one school of painting, known as the Karma gadri, in which landscape elements predominate (see nos. 99, 101, 102, 110). Thus three of the more important religious orders that dominated Tibetan life until the rise of the Gelukpas (*dGe-lugs,* or Order of the "Model of Virtue") in the 1400s were established before the end of the eleventh century. The fourth was the Nyingmapa (*rNying-ma,* or Old Order), which absorbed practices and doctrines introduced by Padmasambhava.

By the time Atīśa Dīpankara Śrījñāna, the best-known Indian Buddhist scholar of his time, had accepted the invitation from the royal family of Guge and come to Tibet, the ground for a revival of Buddhism had already been prepared. Interestingly, when Atīśa arrived after stopping in Nepal for a year, he was greeted with, among other things, an enormous *thanka,* either painted or embroidered, representing the forty-armed Avalokiteshvara.[4] If this was a painting, it is likely to have been rendered in the strongly Kashmiri style introduced into the region by Rinchen Sangpo and his Kashmiri artists. After two years in Guge, Atīśa moved on to central Tibet, where he taught and introduced reforms until his death.

Most of the pre-fifteenth-century Tibetan art in the exhibition was commissioned by patrons belonging to one or another of the pre-Gelukpas orders. The dominant artistic style in central Tibet, which was adopted by all the orders, was derived from that prevalent in the monasteries of Bihar and Bengal under the rule of the Pāla dynasty. The Pāla rulers ardently supported Buddhism. Monasteries such as Nalanda, Vikramaśīlā (founded by royalty), Odantapuri, and Somapuri were the chief sources of Buddhist religion and art for most of Tibet except the west. There, at least until the thirteenth century, the Kashmiri tradition remained paramount. Chinese influence during this period seems to have been stronger on sculpture than on painting, and even Nepali tradition, which had been a constant presence since the early days, appears to have been set aside in favor of the Pāla style. This is clear not only from mural remnants in temples and monasteries in the central regions but also from the scores of early *thankas* that have come out of the country in recent years. In metalwork and sculpture, however, one encounters a large corpus that bears the stamp of the Nepali aesthetic.

Sculptures and Ritual Objects

In metalwork Tibet has a long tradition going back to the Yarlung dynasty. Chinese literary sources of the Tang dynasty mention the Tibetans' skill with metalwork, especially with gold and silver. The use of silver ritual objects appears to have been particularly popular in Tibetan shrines. The Zimmerman Collection includes two very fine examples (nos. 75, 76) that may have been made in Derge in the east, which for centuries has enjoyed a reputation as the leading center of Tibetan metalwork. Both technically and aesthetically, the impressive trident made of different metals (no. 78) is a rare and striking object. Some Tibetan ritual objects were made from human skulls and bones and used in arcane rites. The collection includes an intricately assembled apron (no. 63) that, like the butter lamp or the traveling shrine (nos. 75, 76), is characteristically Tibetan.

The history of Tibetan sculpture shows a development parallel to that in painting. Tibetan texts classify the styles of sculpture into six schools: Indian, Upper Hor, Hor, Tibetan, "Old Chinese," and "New Chinese."[5] Like their classification of painting styles, this attempt to recognize schools of sculpture is highly inadequate. No "Hor" style can be detected at all in the bronzes, while the predominant Nepali element seems to be altogether ignored by the texts. What is certain is that since the Yarlung dynasty, Nepali tradition has remained a constant presence in Tibet. Newari metal casters, among the greatest in the world, have borne a large share of the responsibility for creating Tibet's rich and varied sculptural output. A much greater variety of metal alloys is discernible in Tibetan bronzes than in Nepal. In addition to gilding and sumptuous surfaces, Tibetans characteristically prefer polychromed sculpture, often using gold paint for faces.

The earliest bronze statue in the Zimmerman Collection is from the twelfth century (no. 54). As with painting, the Pāla style was predominant during this period in central Tibet. Tibetan devotion to Indian models was so ardent that it is often difficult to distinguish between prototype and copy. Several early sculptures in the collection are less dependent on imported styles, however, and reveal a Tibetan taste for less sensuous but more dramatic and powerful forms and the typical penchant for luxuriant surface decorations (see nos. 54, 55, 57–59, 62). For instance, the manner in which the texture and design of the garments in the impressive image of Padmasambhava are detailed (no. 60) is characteristically Tibetan.

As in painting, it is not easy to define the precise extent of Chinese influence on Tibetan sculpture, let alone to distinguish "Old Chinese" and "New Chinese" styles. While one can discern stronger Chinese influence on some of the larger sculptures in situ in Tibetan monasteries that probably were made by invited Chinese artists, smaller sculptures show very limited Chinese features. These are mostly confined to draperies, whose multitudinous folds impart a sense of volume to the figures (see no. 73), or to the exuberant use of flying scarves to enhance the sense of movement. Sometimes the treatment of the peonylike lotus seat or the rocky formation of the base may also reflect a borrowing from the Chinese artistic repertoire. The iconometric and iconographic descriptions included in the sacred texts or those followed by the Newari sculptors (as is now known from their sketchbooks) were based on Indian rather than Chinese tradition. Hence the Chinese influence on Tibetan sculpture remained confined to individual motifs or a few technical details.

In both sculpture and painting, the representation of terrifying deities remains one of the most distinctive and dramatically engaging features of the Tibetan aesthetic. Here again Tibetan artists not only displayed a clinical understanding of the human form and its sculptural possibilities but also allowed their fantasies free rein to produce some of the most disturbingly powerful and theatrical imagery in the world of art. Though the forms were envisioned by the mystics, it was left to artists to transform them into visually exciting images. Rarely in human history has a people displayed such sustained ingenuity in creating such a variety of macabre forms with such dramatic force and aesthetic integrity. What is remarkable about these representations is that no matter how fierce and violent the forms, the composition is always characterized by a sense of harmony and restraint. As Hevajra himself states in the *Hevajratantra:*

> Fearful am I to fear itself, with my necklace made of a string of heads, and dancing furiously on a solar disk. Black am I and terrible with a crossed *vajra* on my head, my body smeared with ashes, and my mouths sending forth the sound HUM. But my inner nature is tranquil, and holding Nairātmyā in loving embrace, I am possessed of tranquil bliss.[6]

The *Hevajratantra* also informs us about the type of person who should paint such images and how: "By a painter who belongs to our tradition, by a yogin of our tradition, this fearful painting should be done, and it should be painted with the five colors reposing in a human skull and with a brush made from the hair of a corpse."[7] We are further told that it should be painted in a lonely spot on a dark night by an artist wearing nothing but a bone apron (see no. 63) and "in a ferocious state of mind," having imbibed wine. In reality, however, Tibetan artists appear to have been fairly normal persons. Along with professional artists, monks also learned how to draw images and mandalas. As in most other Hindu and

Buddhist cultures and in medieval Europe, artists in Tibet preferred to remain anonymous. Nevertheless, many of their names, both Tibetan and Newari, have survived, although nothing much is known about them.

One famous monk who was an accomplished artist was Buton Rinpoche. When a certain temple was being built, Buton Rinpoche himself drew the plans of the numerous mandalas that were to be painted.[8] He also "made various drawings of the lives of the Bodhisattvas, the Twelve Acts (of the Buddha) [see no. 81]," and various other narrative themes. Elsewhere we are informed that "he also made the designs for cast images (lugs ma) of Vairocana, Gūhyasamāja and Mahāmuni, carvings ('brkos ma) of the Vajradhātū etc. and drawings (bris ma) of the Eighty Four Siddhas etc." Such passages are important for the light they throw on Buton Rinpoche and also on the history of Tibetan art in general. From another passage in Buton Rinpoche's biography we learn that "he furnished the instructions (zal ta) for a great temple with an 'inner image' (nanrten) of the sKu zan Chen po having the proportions of the Thub pa ju bo and completely filled with the relics (rin bsrel) of the Tathāgatas, including the images of the Sixteen Great Sthaviras." Not only does this tell us that Kusang Chenpo, prince of Shalu and Buton Rinpoche's patron, was being honored by having his commemorative portrait made in the same proportions and form as that of Śākyamuni in his body of bliss (sambhogakāya) manifestation; it also gives us a vivid description of the materials with which the image was to be filled. This is the first known instance of a portrait being filled with effigies of the sixteen arhats. That there was no hard and fast rule for what went into a bronze is clear from the Padmasambhava (no. 60) in the Zimmerman Collection, which yielded a wide variety of relics. Indeed Tibetans appear to have used both *chötens* and images as reliquaries.

A primary function of a sculpture or painting both in Nepal and Tibet is to serve as an aid to meditation. As the inscriptions on some of the Zimmerman objects inform us, there were other functions as well. The unknown royal donor of the imposing Padmasambhava (no. 60) beseeched that "those who see this statue of the great master attain accomplishment." Further he expressed the wish that because of the statue "the teaching of the Buddha will spread" and his own political dominion would be extended (see Appendix 2). *Thankas* or bronzes were commissioned for both spiritual and temporal benefits. Some were commemorative objects, while still others were for personal use in special rites. But no matter what the immediate purpose, generally every object was dedicated in the hope that the act might contribute toward the liberation of all sentient beings.

Paintings

A number of paintings in the Zimmerman Collection are rendered in the Pāla-derived style, which has been identified as the *mShar-thun,* or Eastern style, of

Tibetan sources.[9] The early, sparsely colored painting (no. 79) is an enigma, for it seems to relate to both the Indian and the Central Asian traditions. Among the others depicting scenes from the life of Buddha Śākyamuni, number 81 shows very few specifically Tibetan features, while the little initiation miniatures (no. 80) could have been rendered by Indian artists, even though they have Tibetan inscriptions. Since most *thankas* are portable, it is probable that some were painted in India and brought back to Tibet along with manuscripts and small bronzes. Texts make it clear that the personal possessions of both Tibetan and Indian monks included books and images as well as religious paraphernalia. In any event there can be no doubt that the charming *thanka* of Vajrasattva in the collection (no. 82) was painted in Tibet. Apart from its iconographic details, it combines stylistic elements from both the Nepali and Pāla traditions. In a similar fashion some of the early bronzes reveal this synthesizing of styles which makes their Tibetan origin a certainty (see nos. 58, 59, 62).

As in Nepal and India and regardless of style, early Tibetan painting is highly figurative. While the principal themes are divine as in Nepal and India, Tibetan paintings differ in one significant way. They frequently include representations of divine and mortal teachers. The Tibetans strongly believe in the theory of reincarnation or emanation, which has led to a kind of apotheosizing of their eminent lamas. For instance, the present Dalai Lama is not only considered to be an emanation of Avalokiteshvara, but he is also regarded as an incarnation of his predecessor. He will in turn reincarnate in his successor, thereby passing on his spiritual lineage until all sentient beings are liberated. This is essentially an application of the altruistic bodhisattva concept, where one postpones one's own nirvana in order to enlighten others. The idea is rooted in the Indian notion of *guruparamparā* (succession of gurus) and the more ancient Tibetan concept of sacred kingship. The ancient kings of Tibet were regarded as the "divine mighty ones" (*lha-btsan-po*) and "divine sons" (*lha-sras*), which is why it was easy to characterize the early kings as emanations of Avalokiteshvara (see no. 79). The concept of reincarnated lamas appears to have originated with the Kagyupas but was soon adopted by the other orders.

This notion of reincarnated and apotheosized teachers expanded the thematic repertoire of Tibetan artists significantly. Since such representations had to emphasize the figures' spiritual qualities rather than their physical appearance, the mode adopted was both formulaic and idealized. This tradition seems to go back at least to the eleventh century, to judge from recent evidence from Tibet. The earliest examples are painted in a uniform style, regardless of which order the lineage belongs to. Even though the style is derived from Pāla India, it is unlikely that the idea of such lineage *thankas* originated there.

Whether painted or sculpted, the teacher is always heavily robed in monastic attire and is usually seated on a lotus in the classic posture of meditation. In sculpture he is always oriented frontally, and his hands make one of the five gestures characteristic of Buddha figures, the most common being that of teaching (see nos. 87, 95, 104). In addition he may hold lotuses supporting such attributes as a bell, a thunderbolt, a book, or a sword, depending on the presiding deity of the lineage. On *thankas* the teacher may be shown frontally or in profile, alone or with a second figure, as if engaged in conversation or discourse. Usually, they are surrounded by a host of similar images of teachers belonging to the same lineage. No matter what style the *thanka* is in, the arrangement is strictly symmetrical. The faces, especially of the principal personages, are probably realistic in instances in which the artist knew his subjects. However, those done after an individual's death or of such legendary figures as Padmasambhava (see no. 60), Tsongkhapa (see no. 115), or Milarepa (see no. 68) are idealized and imaginary like those of arhats and *mahāsiddhas*.

The latter are two other categories of human teachers frequently encountered in Tibetan art but rarely in India or Nepal. The word *arhat* literally means "worshipped one" and was applied to all venerable monks in the monastery. Subsequently, sixteen eminent arhats were selected to form a group. It is believed that they had come down from their heavens at the request of the Buddha to hold the fort, so to speak, until the arrival of the next Buddha (see nos. 73, 91). This concept traveled to China with the famous pilgrim Xuanzang when he returned from India around the time Songtsen Gampo was consolidating his power in Tibet. Very likely the Tibetans adopted the idea from Central Asia and China rather than India, for arhats seem rarely to be included on early Tibetan *thankas*. However, the Tibetan tradition does recognize three manners of depicting them, those of India, China, and Tibet itself.[10] The Chinese tradition is said to have been introduced by Lume, in which case the models would have been Song paintings. No study has yet been done of sculpted representations of the arhats that still adorn Tibetan monasteries, some of which may reflect influences of Song-period sculpture. To date no *thanka* devoted exclusively to arhats has been found that can be dated earlier than the fourteenth century. All are based on Chinese models.

The *mahāsiddha* concept also originated in India. The word *mahāsiddha* means "great perfected being" or "great attainer." In fact it is used to characterize eminent tantric teachers who have attained certain supernatural powers, such as the ability to fly, as well as enlightenment. In the Buddhist context they are regarded as the masters of *mahāmudrā* (great seal), which is the designation of the highest tantric path to buddhahood. This is a form of tantric teaching particularly followed by the Kagyu order. Although the number of *mahāsiddhas* varies in literature, a group of eighty-four had come to be recognized by the twelfth century. Like arhats the *mahāsiddhas* were historical personalities, but they were not monks. Instead they were free-spirited yogis (see nos. 59, 91) who advocated spontaneous rather than highly structured methods for realizing desired goals. Like arhats, *mahāsiddhas* do not appear in Indian Buddhist art, but some of them are revered by the Śaivas. In Tibet *mahāsiddhas* are represented on *thankas* at least as early as the twelfth century. Unlike arhats they are portrayed as Indian yogis and mendicants in a wide variety of postures and engaged in diverse activities. Their unconventional behavior allowed Tibetan artists to depict them with lively imagination and expressive originality.

By the seventeenth century it had become common practice in Tibet to represent both arhats and *mahāsiddhas* serially on *thankas* in rich, visionary landscapes (see nos. 91, 101, 103, 110). While the idea of placing figures in landscapes, often asymmetrically, may have been borrowed from Chinese pictorial tradition, it should be empasized that the exact Chinese source is difficult to pinpoint. Many of the motifs, especially on the early arhat *thankas,* are clearly derived from the Chinese repertoire, including the vegetation, rock formations (especially blue-green boulders and jagged, asymmetrical escarpments), cascading waterfalls, furnishings, and the manner of drawing of both the expressive faces and the volumes of robes. But they are combined and interpreted in a quintessentially Tibetan manner. Landscape in Tibetan painting is much more colorful, romantic, and ethereal than in Chinese arhat paintings and is always uniformly illuminated with clear light. The unrealistic relationship between the figures and their natural surroundings is characteristically Tibetan.

While the exact date is not known, this Tibetan landscape type, expressing a feeling of serenity and harmony through bright, vividly conceived natural forms, was likely created sometime in the sixteenth century. This is clear from the dated *thanka* of *jātaka* (tales of the Buddha Śākyamuni's previous lives) in the Zimmerman Collection (no. 99) in which the fanciful landscape appears in its typical form.[11] The sixteenth century was a highly creative period for Tibetan art, especially in the east, where at least three different styles are said to have originated. One of these is the now-familiar Karma gadri style in which three *jātaka thankas* in the collection (nos. 99, 101, 103) are painted. This highly evocative, refined, delicate, and miniaturistic style is considered to have originated with a master[12] artist named Namka Tashi, probably inspired by the celebrated Karmapa hierarch Mikyo Dorje (1507–1554), who was himself a competent artist.[13] Although this style was used to depict legends and stories composed in India, the locale, characters, and props in the narratives became Tibetanized. Hence, unlike other *thankas,* those in the Karma gadri style remain a major visual source for learning about Tibetan material culture and life-style. This distinctive style probably engendered among the Newars a desire to add landscape elements to their narrative paintings, but with very different results (see no. 51).

The second diffusion of Buddhism in Tibet began in the tenth century, and until the 1200s Tibetan, Nepali, and Indian monks worked together to establish it on a permanent basis. By the time Chog lotsava (Dharmasvāmin) visited Bihar in 1234–36, Muslim invaders from Afghanistan had overrun most of north India, and the major monasteries in Kashmir and eastern India lay in ruins. India thereafter ceased to be the principal source for Tibet's spiritual inspiration. Nepal may have filled the vacuum, but only for a short period. From the thirteenth century on, the Tibetans became increasingly self-reliant and developed an enormous body of exegetical literature, a great deal of which was compiled and systematized by Buton Rinpoche. It was also during the thirteenth century that the Sakyapas and Karmapas became influential at the Mongol court in China. Until the fall of the Yuan dynasty in 1368, the Sakyapa pontiff served as the viceroy of Tibet. Tibetan lamas, especially the Karmapas, remained influential at the Ming court.

Although Atīśa's disciples had founded an order based on strict rules and spiritual discipline, by the fifteenth century the religion was again in need of reform. This was achieved by Tsongkhapa, one of the giants of the Tibetan religious world. Once more, as is the case with all eminent teachers, his immediate disciples founded an order based on his teachings. Known at first as the New Kadam, later it absorbed the old Kadam order and came to be known by the name Geluk. Because of the color of their hats, members are also known as the Yellow Hats. The Gelukpas rapidly became the largest and most powerful religious order in Tibet.

In addition to maintaining a close relationship with the Ming court, the Gelukpas also cultivated the Mongols. In 1578 a meeting between Sonam Gyatso, the head of the Gelukpas, and Altan Khan, the ruler of the Tumed branch of the Mongols, had far-reaching consequences for Tibet. Not only were the Mongols converted to Buddhism, adding to the power and wealth of the Gelukpas, but the Mongol ruler conferred on Sonam Gyatso the title of *ta le* (wisdom). This expression was transformed into "Dalai" by Westerners. In due course Lozang Gyatso (1617–1682), the fifth Dalai Lama, became powerful enough to combine temporal and spiritual authority in the office.

The rise and consolidation of the Gelukpa order thus resulted in the political unification of Tibet. Recognition by the Mongols became a political and spiritual asset, and unification heralded a sustained period of prosperity. The Gelukpa monasteries, even larger and richer than the older establishments, became the new patrons of art. And because the Gelukpas resided all over the country, artistic styles became less regional. Somehow, either through *thankas* or at the hands of traveling artists, the Gyantse style became familiar to those responsible for adorning the Red Temple in Tsaparang in Guge. The Zimmerman Collection has three fine *thankas* rendered in the Guge style (nos. 89, 90, 100). The various styles incorporating Chinese landscape elements that developed in sixteenth-century Kham became familiar elsewhere as well. The Newari artists' sketch-books also helped to disseminate styles. Finally, by the eighteenth century it had become common to produce wood-blocks with the outlines for important series (see no. 105). These wood-block prints could be acquired easily and painted anywhere. Thus from the seventeenth century on it becomes difficult to distinguish the various styles of Tibetan painting.

Yet another type of painting encountered only in Tibet is represented in the collection by several outstanding examples (nos. 88, 94, 108, 109). Essentially linear, they are rendered in gold or silver against a black or red ground. Though very few colors are employed in such paintings, the aesthetic effect is quite stunning. In fact nothing quite like them is known in any other religious tradition. These dynamic, chimerical forms and highly expressive fantasies are among the most brilliant and innovative contributions to Buddhist imagery by unknown Tibetan artists. When and where the aesthetic concept originated is not known, though it was likely inspired by illustrated books. Tibetan literary traditions are surprisingly silent about what may well be the most distinctive type of Tibetan art. Writing in gold or silver on black paper was known both in Nepal and Tibet from at least the thirteenth century. Earlier still, Muslims in western Asia had effectively used the contrast between black ground and gold lettering for manuscripts of the Koran. The Chinese too wrote sutras on black paper, often illustrating the frontispieces in a linear style with few colors. It would appear that some highly innovative Tibetan painter decided to transfer this mode to the *thanka,* realizing how dramatic such representations would look by the flickering lights of butter lamps in the special shrines (*gonkhang*) dedicated to protective deities. In fact protective deities predominate in the black-and-gold *thankas,* known as *gserthang*. In those with red backgrounds one encounters peaceful deities as well. It is generally believed that such *thankas* appeared rather late, but the tradition may have begun as early as the fifteenth century, if the suggested date for one of the black-and-gold representations in the Zimmerman Collection is accepted (no. 92).

Another artistic form that plays an important role in the Tibetan's spiritual quest is the mandala. It is so frequently encountered in Tibetan art, particularly painting, that it has come to be regarded as the very symbol of Tibetan culture. Although mandalas occur in the arts of China, Japan, and Nepal (see nos. 33, 35, and 39), only in Tibet is their use so ubiquitous. The Zimmerman Collection includes a large number of mandalas, from which only a small group has been selected for the exhibition (nos. 83–85, 96, 106). Both in form and content they are more diverse than mandalas used in Nepal. While all are visually striking, some are significant art historically since they are datable (nos. 83, 85) or are iconographically rare (nos. 96, 106). No matter what the configuration, the Tibetan mandala epitomizes the technical virtuosity and artistic resourcefulness of the artists. Most unusual are two symbolic mandalas (nos. 111, 112) whose abstract but compelling forms are aesthetically as arresting as their contents are intriguing. One of them (no. 112) was apparently used in esoteric rites to destroy enemies (*abhichāra*) and is considered so potent and dangerous that all Tibetan lamas consulted about it turned their faces away and would not discuss it.

Ritual Textiles

VALRAE REYNOLDS

Luxurious silk cloth has long played an important role in Tibetan religious life. Shimmering textiles of brilliant color, often enhanced with gold thread, filled the shrine rooms and chanting halls of the country's Buddhist monuments. Tibetan monks wore robes of brilliant silk for ritual ceremonies and dances. Religious festivals were the occasion for processions in which rich silken umbrellas, banners, and garments played important roles. Woven brocades and tapestries, stitched embroideries, and pieced appliqués were all utilized for these fine textiles.

Tibet's proximity to the famed ancient silk routes across Central Asia brought direct access, from at least the seventh century, to silk goods moving from Gansu in the northeast to Sogdiana in the northwest. Between A.D. 677 and 863, Tibetan armies raided and often held control of key oasis cities in Central Asia where textiles were made and traded. Tibet's extensive eastern border with China also enabled contact with silk-producing centers such as Chengdu in Sichuan. Thus either as war booty or through peaceful trade, luxury fabric came into Tibet during the period of the Yarlung dynasty. At this time both Tibetan and Chinese historical documents record immense amounts of silk going to Tibet directly from the Chinese emperor. The Zhol pillar below the Potala Palace in Lhasa, carved around 764 in elegant Tibetan script, cites a yearly tribute of fifty thousand pieces of silk from the Chinese emperor Suzong (r. A.D. 756–763) to the Tibetan ruler Trisong Detsen.

After the fall of the Yarlung dynasty, the importation of silk occurred intermittently, waxing or waning as economic circumstances and trading opportunities allowed. The castles and town houses of the Tibetan aristocracy certainly contained quantities of fine textiles, but as the wealth and power of the Buddhist church grew, the bulk of silk coming into the country, as either "tribute" or trade, went to ecclesiastic uses. With the establishment of a theocratic state under the Great Fifth Dalai Lama in 1642, the monastic centers of the dominant sect, the Gelukpas, came to be vast repositories of textiles.

Traditionally, the chanting halls and chapels of religious institutions across Tibet would have been decorated for special occasions with custom-tailored textile adornments for ceilings, walls, and pillars. After the event these decorations would have been folded up and returned to storage. Other special textiles were made into garments or throne coverings for abbots or important lamas, again to be returned to monastic storerooms after a short period of use. If a particular garment or hanging was associated with a great *tulku* (*sprul sku;* incarnate lama) or other exalted personage, the textile might be displayed on an annual basis following his death. Such sacred textiles would be kept in the monastic treasury. Thus garments and hangings, or fragments thereof, were preserved for centuries in Tibetan religious establishments. The historical situation is analogous to that of Buddhist garments and adornments in Japan. The dry, cold, and pristine air of Tibet was ideal for the conservation of textiles. Displayed or worn briefly inside dark rooms and then stored in trunks in cool, dark chambers, they have survived in some cases for almost a thousand years.

The ritual textiles in the Zimmerman Collection represent work made either in Tibet or China for specifically Tibetan Buddhist uses. (This is in contrast to the great quantity of fabrics preserved in Tibet that were originally made for secular or non-Tibetan purposes but were later recycled for religious use.) Foremost among these textiles are appliquéd silks. Appliqué is a technique in which cut pieces of silk (mixed sometimes with wool, cotton, or leather) are sewn onto a cloth background to produce a pattern or picture much like a painting. Edges and details are commonly emphasized by cording, embroidery, or painting. Appliqué may have been used in Central Asia and Tibet in prehistoric times for animal trappings, tent decorations, and domestic furnishings—uses still seen in the twentieth century. Receiving gifts of Chinese woven, stitched, and pieced banners depicting Buddhist subjects during the Yuan period (and perhaps earlier), the Tibetans adapted their skill in appliqué to this new purpose.

Tibetan appliquéd banners or *thankas* can vary from faithful copies, in pieced fabric, of painted religious subjects (see no. 118) to exuberant banners that are bold in scale (see no. 117). Appliqué was also commonly used for religious dance costumes (see no. 119). To produce the great quantity of appliquéd *thankas,* banners, and adornments they required, monasteries established workshops, and great lamas traveled with personal appliqué masters.

Tibetan craftsmen never achieved the complexity and delicacy of Chinese embroidery, although Tibetan patrons admired and treasured such work. Imperial Chinese embroidered copies of Tibetan Buddhist subjects were favored gifts to lamas and monastic treasuries (see no. 116). In format and iconography the embroidered pieces are identical to painted *thankas* of the period. The somewhat cruder, freer embroidery of the Tshangpa hanging (no. 115) may represent Central Asian or Mongolian traditions.

Still another textile form represented in the Zimmerman Collection is brocade used to make a religious picture (see no. 114). In this instance an ancient Chinese technique appropriate for repetitious patterning has been used to "copy" a painted image. It must have been tremendously laborious to set up a brocade loom for such a textile but, once set, unlimited numbers of repeated images could be produced.

Several of the pieces in the exhibition show evidence of recycling. The Mahākāla brocade (no. 114) has been cut down from an original large (horizontal?) length, pieced, and resewn to a *thanka* format. The appliquéd pair of *ḍākinīs* (no. 117) probably once danced across a long banner in company with other figures but were separated and sewn into a small silk frame at some point. Such "adaptive reuse," common in Tibet, is evidence of the reverence shown to precious textiles, which were never just thrown away. When damaged or, perhaps, needed for a particular ritual, fabric would be creatively cut, pieced, and resewn to allow continued use.

NOTES

1. Snellgrove and Richardson 1968, p. 23.
2. Roerich 1976, p. 70.
3. Ibid., p. 74.
4. Das 1965, p. 81.
5. Tucci 1959.
6. Snellgrove 1959, vol. 1, p. 110.
7. Snellgrove 1959, vol. 1, p. 114.
8. See Ruegg 1966, pp. 114–17, for material about his artistic process and for the quotes that follow.
9. I characterized this style earlier (see Pal 1984) as the Kadampa style. See Huntington and Huntington 1990 for a discussion of these styles. Unfortunately, Tibetan traditions for the classification of styles are not always dependable.
10. See Pal 1990 for an extensive discussion of arhat and *mahāsiddha* representations in Himalayan art.
11. See Pal 1984. Earlier still we encounter this landscape type in a scroll in the Virginia Museum of Fine Arts, Richmond, and rudimentary sketches occur in a fifteenth-century book of iconographic drawings.
12. See ibid. for an extensive discussion.
13. See Tucci 1959.

SCULPTURES AND RITUAL OBJECTS

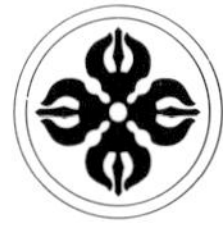

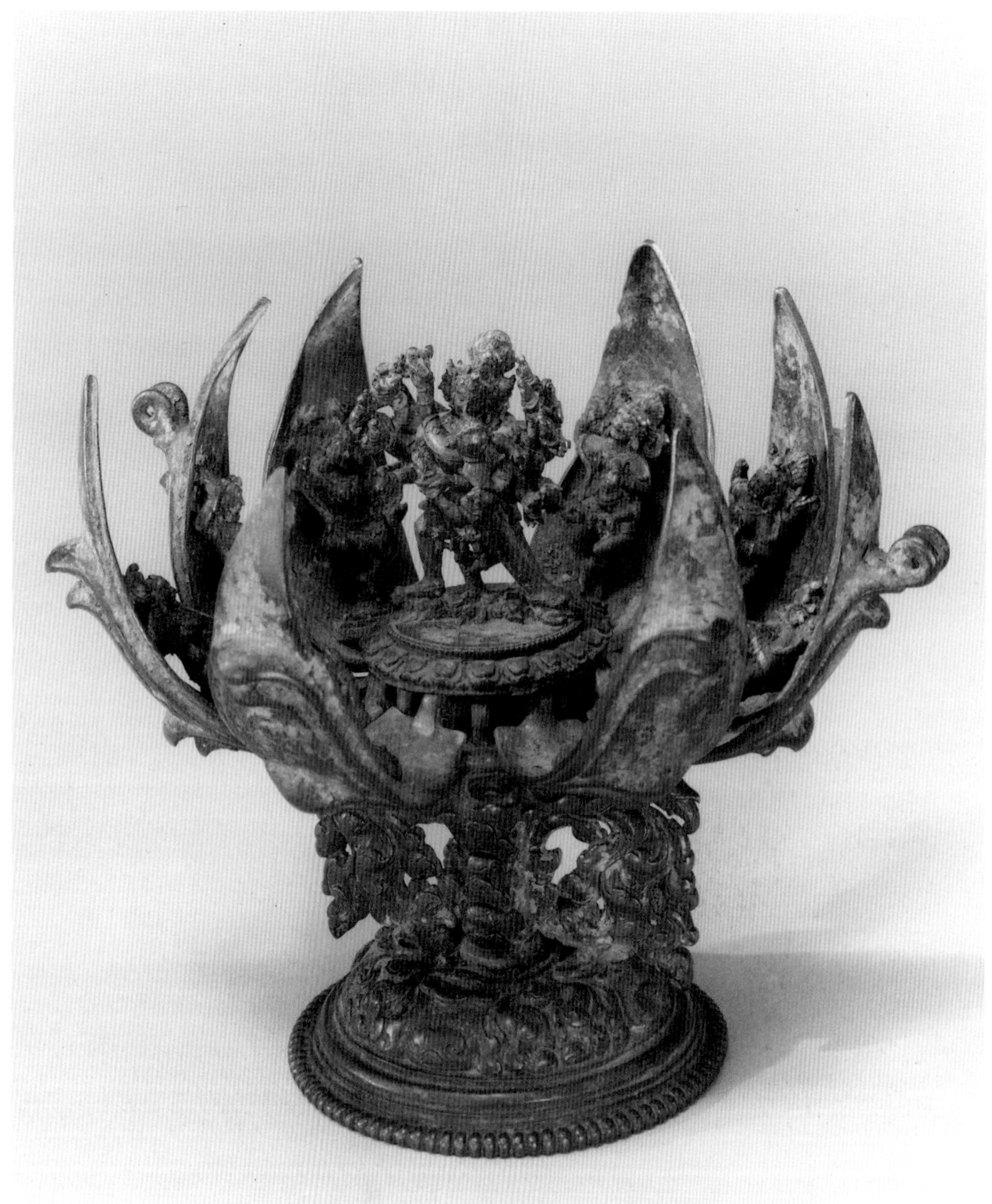

52

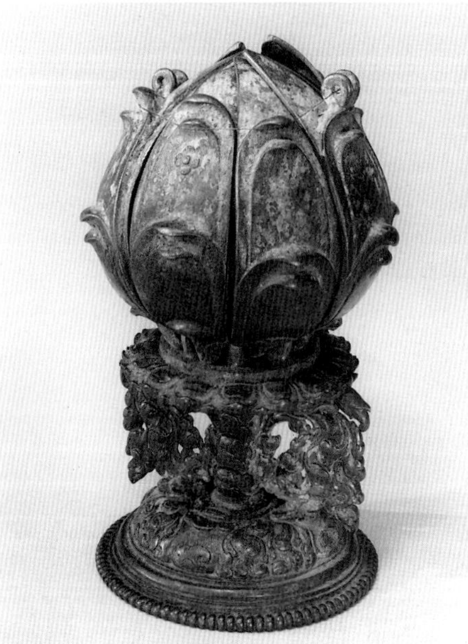

52

52

Lotus Mandala

EASTERN INDIA OR TIBET, TWELFTH CENTURY

COPPER ALLOY CAST IN SEVERAL PIECES

H. (CLOSED): 6¼ IN. (15.9 CM); W. (OPEN): 6 IN. (15.2 CM)

This three-dimensional mandala takes the form of a lotus. When closed, the object resembles an unopened flower. It is opened only during worship, and then only the initiated can see the images inside. The base is richly adorned with exuberant floral motifs that have nothing to do with the main flower, whose petals are naturalistically modeled.

Inside, the esoteric deity Hevajra, the focus of the *Hevajratantra,* ecstatically embraces his spouse, Nairātmyā (see no. 53) on a central lotus. From their union emerge eight goddesses, who are represented on the eight petals of the lotus and whose duty it is to arouse Hevajra. Like all other tantras of high realization, the *Hevajra* offers a method of mental and physical control which, if practiced properly and sincerely, leads the practitioner to a state of bliss or spiritual equipoise. The name or title *Hevajra* is explained in the *Hevajratantra* by the Buddha himself as follows: "By HE is proclaimed great compassion, and wisdom by VAJRA" (Snellgrove 1959, vol. 1, p. 47).

Very likely the object was made in either Bihar or Bengal and taken to Nepal or Tibet. It could also have been made in Tibet following an Indian model. Both the metal content and the figural style make this unlikely, however. Most such lotus mandalas, whether made in eastern India or in Tibet, have emerged from Tibet in recent years. It would have been quite simple for such a small object to have been carried into Tibet by either an Indian monk visiting the country or a returning Tibetan pilgrim. Such objects would at first have been copied diligently by Tibetan artists and then served as general models.

Literature Pal 1975, no. 30.

53

Hevajra and Nairātmyā (?)

WESTERN TIBET (?), TWELFTH CENTURY

BRASS WITH SILVER AND COLORS

H: 12½ IN. (31.8 CM)

The two figures interlocked in a vigorous sexual embrace are very likely Hevajra and his consort, Nairātmyā (see no. 19). Usually, he is shown with more arms, but here a simpler form with only two is represented. He stands resolutely with his legs outstretched in the posture known as *pratyālīḍha*. Nairātmyā's left leg stretches parallel to his right one, but the other encircles him over his left thigh. Below their feet are supine beings symbolizing evil spirits, who are being trampled and destroyed. His hands holding the thunderbolt and the bell are crossed behind her back. She holds a thunderbolt and skull cup filled with blood. Against his chignon is a tiny effigy of the transcendental Buddha Vairochana, and just below is the *viśvavajra* (double thunderbolt).

Except for their ornaments, including some made with severed heads and skulls, both figures are naked. The ornaments across Nairātmyā's rump and on both figures' legs are silver-plated. These and the orange hair on their heads add interesting texture to the otherwise mellow golden surface. Both figures are strongly modeled and have distinctive, expressive faces. Their bodies move in the same direction in rhythmic unison with the perfect timing of two expert dancers.

The earliest Tibetan sculpture in the Zimmerman Collection, this work, although reflecting affinity with Kashmiri tradition, is recognizably Tibetan in style. The modeling is not quite as naturalistic nor the proportions quite as elegant as one encounters in Kashmiri figures. The masklike, distinctive face of the god with its fangs and moustache is reminiscent of an expressive Kashmiri figure of Samvara in the Los Angeles County Museum of Art (Pal 1975, p. 174).

Literature Beguin 1977, no. 197; Reynolds 1986, p. 168, fig. 3; Rhie and Thurman 1984, no. 113 (no ill.); 1991, no. 68.

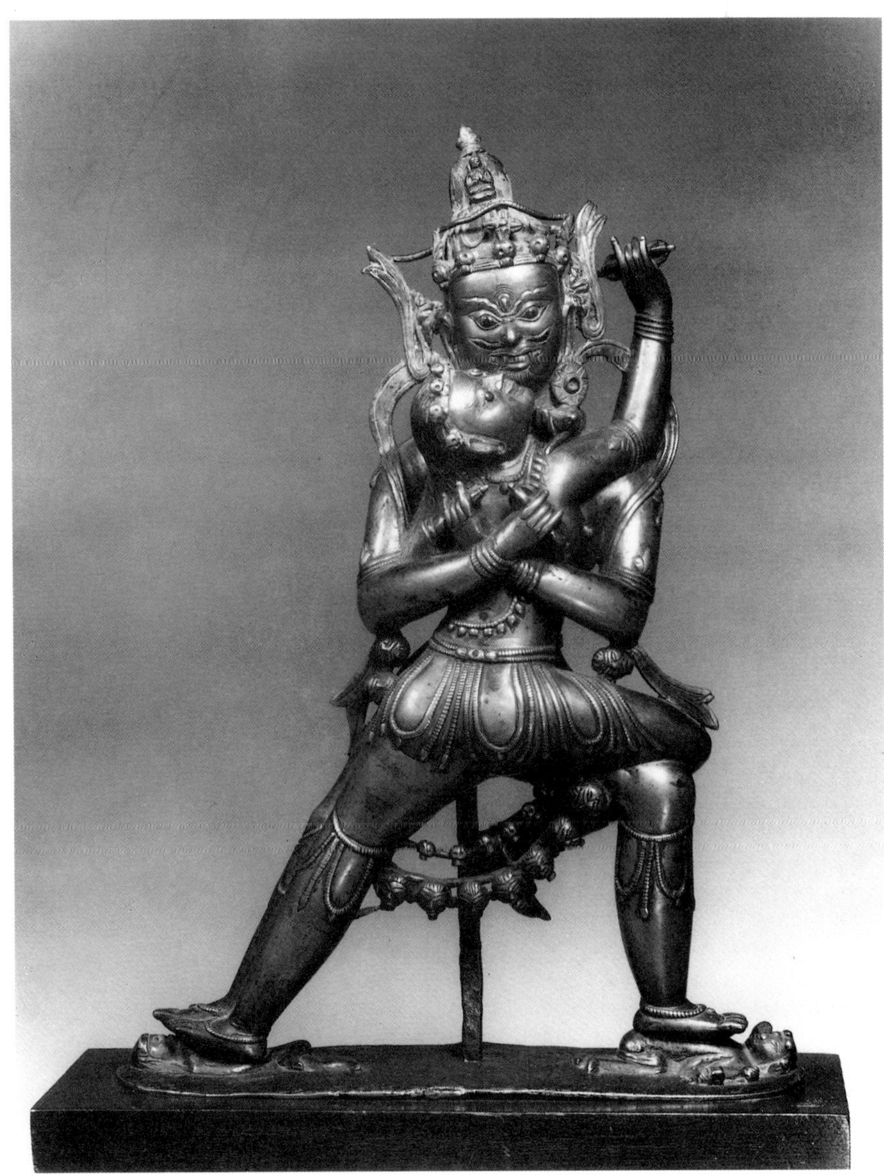

53

54

Buddhist Hayagrīva

TWELFTH CENTURY
COPPER ALLOY WITH COLORS
H: 13 IN. (33.0 CM)

Both Hindus and Buddhists have a deity called Hayagrīva (Horse-Headed One). In Tibet he is called Tamdin (*rta-mgrin*). The Hindu Hayagrīva, an avatar of Vishnu, is the earlier of the two. Whether the Buddhist Hayagrīva was influenced by his Hindu namesake is not known and probably unlikely. While they do share a horse's head, their iconography is different.

In Tibet Hayagrīva is one of the eight Dharmapālas, or Defenders of the Faith, whose cult is very strong. In a less menacing form he is an acolyte of the Bodhisattva Avalokiteshvara (see no. 37). Independent images of Hayagrīva are rare in India and Nepal. In a solitary example from Kashmir (Pal 1975, pp. 204–5), he is depicted as a peaceful deity, as is the case with the Hindu Hayagrīva (see van Gulick 1935).

In this particular representation, Hayagrīva stands in the militant *pratyālīḍha* posture, wearing a short *dhoti* decorated with a whirligig pattern. He has a prominent belly and a

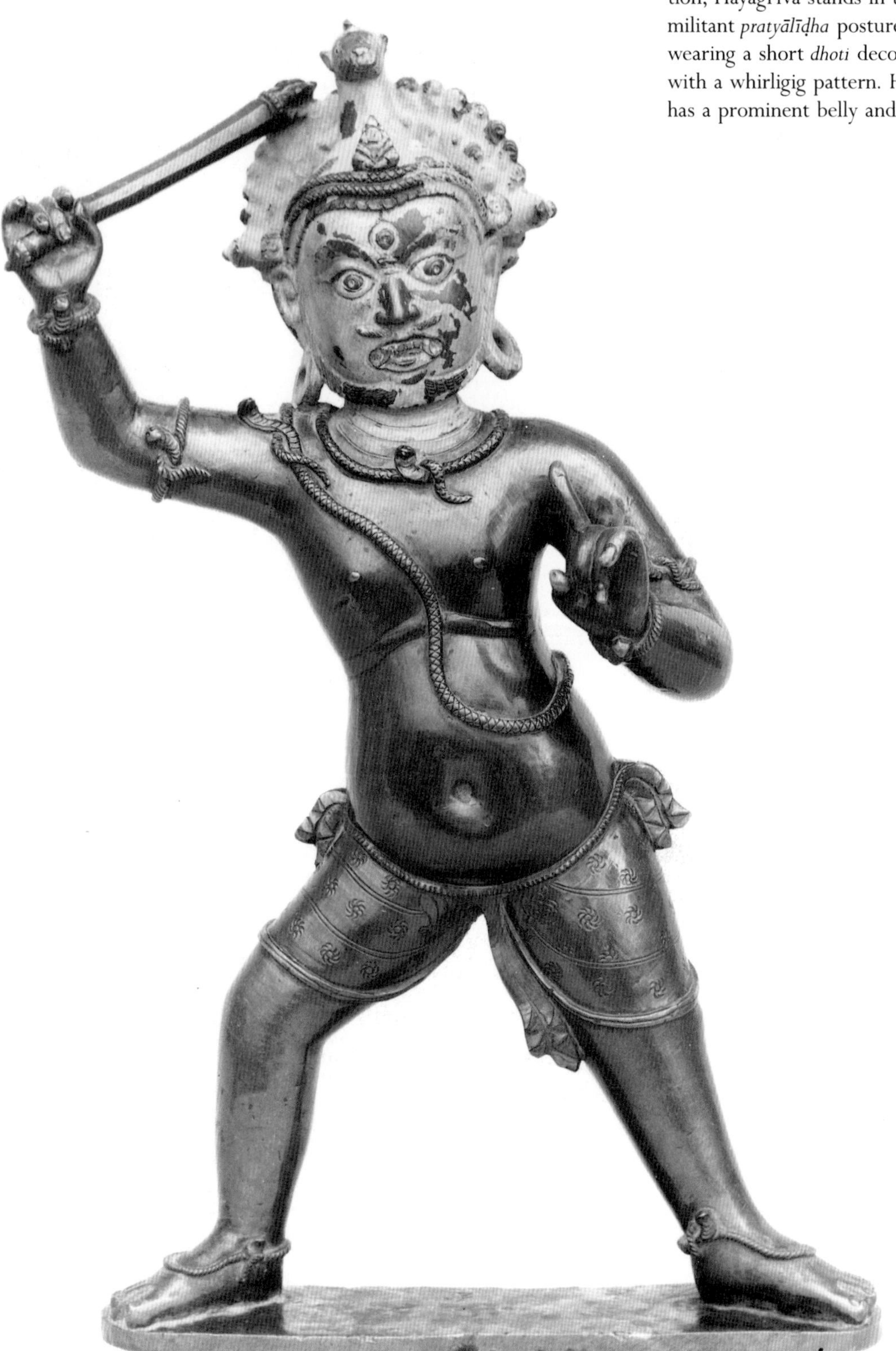

54

terrifying face with beard, moustache, and three bulging eyes. His open mouth shows his teeth and fangs. His hair is arranged in upright curls that look like snake hoods. Except for his earrings and modest tiara, snakes form his ornaments and sacred cord. A horse's head sticks prominently out of his hair. In keeping with his role as a guardian, Hayagrīva brandishes a staff or club with his right hand and displays the gesture of admonition (*tarjanīmudrā*) with his left. As was customary in Tibet, the hair was painted in orange and the face in gold.

Despite his prominent belly, the figure is well proportioned and smoothly modeled. Conceived in the round, stylistically it is reminiscent of tenth–eleventh century sculptures of Bihar and Bengal (see Bhattasali 1929, pl. 23). The fanlike spread of the hair is very similar to that seen in a Garuḍa figure from Bengal (ibid., pl. 41, 1).

Literature Beguin 1977, no. 196.

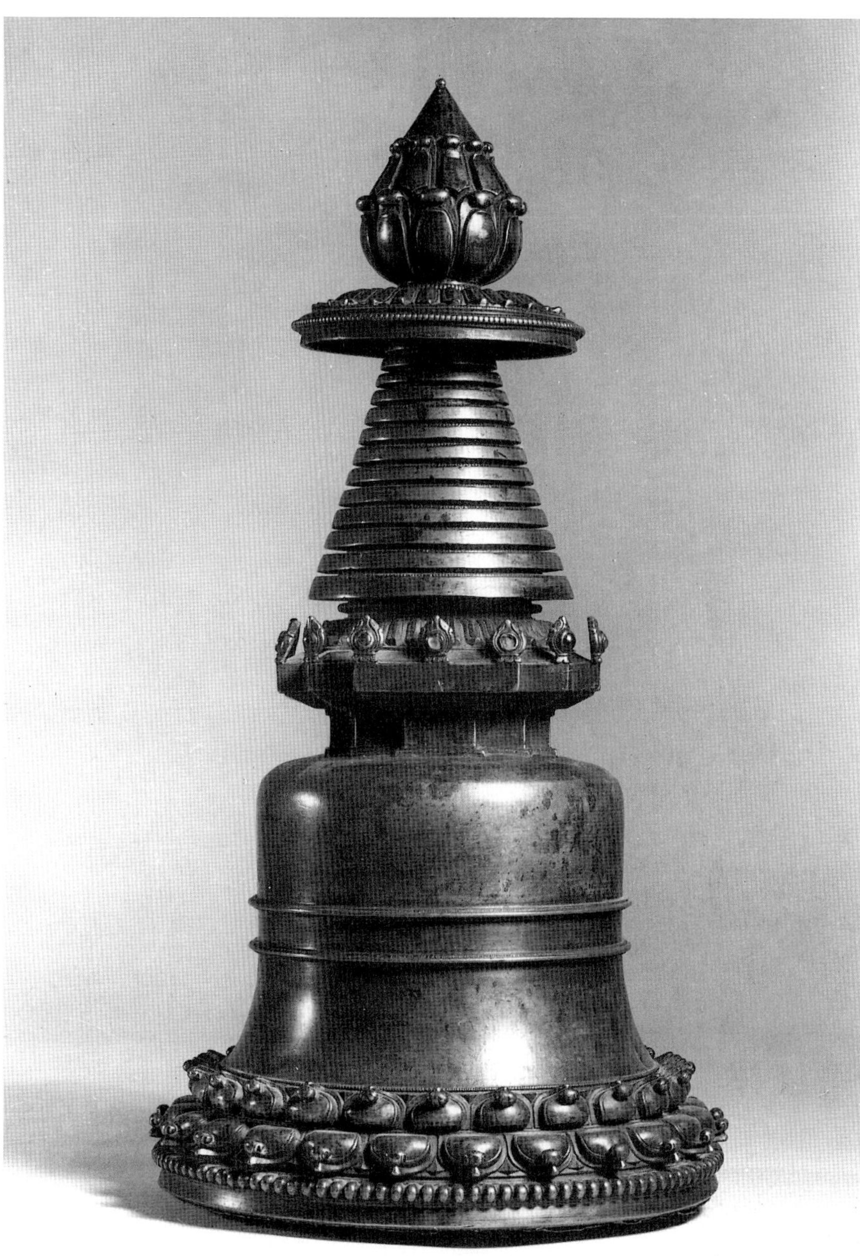

55

55

Commemorative Stūpa

CENTRAL TIBET, THIRTEENTH CENTURY

COPPER ALLOY

H: 17¼ IN. (43.8 CM)

The *stūpa* (Tibetan: *chöten*) is the most ancient symbol of Buddhism and originally had a funerary or commemorative connotation. For instance after the Buddha's death, his body was cremated and the ashes gathered and divided into portions, over each of which a *stūpa* was built. In the early history of Buddhism, the *stūpa* acted as a bond or focal point of the faith and served as its most tangible symbol. Tibetans came to regard the *chöten* as the symbol of the Buddha's mind. It is found in a great variety of forms and sizes. Such portable examples were made for commemorative purposes and may contain the remains and relics of a pious religious figure.

This particular form of *chöten* may have been introduced by Atīśa, for it was particularly popular with the Kadampas. The shape and form of these Kadampa *chötens* are consistent. With a slightly flaring, almost squarish drum, they always rise from a lotus base. The entablature, or *harmikā*, is cruciform with projections on each side, giving the impression of the gateways of a mandala. From the *harmikā* rises the pyramidal arrangement of the ten or thirteen tiers of the umbrella, which is protected by a wider parasol or disc. The finial here is a closed lotus like the lotus mandala in the Zimmerman Collection (no. 52).

This particular example is quite large for such portable *chötens* and remains unopened, its relics intact. For other examples with extensive discussion, see Hatt 1980 and Reynolds et al. 1986, no. 59.

Literature Beguin 1977, no. 352.

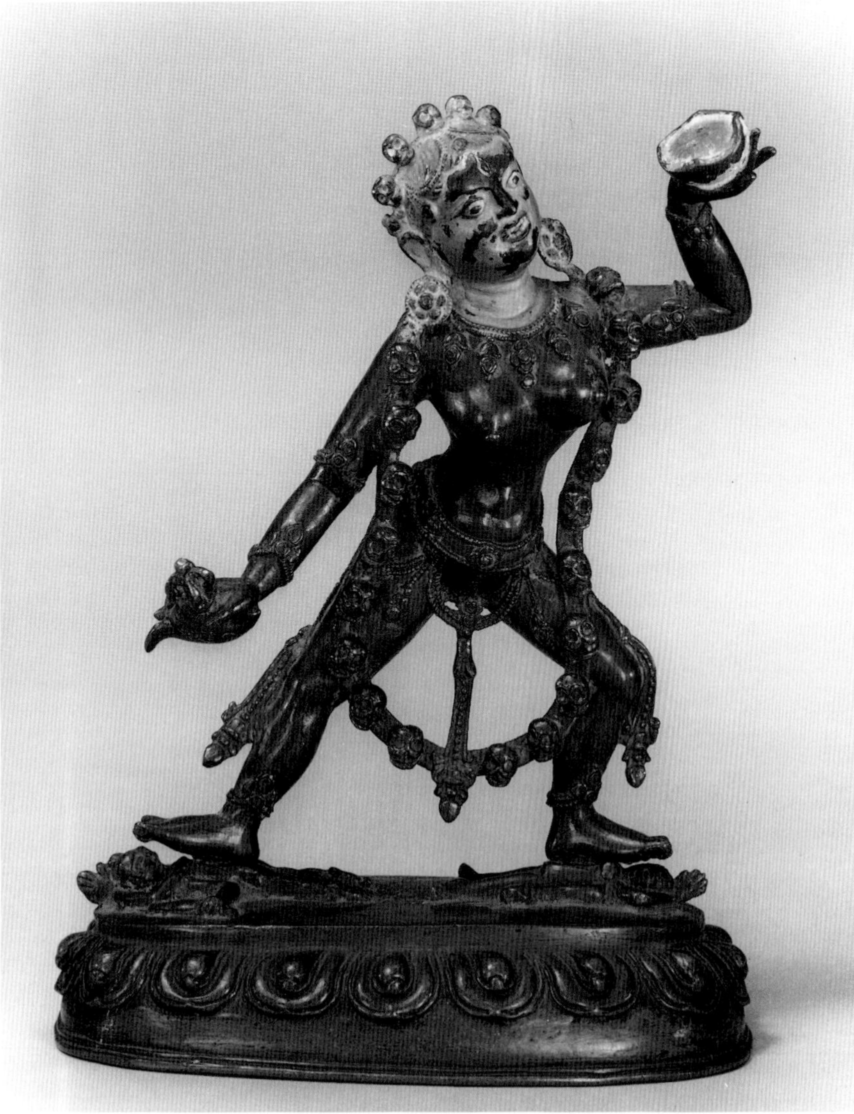

56

56

Goddess Sarvabuddhaḍākinī

CENTRAL TIBET, THIRTEENTH CENTURY

COPPER ALLOY WITH COLOR AND GOLD

H: 8⅝ IN. (21.9 CM)

This goddess is called Sarvabuddhaḍākinī, which means "*Ḍākinī* of All Buddhas." The word *ḍākinī* cannot be translated literally into English. Although it may imply a female imp, in tantric Buddhism the word is also used—as is *mahāsiddha* (see no. 64)—to denote an initiated female partner and a spiritual guide, who may be supernatural. In this instance, however, Sarvabuddhaḍākinī is represented as a goddess symbolizing wisdom. In Tibet she is called Naro Khachoma (*na-ro-mkha'-spyod-ma*). An important goddess, she often appears on *thankas* among tutelary deities. She also is shown in *yab-yum* with Heruka, a manifestation of Hevajra (see no. 53).

Both conceptually and iconographically Sarvabuddhaḍākinī is no different from either Nairātmyā or Vajravārāhī (see no. 57). She is shown naked except for her ornaments, has an awesome visage but a beautiful body, and carries a chopper, a skull cup, and a cot's leg. Usually the cot's leg, missing here, is placed horizontally across her shoulders. Her posture is different, however. While Nairātmyā and Vajravārāhī dance in *ardhaparyaṅka* posture, Sarvabuddhaḍākinī strikes a militant *ālīḍha* pose and tramples two four-armed figures (Hindu gods?) under her feet. Both figures lie on their bellies. Moreover she holds the skull cup high with her left hand as if she is about to drink from it. Her posture and this gesture are very similar to those given to the Hindu goddess Chhinnamastā (no. 50).

The hair of the goddess bears traces of orange-red pigments, while her face is painted in gold. Her eyes are particularly expressive, and her figure is strongly modeled with large, full breasts. This emphasis on curves and volumes is reminiscent of Indian sculpture, and it is difficult to see why the figure has been dated as late as the seventeenth century (see von Schroeder 1981, no. 137F). A thirteenth-century date seems more likely in view of the stylistic evidence and the figure's similarity in metal color and use of paint to the Hayagrīva (no. 54) in the Zimmerman Collection.

57

Two Representations of Goddess Vajravārāhī

CENTRAL TIBET, THIRTEENTH CENTURY

A: COPPER ALLOY WITH SILVER INLAY
H: 11¼ IN. (28.6 CM)

B: COPPER ALLOY WITH TURQUOISE, SILVER, AND COLORS
H: 9 IN. (22.9 CM)

The goddess represented in these two bronzes is Vajravārāhī (Diamond Sow), known in Tibetan as Dorje Phagmo. One of the most powerful figures in Vajrayāna Buddhism, she is the consort of Samvara or Chakrasamvara, the presiding deity of the important Vajrayāna spiritual empowerment embodied in the

Chakrasamvaratantra (nos. 20, 41). Vajravārāhī is worshipped in her own right, however, and is especially venerated in Tibet. Apart from her significance for the Drukpas, a subsect of the Kagyupas, she is the patron deity of the nunnery of Semding, where every nun is said to be her emanation. She is also included on *thankas* as a tutelary deity.

Except for her ferocious visage and the sow's head projecting from her own head, in both bronzes she is modeled as an attractive woman dancing. Wearing a long garland of severed human heads and a tiara of skulls, she steps lightly on a corpse. Except for the ornaments, she is naked. With her right hand she brandishes a chopper and with the other holds a skull cup. In the crook of her left arm rests a cot's leg (missing in B).

It will be evident that, but for the sow's-head excrescence, this goddess is no different from Nairātmyā, the consort of Hevajra (no. 53). The sow's head links her with the Hindu Vārāhī, one of the mother goddesses, though conceptually they are not related. However, since the Hindu Vārāhī enjoyed an independent cult and was regarded as a powerful goddess in eastern India, it is not improbable that she influenced the Buddhists to conceive their own Vajravārāhī. It may also be noted that in Tibet, Vajravārāhī is considered to be a form of Mārichī, the goddess of light, who rides a chariot drawn by seven pigs and is sometimes represented with a sow's head.

Although stylistically the two bronzes are similar and are very likely coeval, there are differences in detail that clearly reflect the artists' individual preferences. Most noteworthy are the variations in the features and expressions of the two faces and in the treatment of the hair and the head ornaments. In A the goddess's long hair comes down over both shoulders, and a conelike oval object crowns her head. In B all the hair is gathered into a topknot crowned by a thunderbolt. In addition a flying scarf encircles her shoulders. More significant are the manners in which support for the folded right legs is provided. In A what appears to be a piece of cloth or scarf rises from the base like a serpentine armrest, but in B a beautifully conceived

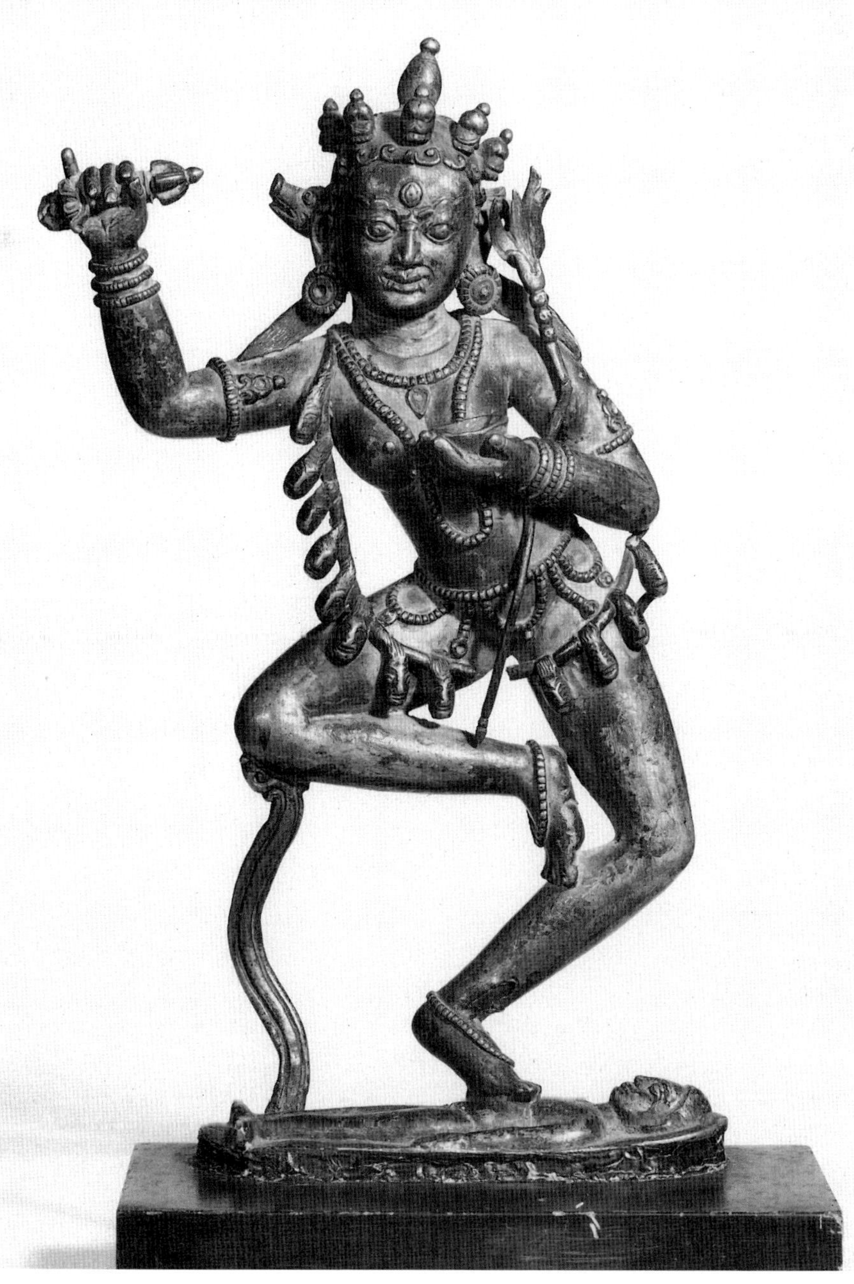

57A

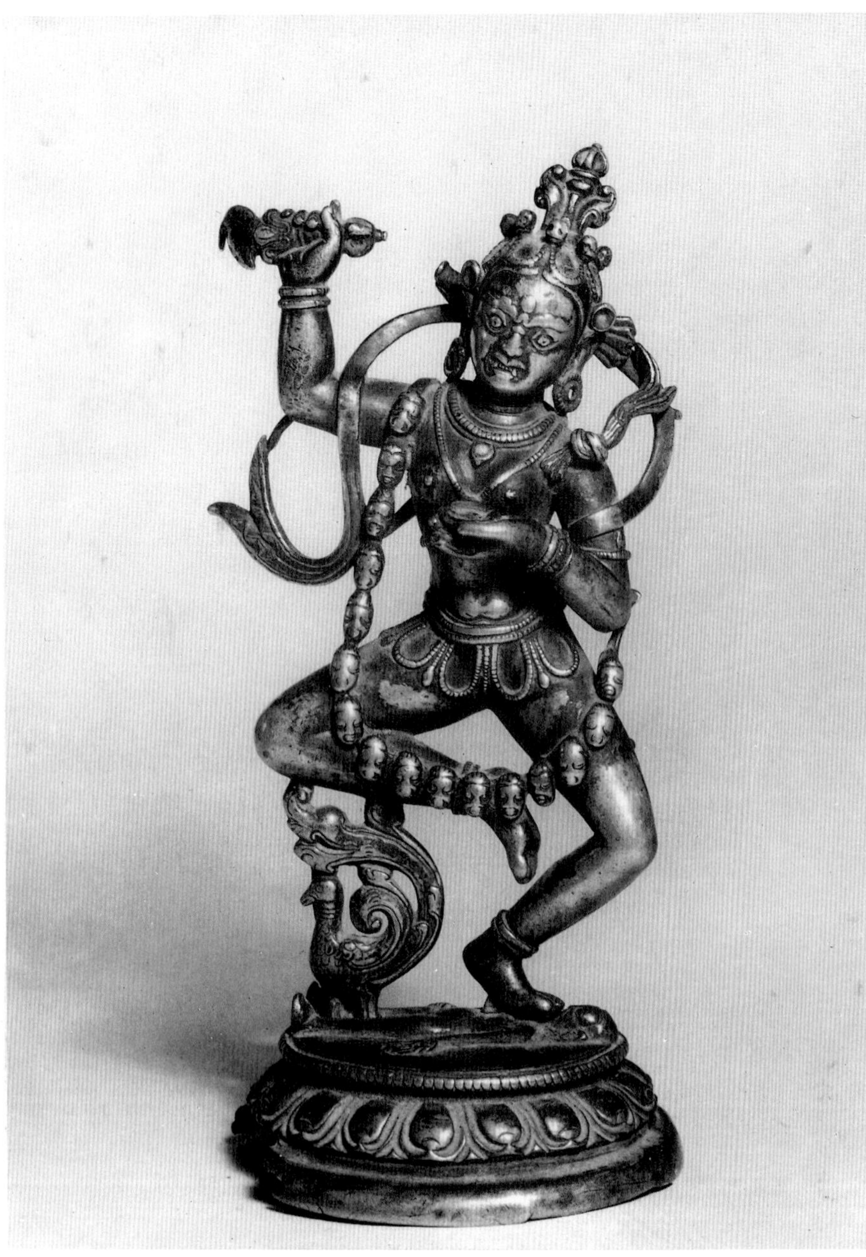

57B

bird, perhaps a peacock, keeps the leg in position with the sweep of its elegant tail feathers. In no other known image of the goddess is such a bird used in a similar fashion. No known textual description includes the bird as the goddess's iconographic emblem either.

Literature B: Beguin 1977, no. 124.

58

Buddha

CENTRAL TIBET, THIRTEENTH CENTURY

BRASS WITH COLORS

H: 15½ IN. (39.4 CM)

This impassive and impressive figure of the Buddha is seated in the meditating posture. His left hand is placed on his lap, and his right is extended with the palm resting against the knee. The middle finger of this hand would have touched the lotus base, which is missing here. This gesture is known as touching the earth (*bhūmispar-śamudrā*). It symbolizes the occasion when the Buddha Śākyamuni called the earth to witness his victory over Māra and his retinue immediately before his enlightenment. The gesture is also given to the transcendental Buddha Akshobhya (Imperturbable), which really is an epithet of Śākyamuni as the conqueror of Māra. Thus the exact identification of this Buddha cannot be determined without knowing the context in which the image was used.

As is characteristic of Buddha images, his neck is marked with three lines, the lobes of the ears are elongated, and a dot adorns his forehead. His hair is in short curls, and the cranial bump known as the *ushṇīsha* is a prominent cone crowned with stylized flames. All these are signs of the Buddha's supernatural character. The hair is painted black, and the face and neck were once covered in gold, some of which remains attached. The upper garment leaves the right shoulder and arm undraped and billows near the left forearm in a manner seen in earlier Buddha images from Bihar. Indeed this figure suggests the influence of eastern Indian sculptures of the Pāla period in both the articulate modeling of the torso and the naturalistic treatment of the feet and hands. The toes and fingers are especially sensitively delineated. The broad face, stylization of the hair, elongation of the conelike *ushṇīsha,* and the latter's crowning elements (flames symbolizing knowledge) are, however, local characteristics.

Literature Von Schroeder 1981, no. 36c; Rhie and Thurman 1984, no. 77 (no ill.); Rhie 1985, fig. 10; Rhie and Thurman 1991, no. 2.

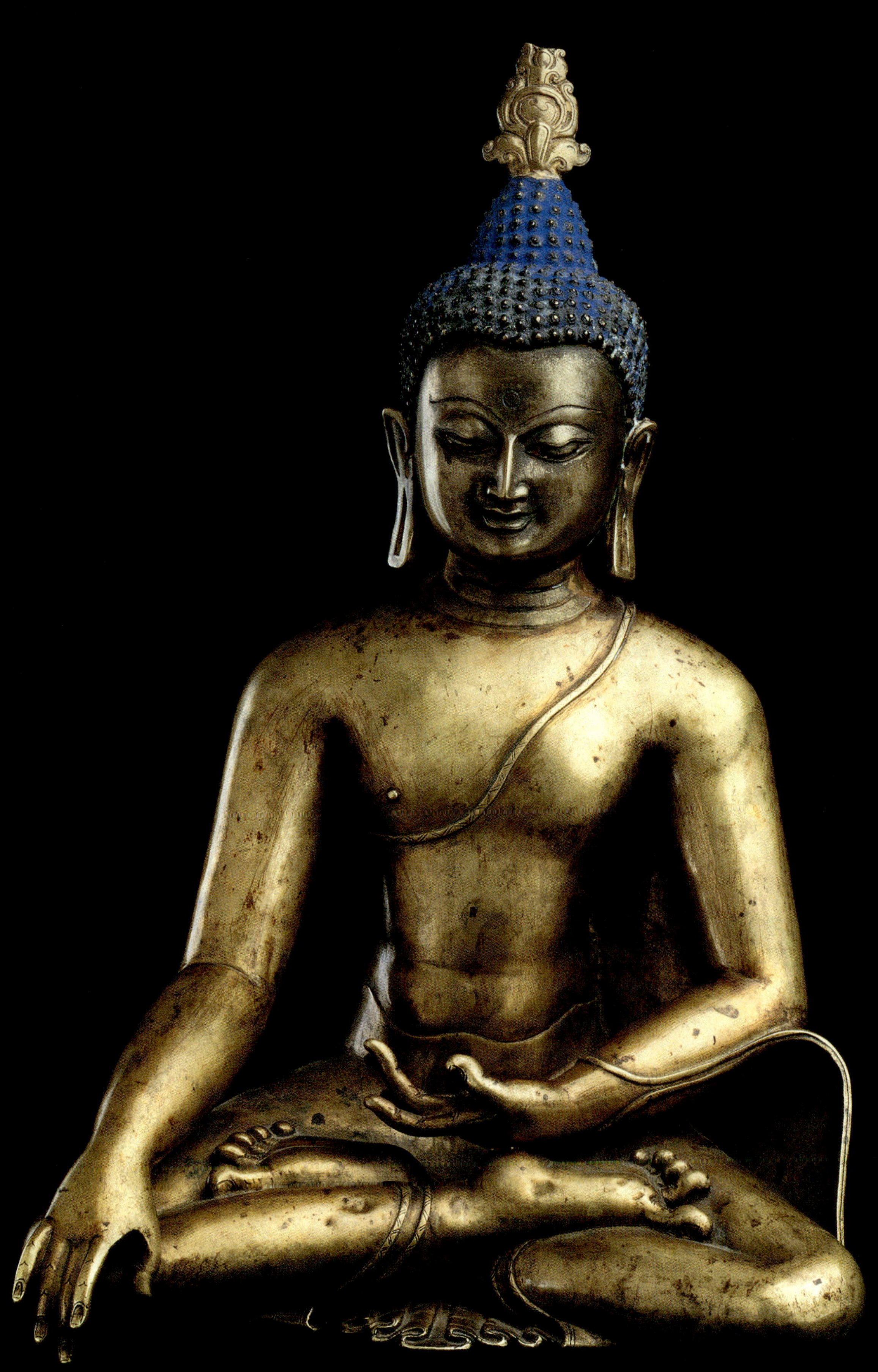

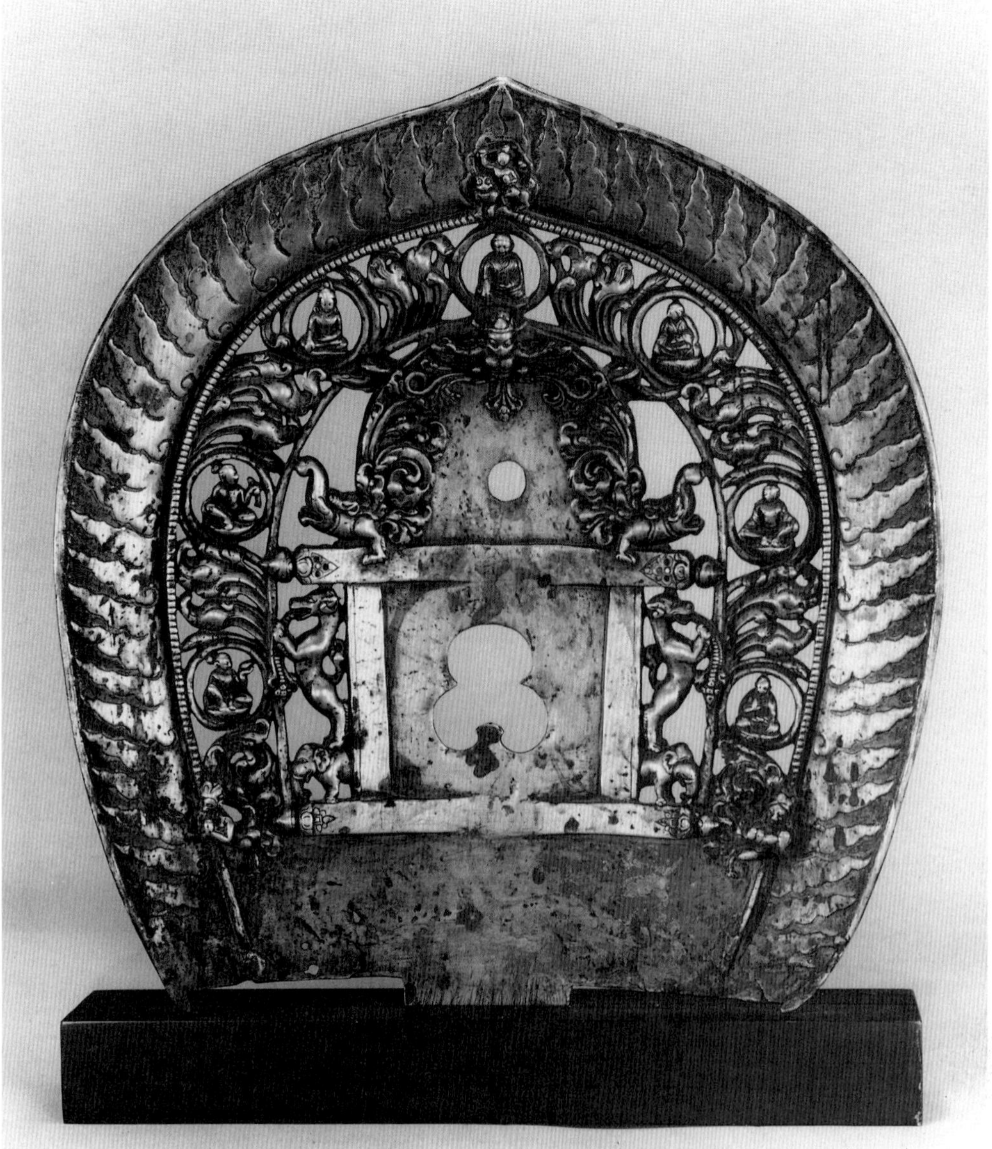

59

59

Aureole

CENTRAL TIBET, CA. 1300
BRASS WITH COLORS
H: 11½ IN. (29.2 CM)

The absence of the figure which the aureole (*prabhāmaṇḍala*) once adorned makes it possible to get an unencumbered view of the object. The fine craftsmanship betokens the excellent quality of the missing image and base. When complete the ensemble must have been impressive. Apart from the fact that the figures, animals, and vegetal motifs gain added volume because of the surrounding space, the contours of the form are crisp and articulate. The outlining of the flame motifs is rather unusual and seems to continue the bold, jagged shapes seen in Pāla styles rather than the more delicate, stylized tongues of flame preferred by Nepali artists. The flames have been given clearer definition by raising them above a red ground. Though this superbly crafted, highly animated aureole reflects Pāla influence, its Tibetan character cannot be doubted.

On both sides the throne back is adorned with the motif known as *gajasiṃha,* in which an elephant (*gaja*) supports a rampant lion (*siṃha*) who is busy extracting pearl strings from his mouth. Above the crossbar are two lively *makaras* whose decorative tails rise to form an arch with a female *garuḍa*(?) at the apex. At the base of the inner circle are a *kinnara* couple. Their tail feathers rise to meander upward, forming roundels along the way. Within each roundel is a human figure. Two on the lower left appear to be *mahāsiddhas*. The second figure, who holds a fish, must represent Luipa. The figure above him is perhaps the crowned transcendental Buddha Akshobhya. The corresponding three figures on the other side are very likely Tibetan monk-teachers, perhaps of the Sakya order. At the top of the outer band of flames is the Bodhisattva Mañjuśrī brandishing his sword and riding a lion.

60

Teacher Padmasambhava

WESTERN TIBET OR LADAKH, CA. FOURTEENTH CENTURY

COPPER ALLOY

H: 24 IN. (61 CM)

According to the dedicatory inscription on its back (see Appendix 2), this bronze figure of Padmasambhava (Lotus-Born) was dedicated by Kunga Gyalpo, who was a ruler of some kind. As the name of his kingdom is not given, he cannot be identified precisely. Therefore it would be imprudent to suggest an exact date for the sculpture, but it is unlikely to be later than the fourteenth century. Both technically and stylistically, it is similar to another equally imposing portrait dedicated in a hermitage in Ladakh and now in the Newark Museum (Reynolds et al. 1986, p. 530). Although the figure was viewed generally from the front, the surface designs of the garment and hat have been continued on the back.

The figure represents the great Indian tantric teacher and mystic who is said to have visited Tibet in the last quarter of the eighth century at the invitation of King Trisong Detsen. Padmasambhava's patron in India was the ruler of Uddiyana (usually identified with the Swat Valley now in Pakistan). With his special knowledge and powers,

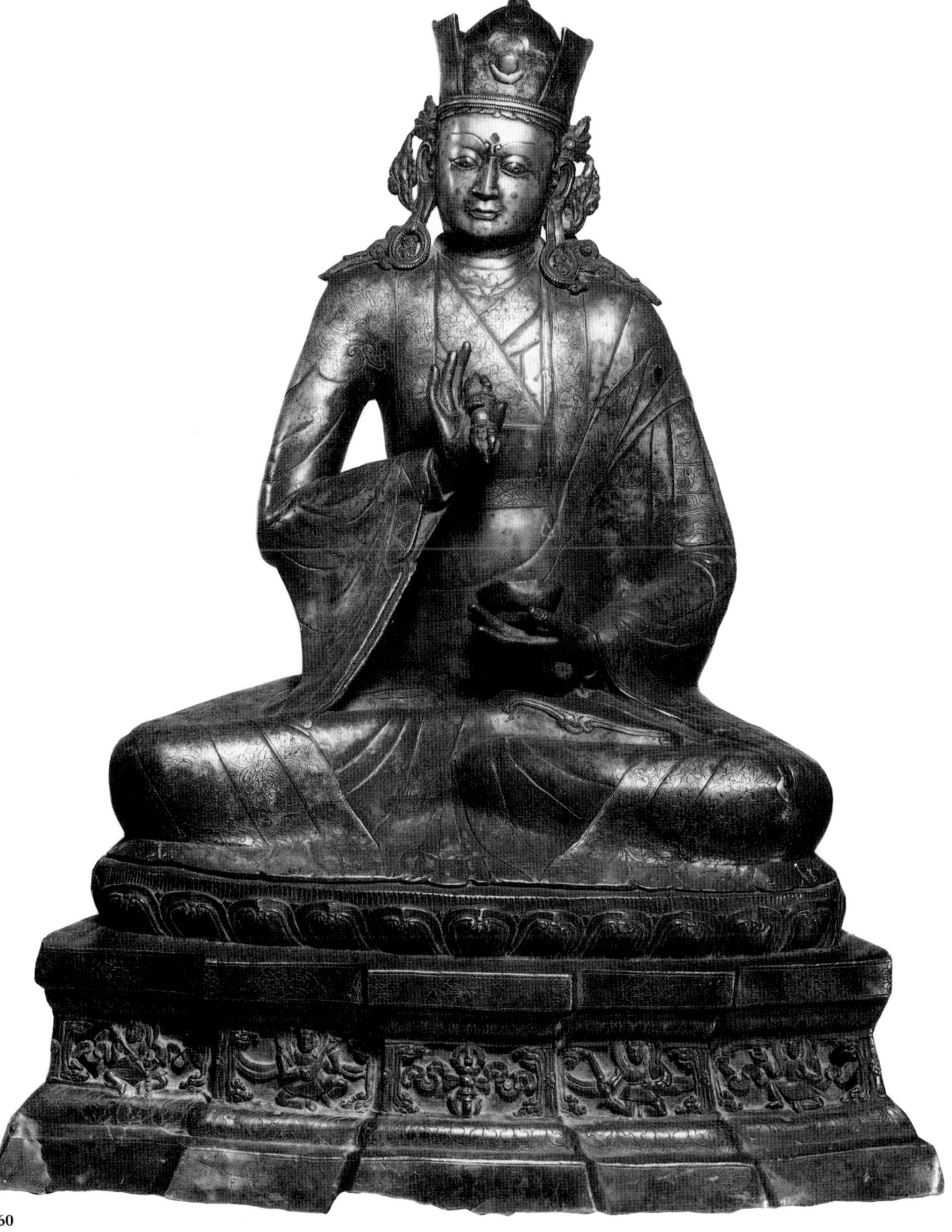

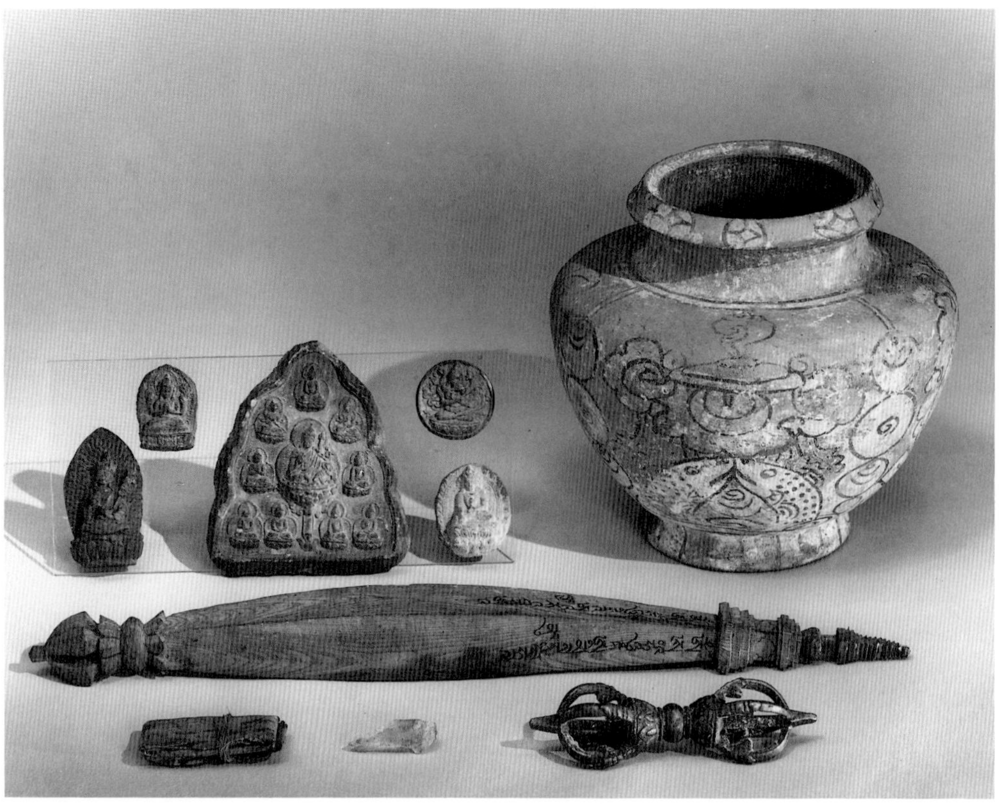

60

Padmasambhava subdued the local spirits and demonic forces in Tibet, helped to found the first Buddhist monastery at Samye, and established Buddhism on a firm footing. Although he is revered by all Tibetans, who fondly refer to him as Guru Rinpoche, he is the patron saint of the Nyingma order. The Nyingmapas regard him as the second Buddha.

Padmasambhava is depicted in a variety of iconographic forms, but this is his most characteristic one. Like all buddhas and monks, he is seated on a lotus in the meditative posture. He is clad in the garments of a monk but with a few distinctive differences. He is distinguished by his earrings, shoes, a cape called the "cloud collar," and his characteristic hat with up-turned flaps. The shoes and "cloud collar" are probably meant to emphasize his regal character. This is also evident from the sumptuous textiles that make up his garments. An unusual feature of this bronze is that the lotus is placed on a pedestal adorned in front with a double thunderbolt (*viśvavajra*) in the middle and the four royal guardians of the directions to either side. This demonstrates that Padmasambhava is being depicted as a universal spiritual sovereign. His attributes are the thunderbolt, skull cup, and cot's leg (also described as a magic staff) in the crook of his left arm (missing here but included on the terra-cotta representations inside the hollow sculpture).

That the royal donor of the image wanted to make certain of its efficacy is clear from the number and variety of objects placed inside it. As the accompanying illustration shows, they include five terra-cotta plaques, known as *tsha-tsha* in Tibetan, of different shapes and sizes. On the largest, Padmasambhava is surrounded by nine figures, seven of whom are buddhas and two bodhisattvas. A second *tsha-tsha* (at the far left) shows his image against rays of light. The four-armed figure on the *tsha-tsha* between the two just mentioned is very likely Shadakshari Lokeśvara or the personification of the bodhisattva's mantra of six syllables (see no. 80). The figures engaged in *yab-yum* on the top right *tsha-tsha* are Vajradhara and Vajrasattvātmikā, and the fifth figure just below it may be a crowned Akshobhya. These five *tsha-tshas,* together with a wooden implement with half a thunderbolt at one end and a stūpa at the other, a piece of crystal, a metal thunderbolt, and a piece of brittle bark tied with string, were all placed in a painted clay pot. The pot is adorned with cloud patterns, jewels, conch shells, and abstract motifs. To my knowledge no other bronze has been found containing such a pot. Thus apart from being one of the most imposing bronze images of Padmasambhava outside Tibet, the sculpture is of considerable cultural significance for both its inscription and its contents.

Literature Beguin 1977, no. 162; Rhie and Thurman 1984, no. 5 (no ill.); Rhie 1985, pp. 82–83, fig. 1; Rhie and Thurman 1991, no. 47.

61

Monk Champa Phuntshok

INDIA, LADAKH, FOURTEENTH CENTURY

COPPER ALLOY WITH TRACES OF GILT

H: 9 IN. (22.9 CM)

The inscription on the front of this object offers salutations to Champa Phuntshok (*byams-pa phun-tshogs*), who is characterized as omniscient. A second inscription on the back informs us that the bronze portrait was commissioned by Gyaltshen Zangpo. According to Stoddard (see Appendix 2), Champa Phuntshok was twentieth in one of the Kagyupa lineages, after Gotshen repa (1189–1258). Hence he must have flourished in the second half of the thirteenth century.

Clothed in his monk's garb and wearing the characteristic hat of Kagyupa lamas, Champa Phuntshok is seated on a lotus in the classic meditating posture. His right hand makes the teaching gesture, and his left holds a book. Interestingly, an effigy of an animal, perhaps a lion, has been added to the lotus base. The exact significance of this attribute remains unknown.

How formulaic and idealized such portraits were can be determined by comparing this representation with one of Champa Phuntshok's immediate predecessor now in the Newark Museum (Reynolds et al. 1986, no. 53). The principal differences are that neither the book nor the animal is included in the Newark bronze, whose face is fleshier and more rounded. The wide-open, staring eyes with prominent black pupils are common to both. In both bronzes too the garments are treated similarly with a section of the upper piece folded back over the left arm. There are only minor differences in the designs of the garments' borders and treatment of the lotus bases. Although the Newark bronze is much larger, the close similarities indicate that both were very likely made in the same workshop. Since the Zimmerman piece was made for the denizens of Gotsang Drubdeh, a hermitage near Hemis monastery in Ladakh, it is probable that both objects were made in that area.

Literature Von Schroeder 1981, no. 135D.

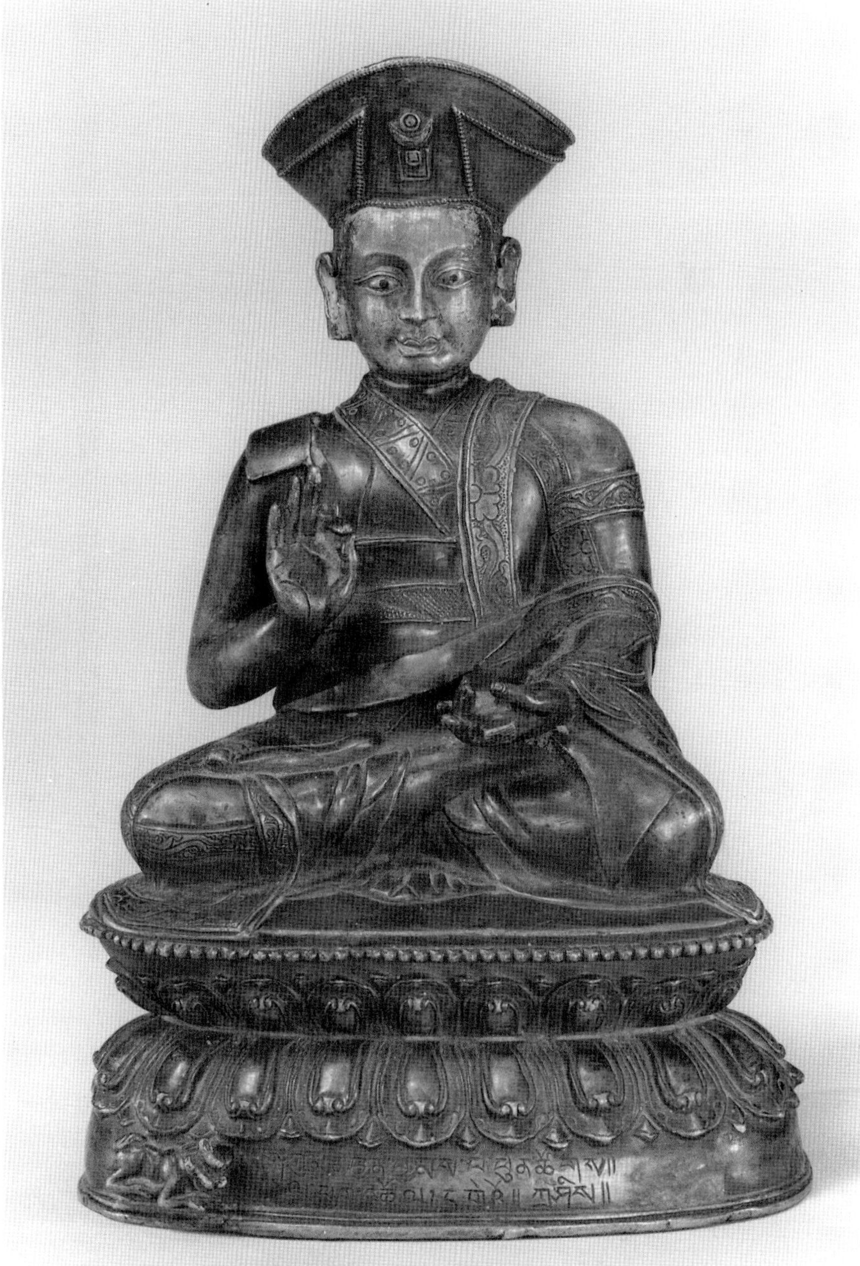

61

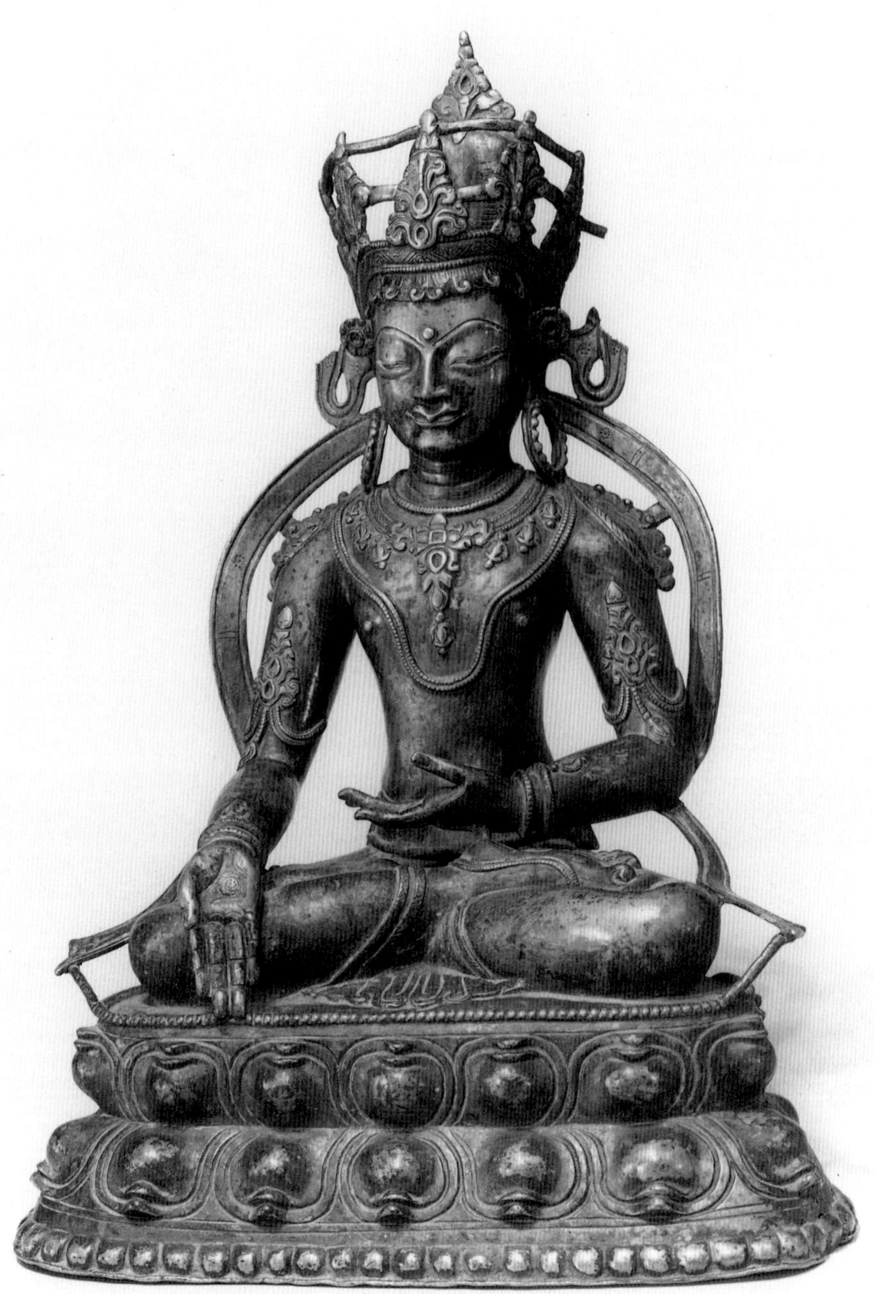

62

62

Buddha Ratnasambhava

CENTRAL OR WESTERN TIBET, CA. FOURTEENTH CENTURY

BRASS WITH TRACES OF COLORS

H: 16½ IN. (41.9 CM)

The dress, ornaments, tiara, and hairstyle all suggest that this figure is a bodhisattva, but he may represent a transcendental Buddha in his *sambhogakāya* (body of enjoyment) form. The gesture of the right hand, that of giving a boon or charity, would then make this a representation of Ratnasambhava (Jewel-Born). The left hand is held in suspension above the lap in the gesture of meditation (*dhyānamudrā*).

This bronze was once painted and possibly encrusted with stones. Many bronzes in this style, ranging in date from the eleventh to the fourteenth century, have come out of Tibet in the last two or three decades, and generally they have been attributed to western Tibet (von Schroeder 1981, pp. 156–93). It is doubtful that all of them were produced in the one region. Surprisingly, they show little influence from Kashmiri sculpture, as one would expect if they had been made in the west, and seem more directly linked to the Pāla style of Bihar. They are also stylistically related to figures painted on early Tibetan *thankas* that certainly derived from the Pāla style and were executed in central rather than western Tibet (see nos. 80, 81; Pal 1990A, p. 135, nos. P1, P2). However, the modeling is more abstract than one encounters in the Pāla style. The design of the tiara is different from that seen in Pāla examples; the flame crowning the chignon has become a floral design.

Literature Von Schroeder 1981, no. 34A; Rhie 1985, fig. 11; Rhie and Thurman 1991, no. 139.

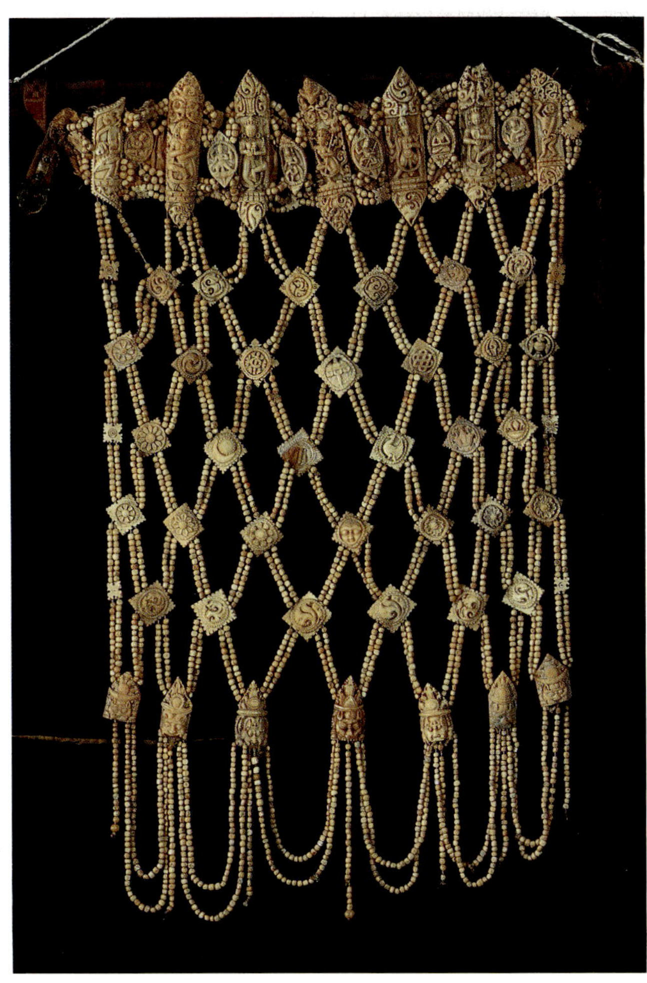

63

63

Ritual Bone Apron

FOURTEENTH–FIFTEENTH CENTURY

BONE, CLOTH, LEATHER, AND BRASS

H: 32½ IN. (82.6 CM)

This type of apron with bone ornaments, often made from human bone, is essential apparel in some forms of tantric ceremonies (see David-Neel 1971, p. 292). In both sculpture and painting, it is often encountered as an ornament worn by esoteric deities (see nos. 88, 93), although such aprons are rarely as elaborately figural as the present example. The bone ornaments here are mounted on a cloth with elaborate decorations on the back. A serpentine motif resembling a boa constrictor meanders across four registers, going through either an eye or the mouth of skulls or human heads. The exact significance of this fascinating motif is not known.

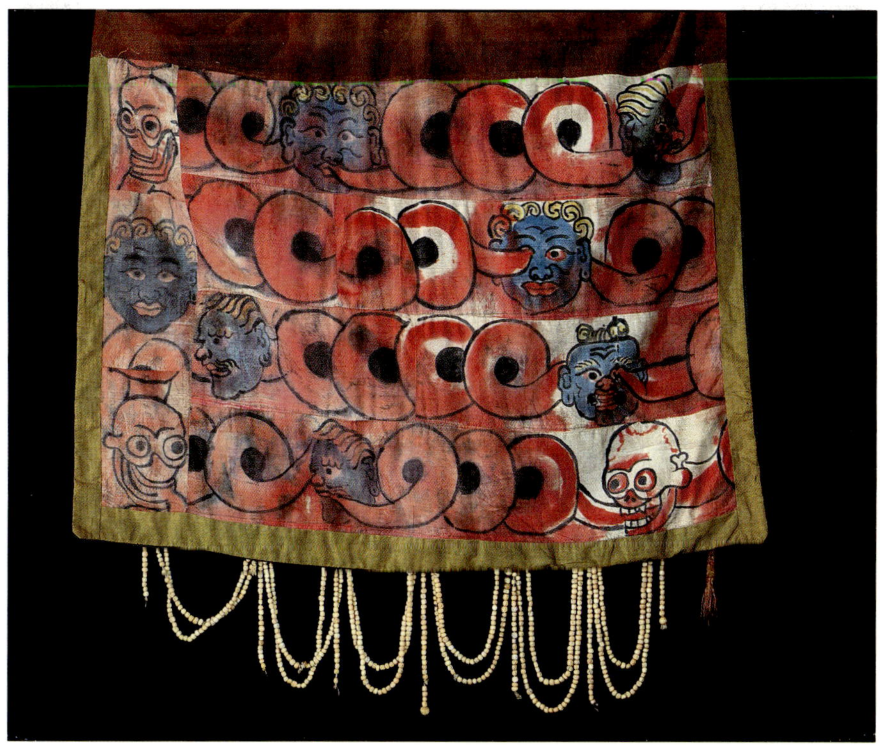

63

The form of this apron is fairly standard. At the bottom the strung beads form garlands. In the middle they are arranged in diamond patterns and the crossings covered by plaques decorated with a wide variety of swirling vegetal motifs, the sacred gander, and auspicious symbols such as the flowering vase, the wheel, the knot of immortality, the yang and yin (confused with the pair of fish?), and so on. Along the top, seven rectangular convex plaques with pointed ends alternate in a row with smaller oval plaques to form a band. The two plaques at the ends are carved with two dancing skeletons, perhaps representing Chiti-Pati, the companions of Mahākāla and guardians of the cremation grounds. All the others are adorned with figures of various deities.

The carving in this complete example is particularly fine. Not only are all details exquisitely rendered, but the figural forms are sensitively modeled and well proportioned despite the diminutive size of the plaques. All the figures are highly energized as they dance or strike militant postures. Especially engaging are the two dancing skeletons, who are both animated and amusing.

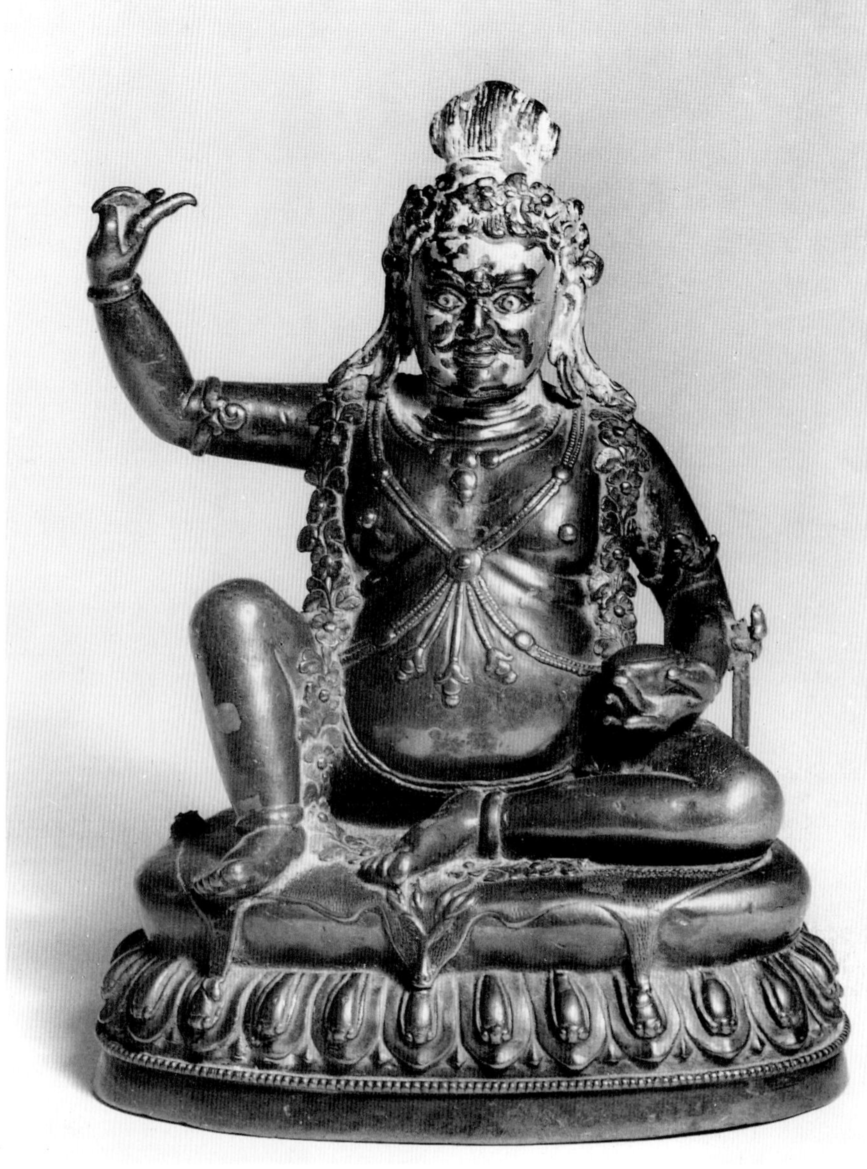

64

64

Mystic Master Virupā

CENTRAL TIBET, FIFTEENTH CENTURY

COPPER ALLOY WITH SILVER INLAY AND COLORS

H: 6½ IN. (16.5 CM)

This figure represents the Indian *mahāsiddha* Virupā (Tibetan: Bir-va-pa). Although his exact dates are not known, he may have lived in the eighth or ninth century. He joined the great monastery of Somapuri (Paharpur in Bangladesh), where he received the initiation and empowerment of Vajravārāhī (see no. 57). Thereafter he recited her mantra for twelve years but remained dissatisfied. Then a *ḍākinī* appeared to him and asked him to persevere and strip his mind of all mental fiction. After another twelve years he became enlightened. He then began to drink alcohol and eat meat. Upon being discovered he was thrown out of the monastery. Giving up his monk's robes, he became a wandering yogi but continued to convert "heretics"—Hindus—to Buddhism. Once in the city of Kanasati a tavern girl refused to serve him liquor unless he could pay. With his magical powers he pledged the sun and prevented it from moving for two days. The local king was alarmed, and on learning the cause of the sun's strange behavior paid the price of the *mahāsiddha*'s drink, thus freeing the sun.

This incident has been encapsulated in this object. With a skull cup in his left hand, the lightly clad *mahāsiddha*'s ample body is seated informally on an animal skin above a lotus. He raises his right hand in the threatening gesture (*tarjanīmudrā*), ordering the sun not to move. Apart from the crossbelt-like ornaments across his chest, which are often given to *mahāsiddhas,* he is distinguished by the garland and tiara of flowers. His hair is arranged in a topknot characteristic of ascetics but does not enclose a book (see no. 95). His round face with rolling eyes expresses his anger at not being served in the tavern. The eyes have been made more menacing by silver inlay, and the face still bears much of its original gold paint.

Literature Beguin 1977, no. 150.

65

Bodhisattva Mañjuśrī

CENTRAL TIBET, FIFTEENTH CENTURY

GILT COPPER ALLOY WITH SEMIPRECIOUS STONES

H: 12 IN. (30.5 CM)

The youthful, elegant Mañjuśrī (Tibetan: 'jam-dpal), though not a boy as in the collection's Nepali bronze (no. 6), is seated on a lotus in the *lalitāsana* posture with his right foot resting on a smaller lotus. He is attired and adorned like a prince, and his two hands hold the stems of lotus flowers even as they form the gesture of turning the wheel of law. The flowers rise to his shoulders and support a sword on his right and a book on his left. The sword, whose blade is broken here, is said to cut through the fog of ignorance, and the book is emblematic of wisdom.

Strongly Nepali in style, the bronze may have been cast by a Newari artist in Tibet. However, a couple of features reflect its Tibetan character. One is its ornamental exuberance, apparent particularly in the inlaid floral pattern of the dhoti. In Nepali figures such floral or geometrical designs are usually etched and not encrusted with semiprecious stones. The other feature is the floral design along the bottom of the lotus base with two rampant lions. This type of border is commonly seen in Sakyapa paintings but almost never on Nepali bronzes.

Literature Rhie and Thurman 1984, no. 82 (no ill.); *Arts of Asia* (January 1985), fig. 15; Reynolds 1986, p. 169, fig. 5; Rhie and Thurman 1991, no. 31.

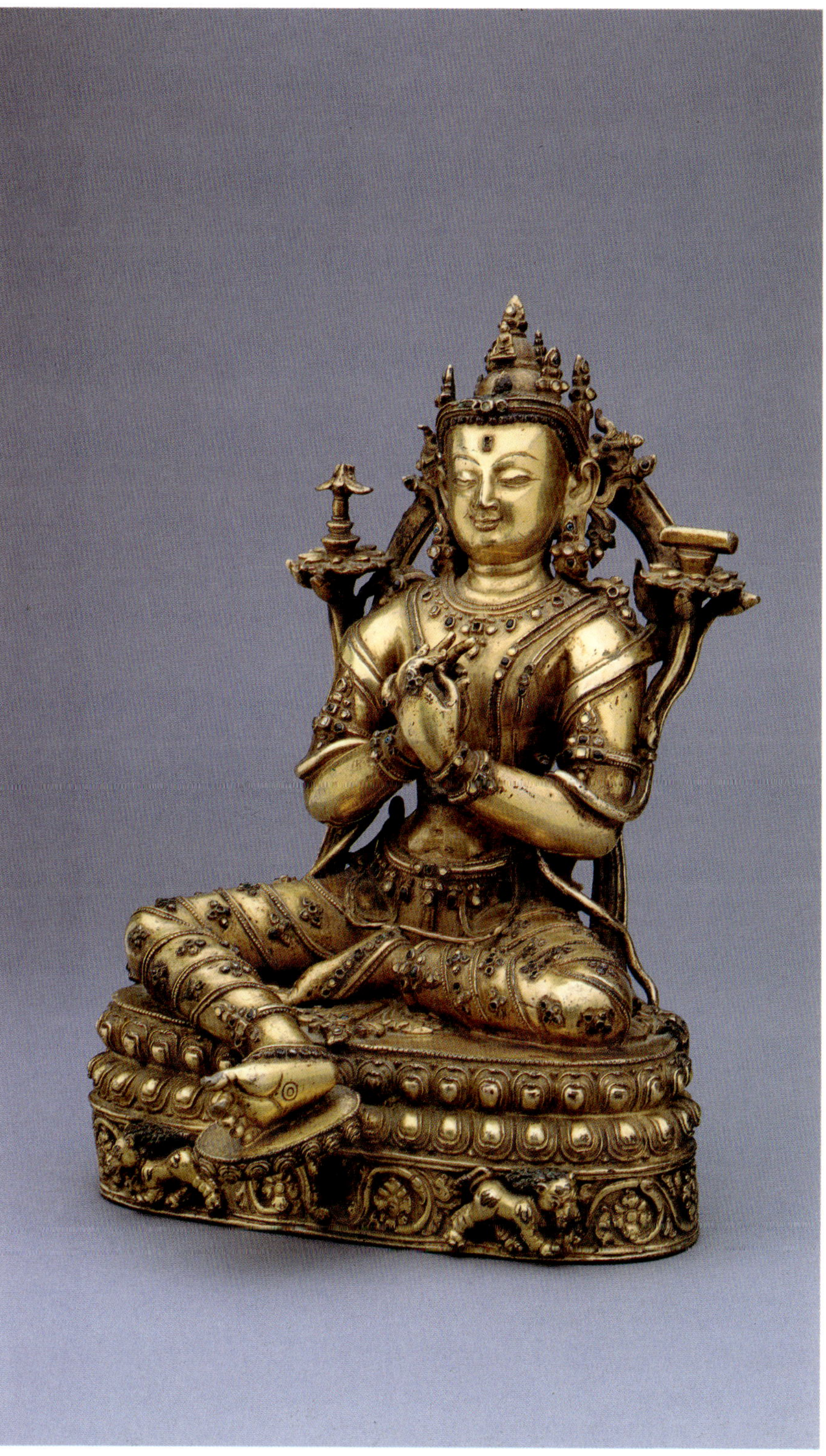

65

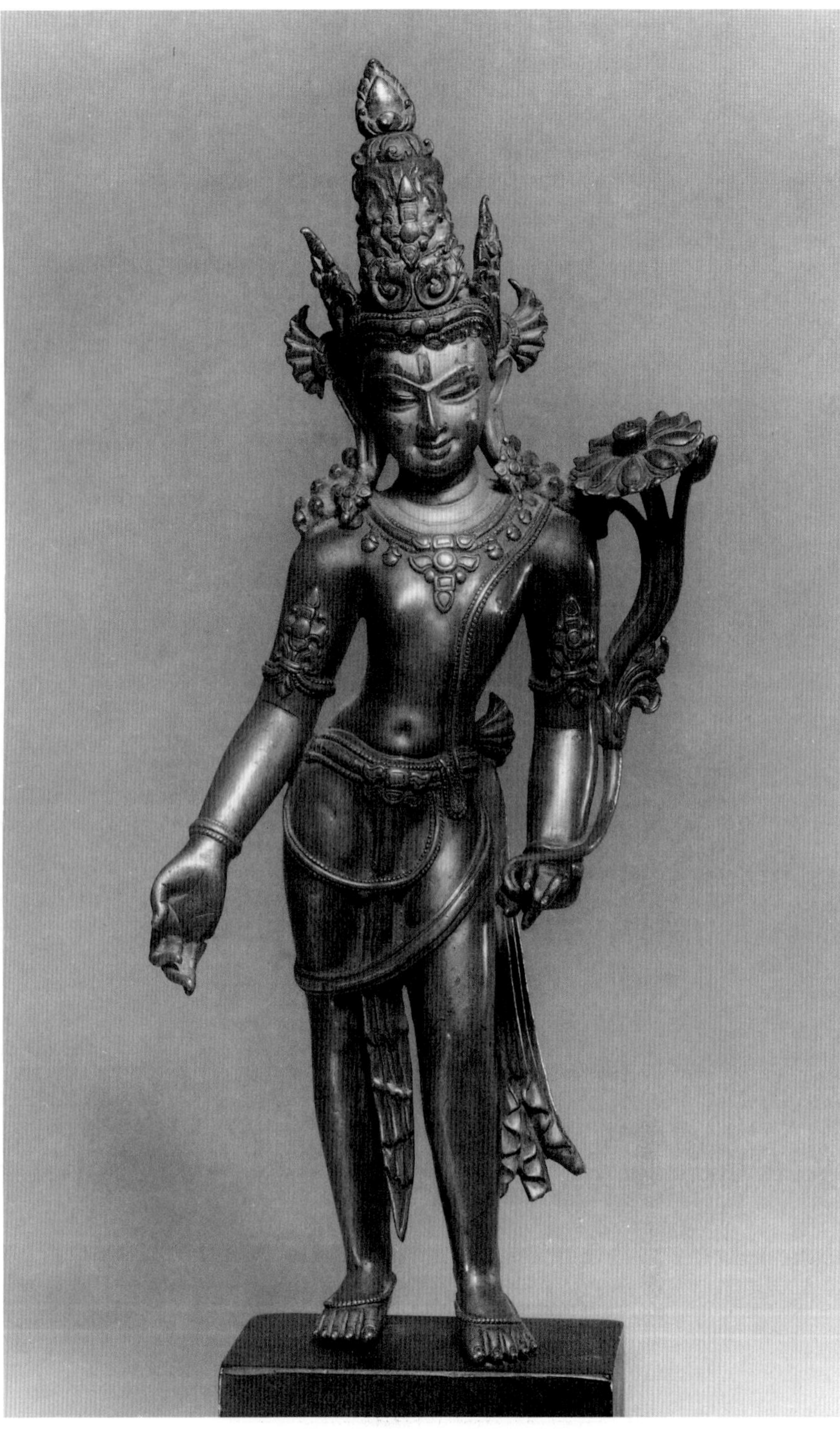

66

ments do not seem Tibetan. However, the proportionately tall chignon is reminiscent of eastern Indian bodhisattva figures rather than Nepali ones. Beguin (1977, pp. 143–44, no. 128) has suggested that the lotus flower held by the bodhisattva may reflect Indian influence. These minor details may indicate a Tibetan origin.

Although the parental Buddha is not represented on the figure's head, the lotus is sufficient to identify him as Avalokiteshvara (Tibetan: Spyan-ras-gzigs), also known by his epithet Padmapāṇi (Lotus-in-Hand). The right hand displays a certain awkwardness in expressing the gesture of charity appropriate to a being whose essence is compassion. The well-proportioned, suavely modeled figure stands gracefully. His soft, smiling countenance further accentuates his altruistic nature. An interesting detail is the jewel crowning the summit of his chignon.

Literature Von Schroeder 1981, pp. 180–81, pl. 34e; Huntington and Huntington 1990, pp. 378–79, no. 143.

66

Bodhisattva Avalokiteshvara

CENTRAL TIBET (?), FIFTEENTH CENTURY

COPPER ALLOY WITH COLORS

H: 13¾ IN. (34.9 CM)

The gold paint on the face and neck are sure indications that this bronze was once used in Tibet. Whether it was made there by a Newari artist or made in Nepal and transported to Tibet is more difficult to establish. The style of the figure is strictly Nepali, as may be seen from a comparison with similar figures from Nepal (see no. 15). The garment and orna-

67

Vajrapāṇi and Spouse

CENTRAL TIBET, FIFTEENTH CENTURY

GILT BRONZE WITH PAINT

H: 15 IN. (38.1 CM)

The Bodhisattva Vajrapāṇi (Tibetan: *Phyag-na rdo-rje*) is shown here in one of his terrifying forms, which is frequently represented in Tibet but is less familiar in Nepal or India. Tantric texts explain this emanation of the bodhisattva in the following way. Once the divine guardians were alarmed by the way evil was triumphing over good. The Buddha re-

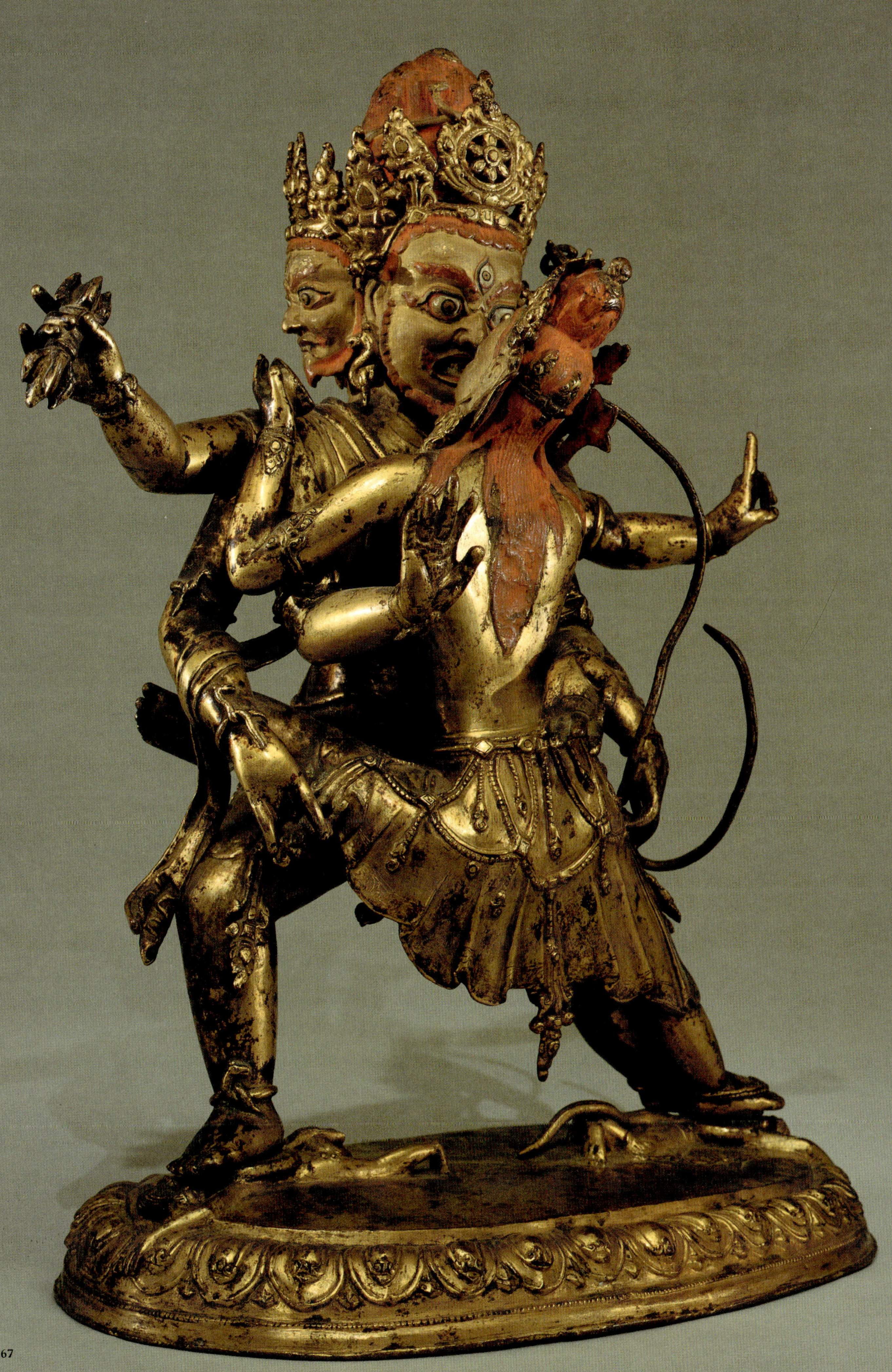

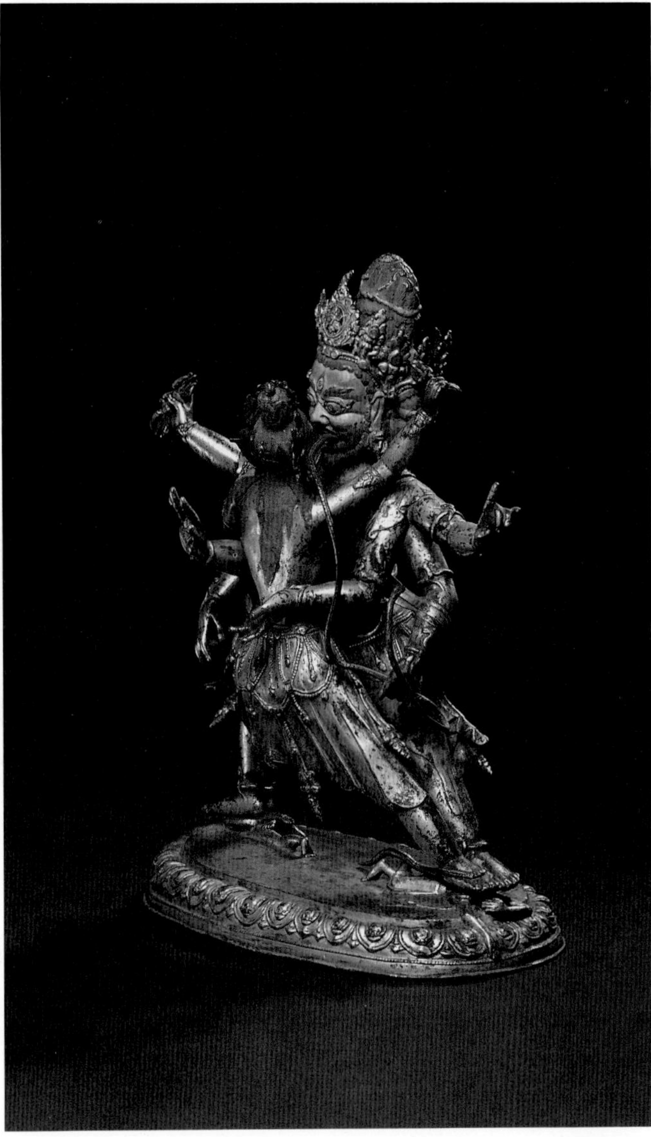

67

quested his personal bodyguard to assume an appropriate form and protect the innocent and the faithful. Accordingly, Vajrapāṇi, like Superman or Captain Marvel, assumed his impediment-shattering (*vajravidāraṇa*) body.

In this powerfully modeled, expressive gilt bronze, the god is shown in *yab-yum* with his Wisdom. He has three heads and six arms, while she has the normal number of limbs. Both, however, have demonic faces, which have been made even more awesome with gold paint. Except for snakes, which serve as his ornaments, and weapons, he is naked, but her midregion is draped in a skirt. All the faces are painted in gold; the hair in orange; the eyes in white, blue-gray, and orange; and the teeth in white. The enemies, humans with serpent hoods (*nāgas*), are crushed underfoot. Vajrapāṇi also brandishes a thunderbolt and displays the gestures of reassurance and admonition. Like most other wisdom deities, she holds a chopper and skull cup.

Literature Rhie and Thurman 1991, no. 56.

68

Ascetic Milarepa

CENTRAL TIBET, FIFTEENTH CENTURY

COPPER ALLOY WITH COLORS

H: 18 IN. (45.7 CM)

The cotton-clad (*ras pa*) Mila is probably the most colorful of the many mystics and eccentric saints venerated in Tibet. Although belonging to the Kagyupa order, he is universally popular. His poems and songs are widely read and sung. Milarepa was the principal disciple of Marpa, the founder of the Kagyupa order. It would be wrong, however, to think of either of them as conventional monk-teachers. Although Milarepa was celibate like a monk, he did not teach in a monastery. He was essentially an itinerant yogi who preferred to live in caves and forests and preach through his songs. Fortunately, there is a richly detailed biography of this popular Tibetan saint as well as a compilation of his poems, both of which are available in English translations (see Evans-Wentz 1951; Chang 1977). Milarepa was particularly gifted at taking abstruse Buddhist ideas and introducing them lucidly through simple folk songs, using local images familiar to ordinary people.

In this impressive metal representation the saint is portrayed in his most characteristic form. As befits an ascetic he is seated on an animal skin placed on a lotus. However, his posture is that of royal ease rather than that of a yogi. He wears his characteristic cotton raiment, which is hardly in tatters. He has several of the attributes of a Buddha such as pierced, extended earlobes; short, curly hair; and a prominent circle (*urṇā*) on his forehead that almost looks like a third eye. His left ear is adorned by a disc, and his left hand holds an alms bowl.

More characteristic is the gesture of the figure's right hand, which is placed close to his right ear. The hand should really be cupping the ear, a gesture made by classical singers in India. Either it refers to Milarepa's fondness for singing, or it signifies the arcane nature of tantric teaching, which is supposed to be whispered from ear to ear. In any event this is the most distinctive feature of Milarepa's iconography.

The face is particularly expressive, with large, staring eyes and almost realistically painted pupils. The paunch is a usual feature, but the arms are slender. The hands, with long, well-articulated fingers, are delicately modeled. The hollow cast bronze was filled with a variety of objects, including rolls of paper printed with mantras—some on black paper—a red wooden staff with a crystal tied to it, a packet of beads, small gems, and a Tibetan coin wrapped in paper.

Literature Rhie and Thurman 1991, no. 78.

69

Earth Spirit Ḍāka

CENTRAL TIBET, FIFTEENTH–SIXTEENTH CENTURY

COPPER ALLOY

H: 6½ IN. (16.5 CM)

The Tibetan name of this figure is Tokye Chenpo (*Lto-'phye chen-po*), while Ḍāka is the Sanskrit appellation. The Sanskrit word is the masculine form of *ḍākinī*. In folklore both words refer to imps who reside in forests skirting villages and are believed to entice their victims by calling (*ḍāka*) them at night in alluring voices. In Buddhist literature there is a realm of *ḍākas* where the *ma-*

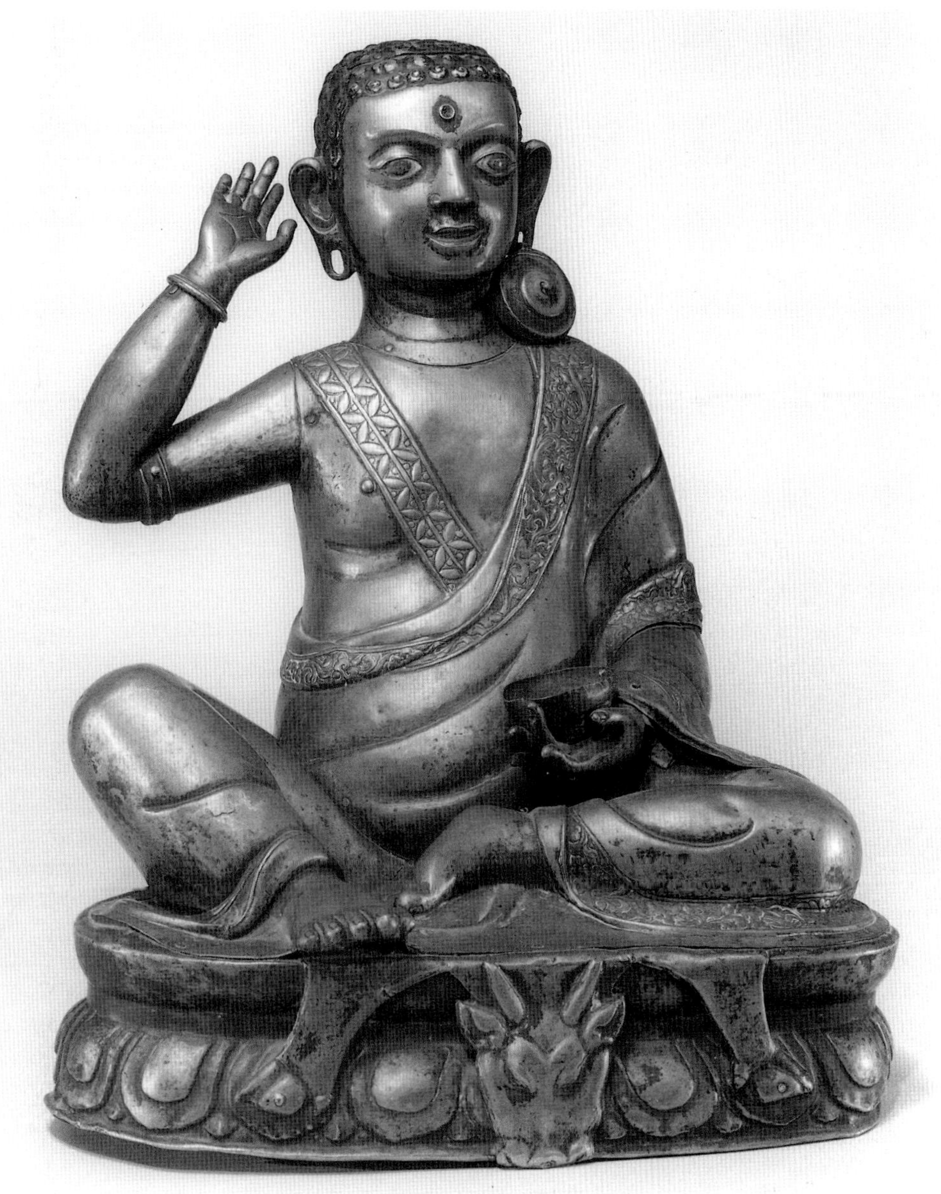

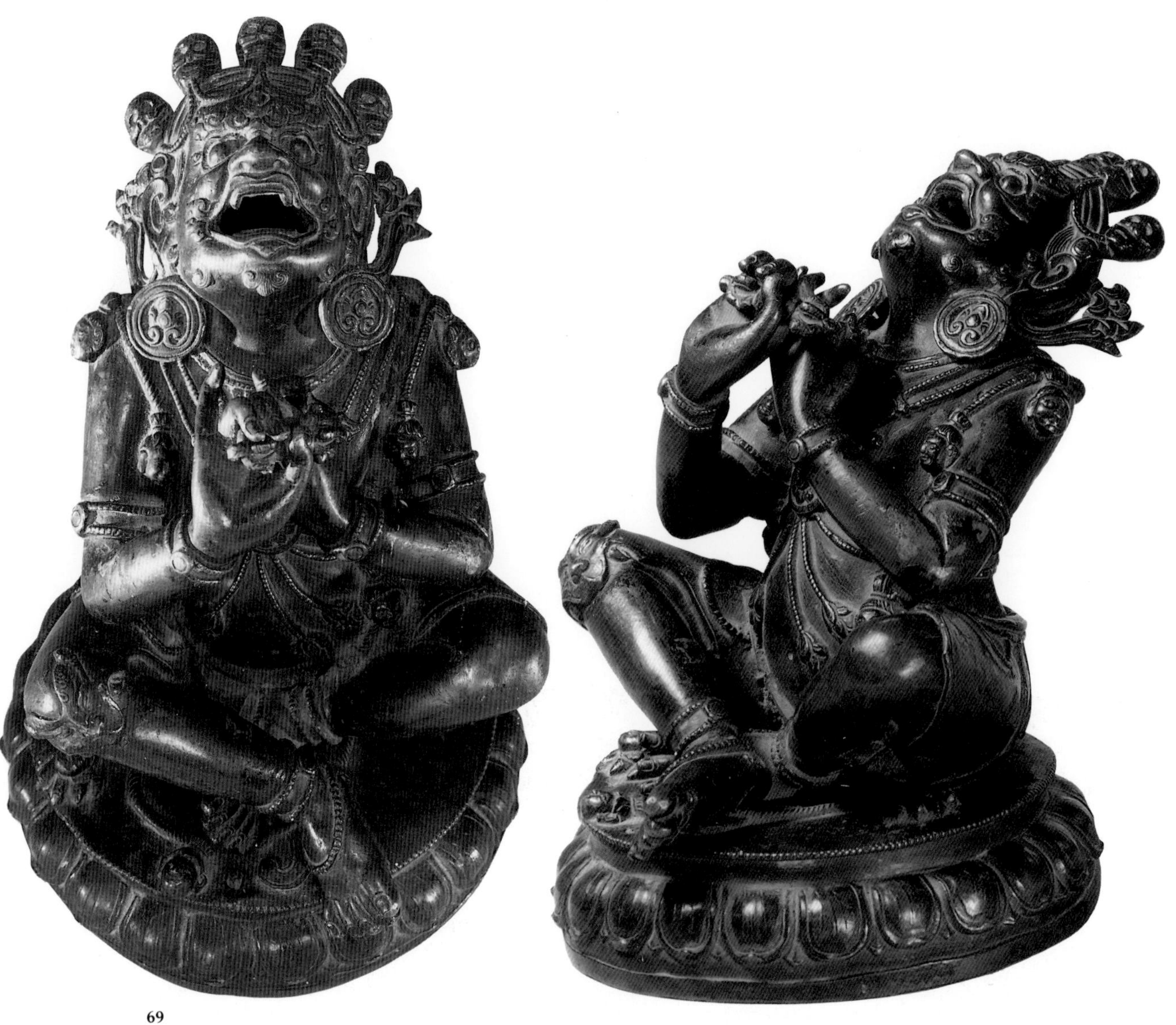

69

hāsiddhas go once they are finished with their earthly tasks.

In Tibet Ḍāka is regarded as an earth spirit who devours all evil influences (Essen and Thingo 1989, p. 210, no. II-440). He is invoked in medical rituals, and when a person is ill a Ḍāka image is held up to his mouth so that he can imbibe medicines from the deity's mouth. Tibetans also believe that Ḍāka is a dwarf who moves on his stomach like a reptile.

Although the name of this figure may have been borrowed from India, everything else, including his function and iconography, seems to be purely Tibetan, for neither the medical association nor the figural form is known in India. Clad in a feline skin, the god sits on a lotus with his legs crossed and knees raised. His head is thrown back, so that he looks up at the sky, and his mouth is open. His visage is that of a terrifying deity, and he wears a tiara of two skulls and a garland of human heads. His hands, holding a thunderbolt and bell, appear to make the gesture of turning the wheel of law; in other examples they are crossed against his chest.

70

Bodhisattva Vajrasattva

TIBET OR NEPAL, FIFTEENTH–SIXTEENTH CENTURY

GILT COPPER ALLOY WITH TURQUOISE INLAY

H: 16¼ IN. (41.3 CM)

Richly ornamented and crowned, Vajrasattva, or Dorje Sempa (Tibetan: *Rdo-rje sems-pa*) is represented here by himself (see no. 82). According to the *Advayavajrasaṃgraha,* an important Vajrayāna text, an alternative name is Dharmadhātū, or Essence of Religion (B. Bhattacharya 1958, p. 75). Dharmadhātū is also an epithet of Mañjuśrī. The

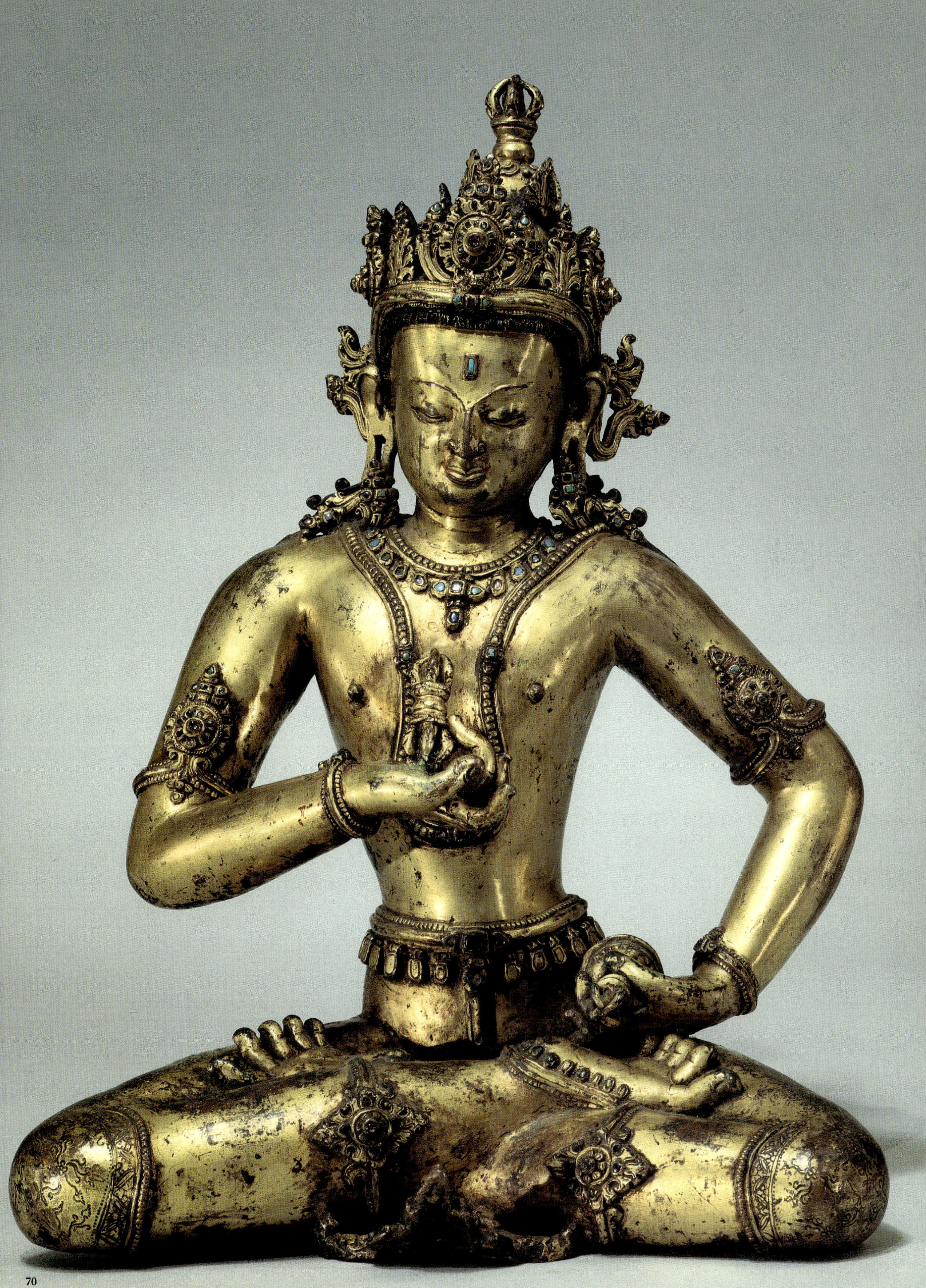

text further informs us that Vajrasattva "represents a stringent taste, the autumn season, the letters of the alphabet ya, ra, la, and va, and the part of the night from midnight to day break." In both Nepal and Tibet he is regarded as the sixth transcendental Buddha. Although he sits in the posture of a Buddha, he is sumptuously adorned like a bodhisattva. His right hand holds a thunderbolt in front of his chest, and his left holds a bell.

As is the case with the Mañjuśrī (no. 65), it is not easy to determine whether the sculpture was cast in Nepal or in Tibet by a Newari artist. Except for the fact that the figure is exuberantly adorned and richly inlaid with turquoise, there is nothing to distinguish it as Tibetan. No matter where it was cast, it is gracefully modeled, and the gentle, serene face must have had a calming effect on devotees.

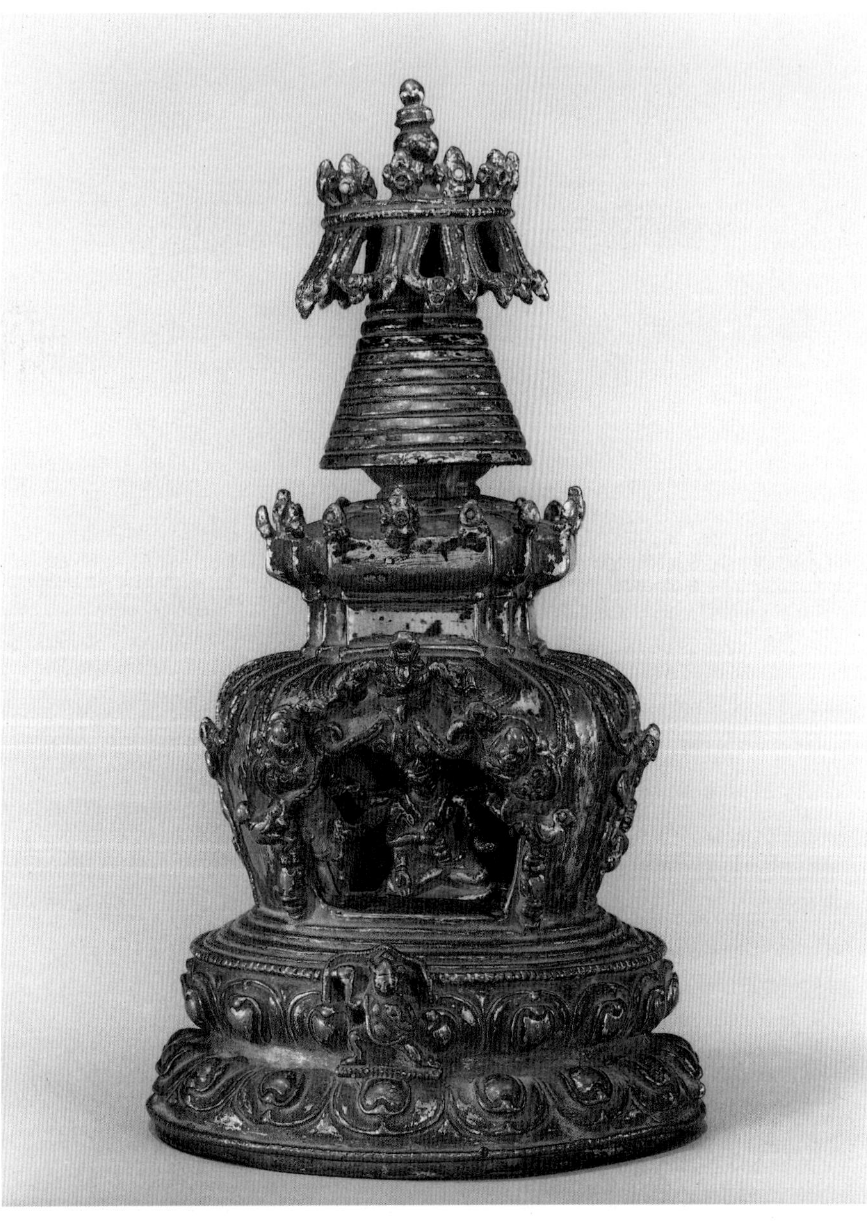

71

71

Ushnishavijaya Stūpa

CENTRAL TIBET, SIXTEENTH CENTURY

GILT COPPER ALLOY WITH TURQUOISE

H: 8¼ IN. (21 CM)

The flaring dome (*aṇḍa* = egg) of the stūpa rises from a lotus base. Above the dome is the *harmikā,* which serves as the base for the elaborate *chhatrāvalī* (parasol) of thirteen receding rings shaped like a cone. The *chhatrāvalī* is protected by a disc with garlands and what appear to be rather crude double-thunderbolt motifs. At the summit is the auspicious waterpot.

Within the womb of the stūpa is the goddess Ushṇīshavijayā, known in Tibetan as Tsugtor Nampar Gyalma (*Gtsug-tor rnam-par gyal-ma*), who is worshipped for long life (see no. 36). She is flanked by two standing males. The cavelike opening is embellished with an elaborate arch of typically Newari design. The dome is further adorned with garlands, and figures of three protective deities are added on the three remaining sides, the fourth being accommodated in front, on the lotus below the throne.

72

Cosmic Deity Vajrabhairava

EASTERN TIBET, SEVENTEENTH CENTURY

GILT BRONZE WITH COLORS

H: 13¾ IN. (34.9 CM)

Especially venerated by the Gelukpas, Vajrabhairava, along with a conceptual twin, Yamāntaka (Destroyer of Yama), is both the angry and the cosmic manifestation of the

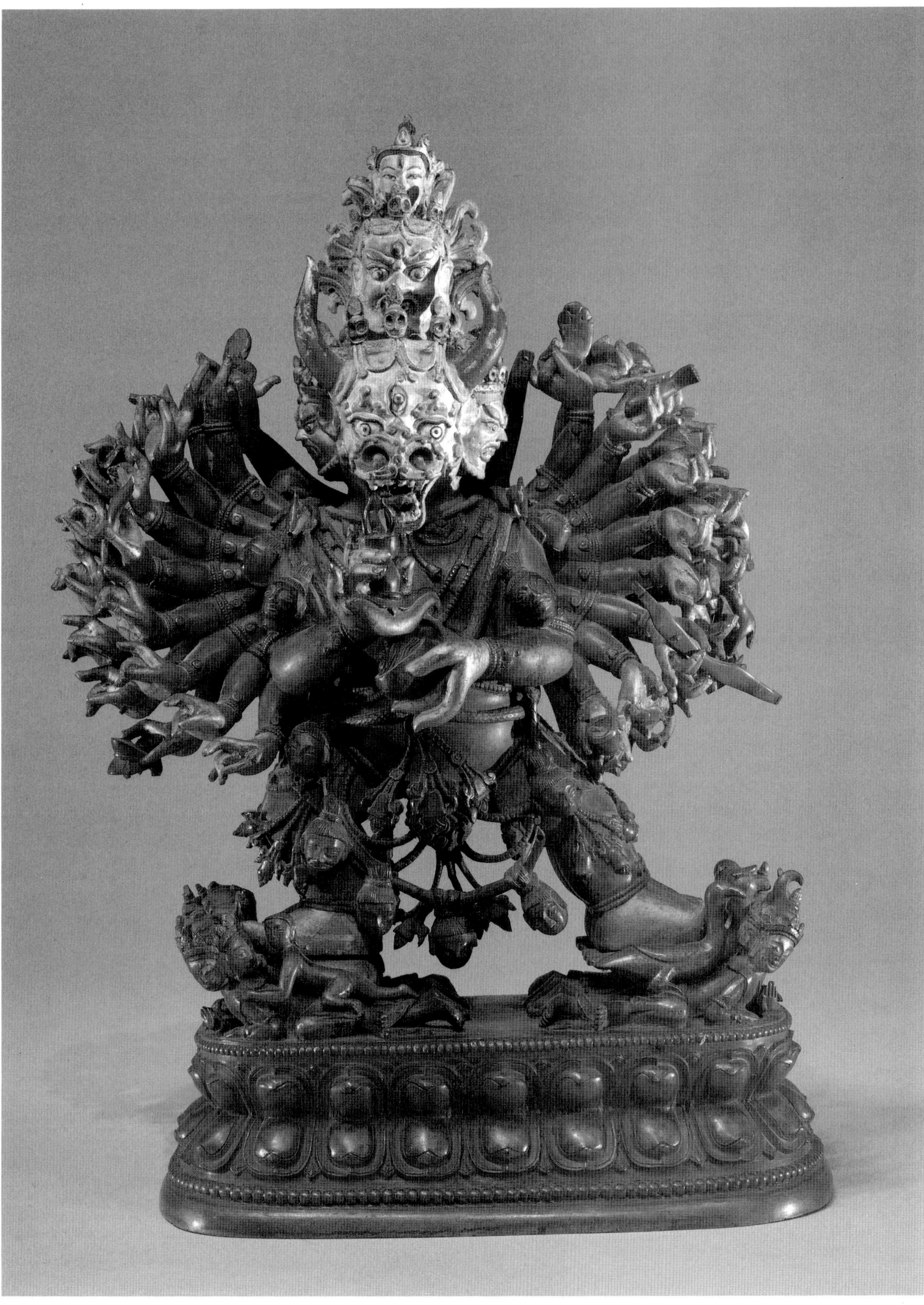

Bodhisattva Mañjuśrī, the god of knowledge and wisdom. In a sense this is not inappropriate, since death is equated with ignorance. Curiously, Mañjuśrī is identified with several Hindu deities such as Kumāra, the divine general; Kāma, the god of love; and Siva, whose angry form is known as Bhairava. Iconographically, however, Vajrabhairava has less in common with Bhairava than with other death-related Buddhist deities such as Yama, Yamāri, and Yamāntaka. All are distinguished by the buffalo head. The buffalo is the mount of the Hindu god of death, Yama, while the buffalo-headed demon symbolizing evil is destroyed by the Goddess Durgā (see no. 18). In Tibetan the god is known as Dorje Jigdje Pachig (*Rdo-rje 'jigs-byed dpa'-gcig*), which means Ekavīra (Sole Hero) Vajrabhairava.

The cosmic nature of Vajrabhairava is clearly demonstrated by his multiple limbs and attributes. The pyramid of angry heads with remarkably varied expressions is surmounted by the placid head of the benign Mañjuśrī. His many hands hold an impressive assortment of weapons and emblems, while his several feet crush creatures large and small. His multiple limbs and attributes were succinctly explained by Tsongkhapa as follows: "His many faces point to the nine fold classification of the scriptures, his two horns to the two truths (conventional and ultimate); his thirty-four arms together with his spirituality, communication and embodiment in tangible form to the thirty-seven facts of enlightenment; his sixteen legs to the sixteen kinds of no-thing-ness" (Tsong-ka-pa 1977).

Apart from demonstrating the skillful manipulation of a highly complex form into a coherent visual design, this image is unusual for the way in which the artist has used color to make a strong visual statement. While much of the body and the limbs reflect the reddish copper color of the basic metal, the hands and feet have been highlighted with dull gold. The dramatic expressiveness of the faces of Vajrabhairava has been enhanced with bright yellow-gold, orange, blue, white, and black pigments. Both as a touch of whimsy and to enhance the terrifying nature of the figure, the unknown artist has cleverly made the snout and open mouth so as to create the impression of a skull. Such double entendre is rarely encountered and clearly demonstrates the sculptor's inventiveness.

Literature Rhie and Thurman 1984, no. 111 (no ill.).

73

Arhat Bakula

CENTRAL OR EASTERN TIBET, SEVENTEENTH CENTURY

GILT COPPER ALLOY WITH COLORS

H: 4¼ IN. (10.8 CM)

The inscription on the back identifies this figure as Bakula and gives its serial number as fifth (see Appendix 2). Originally, it was one of sixteen or eighteen figures. The Zimmerman Collection has seven others from the series. In East Asia and Tibet, apart from sculptural representations of arhats in temples, sets of portable bronzes and *thankas* (see no. 91) were frequently com-

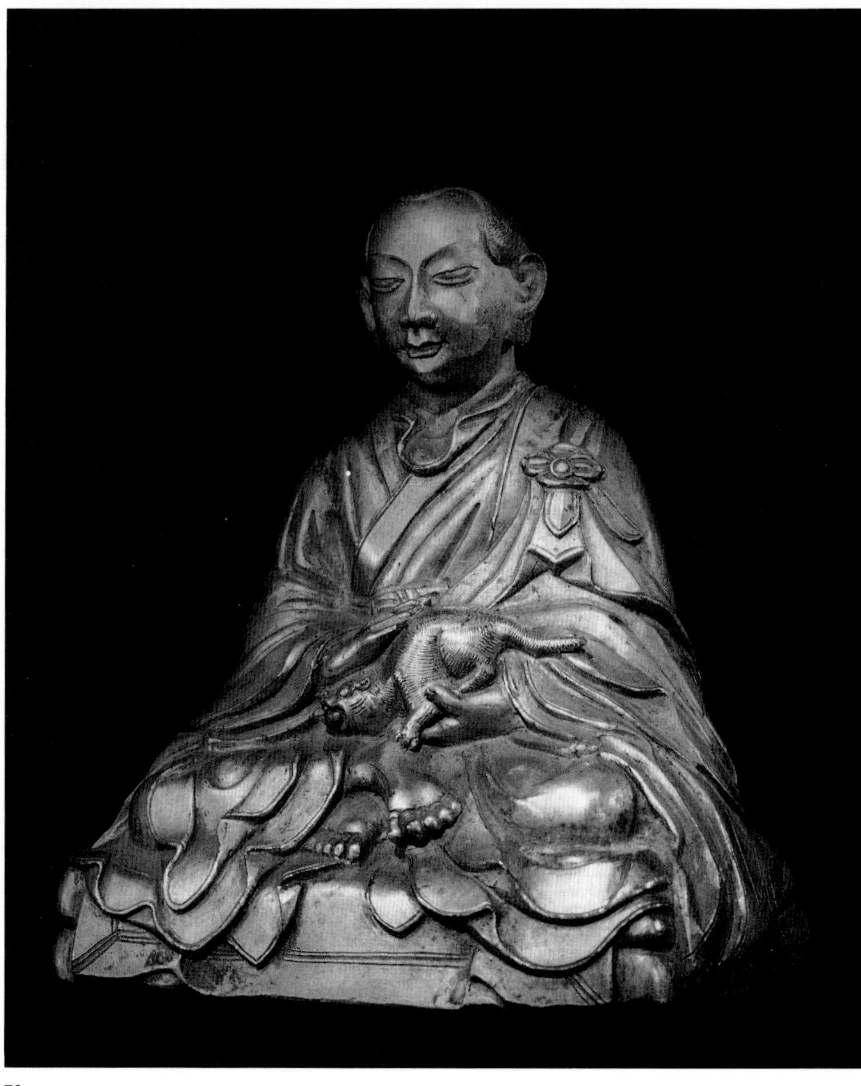

73

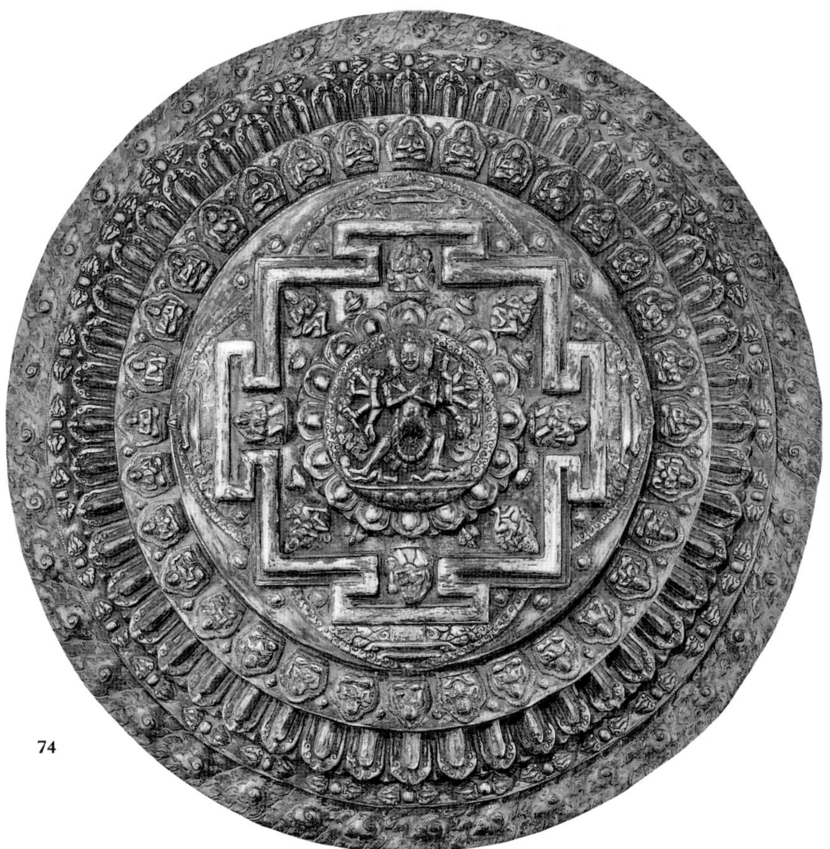

74

missioned as personal acts of piety.

The Sanskrit word *arhat* literally means "one worthy of worship." Originally, it was applied to venerable elder monks and teachers of the faith. At some point a group of them came to be regarded as more important than others. Numbering sixteen, the group consisted of historical and mythical personages. It was further declared that the Buddha Śākyamuni himself had selected them to spread the doctrine all over the universe. Like the bodhisattva, the arhat postponed his own nirvana for the sake of the religion, which is why the group continued to be venerated by later Buddhists. The cult of the arhat seems to have flourished only in East Asia and Tibet. Its popularity in China, whence it spread to Korea, Japan, and Tibet, is very likely due to the fact that the arhats formed a group of human teachers who suited the ideal of both Confucian patriarch and Taoist immortal.

Chinese influence is evident in the drapery of this particular figure. Both the form of the garments and the naturalistic delineation of their folds and volume are distinctly Chinese. Although the figures in the group represent ideal types—when they are not portrayed as ugly and repellent—the faces, as in this instance, appear to be particularized. The arhat sits in the meditating posture and strokes the soft fur of his attribute, a jewel-spitting mongoose. Here again the compassionate nature of the arhat is emphasized by the way he treats the animal, like a pet. The arhat's name originally was Nakula, meaning "Mongoose," which is also the attribute of Vaiśravaṇa or Kubera, the lord of wealth and of the Northern Region, or Uttarakuru, the area assigned to Bakula.

74

Mandala of Chakrasamvara

CENTRAL OR EASTERN TIBET, SEVENTEENTH–EIGHTEENTH CENTURY

GILT COPPER ALLOY

DIAM: 16 IN. (40.6 CM)

This is a rare example of a metal mandala of Chakrasamvara (see nos. 20, 41, 88). Here he is represented in his most familiar form with four heads and twelve arms within a sixteen-petaled lotus but without Vajravārāhī. Eight other deities are depicted in the corners and four projecting gateways of the mandala. This "palace" is surrounded by a circle of thirty-two seated figures, who appear to be indistinguishable. Then comes a lotus of forty-eight petals, which is surrounded in turn by a row of thunderbolts that secure the mandala. The final circle is one of flames.

For a similarly dated metal mandala from Nepal, see Beguin 1981, no. 15.

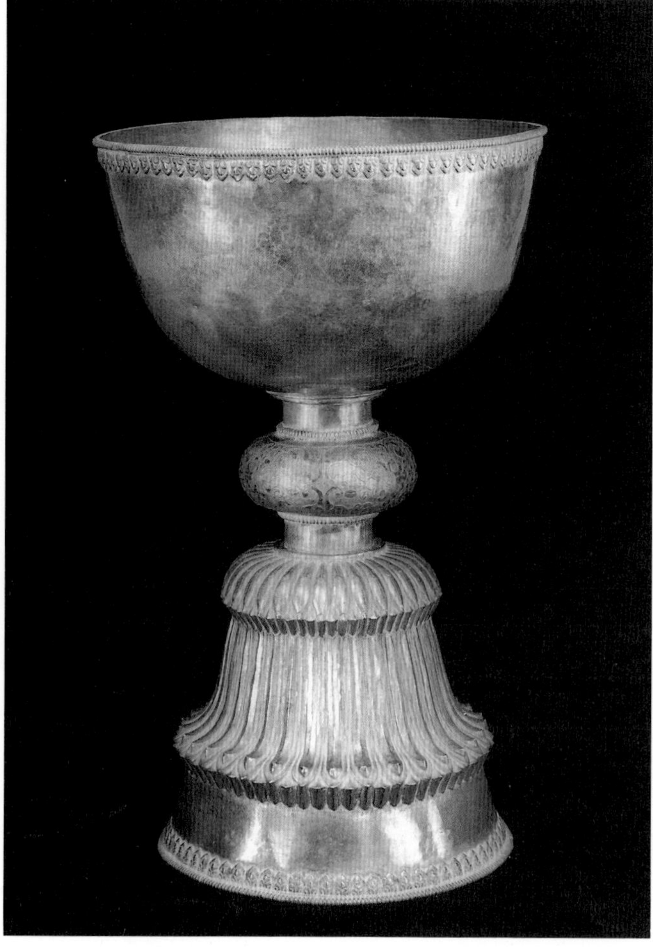

75

75

Butter Lamp

EASTERN TIBET, SEVENTEENTH–EIGHTEENTH CENTURY

SILVER

H: 12 IN. (30.5 CM)

This type of butter lamp, reminiscent of the form of a Christian chalice, is characteristic of Tibet, and no altar, whether at home or in a monastery, is complete without a pair. It is not known when the form became popular or whether in fact it was derived from a chalice. If it was, this must have been due to contacts with Nestorian Christians in Central Asia. Once adopted, the basic form remained fundamentally the same for centuries, and hence it is difficult to ascertain the exact age of such objects.

The most important center of Tibetan metalwork is Derge in the eastern part of the country, and the Tibetans have been renowned for their works in silver from ancient times.

This particularly handsome example is elegantly simple in its decoration. The base and the rim around the lip are decorated with a stylized leaf motif. The stem consists of two sections: a larger, fluted, bell-shaped portion with a canopy of lotus petals and a ring supporting a cushion-shaped section below another plain ring that supports the cup. The cushion is enriched with vegetal arabesques.

76

Portable Shrine

EIGHTEENTH CENTURY

H: 9 IN. (22.9 CM)

Called a *gau,* such portable or traveling shrines are encountered only in Tibet and in areas influenced by Tibetan Buddhists. Nothing quite like them is known in any other Buddhist country, although some sort of portable shrine to protect travelers must have been used by devout Buddhists elsewhere. It is not known how old the custom is in Tibet. Most known examples are generally dated to the last two or three centuries, although some may be earlier. Mostly, they are silver or silver gilt.

Made in two parts like a box with a cover, the *gau* has loops on the sides to attach it to a crossbelt during travel. Generally, it is trefoil shaped with all decoration confined to the front. The sides and back are usually unembellished. A small window in the front allows the owner to view the tiny silk-wrapped image of the personal deity inside. When not in use the *gau* is kept reverently on the domestic altar.

In this particular example the aperture at the front is surrounded by a border adorned with a bowl of fruits or jewels at the bottom center and the seven jewels indispensable for a universal ruler (see no. 82) against a background of fine meandering vines. Following ancient Chinese practice, these seven are symbolized by the following objects (clockwise from top): a discoid ornament called *khyi-sna* for the wheel; two interlocked rings for the wishing gem; a *svastika* instead of swords for the general; coral for the queen; a pair of tusks for the elephant; a unicorn

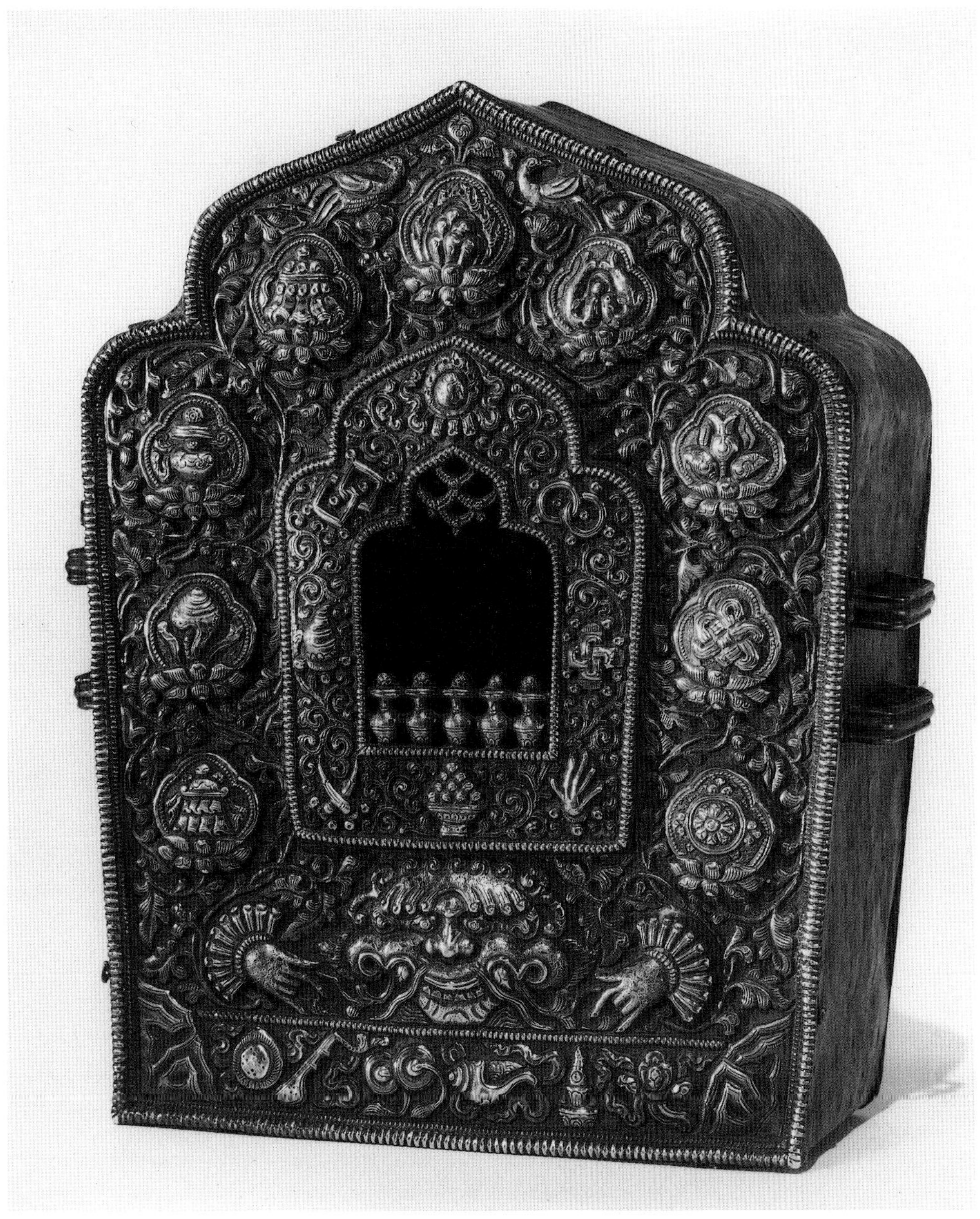

76

horn for the horse; and a pair of interlocked square ornaments (*rgyan*) for the minister. In the larger segment, bolder flowering vines form medallions enclosing the eight symbols of good luck with the three jewels at the top. These eight symbols are as follows (clockwise from one o'clock): a pair of fish, a lotus, an interwoven knot of life, a wheel, a banner, a conch shell, a water pot, and a parasol. Between the window frame and the register at the bottom is the monster head known as *kāla* (time) or *kīrttīmukha* (face of glory) extracting foliage from its mouth. This same foliage meanders up the surface of the *gau*. The register at the bottom contains a third group of five senses usually seen on a Tibetan altar. They are a mirror (sight), cymbals (sound), a conch shell with perfumed liquid (smell), peaches (taste), and a textile (touch). Clearly, all these symbols constitute a permanent offering to the deity inside that would otherwise be difficult to make while traveling.

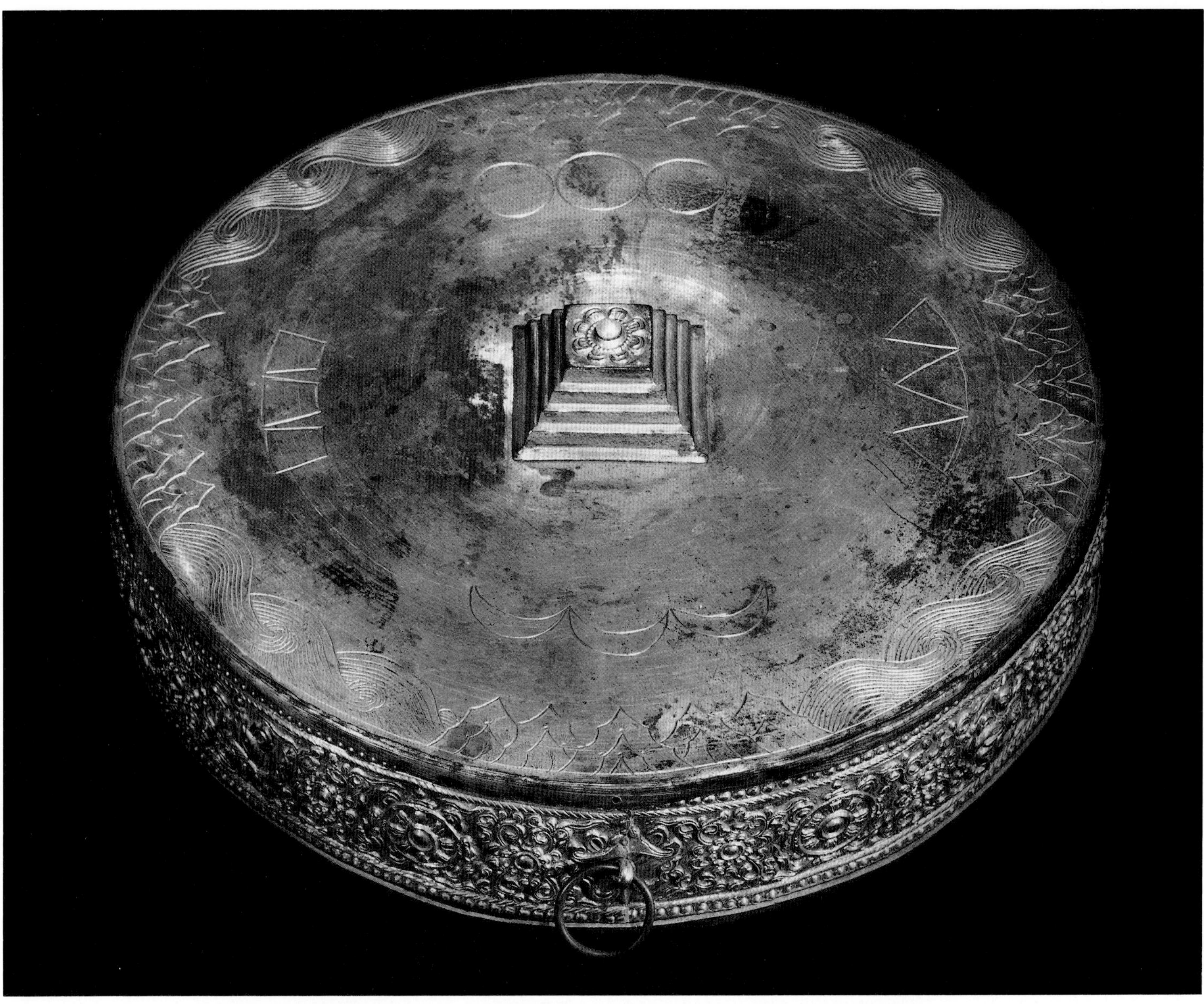

77

77

Meru Mandala

EASTERN TIBET, EIGHTEENTH CENTURY

GILT COPPER ALLOY AND CRYSTAL

DIAM: 12¼ IN. (31.1 CM)

This is a metal mandala of the cosmic mountain known in Sanskrit as Meru (Wayman 1973, pp. 101–9). Situated at the center of the universe, it also serves as the *axis mundi*. In the mandala within the human body, the spinal column is the corresponding microcosmic element, for it is called in Sanskrit *merudaṇḍa*.

The edge of the mandala is decorated with luxuriant floral motifs interspersed with auspicious symbols. On the top, around the periphery, are represented four major continents, symbolized by iron mountains alternating with the four oceans. Within this circle are four groups of symbols, two of which are easily recognized. The three contiguous circles represent the sun, the three contiguous crescents the moon. The significance of the three triangles and three rectangles is not known. Nor is it clear why each symbol is depicted in a group of three. All these forms and symbols are incised. In contrast, the central mountain is represented three-dimensionally. It is of pyramidal shape and consists of five terraces. The first four are square, while the fifth is an eight-petaled lotus, which is surmounted by a circular piece of crystal. The mountain's shape is reminiscent of the great stūpa Borobudur in Indonesia.

Such a three-dimensional mandala is one of the items with which an important visitor to a monastery is greeted on arrival. When presented, multicolored ribbons are attached to the ring. Thus the function of such mandalas is largely ceremonial and probably symbolizes the recipient's homology with the cosmic mountain. (For another example of such a mandala, see Beguin 1981, no. 33.)

78

Flaming Trident

EIGHTEENTH CENTURY OR EARLIER

GILT COPPER, IRON, AND SILVER

H: 21 IN. (53.3 CM)

This striking object is a trident that has been embellished with a grinning skull at the base of the three prongs or blades to which stylized, gilded flames are attached. The skull rests on a simple lotus supported by a polished square stem or handle that rises from an openwork knob. The knob may represent part of a thunderbolt. A trefoil-arched plate serves as a bridge between the skull and the flaming prongs.

The exact function of this implement is not known. Almost certainly, it was used on ceremonial occasions requiring a certain amount of pomp and circumstance. It could have been dedicated to a temple as an offering. While a trident is held by many different Buddhist deities, one of whom is Chakrasamvara (see no. 41), it is not as common a ritual object as the *phurpa*—a magic or ritual dagger—or thunderbolt. In the Hindu context a trident is a powerful and ubiquitous symbol of Siva and Śakti. In this instance, however, the addition of flame almost certainly indicates that the object was meant for Buddhist usage. The object may well represent a combination of a trident and a cot's leg, which is usually adorned with a skull.

The use of various colored materials not only reflects the skill of the craftsman but also creates an interesting aesthetic effect. The shaft has the texture of pewter, the teeth of the skull are in shiny copper, and the flames are gilded.

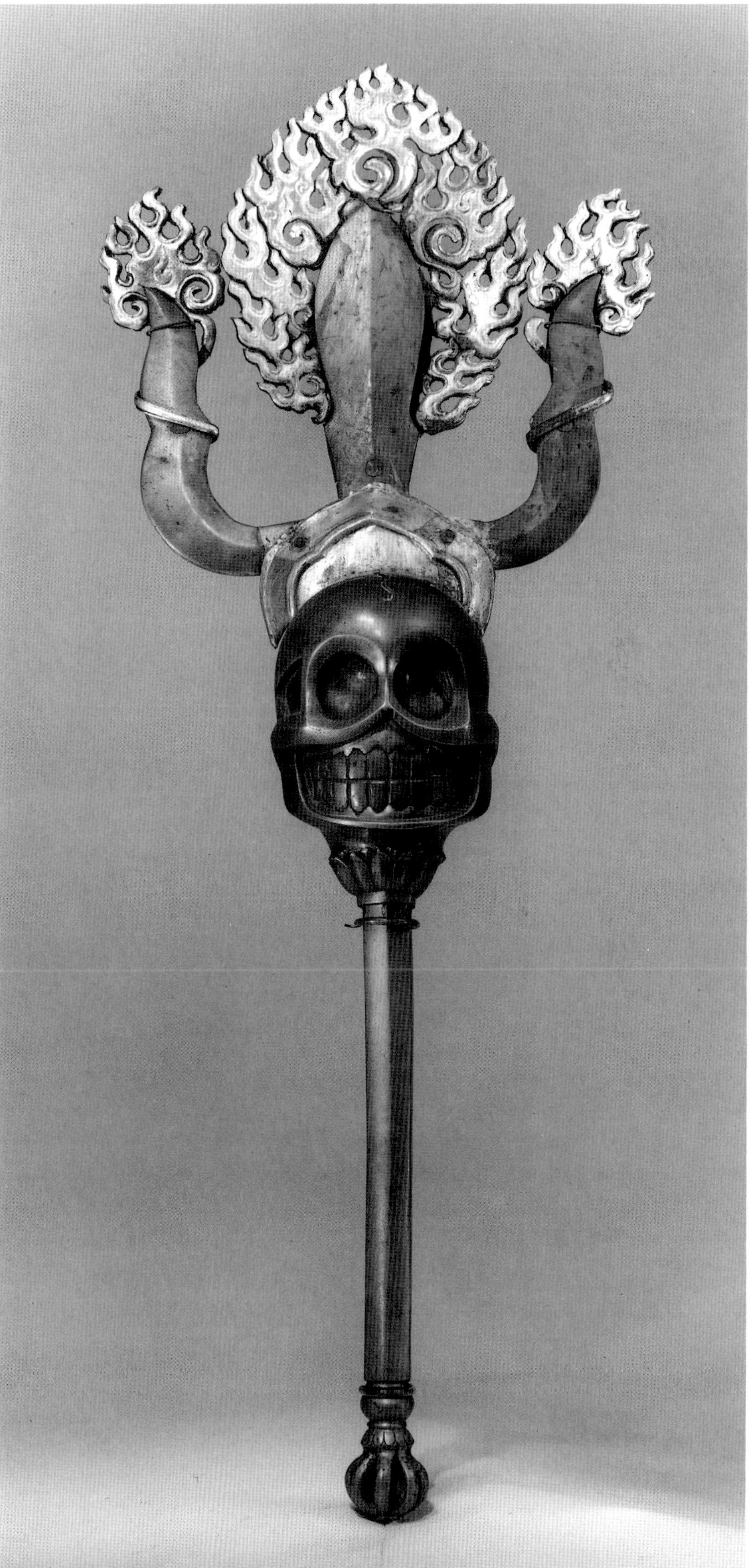

78

PAINTINGS

All Tibetan paintings are rendered on cotton or linen supports in opaque watercolors unless otherwise noted. Readers interested in the technique of Tibetan painting should consult Jackson and Jackson 1984.

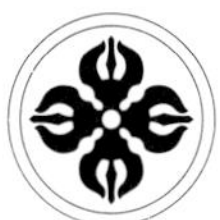

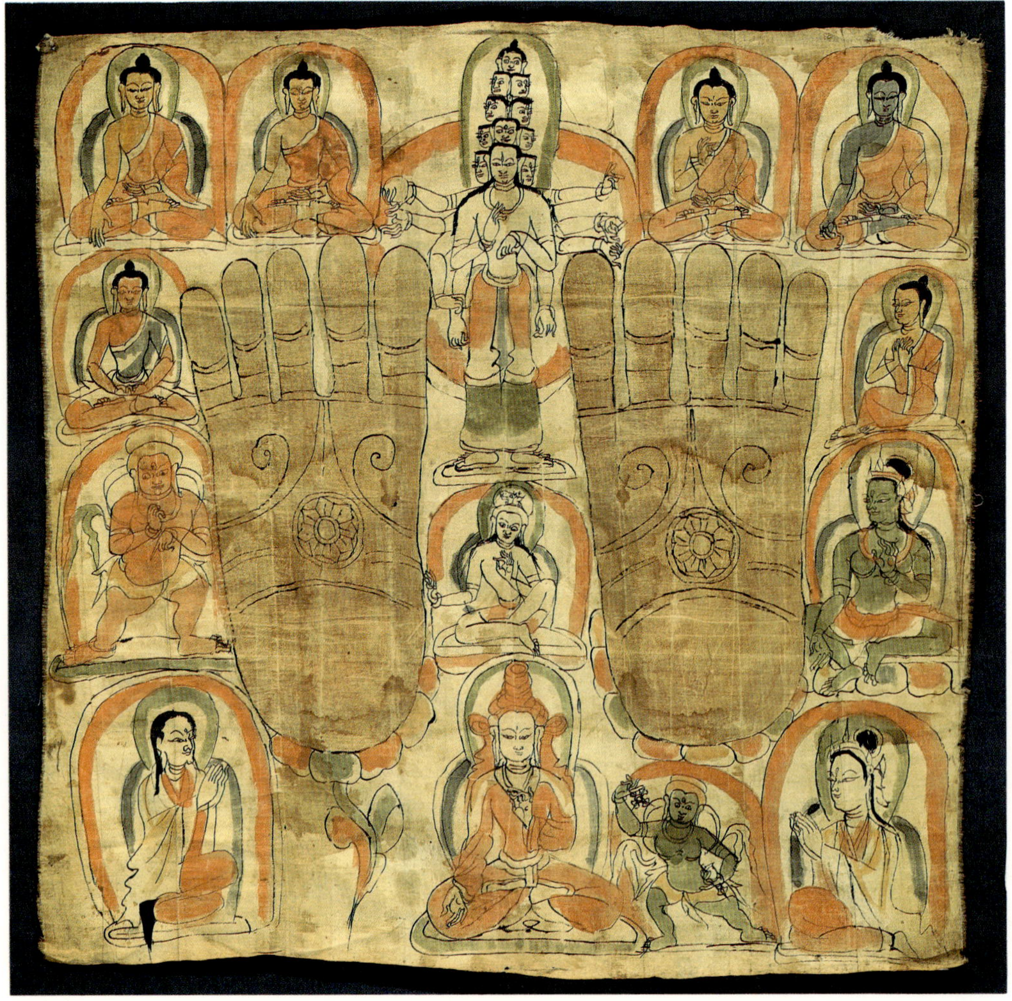

79

79

Footprints and Deities

TENTH–ELEVENTH CENTURY

COLORS ON SILK

21 × 21¼ IN. (53.3 × 54 CM)

The earliest and perhaps most unusual Tibetan painting in the Zimmerman Collection, this *thanka* may prove to be of great art-historical significance. Unlike most *thankas* it is painted on silk. Furthermore the technique of drawing and the application and tonality of the colors differ noticeably from most known forms of Tibetan painting. On the other hand the somewhat free, cursive drawing is encountered in small, rapidly sketched figures on paper inserted into metal images (Pal 1969, fig. 4, where they are incorrectly dated; Huntington and Huntington 1990, no. 114) and in Central Asian banners and drawings. The light application and thin consistency of the colors are also reminiscent of paintings with Tibetan inscriptions, perhaps rendered by Tibetan artists, at Dunhuang (see Whitfield 1983, vol. 2, nos. 48, 49). Also comparable for cursiveness of drawing (Beguin et al. 1977, nos. 22–26), especially of Buddha figures, is material from Karakhoto (Gansu in China). Indeed the style of the Buddha figures here, relating to tenth- to eleventh-century Pāla images, precludes a date earlier than the tenth century.

The most prominent iconographic feature of the composition is the pair of feet placed like icons on lotuses. Supposed to be golden, the soles are also marked with lotuses, a sign of auspiciousness. Very likely the feet represent the footprints of the Buddha Śākyamuni. Between the footprints are three figures. The standing figure at the top with eleven heads and ten arms is Eleven-Headed Avalokiteshvara; the seated figure in the center is that of a bodhisattva, very likely Avalokiteshvara in his simplest form; and the figure seated at the bottom, dressed in Tibetan costume and wearing the turban typical of the rulers of the early Yarlung dynasty, is almost certainly Songtsen Gampo. His position is appropriate, since he is considered to be an emanation of Avalokiteshvara. The two figures flanking him at the bottom corners are very likely the two wives of the deified king. Their hairstyles and attire are typically Tibetan.

The six buddhas seated around the toes of the footprints can be identified as (at the left) Buddha Śākyamuni, Akshobhya, and Amoghasiddhi and (at the right) Ratnasambhava, Amitābha, and Vairochana. It should be noted that they are identified from their gestures rather than their complexions, which do not follow textual prescriptions. For instance all of them except Ratnasambhava, who is painted gray, have peach-colored complexions. They all also wear orange garments except Amitābha. The upper part of his garment simply shows swaths of gray. In fact the colors have been applied in what appear to be careless dabs, indicating the painting's unfinished state. The orange-complexioned angry deity at the left in the third row cannot be identified, as he has no attributes, but the green female across from him is the goddess Tārā. The green militant guardian figure to the left of Songtsen Gampo may represent Vajrapāṇi.

80

Four Buddhist Deities

CENTRAL TIBET, TWELFTH CENTURY

COLORS ON PAPER

A, B: EACH, 6¼ × 6 IN. (15.9 × 15.2 CM); C: 8½ × 8 IN. (21.6 × 20.3 CM); D: 9 × 8⅛ IN. (22.9 × 20.6 CM)

Except for one, the inscriptions on the fronts of these paintings identify the deities portrayed, and those on the backs consist of the usual Buddhist creed and mantras of those deities (see Appendix 2). Moving clockwise from the top left, the divinities can be identified as follows: A) Vajravārāhī; B) Ushṇishachakravartin; C) Shaḍaksharī Lokeśvara or Avalokiteshvara; and D) an angry deity.

Vajravārāhī (see no. 57) is of red complexion and dances on a yellow corpse with one leg raised and bent. Her attributes are a chopper, a skull cup, and a cot's leg. A tiny sow's head protrudes from her skull.

Less well known is Ushṇishachakravartin. The word *ushṇīsha* refers to a headdress such as a turban or

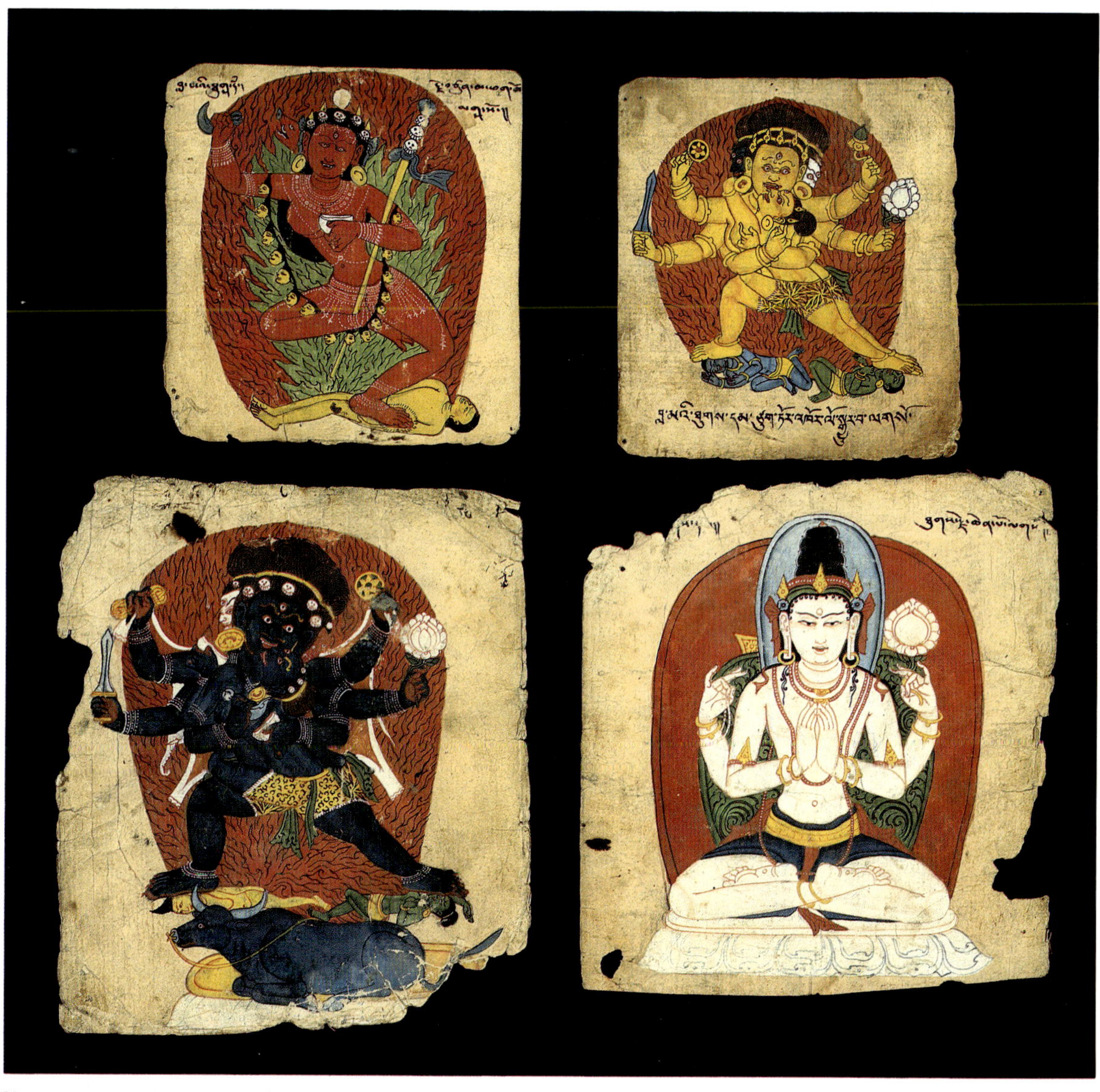

crown. In Buddhist iconography it is also used to denote the cranial bump on the Buddha's head. It is obviously a reservoir of transcendental wisdom. *Chakravartin* literally means "One Who Turns the Wheel" and also denotes a just and universal monarch. The specific deity known as Ushṇishachakravartin is included in some mandalas as a god of direction. His description is as follows: "In the upper region there is Ushṇishachakravartin of yellow color. His three faces are yellow, blue and red. He holds the yellow discus, the sword, the jewel and the lotus" (B. Bhattacharya 1958, p. 256). Like the other directional deities, he embraces his female partner. The inscription on this painting identifies him as the protective deity of a lama, presumably the owner of these paintings.

The word *shaḍaksharī* literally means "six syllables" and refers to the classic six-syllabled mantra of Avalokiteshvara: *om mani padme hum*. The deity is the personification of the mantra. White-complexioned, his principal hands form the gesture of greeting or offering, and the other two carry a rosary and a lotus.

The fourth figure is not identified by an inscription. He and his spouse are blue-complexioned. He has three heads, the other two being red and white. His six arms hold a thunderbolt, a wheel, a lotus, a skull cup, a chopper, and a sword. He uses an elephant skin as a cape, and she is clad in a tiger skin. The two figures below his feet are yellow and green. In front of the couple a water buffalo sits on a yellow mat. Although the figure does hold an elephant skin, thus recalling Chakrasamvara (see no. 88), nothing else conforms to that deity's iconography. His form, his two principal attributes, and the manner in which they are held rather suggest Mahākāla (see no. 93). The buffalo, however, is a mount of Yama, the god of death. Thus the male figure here seems to be a composite deity who may be related to Avalokiteshvara because of the lotus he holds.

From their sizes it is clear that the four paintings belong to two different sets. They represent what is known in Tibetan as *tsakali,* miniature paintings rendered on cloth or paper and generally used in initiation rites (see no. 97). No matter what their function, there seems little doubt that all four were painted by the same person. Moreover they are among the finest examples of Kadampa-style painting. The contrasting use of strong, glowing colors adds a solid sense of volume to the figures. The white figure of Shaḍaksharī Lokeśvara gains added depth because of the green cushion behind him that is surrounded by a plain red arc. Apart from their lively postures, the other three figures are animated by their fiery aureoles. The design of the leaping tongues of flame is strongly reminiscent of that seen in Pāla manuscript illuminations (Pal and Meech-Pekarik 1968, pls. 10, 11, fig. 27a). Note, however, that the artist has provided a green aureole immediately behind the red Vajravārāhī to make her figure more prominent. Indeed greater plasticity is perceptible in the modeling of these three figures, and in the astonishingly naturalistic buffalo, than is commonly encountered in such early Tibetan paintings.

81

Scenes from the Life of the Buddha Śākyamuni

CENTRAL TIBET, TWELFTH CENTURY

30⅛ × 23 IN. (76.5 × 58.4 CM)

The predominant central tableau of the enshrined Buddha represents the enlightenment of Śākyamuni at Bodhgaya after his victory over Māra, the god of desire, as well as the famous temple at the site. The partly effaced figures representing Māra's retinue attacking the Buddha are depicted on either side of the temple's superstructure. The golden complexion of the Buddha, as well as the two attendant bodhisattvas, indicates that this is not an event from his physical life but a transcendental or cosmic occasion. This type of image is also known as Vajrāsana Buddha (Buddha of the Diamond Seat).

Surrounding the central composition are narrative panels succinctly depicting the principal events from the Buddha's life. J. Huntington (Huntington and Huntington 1990, pp. 316–18, no. 107) has suggested that the painting combines two different iconographic traditions, one recounting the eight great miracles popular in Pāla art and the other a sequence of twelve acts described in the biography of the Buddha known as the *Lalitavistara*. Some of the acts, such as the Victory over Māra and the First Sermon, overlap in the two lists and apparently have been represented twice in the painting. In addition a row of buddhas and bodhisattvas stands at either end of the second register, while eight stūpas are depicted in the top register. Huntington has identified these as the eight stūpas containing the Buddha's relics, although there is a ninth stūpa at the left of the shrine's apex in the second register.

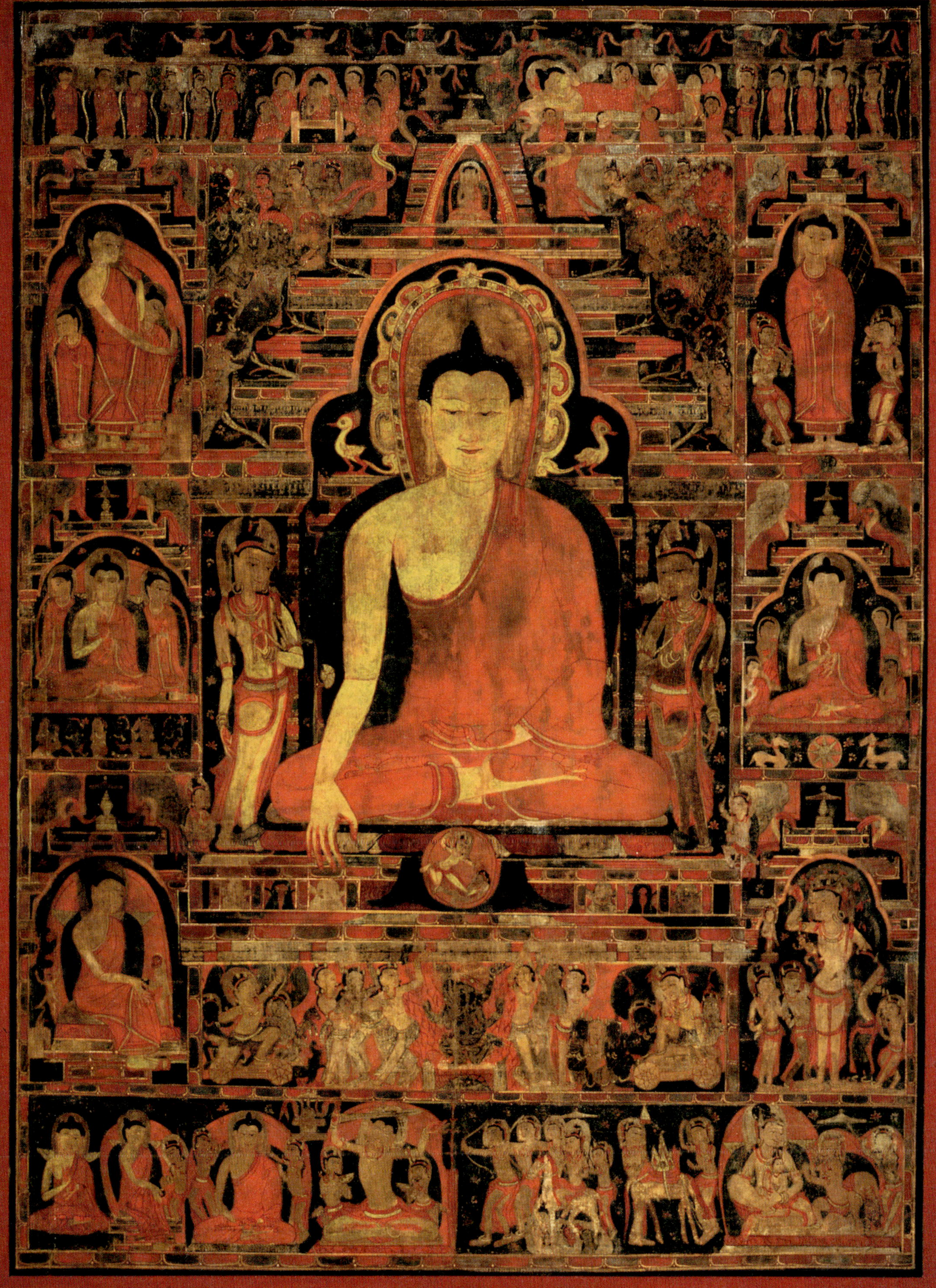

It is difficult to agree with Huntington that "an iconographic synthesis of two iconographic programs" in a single *thanka* is "a feature that is apparently wholly Tibetan," and that "this supports an emerging intellectual maturity among the Tibetan teachers that is beyond what one would expect in the new reproselytized Tibetans" (ibid.). There is almost nothing in this painting to indicate its purely Tibetan origin, no portrait of a Tibetan donor, and no Tibetan inscription on the back, as on most such early *thankas*. Even Śuddodhana, the father of Śākyamuni, is portrayed as an Indian prince and has not been Tibetanized. Thus it could have been painted in India and taken to Tibet, it could have been painted in Tibet for an Indian patron, or it could be a close copy of an Indian original done in Tibet. Moreover, since no such cloth paintings of the Pāla period have yet been firmly identified, one cannot conclude that the two "iconographic programs"—if Huntington's identification is conclusive—were not employed together in Indian representations.

What is clear is that this is one of the earliest *thankas* from Tibet to represent scenes from the life of Buddha Śākyamuni, and its stylistic implications are intriguing. It is a fine example of the early style with well-preserved, vibrant colors. The elegantly modeled central figure has been delineated with great care, strictly adhering to canonical proportions. The narrative panels, however, are more freely rendered, with greater animation than one encounters in contemporary Pāla manuscript illuminations.

Literature Pal 1975, no. 3; 1984, no. 11; Reynolds 1986, pp. 176–77, fig. 1; Huntington and Huntington 1990, no. 107.

82

Vajrasattva with Spouse

WESTERN TIBET (?), CA. 1300

14¼ × 12¼ IN. (36.2 × 31.1 CM)

The enthroned couple in the center represents Vajrasattva (Adamantine Being or One Whose Essence Is the *Vajra*) and Vajrasattvātmikā (Soul of the *Vajra* Essence) and not Vajradhātvīśvarī, as has been suggested elsewhere (Huntington and Huntington 1990, no. 116; see B. Bhattacharya 1958, pp. 74–75). Vajrasattva is one of the principal mind-born deities of Vajrayāna Buddhism, and although portrayed generally as a bodhisattva, he is no less important than a transcendental Buddha (see no. 70). His distinctive emblems are a thunderbolt and a bell, two of the most important symbols of Vajrayāna Buddhism. Vajrasattva here holds only a bell with her left hand while lovingly embracing her spouse with her right hand. They are surrounded by sixteen deities and ten buddhas, thereby probably constituting a mandala. In the bottom row, only the three figures on the left represent divinities. At the other end are an officiating monk and the group of seven jewels of a universal monarch: a lance- and sword-bearing general, a white elephant carrying the wheel of law, a horse bearing gems, a minister, and a queen. They are being offered to Vajrasattva, whose sumptuous ornaments make him a regal figure.

The attire and physiognomy of the minister, the queen, and the general are unambiguous indications that the *thanka* was painted in Tibet. Whether the officiating monk, who may be either Indian or Tibetan, is also the donor cannot be determined. Stylistically, the *thanka* is closely related to one in the Los Angeles County Museum of Art (Pal 1990A, no. P3), and very likely both belong to a series of lineage *thankas* of which the Zimmerman example served as the frontispiece. Vajrasattva is often considered to be the originator of a particular teaching and hence of the lineage related to it.

Although rendered in the same basic style as the *thanka* depicting the life of the Buddha (no. 81), the delineation here is more free and vivacious. Neither the forms nor the outlines are as carefully drawn, and the colors are more strident. The generous use of brilliant blue adds significantly to the *thanka*'s visual appeal. The loose manner of the drawing is particularly reminiscent of Kadampa-style paintings seen in western Tibet (Pal and Fournier 1982, pls. LS1-LS32) and Ladakh (Copeland 1980; Huntington and Huntington 1990, no. 109). While J. Huntington is correct in pointing out that this painting possesses qualities—mostly in the use of specific motifs and details—that are more familiar in Nepali paintings, the overall style is not Nepali. Rather the salient stylistic features derive from the Pāla-dependent style. The "imprecision bordering on crudeness" that he observes in the rendering of details is certainly not a Nepali feature. In fact early Nepali paintings are admirable for their precise delineation of details and their sure and elegant drawing. Rather than considering this as an example of the Nepali (or Bal) style, it seems more probable that the artist created a synthesis of the two modes in a characteristically Tibetan manner.

The representation of the smiling couple in the center of this lively *thanka* is especially engaging. Their gestures and postures make them a couple suffused with love, as is seen in

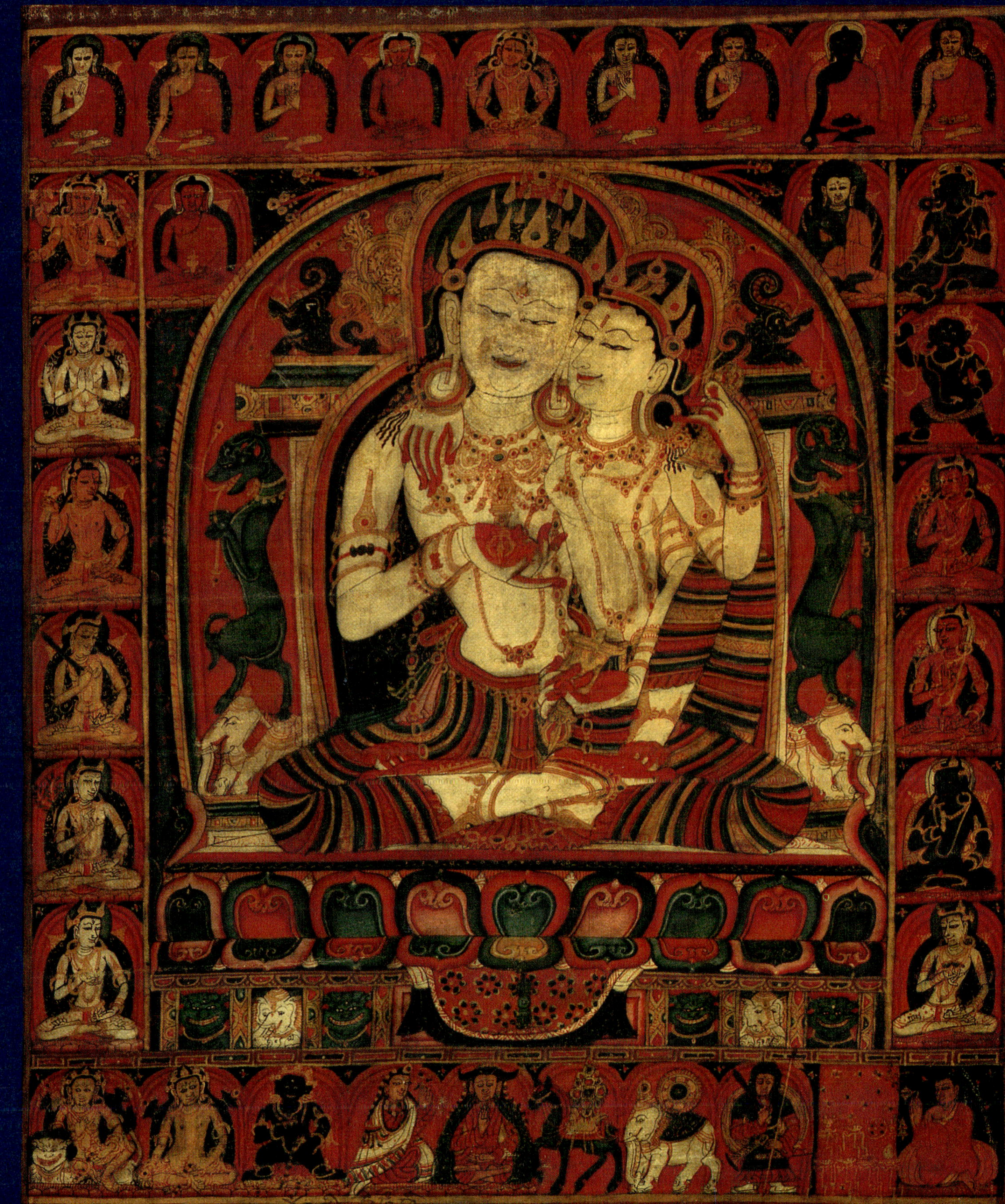

Umā-Maheśvara images in Pāla India rather than Nepal (see no. 16). The emphasis given to the goddess's swelling breasts is also more characteristic of Pāla than of Nepali modeling. Also noteworthy are the whimsical delineations of the animals on the throne base, which provide a strong contrast to the sober, dignified divine figures in the borders. Along with the central couple in dalliance, they considerably enliven the composition.

Literature Pal 1975, no. 29; Beguin et al. 1977, no. 117; Pal 1984, pp. 43–44, pl. 17; Huntington and Huntington 1990, no. 116.

83

Hevajramandala

CENTRAL TIBET, SAKYAPA ORDER, THIRTEENTH CENTURY

21¼ × 15½ IN. (54 × 39.4 CM)

In the center of the mandala, Hevajra unites with Nairātmyā (see no. 19). He has eight faces, sixteen arms, and four legs that trample on the four *māras*. Surrounding him are eight goddesses, all of whom originate from the union of Hevajra and Nairātmyā. They are Gaurī, Chaurī, Vetālī, Ghasmarī, Pukkasī, Savarī, Chaṇḍālī, and Ḍombinī. Each is depicted in an identical dancing posture but holds different emblems. Immediately outside this ring are eight waterpots with plants—a pair at each corner—and in the next square are sixteen dancing goddesses.

Beyond the four gateways of the mandala is the circle of eight cremation grounds representing the phenomenal world. Each cremation ground is occupied by a *Dikpāla,* or Protector of a Direction, and a *mahāsiddha* with worshippers, a stūpa, a burning corpse, and carrion eaters. Each ground is protected by a circle of thunderbolts and an outer ring of multihued flames. Beyond the mandala proper are twelve more deities, three in each corner, and two registers of figures at the top and one at the bottom. The two upper registers contain representations of deities, *mahāsiddhas,* and monks of the lineage, while at the bottom are twelve protective gods.

The closest stylistic parallels for this mandala may be seen in Nepali paintings and manuscript illuminations of the twelfth and thirteenth centuries. The modeling and proportions of the figures, the manner of fortifying their outlines to impart greater plasticity, the rendering of the trees, and the coloring in general are similar to the lively representations in some illuminated pages of a *Prajñāpāramitā* manuscript (Pal 1985, p. 59), as well as the two earliest known Nepali *paubhās* (see Pal 1978, figs. 68–70). One of the earliest surviving mandalas from Tibet and probably rendered for a major Sakyapa monastery, this is also one of the finest for its technical virtuosity.

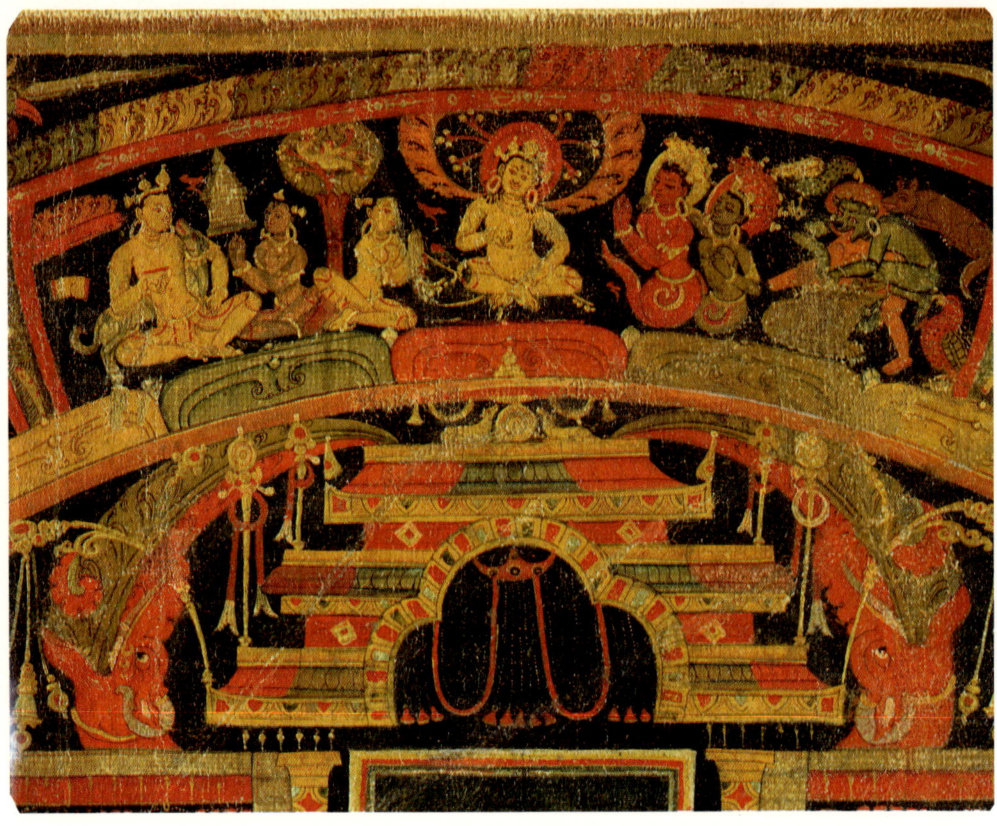

83

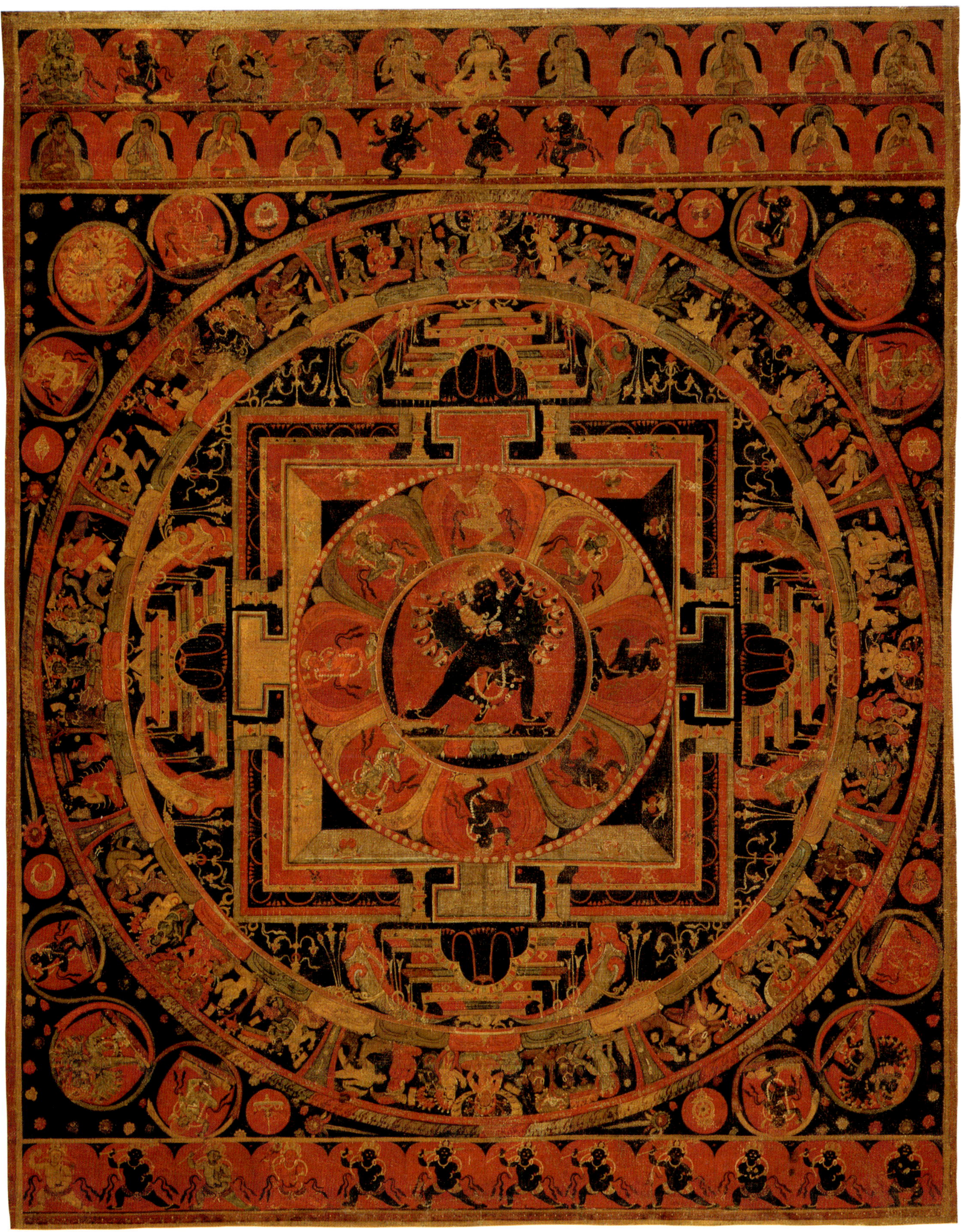

83

84

Four Mandalas

CENTRAL TIBET, SAKYA ORDER, LATE FOURTEENTH CENTURY

36 × 29 IN. (91.4 × 73.7 CM)

This group of mandalas belongs to a series from which another example also is in the Zimmerman Collection (see Rhie and Thurmon 1991, no. 73). The inscriptions praise the holy lama Sazang Phakpa, whose wishes it is hoped will be realized, and desire blessings for the monk Kunga Zangpo (see Appendix 2). From the companion *thanka* in the collection we know that the series was commissioned by Kunga Zangpo after the death of Sazang Phakpa. Fortunately, it is known that Sazang Phakpa, a Sakya lama, was one of Tsongkhapa's teachers and died in the 1380s. Thus the series, based on a tantric text called the *Vajrāvalī,* must have been painted soon after his death. Interestingly, Tsongkhapa himself is said to have heard the *Vajrāvalī* at the age of seventeen at the Drigung monastery (Tucci 1949, p. 436).

The two Sakyapa hierarchs in the center of the *thanka* are identified as Drakpa Gyaltsen and Sherab Gyaltsen. There are several teachers with these epithets, so their exact identification is difficult. The former may well be the Yarlung translator, while the latter may be either the translator from Dolpo (1292–1361) or a contemporary of the translator of *The Blue Annals*. Stylistic considerations make it likely that the former is represented here.

With the exception of the mandala at the lower right, the other mandalas are identical with only one difference: the central goddess is shown in three different colors, red, yellow, and blue. She is either Vajravārāhī or Nairātmyā, the former being the spouse of Chakrasamvara (nos. 20, 41, 88) and the latter of Hevajra (nos. 19, 53). The sow's head is not clearly distinguishable. In each mandala twenty-eight other manifestations of the goddess are represented along the arms or prongs of the thunderbolt configuration. The fourth mandala, however, is quite different, consisting of eleven lotuses within the palace, each enclosing a different pair of deities in *yab-yum*. Here again, without the relevant texts the figures are difficult to identify. Nine of the lotuses are of the same size; the other two are smaller and accommodated within the upper and lower gateways. None of the gateways is guarded. Along the top and bottom of the set of mandalas are two arcaded registers, each column supporting a stūpa. In the upper register each arcaded

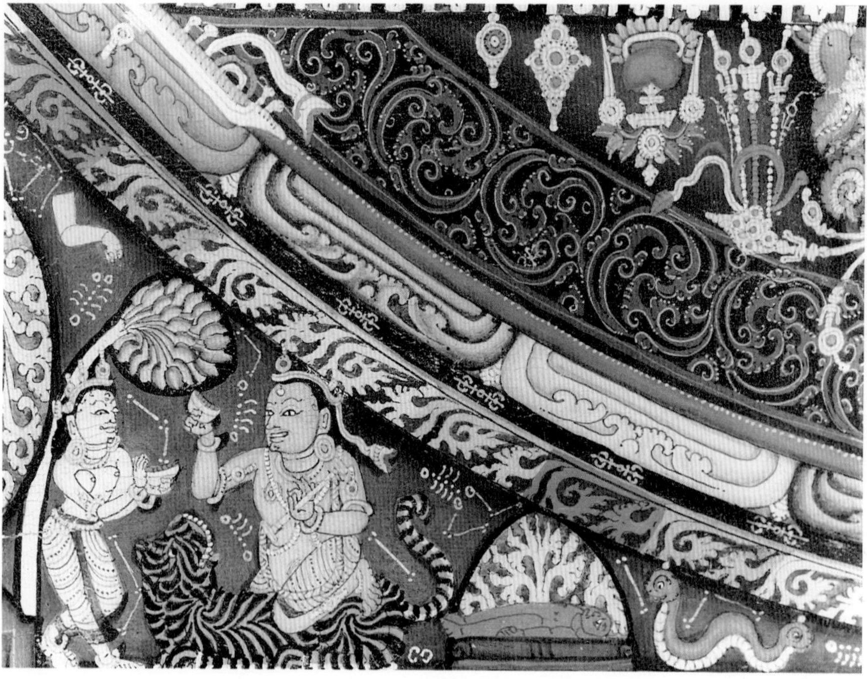

84

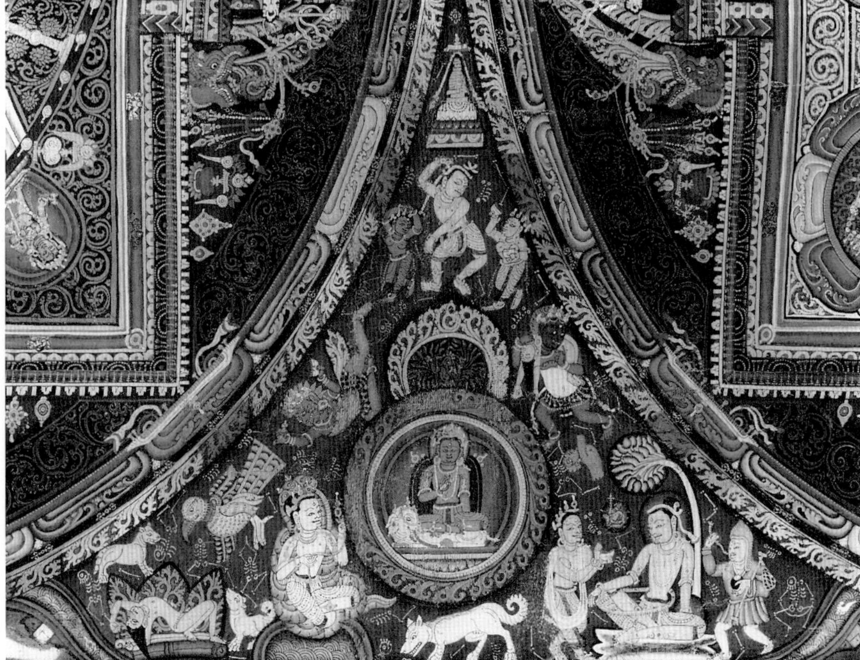

84

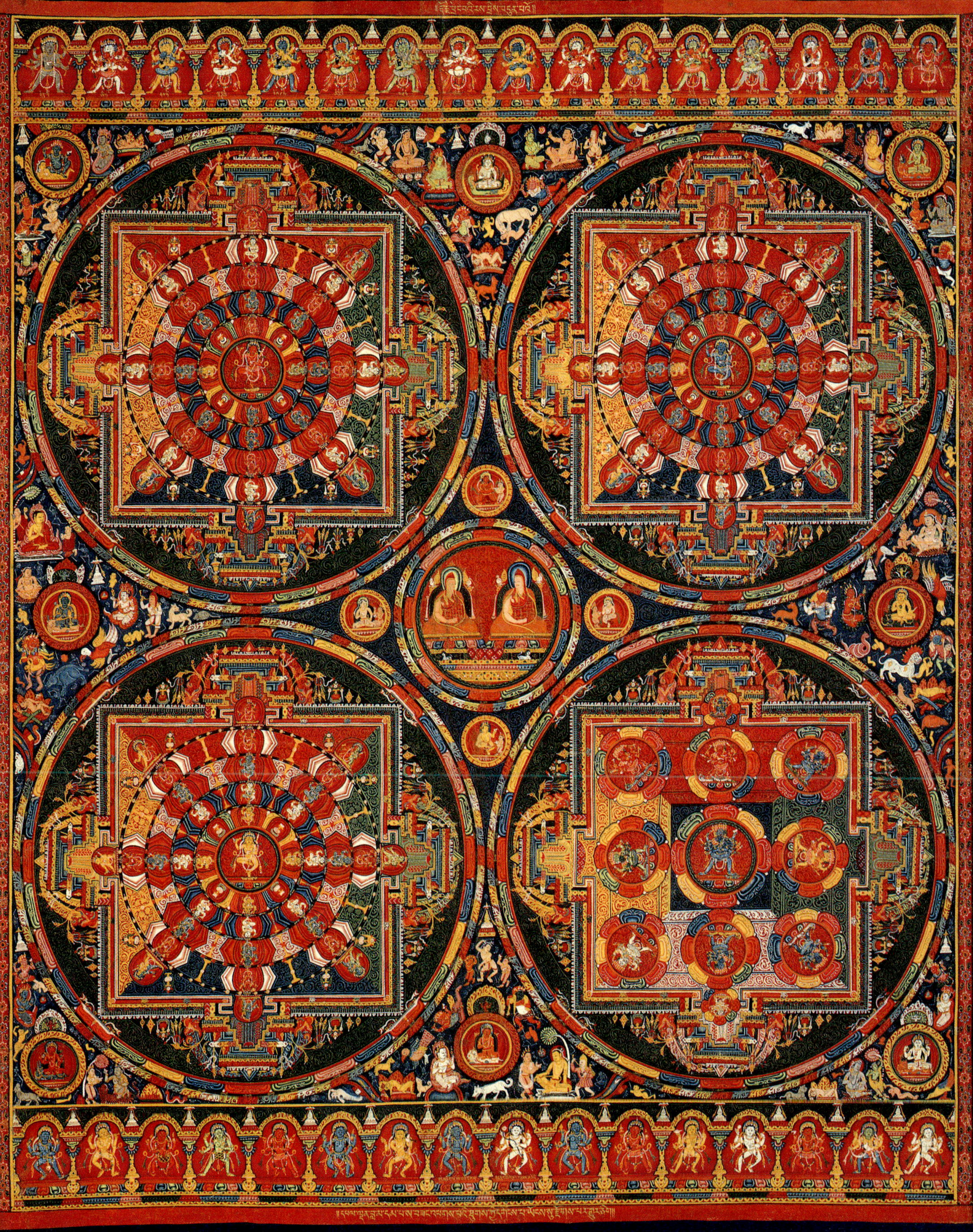

shrine contains a deity. In the top register all are in *yab-yum* except for those at the two ends. On the left is a gray god and on the right the red Vajravārāhī or Nairātmyā. Along the bottom are sixteen female offering deities, each with a different object.

Lively as these representations are, even more fascinating are the eight cremation grounds represented outside the four mandalas. Among the most elaborate known in Tibetan paintings, they are rendered with imagination and verve. The formula and style are purely Nepali, and very likely the series was executed by Newari artists. Although the scenes depict charnel fields with macabre goings-on, there is little that is gruesome. Rather it seems as if a merry, if somewhat bizarre, party is in progress. A *mahāsiddha* is being offered liquor, while another eccentric plays a bone trumpet; elsewhere a group dances joyfully, and a masked figure tries to slip by with a corpse on his shoulders, even as ghouls with sharpened choppers and scavenging birds soar through the sky toward a body being cremated (or barbecued, in the world of ghouls). In fact the flames are so stylized that they look like the back of a couch, while the corpse appears to be a drugged or drunken man rather than a dead one. Especially interesting is the subtle delineation of white pieces of bone and skeletons strewn over the dark background.

85

Mandala of Raktayamari

BY MIKYO DORJE

CENTRAL TIBET, SAKYA ORDER, CA. 1400

WITH SILK SURROUND: 37½ × 30 IN. (95.3 × 76.2 CM)

The principal deity in this mandala is Raktayamāri (Red Yamāri), the enemy of Yama, the god of death. He is shown in *yab-yum* with his spouse, who is his own emanation. Both are colored red and

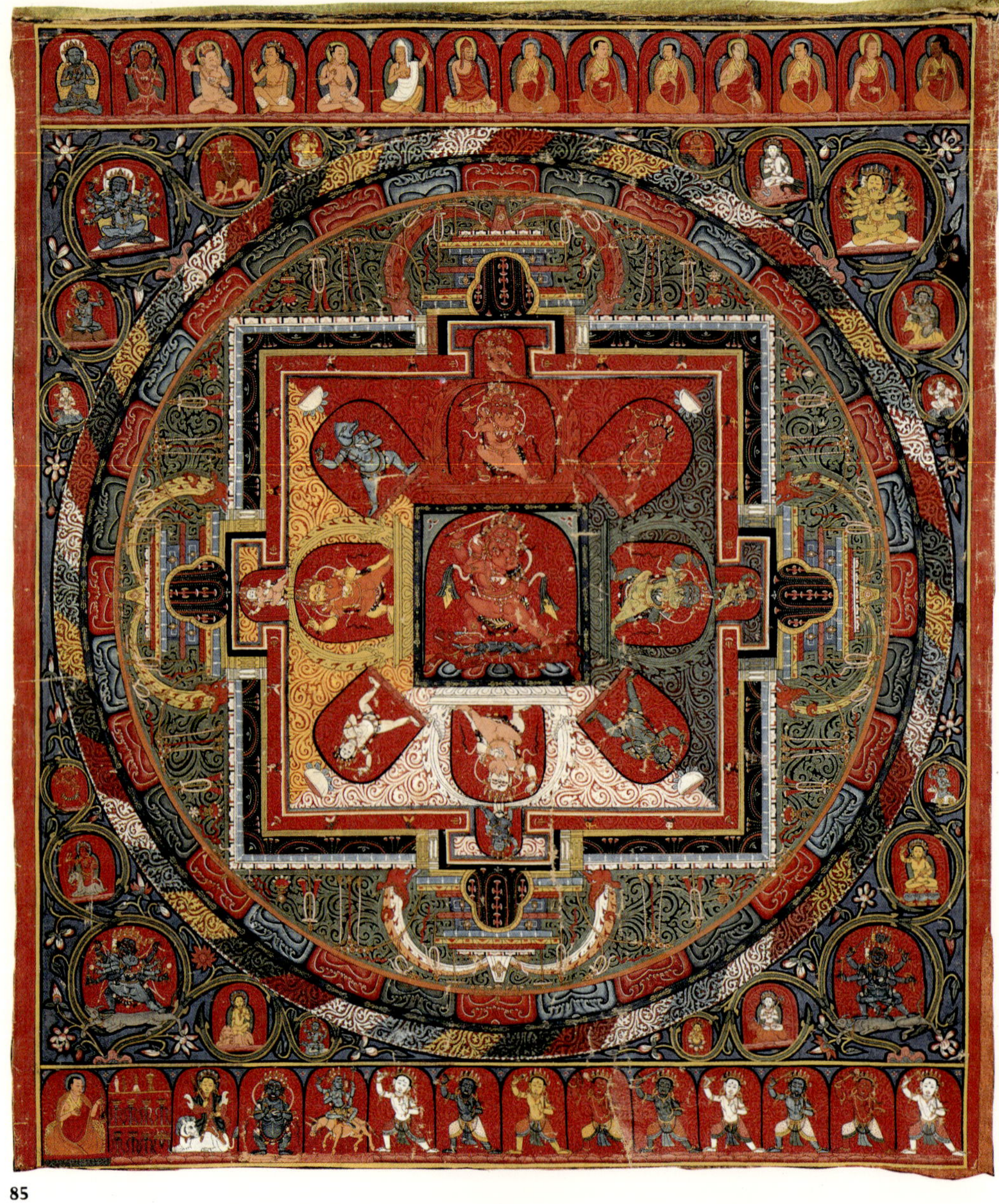

85

stand over the figure of Yama stretched out on a red bull. (Normally, Yama rides a blue buffalo.) His right arm brandishes a staff, and his left holds a skull cup. The four deities in the four cardinal directions are different-colored forms of Yamāri himself, also depicted in *yab-yum*. In the four corners are the goddesses Vajracharchikā, Vajravārāhī, Vajrasarasvatī, and Gaurī. The gates of the mandala are guarded by four other forms of Yamāri known as Mudgara[club]yamāri, Daṇḍa[staff]yamāri, Padma[lotus]yamāri, and Khaḍga[sword]yamāri. Outside the mandala's outer fiery ring is another group of sixteen deities which seems to include four important gods, possibly Gūhyasamāja, Gūhyamañjuvajra, and two other forms of Yamāri, as well as the eight keepers of the directions. The lineage in the top register is composed of Vajradhara, *mahāsiddhas,* and Indian and Tibetan monks. Along the bottom the officiating monk with his offerings is at the left corner, followed by the three protector deities Vaiśravaṇa, Mahākāla, and Lhamo and then nine militant divinities. Each of the latter is differently colored but posts and brandishes his weapon in the same manner.

According to the dedicatory inscription, the *thanka* was the precious possession of the learned monk Kunga Legpa, the holy lama of Changphuk (see Appendix 2). While it is possible that it was painted in Changphuk itself, it may have been acquired elsewhere, perhaps on a visit to Sakya. Kunga Legpa has been identified as one of Tsongkhapa's teachers who lived in the latter half of the fourteenth century (Rhie and Thurman 1991, no. 75). The *thanka* is a fine example of Sakyapa-style painting showing strong Nepali influences. The practice of enclosing figures within roundels composed of vines is typical of Tibetan paintings in this style and is rarely encountered elsewhere.

Raktayamāri was a tutelary deity for several important Tibetan monks. According to *The Blue Annals* (Roerich 1976, p. 379), these included such illustrious figures as dPyal Chos-bzangs, Chag lotsawa, and Buton Rinpoche. The text also informs us that "gLo-po lo-tsa-va Shes-rab zin-chen, a disciple of the siddha Dar-pan and Revenda, spread in Central Tibet the texts of the precepts of the Red Yamāntaka (= Yamāri) according to the teaching transmitted through the lineage of Viru-pa" (see no. 64).

Literature Rhie and Thurman 1984, no. 128 (no ill.); 1991, no. 75.

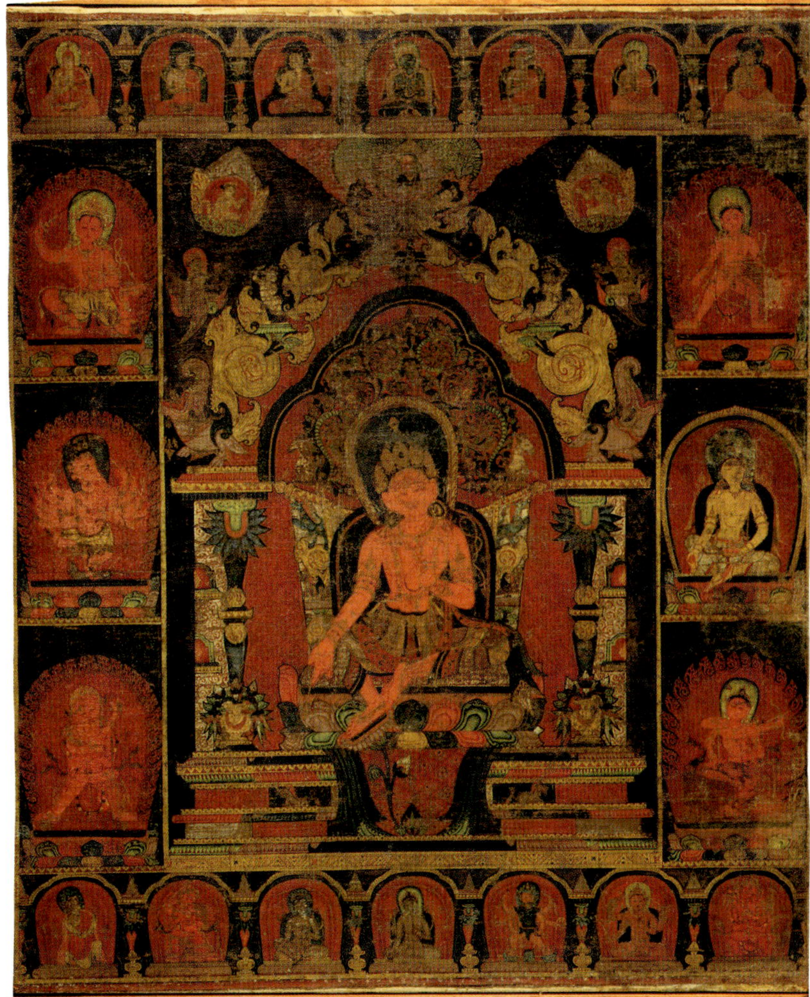

86

86

Goddess Tārā

CENTRAL TIBET, SAKYA ORDER, CA. 1400

22½ × 19¾ IN. (57.2 × 50.2 CM)

The red figure seated within an elaborate shrine in the center of this *thanka* is Tārā, the savior goddess of Vajrayāna Buddhism, whose cult is particularly popular in Tibet (see Beyer 1978). She is surrounded by various deities, including a red Gaṇeśa dancing ecstatically in the middle of the border at the right. Immediately above him is a red emanation of Achala (see no. 38). The figure at the bottom of the column on the other side is Kurukullā, the goddess of love. In the register above are represented Vajradhara in the center and six monks, two of whom wear the Indian pundit's cap. Vajradhara (Thunderbolt Holder) is considered to be a supreme deity in some systems of Vajrayāna Buddhism and is particularly important for the Sakyapas. Along the bottom the effigy of the officiating monk is followed by images of six other divinities.

There can be little doubt that this *thanka* was painted by a Newari artist for a Sakyapa monastery, perhaps even at Sakya. The presence of the monks in the top register is the only reason it can be attributed to Tibet or a Tibetan patron. Otherwise most of the salient features, such as the blue background filled with subtle scrollwork, the textile patterns, the elaborate design of the central shrine, the arcaded registers at top and bottom, and the rather delicate frame and small proportions of the figures are all characteristic of Nepali painting. Especially noteworthy are the delicacy and refinement of the aureoles and the shrine with its exquisitely detailed arch (*toraṇa*) consisting of swirling animal and vegetal forms.

Literature Pal 1978, p. 149, fig. 205; 1984, pp. 64–65, pl. 25.

87

Sakyapa Lineage

CENTRAL TIBET, SAKYA ORDER, 1450–1500

34½ × 31½ IN. (87.6 × 80 CM)

One of the most impressive *thankas* in the Zimmerman Collection, this is also one of the finest examples of a Sakyapa lineage *thanka* outside Tibet. While the composition itself is not unusual, the finesse of the drawing, sumptuousness of the colors, and striking design of the throne make this an outstanding example of the genre. Especially attractive is the generous use of gold, which—together with the rich yellow and orange—creates a dazzling visual effect.

As is customary in such portraits, the principal figures share a lotus on an elaborate throne consisting of ornate arches supported by slender columns. It is interesting to note how some of the important symbols of the religion have been smoothly integrated into the complex design of the columns and arches. At the base of the columns are auspicious waterpots, in the middle is a thunderbolt, and above the capitals are flaming mirrors. At the apex of each arch is the symbol of the three jewels. In addition the eight auspicious symbols are lightly drawn in white like delicate lacework against the blue background just above the arches.

Another unusual feature of this *thanka* is that minimal attempts have been made to distinguish between the two central personages. Both are given identical attributes: the hands form the gesture of turning the wheel of law and hold lotus stems, the blooms supporting bells and thunderbolts. Both have almost identical faces, like twins. Only the left eye of the figure at the right has been made round to express a sense of wonder. Also unusual is the placement of the four bodhisattvas led by the blue Vajrasattva, with Achala and Mahākāla, the two protective deities, along the bottom of the *thanka*. Usually, Vajrasattva leads the lineage in the top register. Here the first figure at the top left is the Buddha Śākyamuni. All the other figures represent Indian and Tibetan teachers.

One of the distinctive features of some Sakyapa lineage *thankas* is that they depict subsidiary figures against red aureoles enclosed within medallions of meandering vines. The vines in fact originate from a waterpot at the bottom center of the entire composition and rise up on either side. The idea occurs earlier on murals in western Tibet, as may be seen in Tsaparang (Weyer and Aschoff 1987, pls. 13, 14). Although all the figures are seated here in the same manner, there is considerable variety in their facial features and gestures, making them an animated group.

Of the two main figures, one is named by the inscription as Gyaltsen Peljor Zangpo (see Appendix 2), but he has not been identified yet. All the others are identified by small inscriptions in gold. One of the labels (on the fourth figure in the second row from the top, counting from left to right) reads *bsam-gtan-pa chen-po kun-dga' bzango-po,* which means "great meditation master Kunga Zangpo." Kunga Zangpo was very likely the ascetic and scholar who lived from 1382 until 1444 and founded the Nor monastery. If this is correct, the *thanka* could not have been painted earlier than 1444. A date in the second half of the fifteenth century is stylistically consistent. Closely comparable is an equally impressive Sakyapa lineage *thanka* in the Los Angeles County Museum of Art (Pal 1990A, no. 13).

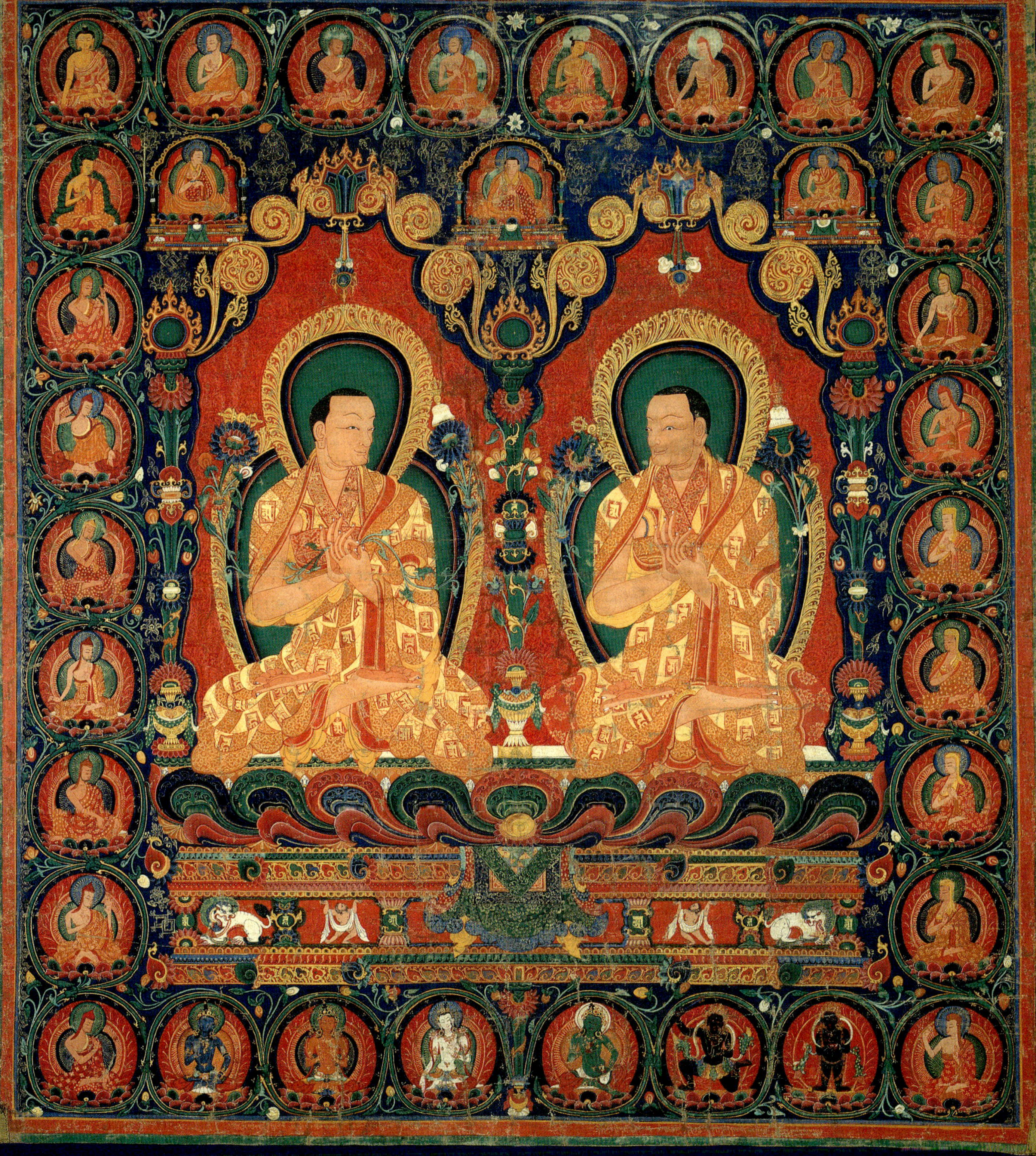

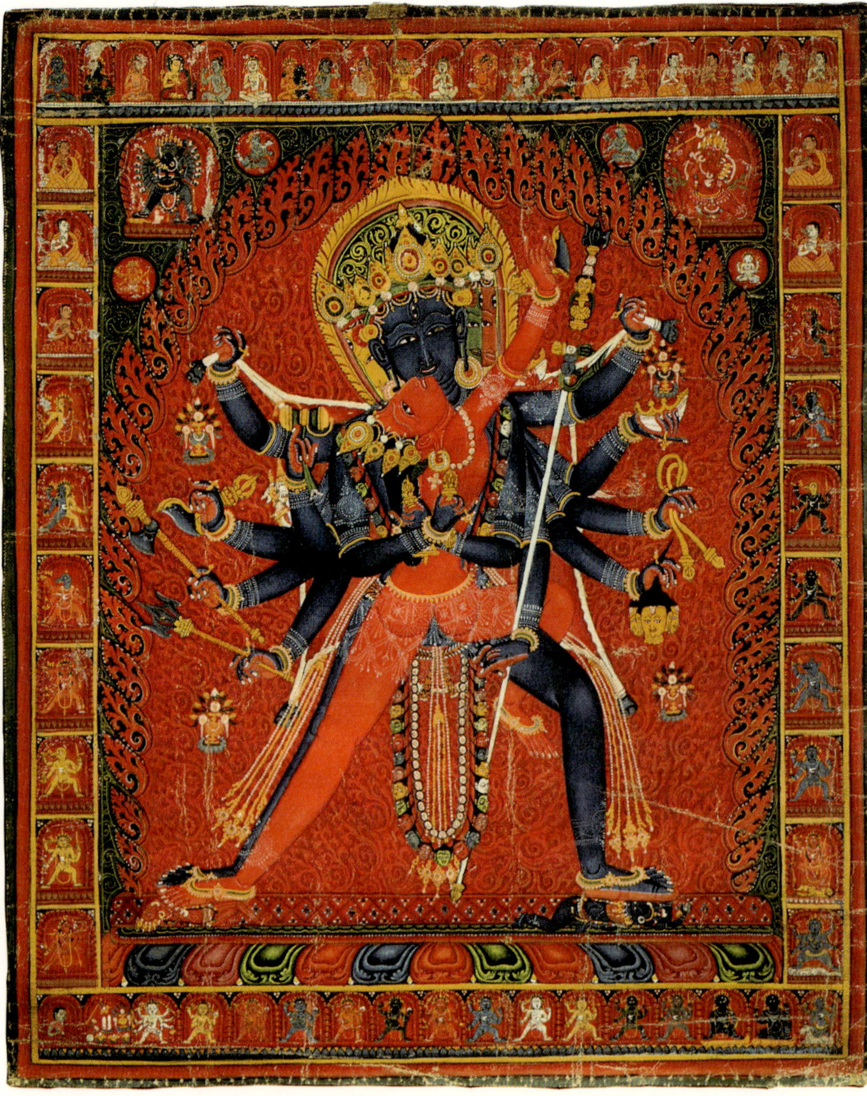

88

88

Chakrasamvara and Spouse

CENTRAL TIBET, SAKYA ORDER, 1450–1500

16 × 13⅛ IN. (40.6 × 33.4 CM)

The embracing figures of Chakrasamvara and Vajravārāhī (see no. 41) are represented against an aureole of leaping flames. The area behind the stylized tongues of fire is filled with a green arabesquelike scroll pattern. The fiery aureole is rendered in two different shades of red, and the subtle design gives it the appearance of a finely woven textile. The yellow, blue, green, and red heads of Chakrasamvara are set off against a nimbus filled with green and yellow scrolls fringed with yellow tongues of flame. His complexion is brilliant blue highlighted with silvery gray patches and intricately rendered filigreelike jewelry to impart a sense of volume.

Both figures are remarkably tall and slim with long, slender legs, as is the case in a later Nepali version of the subject in the Zimmerman Collection (no. 41). Also noteworthy is the oval face of Chakrasamvara with its sharply defined features, as is seen in a contemporary *thanka* representing Bhaishajyaguru in the Binney Collection (Pal 1984, pl. 44). Indeed the patterning of the scroll designs, treatment of the lotus, and tonality of the colors are similar in both. The design and coloring of the mattress-like object above the lotus base here also occur on the border of Bhaishajyaguru's robe. It is possible that the two paintings were rendered by the same artist or in the same workshop.

The concept and iconography of Chakrasamvara and Vajravārāhī have already been discussed (see nos. 20, 41, 57). While the two principal deities do not differ iconographically from the Nepali painted representation (no. 41), the subsidiary figures do, thereby denoting that two different traditions were followed. The Tibetan version not only includes different subsidiary figures in the immediate circle of Chakrasamvara but also is enriched with additional attendant deities as well as the depiction of the lineage that transmitted the tradition. Beginning with divine figures such as Vajradhara and Vajrasattva at the left extremity of the upper register, they include Indian as well as Tibetan teachers. Most of the former are monks. At the bottom another monk makes offerings at the far left, and at the opposite end are Mahākāla and Lhamo, two of the Dharmapālas.

89

Two Forms of the Goddess Tārā

WESTERN TIBET, GUGE, 1450–1500

20¼ × 20 IN. (51.4 × 50.8 CM)

On the left is the White Tārā and on the right the Green Tārā. Each is a different aspect of the savior goddess Tārā, who like Avalokiteshvara is a popular deity in Tibet and who is said to have been born from a tear of Avalokiteshvara (see Beyer 1978).

Apart from their complexions, the two forms of the goddess have other distinguishing features. Both are seated on lotuses rising from a stylized decorative pool with hills in the background. Apart from the central stems, tendrils emerge from the pool to form swirling scrolls enclosing more flowers. The flowers on which the goddesses sit are of two varieties, the white one being more like a Chinese peony than a lotus. The White Tārā sits in the classic meditating posture known as *vajraparyaṅka,* with both legs crossed on her lap and her soles exposed. The green goddess sits more gracefully with the right leg pendant in *lalitāsana*. Although both wear similar garments and ornaments, the textiles and designs are different. The right hand of each is outstretched in the gesture of charity, and the left holds a lotus. A second flower is attached to the Green Tārā's right arm. The white goddess is further distinguished by five additional eyes, one on her forehead and one on each of her palms and soles, to emphasize her compassion and omniscience. Interestingly, each of the lotus flowers, whether rising from the pool or in the goddesses' hands, appears to support a gem on the pericarp.

Above are five deities and two monks, who cannot be identified as their attributes are indistinct. Both monks wear yellow hats, and so one of them may represent Tsongkhapa and the other the founder of the Red Temple at Tsaparang. The central figure is very likely Shaḍaksharī Lokeśvara (Lokeśvara of the Six Syllables), Tārā's consort. The guardian deity at the bottom center is Vighnāntaka, and the figure on the right is very likely the donor.

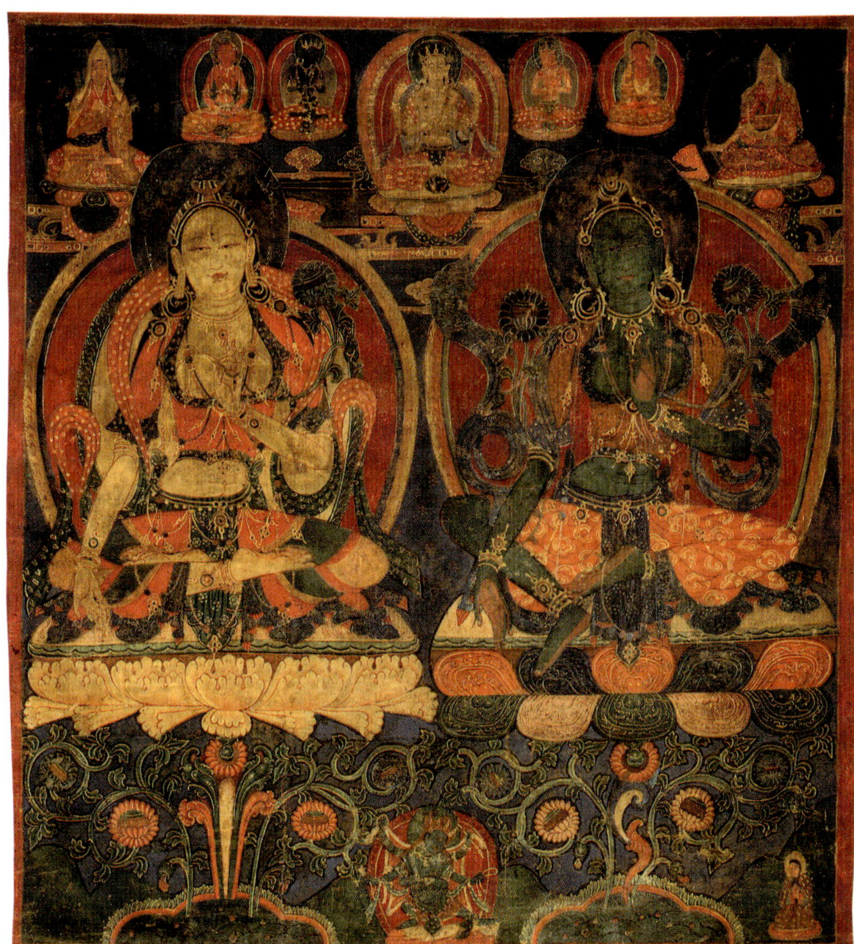

89

As far as is known, this is the only Guge *thanka* that represents the two Tārās in this fashion. Close stylistic parallels may be seen in the Red Temple in Tsaparang in ancient Guge (Weyer and Aschoff 1987, pls. 26, 27, 45, 46) and in the Serkhang at Tapho (Tabo), now in Himachal Pradesh (Huntington 1972, pls. 59b, 60a). Both of these temples were built between 1450 and 1500, so a date in the second half of the fifteenth century seems fairly certain for this *thanka*. It should also be noted that the figure of the White Tārā is formally very close to a goddess on the ceiling of the sTonpa Lhakang at Phugtal in Zangskar (Snellgrove and Skorupski 1980, vol. 2, fig. 30; see pl. 5, figs. 39, 40).

The attire of the goddesses, especially the tailored blouse exposing the breasts, derives ultimately from the Kashmiri tradition and is commonplace on earlier murals surviving at such sites as Alchi (in Ladakh) and Tapho. The proportions and modeling of the two figures also echo the earlier Kashmiri aesthetic, but the coloring is more subdued. However, the tonality of the colors, designs of the flowers, patterns of the textiles, and cloud motifs derive from Chinese tradition filtered through such Sakyapa establishments as Shalu and Gyantse.

90

Amitābha and His Paradise

WESTERN TIBET, GUGE, LATE FIFTEENTH CENTURY

30 × 23½ IN. (76.2 × 59.7 CM)

The red central Buddha seated on a lotus rising from a pool (see no. 89) is Amitābha. He holds a bowl in his hand and wears garments with Chinese brocade borders. He is flanked by the graceful figures of the Bodhisattva Avalokiteshvara on his right and the dark Bodhisattva Vajrapāṇi on his left. Two tiny figures of monks wearing yellow hats are represented in red aureoles on either side of his head.

The rest of the *thanka* is filled with stylized, decorative trees, Tibetan-style buildings denoting pavilions, a large number of monks forming audiences, and some residents of the paradise engaged in various activities. There are also ten seated buddhas, mostly white, who are busy preaching. Six are in the upper section and four in the lower half of the *thanka*.

A classic example of the style that developed in Guge in the second half of the fifteenth century, the *thanka* depicts a theme that seems to have had particular appeal in the region for unknown reasons. It represents the Paradise of Bliss or Happiness (Sukhāvatī) of Amitābha, also known commonly as Western Paradise or Pure Land. Generally, the cult of Pure Land Buddhism, as it is known in China, was not as popular with the Tibetans as it was in Central Asia and China in much earlier times. In the fifteenth century, however, the paradise theme appears to have captured the imagination of the Tibetans in Guge for both wall paintings and *thankas*. The Sukhāvatī of Amitābha was not the only paradise they preferred. One also finds the much rarer paradise of Akshobhya (Pal 1990A, no. P6). Why the concept of paradise became popular in Guge at this time remains unexplained.

Both iconographically and compositionally, the Zimmerman Sukhāvatī *thanka* is less complex than another in the Los Angeles County Museum of Art (ibid., no. P7) or the representation at Tapho (Huntington 1972, pl. 59b). Nevertheless it follows the same basic composition with a central enthroned Buddha surrounded by scenes of preaching buddhas and groups of listeners interspersed with adorned pavilions and trees. I have elsewhere refuted Tucci's suggestion that these fluid, crowded compositions derive from much earlier Central Asian paradise paintings (Pal 1990A, pp. 140–43). Rather, such densely populated paradisiacal compositions are further elaborations of scenes of Buddha preaching found in earlier murals at Alchi (Snellgrove and Skorupski 1980, vol. 1, pl. 9, figs. 23, 47) and ultimately can be traced further back to Ajanta murals.

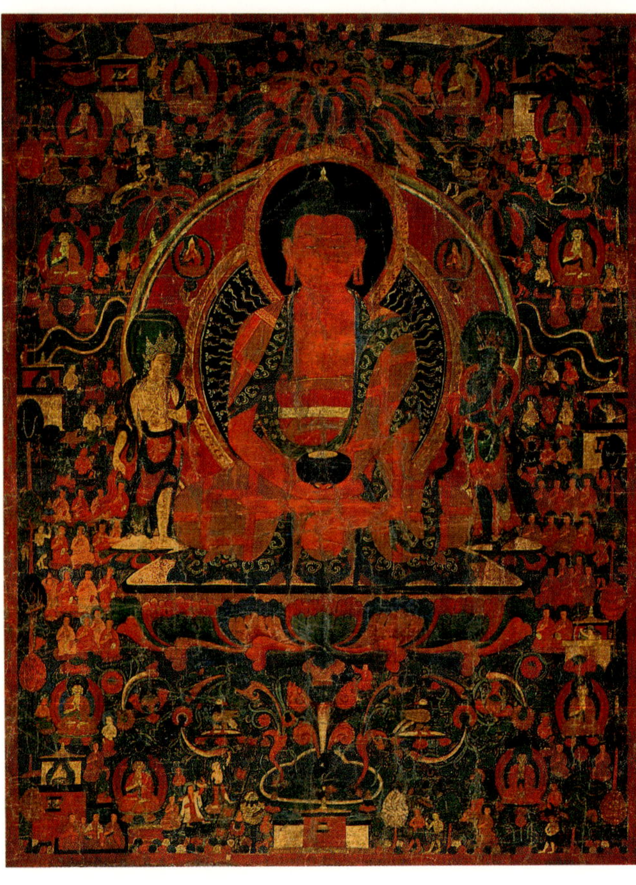

91

Arhat Bhadra

CENTRAL TIBET (?), FIFTEENTH CENTURY

WITH SILK SURROUND: 47½ × 31½ IN. (120.7 × 80 CM)

Wearing colorful robes, Bhadra (Auspicious One), whose realm is Tāmradvīpa, or Copper Island, is seated on an elaborate throne with his elegant Central Asian shoes placed carefully on a footstool. His right hand demonstrates that he is engaged in teaching. Two attendants stand on either side of the throne. The one in front holds a puppy in his arms, and the other brings a bowl of gemstones as an offering. A third figure meditates within a snowy cave, and above are four deities and two parasol bearers floating on clouds. For other examples from the same series, see Pal 1990A, no. P9, and Rhie and Thurman 1991, no. 13.

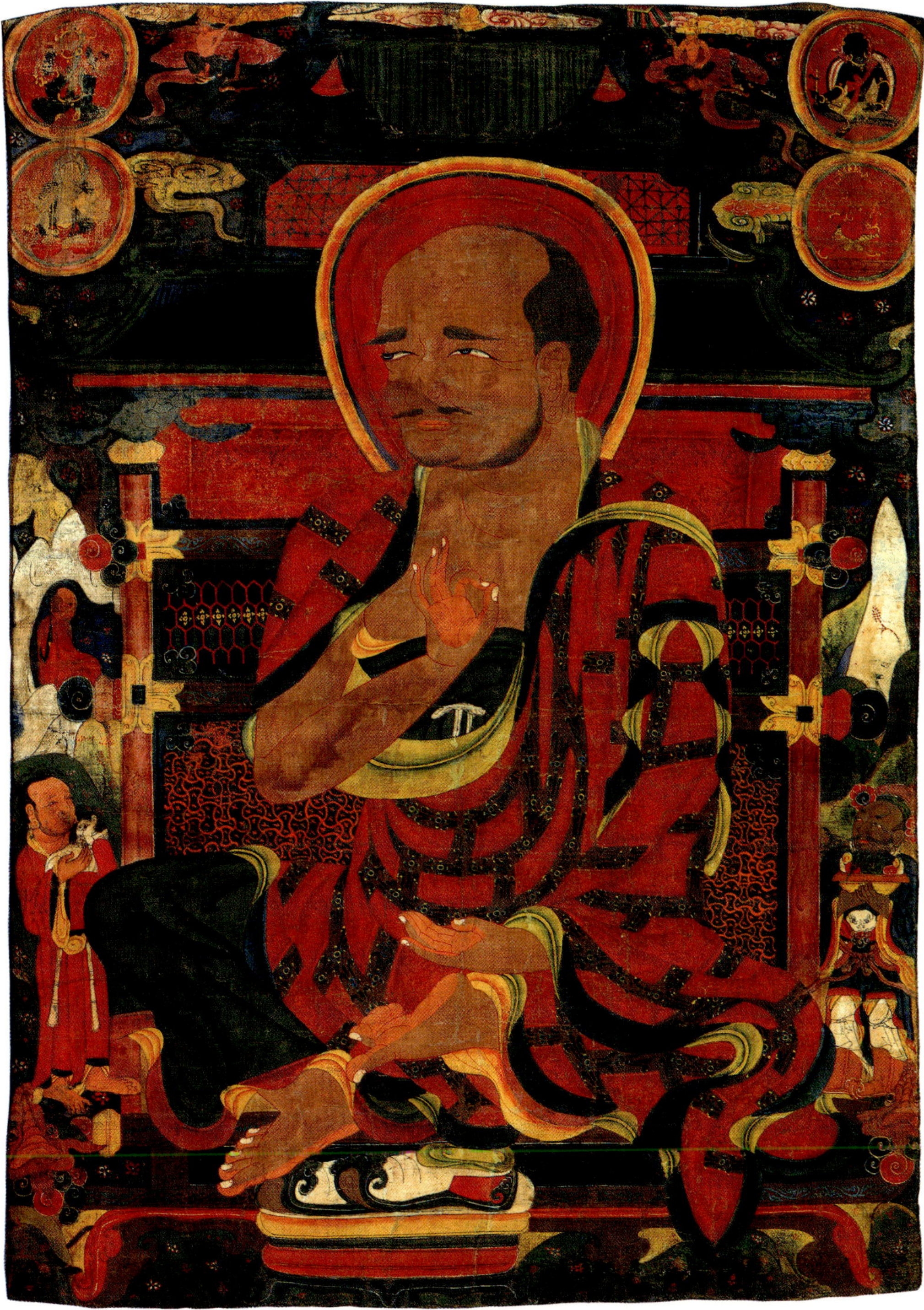

91

Unlike divine figures, arhats are always portrayed as human beings, usually as teachers. Tibetans knew of three basic traditions of arhat paintings: Indian, Chinese, and Tibetan (see Pal 1990). No example of an Indian-style representation of an arhat has yet come to light. Most surviving early Tibetan painted examples, which do not seem to go back earlier than the fourteenth century, indicate that the tradition of depicting arhats may have captured the imagination of the Tibetans during the Yuan period. In any event they also clearly demonstrate that China rather than India was the principal artistic source for Tibetan arhat representations. It must be added, however, that even in the earliest examples one cannot trace a precise Chinese source. It would thus appear that the Tibetans invented their own mode of representation by borrowing compositional devices and motifs from Chinese tradition.

Many of the salient features of this representation, such as the manner of delineating the folds of the garments to convey a sense of volume, the landscaping around the obviously Chinese throne, and the cloud forms, demonstrate a familiarity with Chinese tradition. The naturalistic drawing and delineation of the arhat's flesh also follow Chinese technique. However, the shapes and forms of the mountains as well as their coloring owe little to Chinese tradition, revealing instead a characteristically Tibetan visionary quality. The little figures of deities within the red circles at the top are also Tibetan rather than Chinese. The most prominent difference is the penchant for bright coloring and a rather crowded composition, neither of which is encountered in Chinese arhat paintings.

Literature Beguin 1977, no. 86; Pal 1984, pp. 124–25, pl. 57; Reynolds 1986, pp. 176, 179, fig. 13.

92

Mahākāla in the Form of a Brahman

CENTRAL TIBET, SAKYA ORDER, FIFTEENTH CENTURY

49 × 32⅜ IN. (124.5 × 82.3 CM)

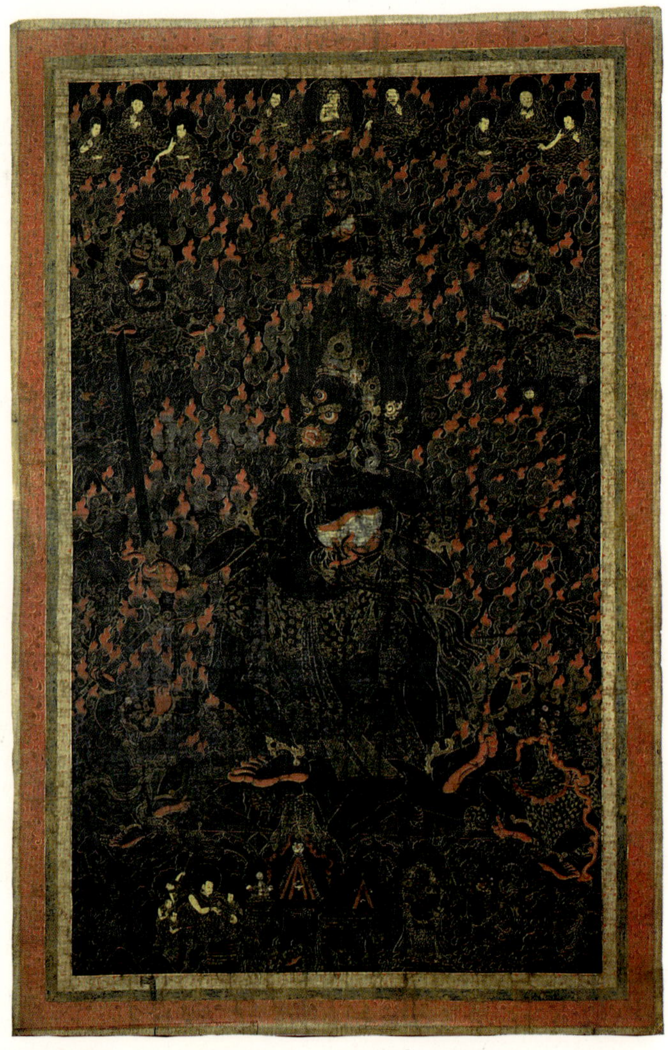

92

This black-and-gold *thanka* depicts a rarely represented form of Mahākāla which would have been difficult to identify without the inscriptions. They make it clear that the *thanka* was meant for Sakyapa usage (see Appendix 2). Although Mahākāla is universally venerated by Tibetans, the largest variety of his forms is known in the Sakyapa tradition (see Nebesky-Wojkowitz 1956, pp. 38–67).

According to the inscription, the name of this form is mGon- po bram-gzugs, which means "Mahākāla in the form of a brahman." It is interesting that he is invoked as the Great Putra (Son), which is used in another description of an attendant of Gur gyi mgon po, or Mahākāla as Protector of the Tent (ibid., p. 50). One of the attendants, known as Putra Nagpo (or gShin rje ma rungs pa mon bu putra), is described as brandishing a long sword with his right hand and holding a skull cup in his left. In fact the cup is supposed to be filled with warm brains and blood. It would appear that the same figure is included in the retinue of Mahākāla on another black-and-gold *thanka* of the deity in the Zimmerman Collection (no. 94). The inscription further informs us that this deity and the others on the *thanka* wear the dress of Mon country, and all have a fierce appearance, with eyes oozing blood and mouths spitting flames. Adorned with human heads, they dwell in the middle of a fire storm. The artist has attempted to convey this by highlighting the dancing flames all over the *thanka* with red. Red is also used for the mouths, eyes, palms of the hands, soles of the feet, and insides of the skulls, no doubt to indicate blood. The only other color employed is white, for the complexion of the Sakyapa monks and the skulls and to highlight the eyes.

Space limitations do not permit a discussion of the other figures on the *thanka,* who are identified by inscriptions. However, some comments are necessary regarding the officiating monk at the bottom left. Identified as Jamyang

Pal Drakpa Lodro Gyaltsen, he may represent a teacher of the same name who lived in the first half of the fifteenth century (see Appendix 2). If so, this *thanka* must commemorate the observance of the special rite dedicated to this form of Mahākāla by the officiant. The date would of course make this *thanka* a landmark in the history of Tibetan painting by pushing back considerably the generally accepted dates for this type of work.

93

Mahākāla and Companions

CENTRAL TIBET, SAKYA ORDER, CA. 1500

64 × 53 IN. (162.6 × 134.6 CM)

One of the largest *thankas* in the Zimmerman Collection, this is also one of the most expressive. The presence of the Sakyapa teachers on the top and the sides makes it clear that it was commissioned for a monastery of that order. The style of the painting, however, differs considerably from other characteristically Sakyapa representations of Mahākāla in his Protector of the Tent form rendered in a strongly Nepali style (see Beguin 1990, no. 26; Pal 1990A, no. P10). For one thing the cremation grounds that are prominent in other paintings have been omitted here. For another, the red is not as ubiquitous here, and the lineage figures are not represented in a single register along the top. The figure of Mahākāla dominates the composition like a colossus, and all the other figures are much reduced in size. Although the cremation grounds are excluded, the

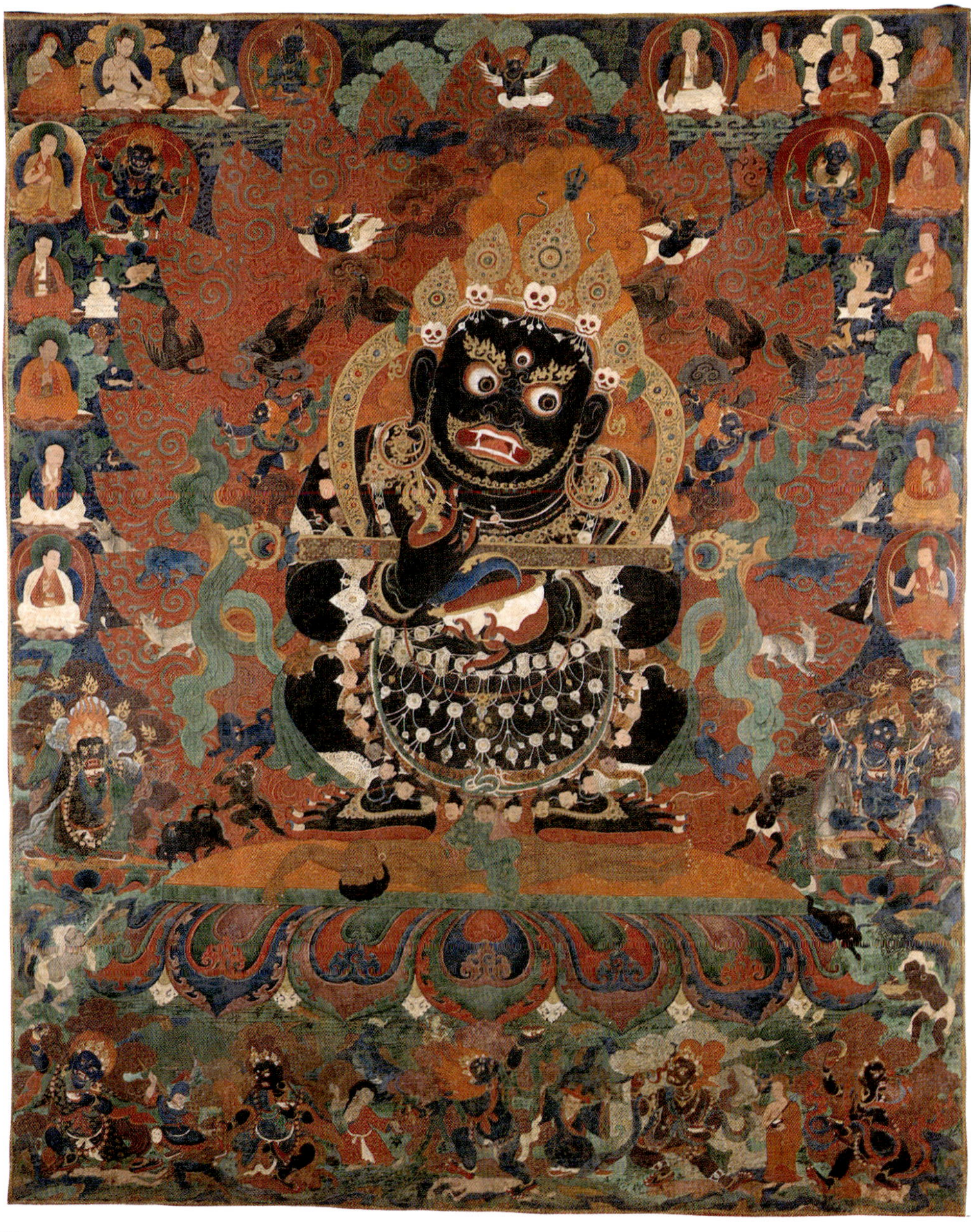

93

composition is more densely packed with bold designs of the fiery aureole, swirling cloud surrounds for most of the other figures, and a much larger supporting cast engaged in a wide variety of activities all around the central figure. Most of the more typical Sakyapa representations of Mahākāla appear to have been done, perhaps by one family of artists, sometime in the fifteenth century. This highly animated example seems to have ushered in a second style that is more distinctly Tibetan. A later painting in this second style is in the Los Angeles County Museum of Art (Pal 1990A, no. P21).

Continuity with the earlier mode was maintained by following the same basic composition. Mahākāla is surrounded by all sorts of scavenging birds and animals as well as militant demons, so that the basic idea that the charnel field is the god's appropriate theater is intact. The god's four principal companions—Palden Remati and Palden Lhamo on his left and Bhūtaḍāmara and Legden Nagpo on his right—are so reduced in size as to be scarcely noticeable. A group of five more prominent figures is included along the bottom. They are all demonic and highly charged in appearance and assume aggressive postures. They also occur on a later *thanka* in the Zimmerman Collection (no. 94) as well as on the seventeenth-century *thanka* of this type in Los Angeles.

Especially impressive is the figure of Mahākāla himself. The beautifully rendered bone apron (see no. 63) is rarely seen in other representations of the deity. His gold ornaments as well as the billowing scarf are also more prominently rendered than usual. Against his black body the gold and white create a rich visual contrast.

Literature Rhie and Thurman 1991, no. 71.

94

Mahākāla and Companions

TIBET, SAKYA ORDER (?), CA. SIXTEENTH CENTURY

GOLD AND COLORS ON SILK

30 × 24½ IN. (76.2 × 62.2 CM)

The two-armed Mahākāla is represented here in the familiar Protector of the Tent image (see no. 93). His retinue, however, differs from the other representation in that two of the four companions have not been included. On his left are the goddesses Ekajaṭā and Lhamo, but the two regular companions on the right are missing. Instead, one of the five dancing deities depicted along the bottom of the earlier *thanka* (no. 92) is placed across from Lhamo. He holds a skull cup and brandishes a chopper. The other four members of this group are painted along the bottom. At Mahākāla's right shoulder is a smaller menacing figure wearing what may be a shaman's or oracle's hat. A small second figure with a similar hat and holding a bowl is represented just below Lhamo's mule. Across from him at the other corner of the lotus is a small militant figure clad in armor and holding a sword. In between are a demonic male and a female who look at Mahākāla as they throw up their arms in ecstasy. Immediately above Mahākāla soars a *khyung* bird, who serves as the god's messenger. The remaining figures are a bearded ascetic with a skull cup in the top left corner and a monk in the other corner. The monk may be a Sakyapa.

While gold remains the principal color, the artist has used a variety of other pigments, though sparingly, to articulate the forms and enhance the painting's psychedelic effect. The gold has been applied in various densities: thin and wiry for all contours, thicker for ornaments, and solidly for the complexion of the lama. Other colors used are red, pink, blue, and white. The pericarp of the lotus has been covered with golden flowering lotus vines, a common motif in fifteenth-century Sakyapa paintings.

95

Two Mahāsiddhas *and Sakyapa Lineage*

CENTRAL TIBET, SAKYA ORDER, SIXTEENTH CENTURY

24 × 19 IN. (61 × 48.3 CM)

The two large figures in the center sharing a pedestal are very likely *mahāsiddhas*. They are surrounded by various other *mahāsiddhas*, buddhas, bodhisattvas, gods, Indian monks, and monks of the Sakyapa order. All the monks on the two sides and the figures in the top register are identified by inscriptions (see Appendix 2). The figures at the bottom of the *thanka* and four divine figures in the second row from the top are not identified, however. Following the animal-headed figure at the upper left corner are the *mahāsiddhas* Dombipā or Ḍombi Heruka riding a tiger and Virupā depicted as ransoming the sun (see no. 64). The fourth figure is Raktayamāri (see no. 85) in *yab-yum*, repeated in the clouds between the two main figures. It would thus appear that the lineage may relate to the transmission of the Raktayamāri teachings (see no. 85). Along the bottom the eight guardians of the directions (*Dikpālas*) can be readily identified because of their mounts. Rather curious are the white figure facing the officiating monk in the bottom register and the solitary figure in the row above on the left. Both are seen to emerge from flowers as is sometimes the

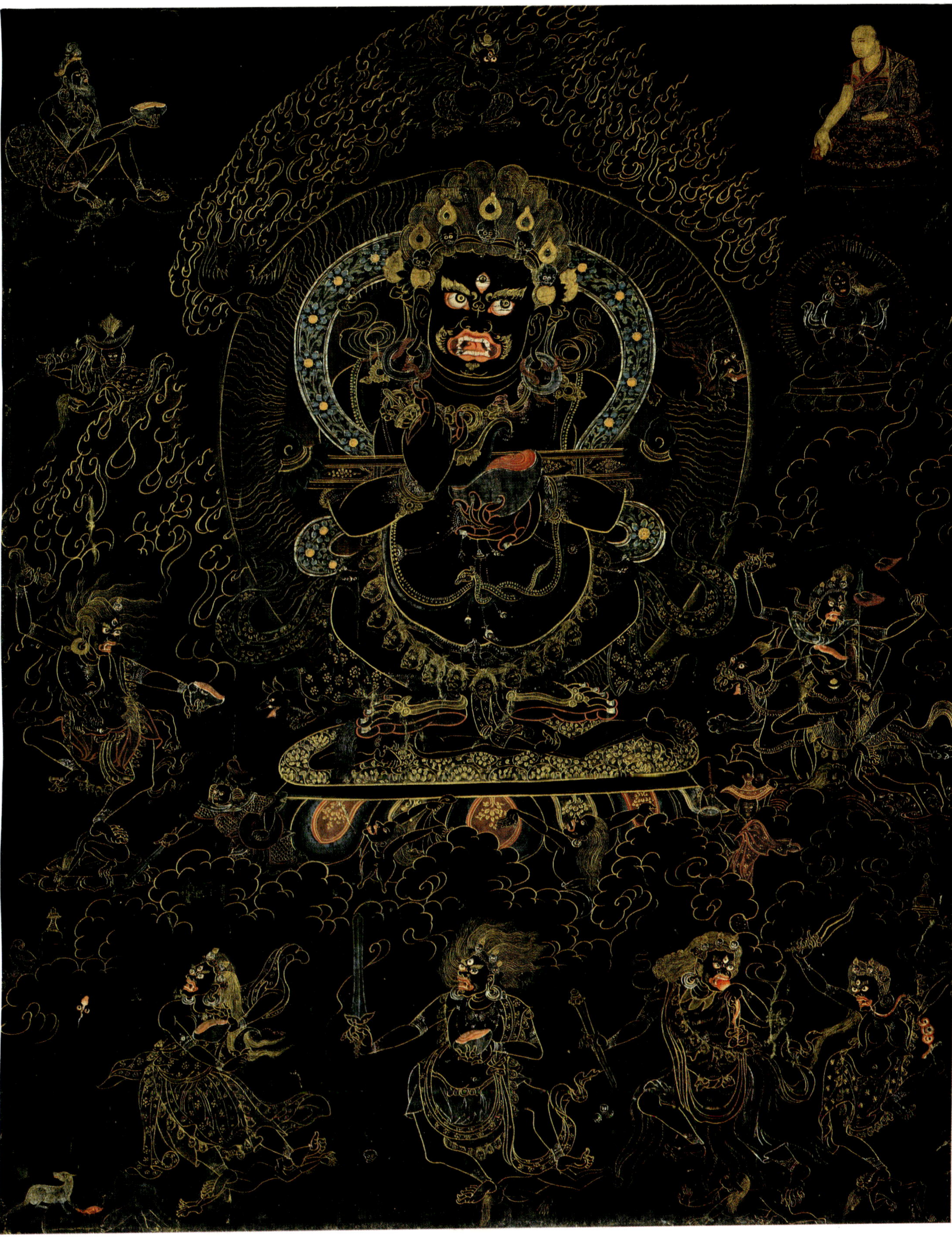

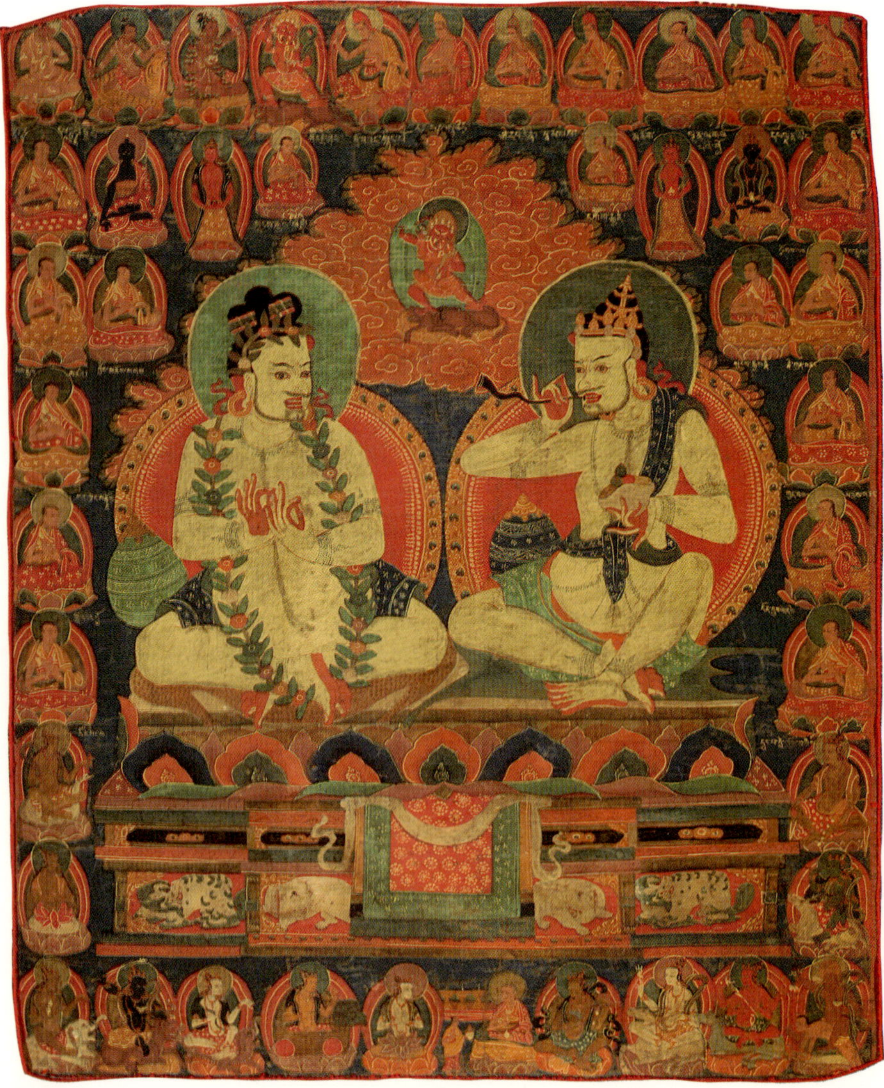

95

case in paradise representations.

Although no inscriptions identify the central figures, the one on the left can be recognized as Virupā by comparison with an inscribed bronze image of this *mahāsiddha* in the Los Angeles County Museum of Art (Pal 1990A, no. S34). There the *mahāsiddha* is seated in an identical posture with his legs loosely crossed at his ankles and making the same gesture with his hands. Furthermore his hair is tied in a similar topknot and, interestingly, around a manuscript. The manuscript is clearer in the painting than in the bronze. Another iconographic attribute common to both representations is the wreath or garland of flowers. This appears to be a distinctive feature of Virupā, as may be seen in the small effigy at the top of this *thanka* and in another representation (Lauf 1976B, pl. 83; Beguin 1977, no. 150).

It thus appears that there were two traditions of representing Virupā, both of which are included here. The more distinctive, of course, is the form in which he holds a cup of liquor in one hand and ransoms the sun in a tavern with the other. This is the Virupā who was a contemporary of the Pāla monarch Dharmapāla (ca. A.D. 770–ca. 810) and of Padmasambhava (see no. 60). There appear to have been two later teachers by the same name, one of whom taught Marpa, the guru of Milarepa. Could the preaching figure represent one of these later siddhas?

The second main figure on this *thanka* is more difficult to identify. There is little doubt, however, that it is the same as a horn-blowing *mahāsiddha* on a *thanka* in the Ford Collection identified by Lauf (1976B, p. 84, pl. 22) as Krishṇāchārya or Kānhapā. Lauf, however, gives no reason for his identification, and no known published iconographic tradition associates Kānhapā with an antelope horn. A horn-blowing *mahāsiddha* is included in a portrait of an identified lama in the Boston Museum of Fine Arts, while a similar ascetic figure, though without the horn, and Virupā are depicted in a painting of Raktayamāri in the same collection (Pal and Tseng n.d., nos. 29, 37). However, neither figure is included in the Zimmerman Raktayamāri mandala (no. 85). In any event, except for this tenuous connection with Raktayamāri rites, there seems to be no historical association between the two *mahāsiddhas*.

No other published *thanka* is known in which two *mahāsiddhas* are shown surrounded by so many monks of a single order. It is also rare to encounter them seated in this particular manner like confronted teachers in lineage *thankas* (see no. 87). Stylistically, this *thanka* is not as decorative as more typical Nepali examples favored well into the sixteenth century by the Sakyapas, nor does it reveal the penchant for landscape features one encounters in seventeenth-century and later lineage pictures. However, some typical central Tibetan features, such as the drawing of the cloud pattern, the garments, and the strongly Chinese design of the pedestal and lotus, indicate a date when the Sakyapa style was beginning to shed some of its Nepali characteristics and adopt motifs from other styles.

96

Mandala of Donkey-Headed Chakrasamvara

CENTRAL TIBET, SAKYA ORDER, SIXTEENTH CENTURY

22½ × 18½ IN. (57.2 × 47 CM)

This rare painting depicts the maṇḍala of a form of Chakrasamvara (see nos. 20, 41, 88) seldom encountered in art. The principal head of the central blue male is that of a donkey or mule (*khara*), and hence the form is characterized as Kharamukha or Donkey-Headed Chakrasamvara. (See Essen and Thingo 1989, vol. 1, no. 118, for another example.)

Several reasons are given for visualizing this form of Chakrasamvara. One is to cultivate detachment both from the god's anthropomorphic form and from one's own human body. Another is to gain the ability to fly, achieved through the realization that one's body is illusory. It is further believed that one of the perfections (*siddhi*) achieved is the ability to see "all the bodies that a person inhabited in his or her previous lives" (Huntington and Huntington 1990, no. 121).

In keeping with the rendering of the principal deity, some of the other figures of the mandala also have animal heads. The outer circle contains stereotyped representations of the eight cremation grounds. In the register at the top are deities and human teachers of the Sakyapa order involved in the transmission of this particular teaching. Along the bottom are various Dharmapālas and tutelary deities. Also included are the eight auspicious symbols of Buddhism. (See ibid. for a more detailed identification of the mandala.)

Especially noteworthy is the skillful juxtaposition of the eight prongs of a thunderbolt

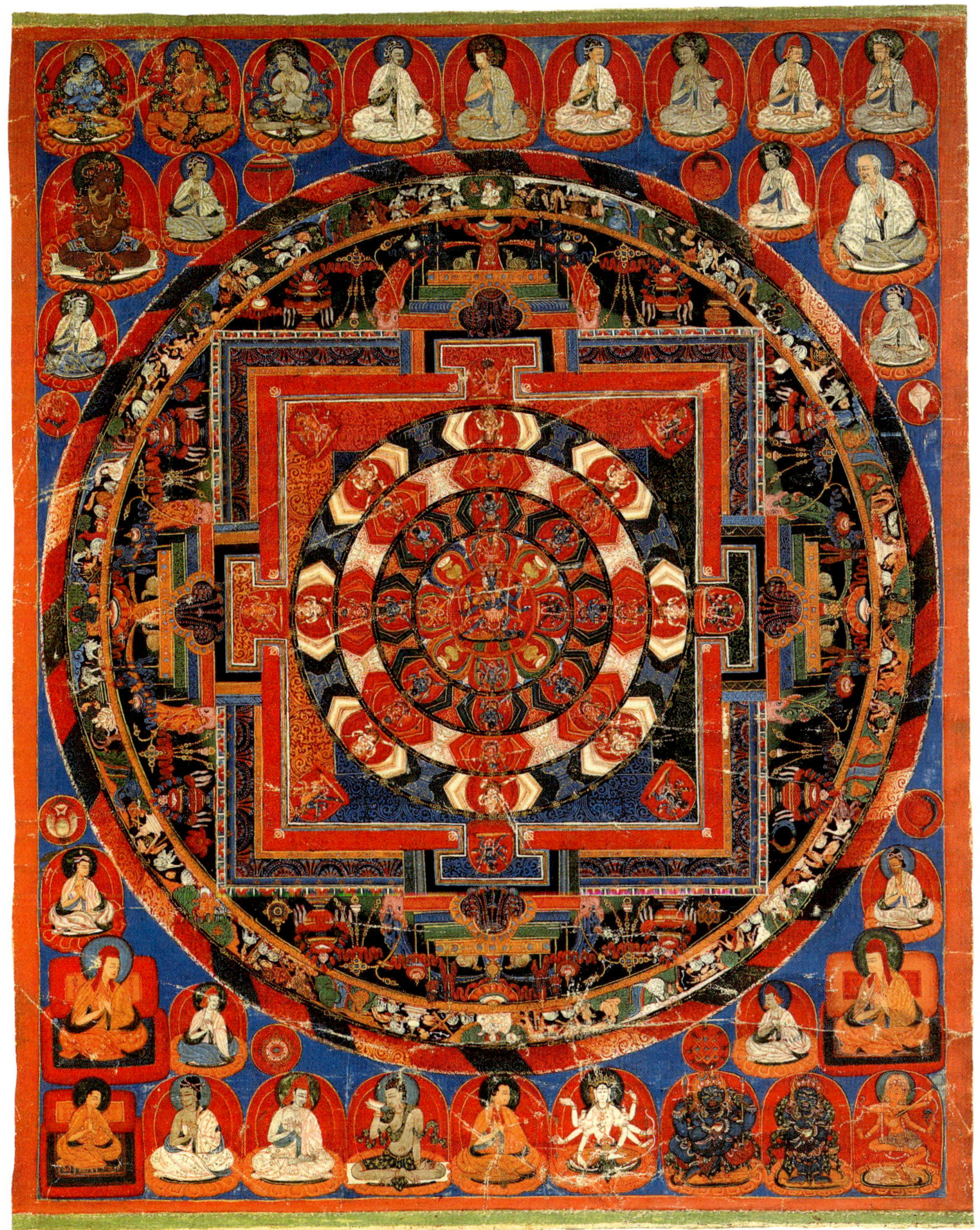

96

over the four inner circles of the mandala. Only the innermost circle is rendered as a lotus. The thunderbolt shapes not only add to the potency of the mandala but also make the design visually compelling. These diamond-shaped prongs have been painted in three different colors in the different circles, thus contributing to the rich variegation of the design. The scrolling pattern of the background and the various festoons, garlands, and banners adorning the walls and gateways of the celestial mansion are rendered with incredible finesse. Yet another unusual feature is the use of ground lapis lazuli for the brilliant blue, whose luster lends vibrancy to the other colors.

Literature Fisher 1974, no. 11.

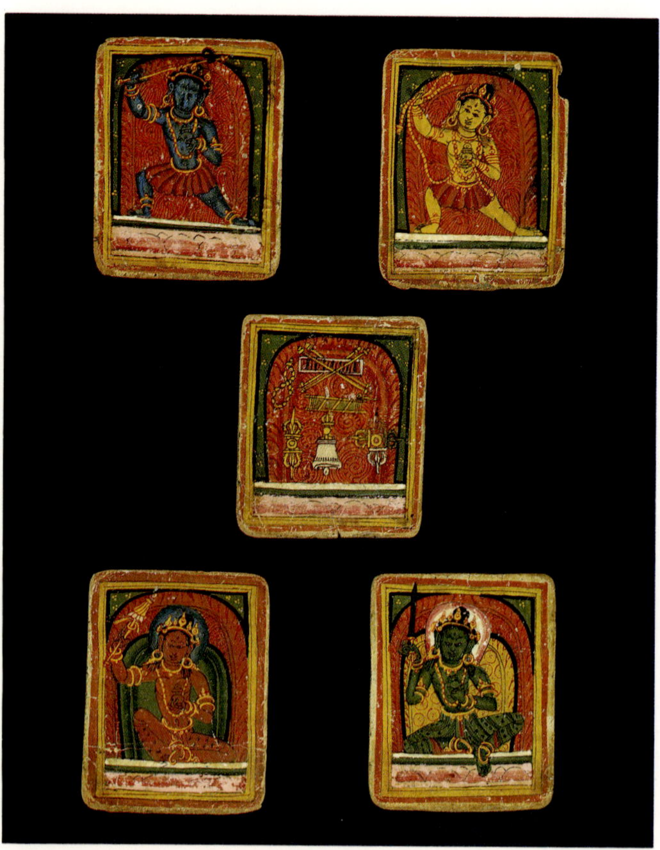

97

97

Five Initiation Cards

CENTRAL TIBET, SIXTEENTH CENTURY

EACH: 4⅜ × 3⅜ IN. (11.2 × 8.6 CM)

These *tsakalis*—small cards with images and symbols—are generally used by gurus or preceptors during initiation ceremonies (see no. 80). A lucid and extensive discussion of the use of *tsakalis* is given by Wayman (1973, pp. 56–59), who writes: "Naturally, the master cannot be expected to carry around with him those large tankas which hang in the temples. For the purposes of permission and initiation of the disciple, the miniature serves handily." Citing a Tibetan text that mentions *tsakalis* in connection with the initiation praxis, Wayman continues, "Here we find that on a platform in front, the performer arranges various offerings and adornments for the deity, including the tsa-ka-li." Penetrating deeper, Wayman demonstrates with passages from the Indian pundit Ānandagarbha that in yoga-tantra praxis the mantras are arranged in the mind while the *tsakalis* serve to arrange the body. For the initiate they function as a helpful "meditative prop." It should be noted that *tsakalis* are also used in ceremonies associated with the ritual recitation of the *Book of the Dead* (Lauf 1977, pl. 3).

The four deities represented in these finely detailed, colorful miniatures cannot be precisely identified. The two upper figures strike militant postures and aggressively brandish a staff and a rope. Although one appears to be male (blue) and the other female, both wear short skirts resembling ballet tutus. The other two figures, both female, are clad more decorously. The red figure holds a banner and the green one a sword. They could be embodiments of the emblems they hold. The card in the center depicts a regular thunderbolt, a bell, a universal thunderbolt (*viśvavajra*), a manuscript, and what appears to be a second manuscript on a book stand. The figures and emblems are placed on purple lotuses and surrounded with aureoles against a green background. The borders are in red and yellow.

The drawing is of very fine quality, and the details have been rendered meticulously. The representation is related to the fifteenth-century murals at Gyantse, where talented Tibetan artists, along with colleagues from China and Nepal, created an eclectic and distinctive style.

98

Arhat Chūḍāpanthaka

EASTERN OR CENTRAL TIBET, SIXTEENTH CENTURY

WITH SILK SURROUND: 58 × 31¾ IN. (147.3 × 80.8 CM)

The arhat represented here is Chūḍāpanthaka, also known as Chullapanthaka (Tibetan: Lamphran bstan). He is said to have lived in the thirty-third heaven and is usually shown seated in deep meditation. He does not always hold any personal attributes but is sometimes shown surrounded by the children of the gods who venerated and served him.

In this *thanka* there are no children, but an attendant dressed in Central Asian clothing carries a puppy in his arms, perhaps as an offering to the arhat. A second dog, of the same blue color, barks at the puppy. Both animals are of the Chinese fu-dog variety. The antics of the canines do not seem to disturb the meditating arhat, whose face is impassive. It is nevertheless the tender face of an elderly man rendered with great subtlety and in a characteristically Chinese naturalistic manner. Elaborately attired in Chinese-style robes, the arhat is seated on a carpet placed on a flat seat of blue-green rocks. Immediately behind him is a table, also formed from a boulder, supporting a vase with flowers, a lacquer box, and a metal incense burner. A twisted pine tree forms a parasol to provide him with shade, and behind him is a tranquil landscape of cascading waterfalls. A golden Buddha floats near the top of the mountains. Except for the liveliness of the two dogs, the landscape adds to the serene mood appropriate to the arhat's meditational practices. For a close stylistic parallel for this *thanka,* see Pal 1984, pl. 59.

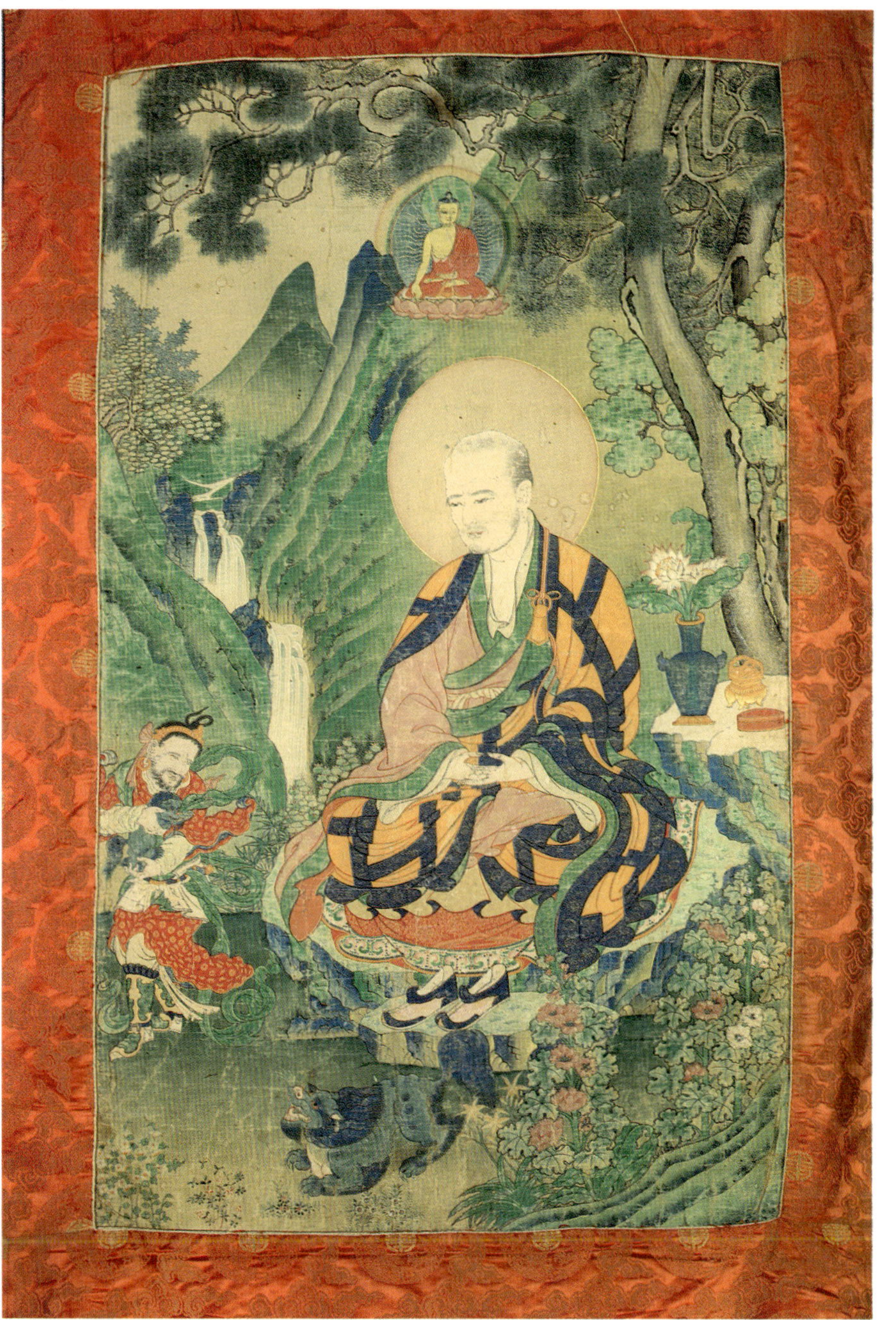

98

A comparison with the earlier arhat *thanka* in the Zimmerman Collection (no. 91) demonstrates how different this representation is stylistically. Whereas in the earlier example the figure of the arhat dominates the composition unnaturally by filling almost the entire surface, here he is of less imposing proportions and better integrated with his surroundings. In the earlier painting the natural forms and landscape elements remain subordinate, while here they are given greater emphasis and clearer definition. In coloring too the somber and subdued tonalities of the earlier style are here eschewed for bright, sparkling colors.

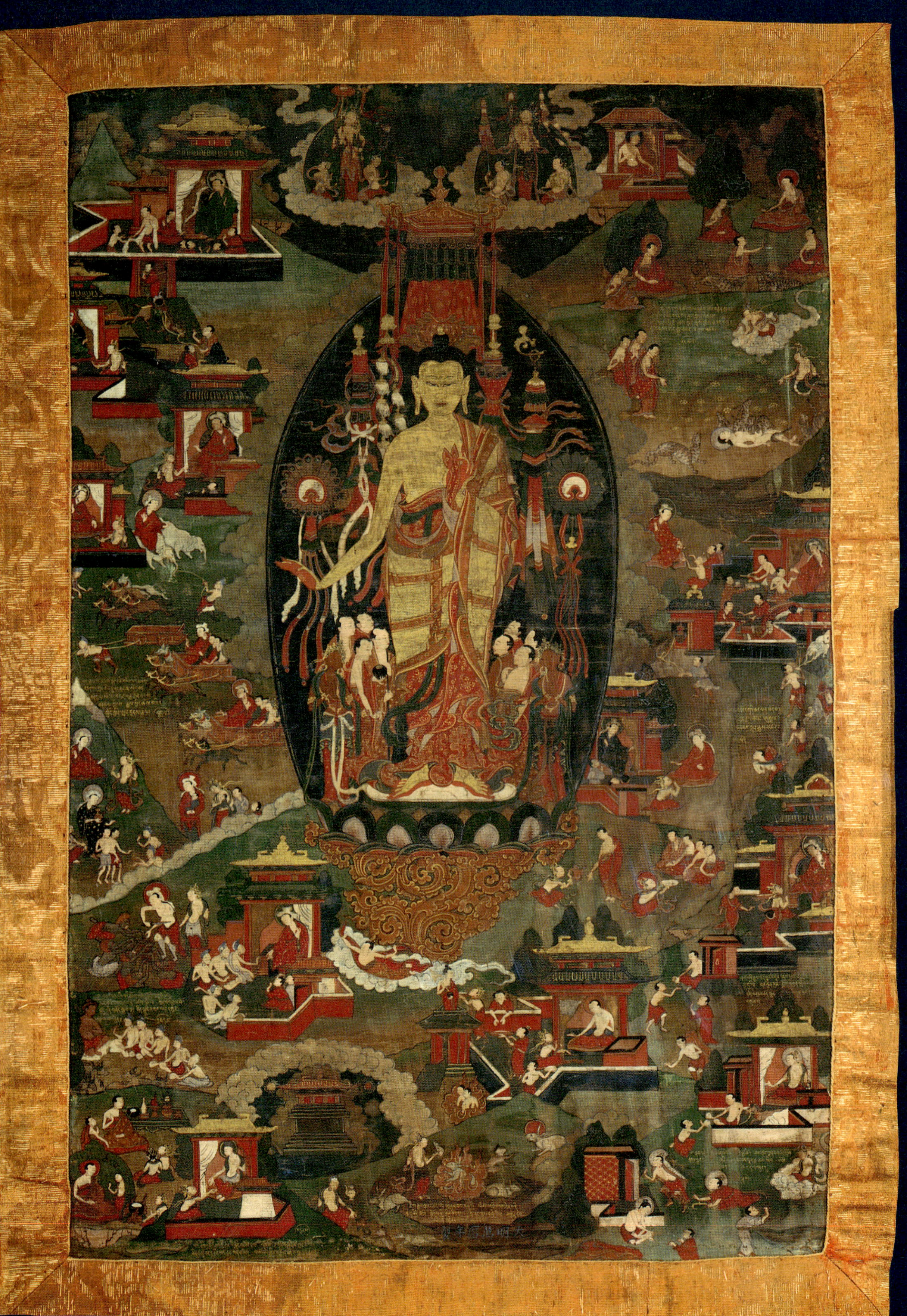

99

Buddha Śākyamuni with Jātaka Tales

CENTRAL OR EASTERN TIBET, 1573–1619

26½ × 18 IN. (67.3 × 45.7 CM)

This is one of the better-known and more important *thankas* in the Zimmerman Collection. It bears a Chinese inscription at the bottom center informing us that it was made in the reign of Wan Li of the Ming dynasty (see Appendix 2). Thus there can be no doubt that the *thanka* was painted sometime between 1573 and 1619. Whether it was executed in Tibet or for a Tibetan monastery in China is less easy to establish. That it was made for Tibetan rather than Chinese patrons is clear from the Tibetan inscriptions used to identify the scenes. Moreover there is a later painting in this style in the Victoria and Albert Museum, London, that was executed in the Ganden monastery (Beguin 1977, no. 272), making it highly probable that this *thanka* was painted in Tibet as well. The Zimmerman *thanka* may be compared to yet another *jātaka* painting in the British Museum, London, also made during the reign of Wan Li (Pal 1969, no. 15). Both size and style indicate that they may belong to the same series.

What is unusual about the Zimmerman *thanka* is the depiction of the Buddha Śākyamuni in the center. In most *jātaka* paintings, whether on *thankas* or monastic walls, the Buddha is shown seated. Here, however, he stands like a colossus, especially when compared to the eight monks and two bodhisattvas who huddle around him. Also unusual are the bracketlike, intricately designed form below the lotus and the abundance of banners and parasols above the Buddha's head. Of golden complexion, he is shown blessing his companions. Around the central tableau are represented various tales of the previous births of Śākyamuni, which are difficult to identify despite the long inscriptions (see Appendix 2).

The various stories unfold here in continuous narrative, one composition telescoping into another with complete disregard for time and space. Most of the figures are represented in architectural settings against a background of rolling green hills fringed with woolly clouds and with an occasional snowy summit added for effect, again with complete disregard for scale. This unnaturalistic treatment of relative size is particularly noticeable in the *jātakas* involving animals.

At the bottom center of the *thanka* is the well-known *Śaśajātaka* (Tale of the Hare), in which the Buddha, born as a hare, lived in the forest with a hermit. Noticing that the hermit was hungry with nothing available to eat, the hare asked his companion to light a fire. The hare then jumped into the fire so that the hermit would have roasted meat to relieve his hunger. In another composition at the upper right corner is depicted the tale of the hungry tigress. On that occasion the Buddha was born as a human being and encountered a tigress who was so starved that she was about to eat her cubs. The bodhisattva offered himself to the tigress, thereby saving the cubs. In both representations there is no attempt to represent the participants at natural size in relation to the human figures. However, in all the compositions the bodhisattva is generally distinguished by a nimbus, which may be seen behind the hare's head as well.

Literature Beguin 1977, no. 270; *Arts of Asia* (January 1984), p. 78; Pal 1984A, no. 132; 1984B, pp. 129–30, pl. 61; Beguin 1990, pp. 94–95.

100

Golden Buddha

WESTERN TIBET, GUGE, KAGYU ORDER, CA. 1650

31¼ × 26¾ IN. (79.5 × 68 CM)

The inscription informs us that this painting of the "Lord of Munis" was dedicated by Lobzang Dondrup. It is interesting that he begs the indulgence of scholars for any errors, even those made by the artist, because he was the cause for the painting. His representation in the lower-left-hand corner (see Appendix 2) suggests that he was a lama of the Kagyu order.

The expression "Lord of Munis" generally refers to the Buddha Śākyamuni, who usually holds a begging bowl in his left hand and makes the gesture of touching the earth with his right hand, symbolizing his enlightenment. His golden complexion indicates his transcendent and cosmic nature. He is seated on a lotus above an elaborate throne with a wonderfully designed arch formed by swirling tails of a *makara* which disappear into the mouth of the *khyung* bird at the summit.

On either side of the central figure stand two golden bodhisattvas, Maitreya at his right and Mañjuśrī at his left. The rest of the painting is filled with twenty-seven identical

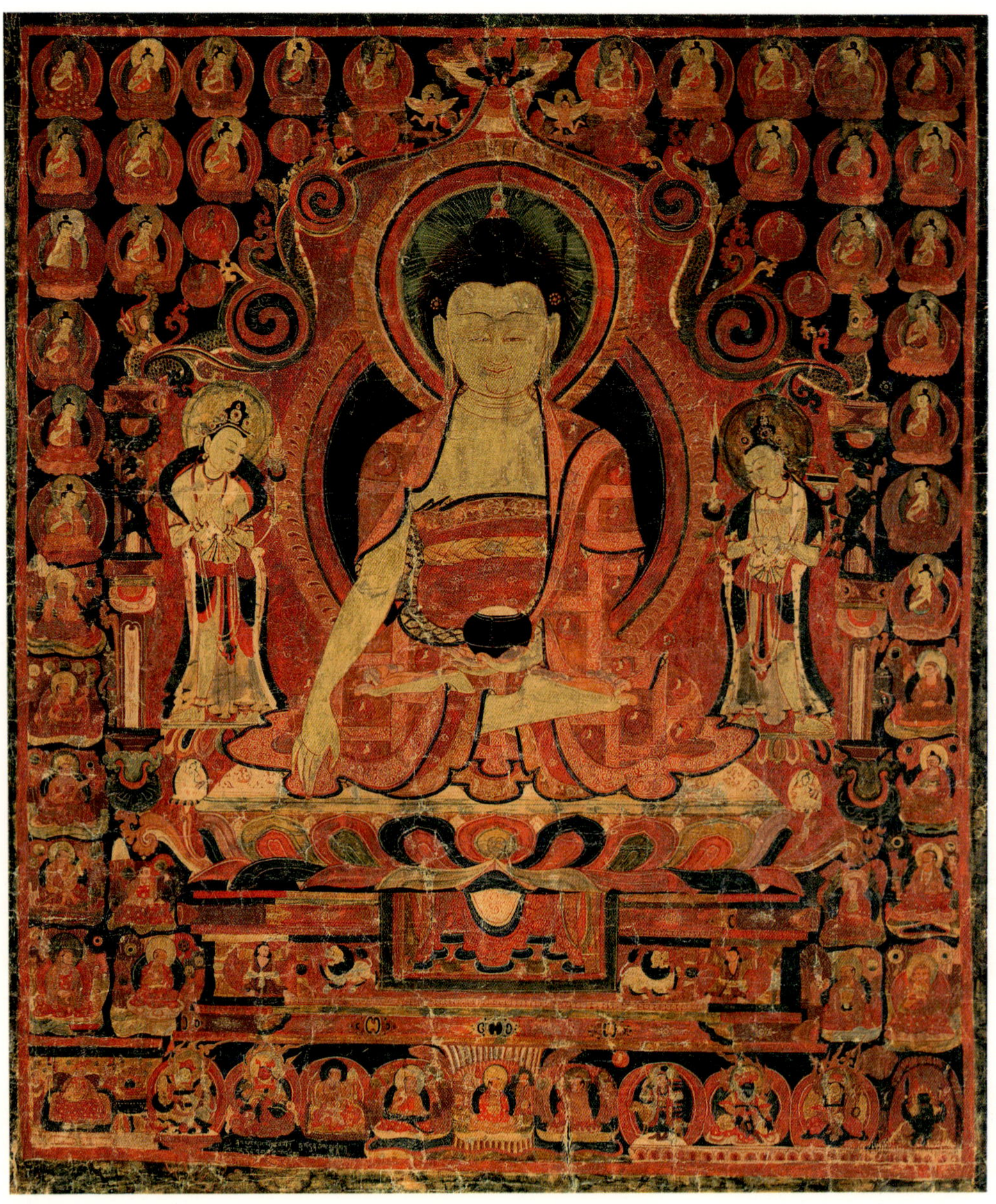

100

Buddha figures in the upper section and sixteen arhats in the lower section. The four kings of the quarters clad in Central Asian attire are included in the bottom register along with Mahākāla and the officiating lama. An interesting group of figures is accommodated in the center of the bottom register. Separated from the others by a low enclosure of yellow and red are three monks, each with a halo. The central monk is seated on a rocky platform and is surrounded by a few attendants. The other two are clearly oriented toward him.

Stylistically, this *thanka* is related to an early-seventeenth-century painting from Ladakh (Pal 1990A, no. P17) and to a representation of Sukhāvatī paradise from Guge dated by Huntington (1972, pl. XLIb) to around 1700. The Zimmerman *thanka* may well have been painted sometime around the middle of the seventeenth century. In most salient features these paintings differ from the fifteenth-century Guge style (see nos. 89, 90) but share formal characteristics with seventeenth-century central Tibetan styles.

Literature Reynolds 1986, pp. 176–78, fig. 12.

101

Buddha Śākyamuni with Jātaka *Tales*

CENTRAL OR EASTERN TIBET, 1650–1700

36 × 24 IN. (91.4 × 61 CM)

According to inscriptions (see Appendix 2), this is *thanka* number eight from a series representing stories of the Buddha's previous lives. The stories, probably from Āryasura's *Jātakamālā,* are numbered seventy-one to eighty and are described at length in inscriptions accommodated in the narrow red horizontal bands below the scenes. Thus these bands serve as dividers between the various compositions. This differs from the two other *thankas* in the Zimmerman Collection (nos. 99, 103) in which vignettes telescope into one another, making it difficult to determine where one episode ends and another begins. Although no vertical dividers have been used, each story unfolds against its own background with buildings and landscape elements, so that each is almost a separate miniature composition. As is customary in such narrative paintings, the middle of the *thanka* is occupied by the figure of the golden Śākyamuni seated on a lotus throne with a bowl filled with golden peaches (?), symbolizing longevity, in his hands. A tray of gems, like multihued gumballs, is placed against the lotus.

Space limitations do not allow us to identify all ten stories, but a couple will be identified, both involving elephants. At the upper-left corner is the story depicting the Buddha's birth as a king who owned a male elephant. Along with its trainer, the king set out on the elephant to hunt. However, on smelling the presence of a cow elephant, the male bolted, and the king and trainer saved themselves by clinging to some branches. When the king questioned the trainer's ability, the latter replied that he could train only the body and not the mind. When the elephant returned to the palace, the trainer had him lift an iron ball to demonstrate his skill. The king demanded to know who could train the mind and was told that only the Buddha had that power. The king then venerated the Buddha.

The second story is depicted at the bottom left. This time the elephant is golden, whereas in the previous tale he is white. The reason is clear, for in this story the elephant is the bodhisattva himself, and it was normal to represent the bodhisattva as a golden figure in these narratives. In this story, when the Buddha was born as an elephant, a king coveted the tusks. So he sent a hunter to kill the elephant and bring him the ivory. The hunter decided to wear a monk's robe and went after the animal with poisoned arrows. However, on seeing the hunter in monk's attire, the elephant willingly surrendered his tusks. This seems to be a variation of the well-known tale of the elephant with the six tusks (*Shadantajātaka*).

Although rendered in the same Karma gadri style as the other two related *thankas* in the collection (nos. 99, 103), the representation here is much more colorful. Vivid orange and gold predominate to make the painting vibrantly bright, but sufficient patches of blue and green help to make the warmer colors less overbearing. The representation is rich in architectural forms as well as in the diversity of the miniature compositions.

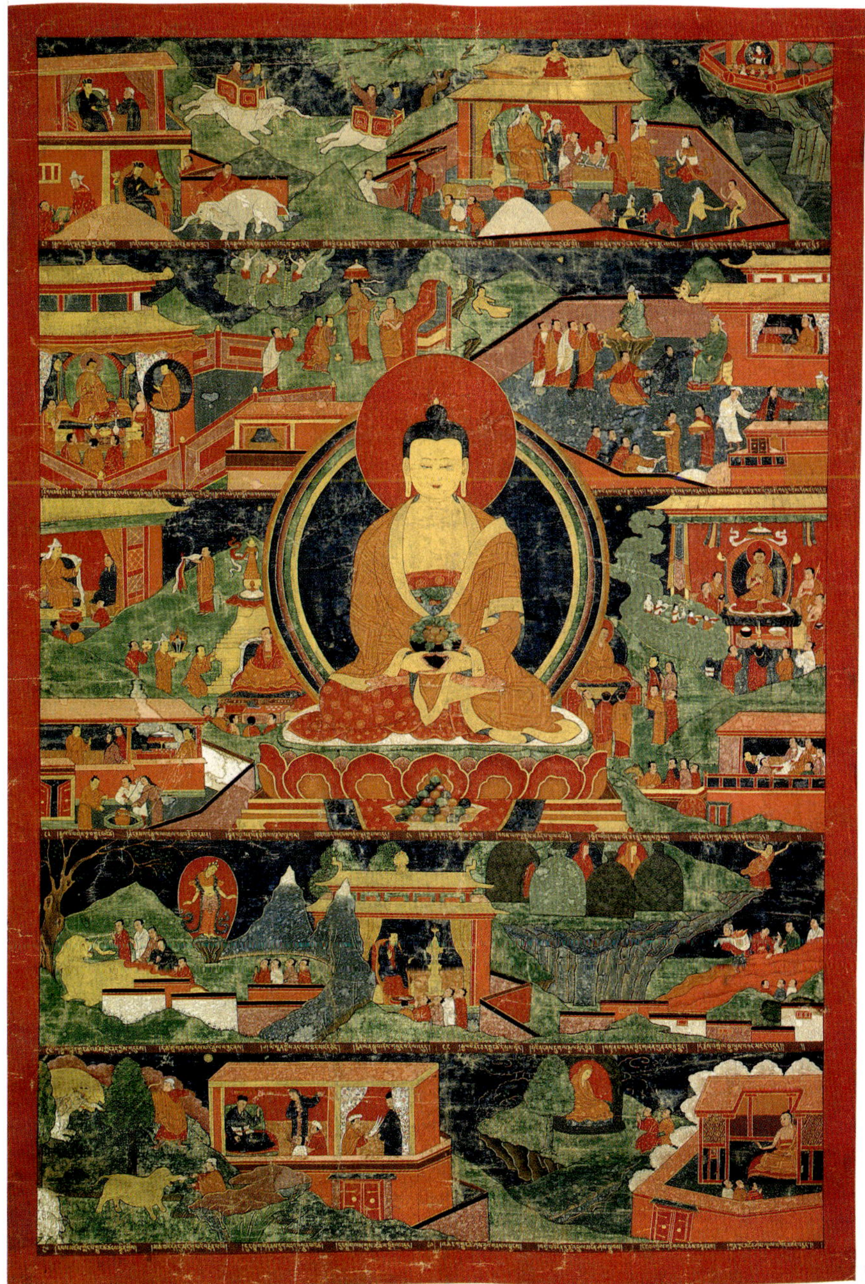

102

Deities of the Bardo

CENTRAL TIBET, SEVENTEENTH–EIGHTEENTH CENTURY

WITH SILK SURROUND: 45 × 44½ IN. (114.3 × 113 CM)

This highly energized, powerful painting portrays deities of the *Bardo*. A typically Tibetan concept, the *Bardo* is the world of the intermediate state through which the deceased wanders for forty-nine days before assuming a new existence in one of the six phenomenal worlds (see no. 113). The *Bardo* is described at great length in the *Book of the Dead,* probably the most familiar Tibetan literary work outside Tibet. During his wandering, "the consciousness of the deceased experiences, in a special (fine-substance) after-death body, the Karmic effects of his former spiritual deeds which now manifest themselves as light, sounds or deities" (Lauf 1976B, p. 149). Both the peaceful and the terrifying deities are apprehended in succession. However, with the help of the lama who reads the *Book of the Dead* for at least a fortnight after a person's demise, one can recognize that all visions of deities experienced in the *Bardo* are unreal reflections of one's own spirit. These visions of deities described vividly in the text were given powerful expression on *thankas* like this one by unknown artists. Such *thankas* were very likely used during the reading of the text.

This particular example is an unusually fine and expressive painting of some of the terrifying deities. All the figures are uniformly painted in gold, even though in the text they are given different colors. The central figures are the six Herukas, terrifying aspects of the five transcendental buddhas and of Ādi-Buddha Samantabhadra, the supreme deity in the *Bardo* pantheon. All six Herukas are similarly portrayed. Distinguished by their wings, they are shown in *yab-yum* with their female partners. Four of the six are depicted against the fiery field, while the remaining two are accommodated below the lotus. Surrounding the field are twenty deities with a group of fourteen at the two top corners and another group of twenty-two along the bottom. They form a very spirited retinue as they dance and prance in a wide variety of postures, brandishing various attributes. A number have animal heads. Very likely they constitute the various classes of *Bardo* mandala deities known as Kenrima, Phamema, and *ḍākinīs* (see Beguin 1977, no. 208, pl. 2; Lauf 1977). The fifty-six-member retinue on this *thanka* appears to fall short by two, for altogether there are supposed to be fifty-eight.

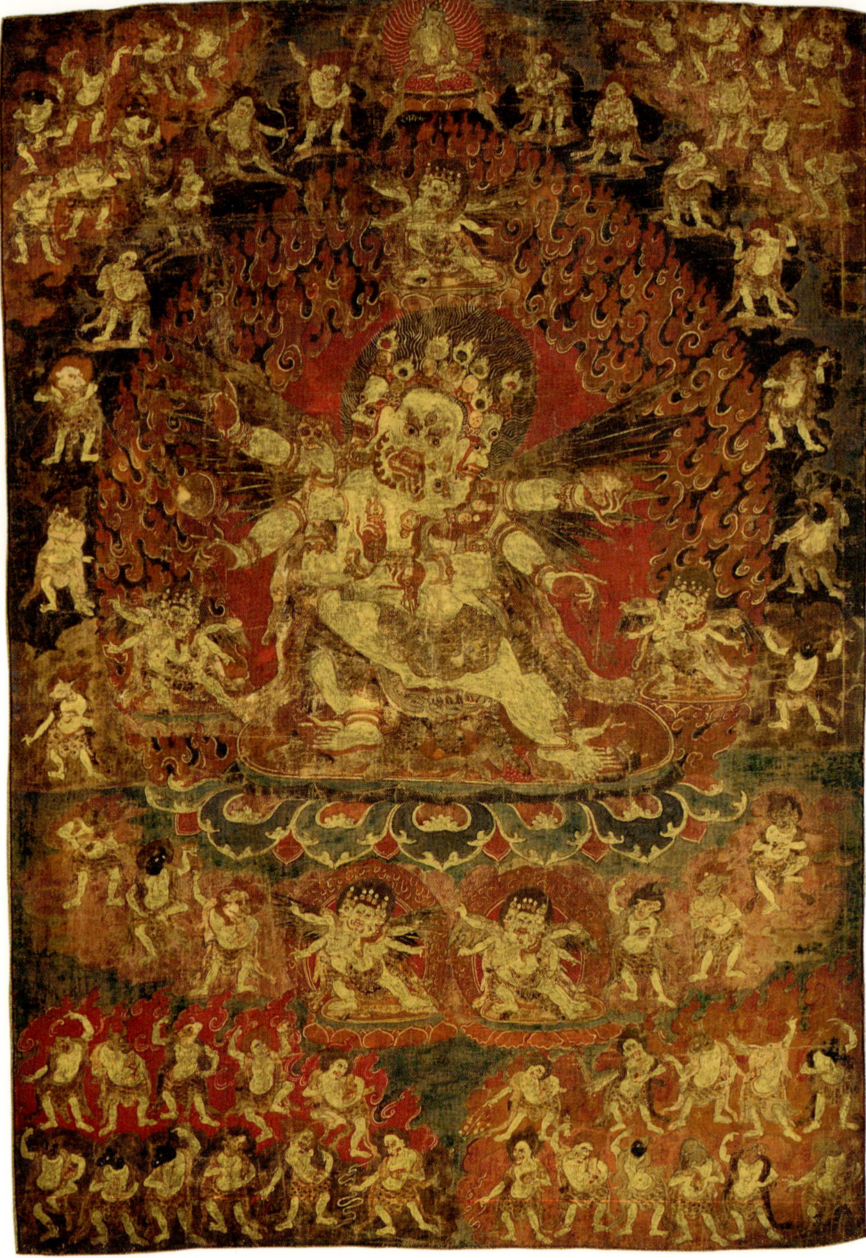

102

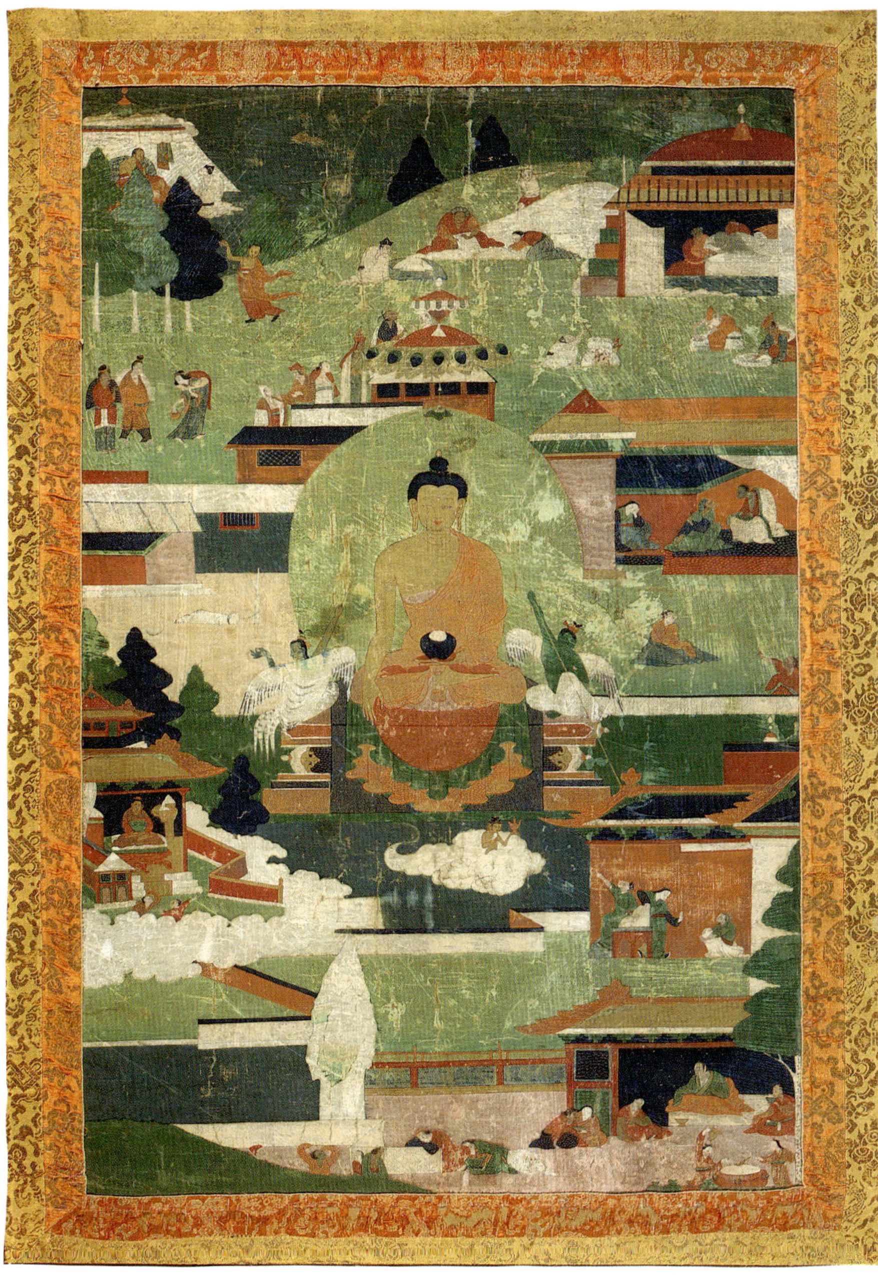

103

103

Buddha with Narrative Scenes

EASTERN TIBET (?), CA. 1700 OR EARLIER

37 × 26½ IN. (94.0 × 67.3 CM)

As there are no inscriptions, the story or stories depicted on this *thanka* are even less easy to identify than those on the two inscribed *thankas* in the Zimmerman Collection (nos. 99, 101). Since the central figure represents the Buddha Śākyamuni, very likely the *thanka* belongs to a *jātaka* or *avadāna* (other moralistic stories of legendary acts of the Buddha) series. The enthroned figure is golden, and his right hand makes the gesture of touching the earth while his left holds an alms bowl on his lap. More interesting are the two winged attendants on either side, whose exact function remains unknown. Both are spirited representations with large white wings. The figure at the right, a green male, appears to be holding a pole as if punting. The other figure, no doubt a female, appears to be clad in a costume and strikes a dancing posture. Most of the surrounding scenes take place within mansions or pavilions and perhaps depict only one or two stories.

The *thanka* was rendered in the same basic style as the other two narrative paintings (nos. 99, 101), but the coloring here is much softer and cooler and the compositions less crowded. The colors have a pastel tonality, with a strong emphasis on different shades of green. Although the figures are expressive, the scenes are less frenzied, and a sense of lyrical serenity pervades each composition. The style is closely comparable to that of a *jātaka* painting in the Musée Guimet, Paris (Pal 1969, no. 23).

104

Reincarnated Monk

CENTRAL TIBET, DRIGUNG KAGYU ORDER, SEVENTEENTH CENTURY

24½ × 18½ IN. (62.2 × 47 CM)

The central figure wearing red robes and a ceremonial hat and seated on a Chinese chair has been identified as a Chetsang Rinpoche of the Drigung Kagyu order (see Rhie and Thurman 1991, no. 87). A suborder of the Kagyu, the Drigung was founded by Jigten Sumgon (1143–1212). The Chetsang Rinpoches, the reincarnations of one of his disciples, are regarded as lamas of the highest status in the order.

The lama's hands form the conventional gestures of a Buddhist teacher, but his smiling face betrays individualistic features and character. One assumes that the artist was familiar with his subject. Moreover, the golden prints of hands and feet are probably his, and therefore the *thanka* may have been painted during his life-

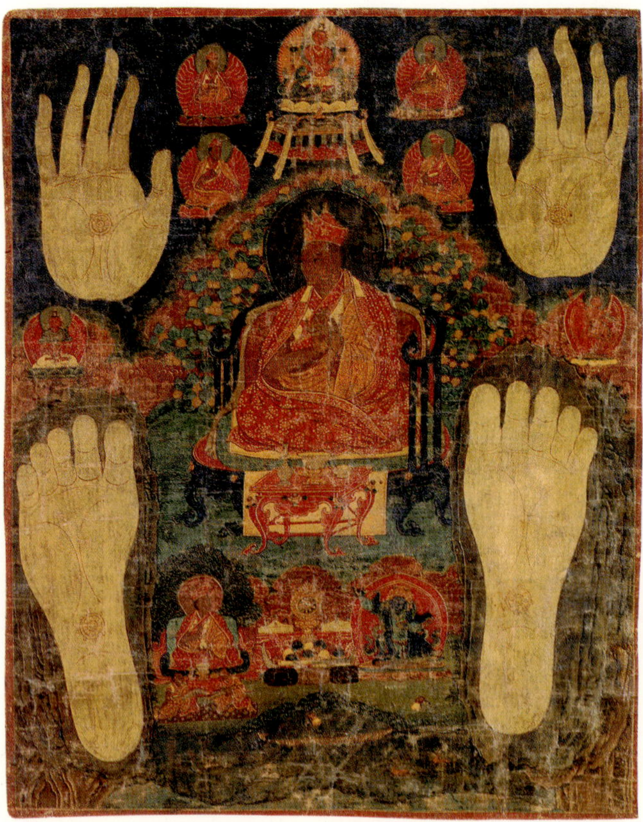

104

time. To indicate his Buddha nature, the auspicious wheel symbol has been added to the palms and soles. Usually, hand prints of venerable lamas who consecrate a *thanka* are added to the back (see Reynolds et al. 1986, no. P42). The cult of the Buddha's footprints is of course very ancient in India, but in Tibet one also finds examples (see no. 79) of the use of foot- and hand prints of eminent teachers both on the back and front of a *thanka* (Beguin 1977, no. 174; Pal 1984, pl. 12; Beguin 1990B, no. 2). The practice is not known in Nepali painting, although footprints of the yogi Gorakhnath are worshipped.

Immediately in front of the Chetsang Rinpoche is a red table, also of Chinese design, on which are a small waterpot, a cup, and a butter lamp. A fruit tree fringed with cloud patterns forms an aureole behind him. Below the table is a Kagyu monk at the left observing what may be an empowerment of the deity on the other side of the offerings in the center. The monk is aided by two other monks holding books. Two deities are represented on either side of the Chetsang Rinpoche between the feet and hands. The one on his right cannot be identified, but the other is almost certainly Vajravārāhī. Above him is an unidentified deity in the center flanked by four Kagyu lamas.

As is characteristic of Central Tibetan *thankas* of the period, the figures have been placed in a landscape setting of muted colors and subtle forms. The manner of superimposing the hands and feet on rocks is interesting and unusual. Altogether the visionary landscape, the large imprints, and the disproportionate figures, both realistic and idealized, contribute a surrealistic flavor to this unique painting.

105

Incarnations of Panchen Lamas

CENTRAL TIBET, NARTHANG MONASTERY, GELUK ORDER, 1700–50

26 × 16½ IN. (66 × 41.9 CM)

This *thanka* is from a series representing the successive incarnations of the head lama of the well-known Tashilunpo monastery near Shigaste. Known as the Panchen Lama and belonging to the Geluk order, he is considered second only to the Dalai Lama in the religious hierarchy of Tibet.

Although there are a number of figures, both human and divine, on the *thanka,* the two incarnated lamas are the two largest ones. That in the lower left is Yunton Dorje Pal (Gyung-ston rdo-rje dpal [1284–1365(?)]). A great authority on the Kālachakra-tantra, he is said to have meditated on the blue Yamāri and to have brought under control Gonpo Legden, a form of Mahākāla, and his retinue. On the *thanka* the venerable lama extends a skull cup with his left hand to the head of Mahākāla which emerges from a cloud of smoke. Note the expression of glee on the monk's face. Two other forms of Mahākāla are represented at the right, while three monks are seated in front. Above the incarnated monk's head is the *yab-yum* image of Raktayamāri (see no. 85). The large seated figure to his left represents Gos Lotsawa, the translator of the 'Gos clan of tanag, a great scholar, and the first disciple of Atīśa in Tsang. Appropriately, he is shown holding a manuscript and perhaps dictating to a scribe. Immediately above his head is his guru, Atīśa. The monk reading a book in the upper-left-hand corner is asso-

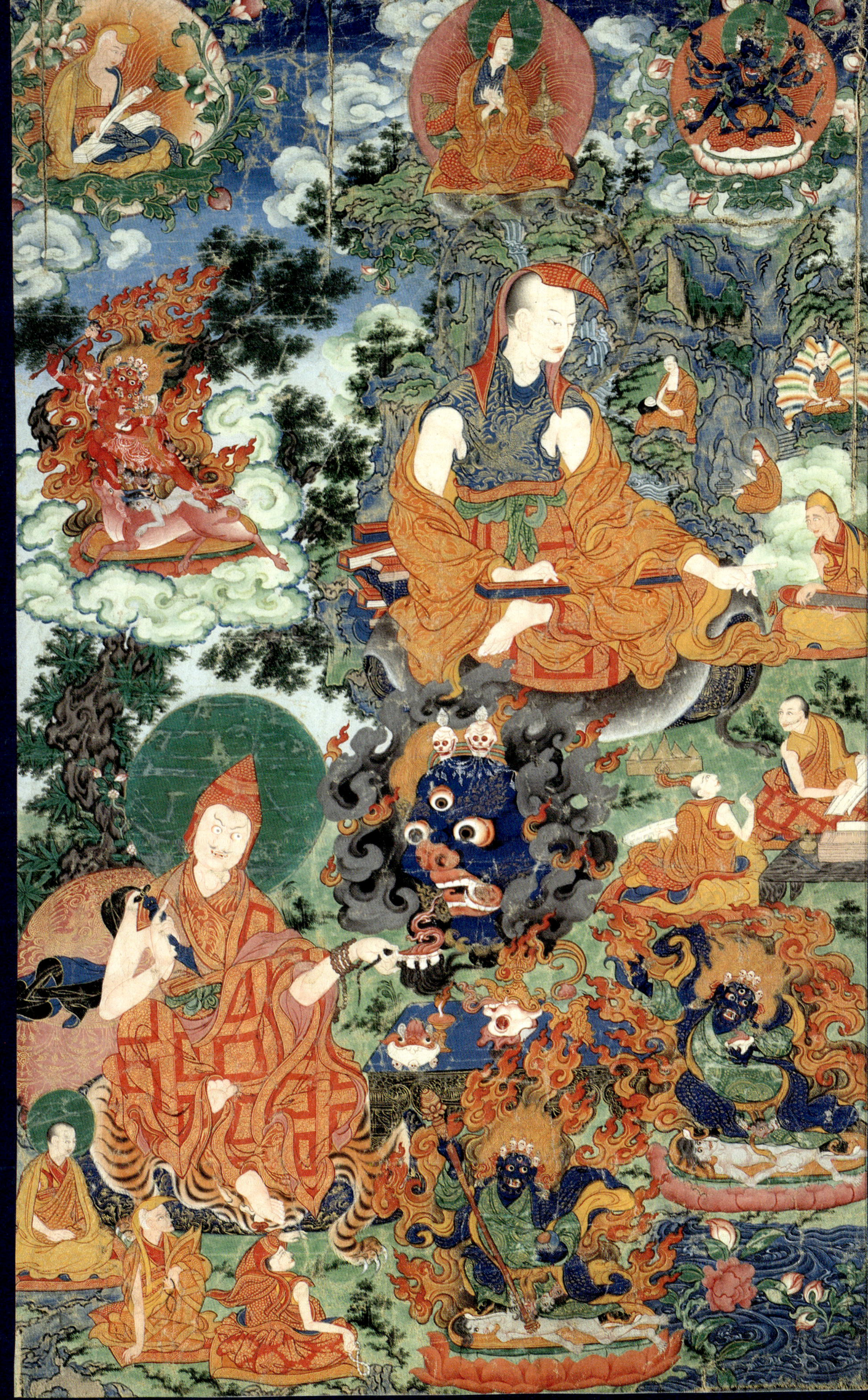

ciated with Yunton Dorje Pal's cycle, while at the opposite corner is Vajrasattva in *yab-yum*.

The *thanka* is stylistically related to the Narthang (a celebrated monastery of central Tibet) woodcuts of the incarnations of the Panchen lamas, now a familiar series in the West and made sometime between 1705 and 1737 (see Hackin 1928, pp. 145–49; Tucci 1949, pp. 410–17; Schmid 1961; Beguin 1990, pp. 106–16). That series, however, depicts one incarnation per *thanka,* whereas in the Zimmerman painting there are two principal lamas. There can be little doubt, nonetheless, that the same workshop was responsible for both series, and that they were rendered at about the same time.

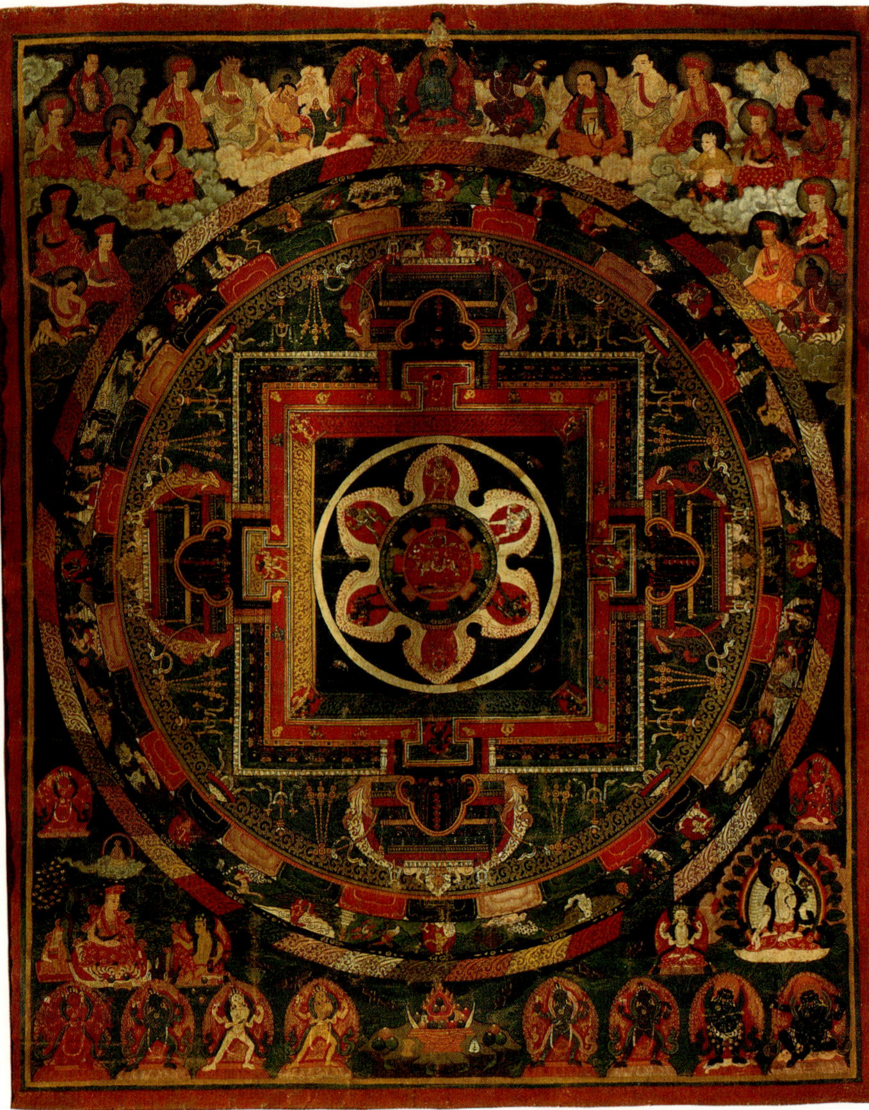

106

106

Mandala of a Red Deity

CENTRAL TIBET, KAGYU ORDER, EIGHTEENTH CENTURY

18¼ × 15 IN. (46.4 × 38.1 CM)

The figure in the center of the mandala is very likely a female, although she is iconographically akin to Chakrasamvara (see no. 88). Multiarmed, she strikes the same posture as that deity and tramples two figures. Like him she has four heads and twelve arms. Her red complexion would make her a form of Vajravārāhī or Nairātmyā (see no. 57), neither of whom is usually portrayed with multiple arms and standing in this fashion, however.

In the second circle are six differently hued but otherwise identical goddesses represented in the more conventional posture for these deities. Eight protectors of directions stand guard at the four gateways and four corners of the palace. Apart from the usual adornments of nets, bells, banners, garlands, and so on, the roof of each portal is embellished with a pair of white antelopes flanking the wheel of law, as is commonly seen on the rooftops of Tibetan temples and monasteries. As is customary, the narrow outer circle accommodates the eight lively cremation grounds.

Outside the mandala are two groups of figures consisting of monks, teachers, and deities. A host of gods and the officiating monk are represented in the lower section against a hilly background with some foliage. Among others, the deities include the White Tārā, two forms of Mahākāla, and a second group of six identical goddesses with different complexions. In the middle is an altar table with multihued gems and two elephant tusks. In the upper section all the figures are shown floating in the clouds against a blue sky. They include *mahāsiddhas,* Kagyupa lamas, Vajradhara, and the goddess Sarvabuddhaḍākinī (see no. 56). Above all of them and directly above Vajradhara is a tiny representation of Milarepa (see nos. 68, 110).

On these later mandala *thankas* and also on those of deities, the rigorous and severely geometrical configuration of earlier mandalas (see nos. 83–85) is relieved somewhat by placing the diagram in a rudimentary landscape setting.

Outside the mandala proper, hills, streams, and grassy knolls with shrubs have been added in the lower section and a blue sky with clouds in the upper one. The lineage figures and divinities too are presented in a less regimented fashion, forming a more lively group that floats in the sky. Very likely these stylistic modifications occurred sometime in the seventeenth century in Gelukpa monasteries in central Tibet.

107

Tsongkhapā with Myriad Tārās

TIBET, GELUK ORDER, EIGHTEENTH CENTURY

31½ × 24½ IN. (80 × 62.2 CM)

This *thanka* differs from the others of its type in that the background here is silver rather than gold. Also, except for the black outlines and hair, no color has been used. Hence this is, strictly speaking, a drawing rather than a painting. The tiny images of Tārā, like those of Amitāyus (see no. 108), omit no essential iconographic feature. Her right hand is extended in the gesture of charity, and her left holds a lotus flower.

Tsongkhapa is represented in his characteristic form, seated in the classic meditation posture on a lotus. His hands form the gesture of turning the wheel of law as they hold the stems of two lotus flowers. The flower at his right supports a sword and that at his left a book. These are the two major attributes of the Bodhisattva Mañjuśrī, whose emanation Tsongkhapa was. The great monk and reformer, born near the famous monastic establishment of Kumbum in northeastern Tibet, is credited with having composed over three hundred treatises. Besides being a learned scholar, he was a gifted teacher and charismatic personality.

The close association of Tsongkhapa with Tārā is not difficult to explain. As the heirs to the Kadam lineage, for whom Tārā was almost a patron deity, the Gelukpas became devoted to her. As a Tibetan scholar informs us, "The holy Tārā made a vow to preserve all the friends of the Kadam who followed after Atīśa. . . . Accordingly all the disciples of Atīśa and of the Conqueror Tsongk'apa took the holy Tārā as their highest deity, and prayed to her alone" (Beyer 1978, p. 14).

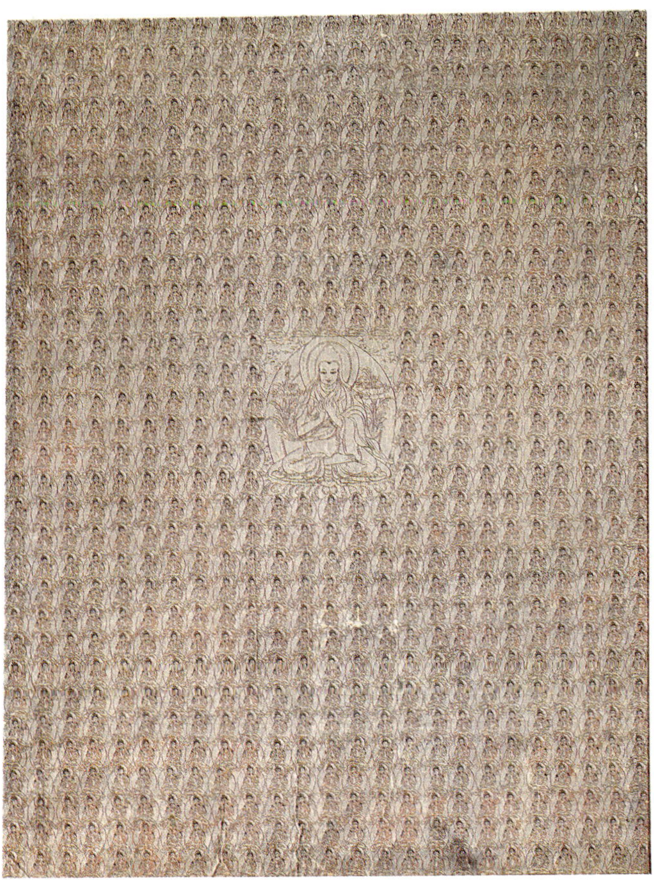

107

108

Myriad Amitāyus

CENTRAL TIBET, EIGHTEENTH CENTURY

36 × 24 IN. (91.4 × 61 CM)

All the figures on this gold *thanka* represent Amitāyus, the Buddha of infinite life. Also known as Amitābha (Infinite Light), and as Amida in Japan, Amitāyus has remained a popular figure in Tibetan Buddhism, even though representations of his western paradise are less familiar (see no. 90). This *thanka* shows a popular mode of representing the Buddha with a large central image surrounded by smaller ones symbolizing limitlessness. Painting such *thankas* is meritorious for both donor and artist, for the greater the number of images, the greater the accumulating merit. Specifically, Amitayus is invoked for a long life, and such *thankas* may have been consecrated during the observance of the appropriate rites of longevity associated with the Buddha.

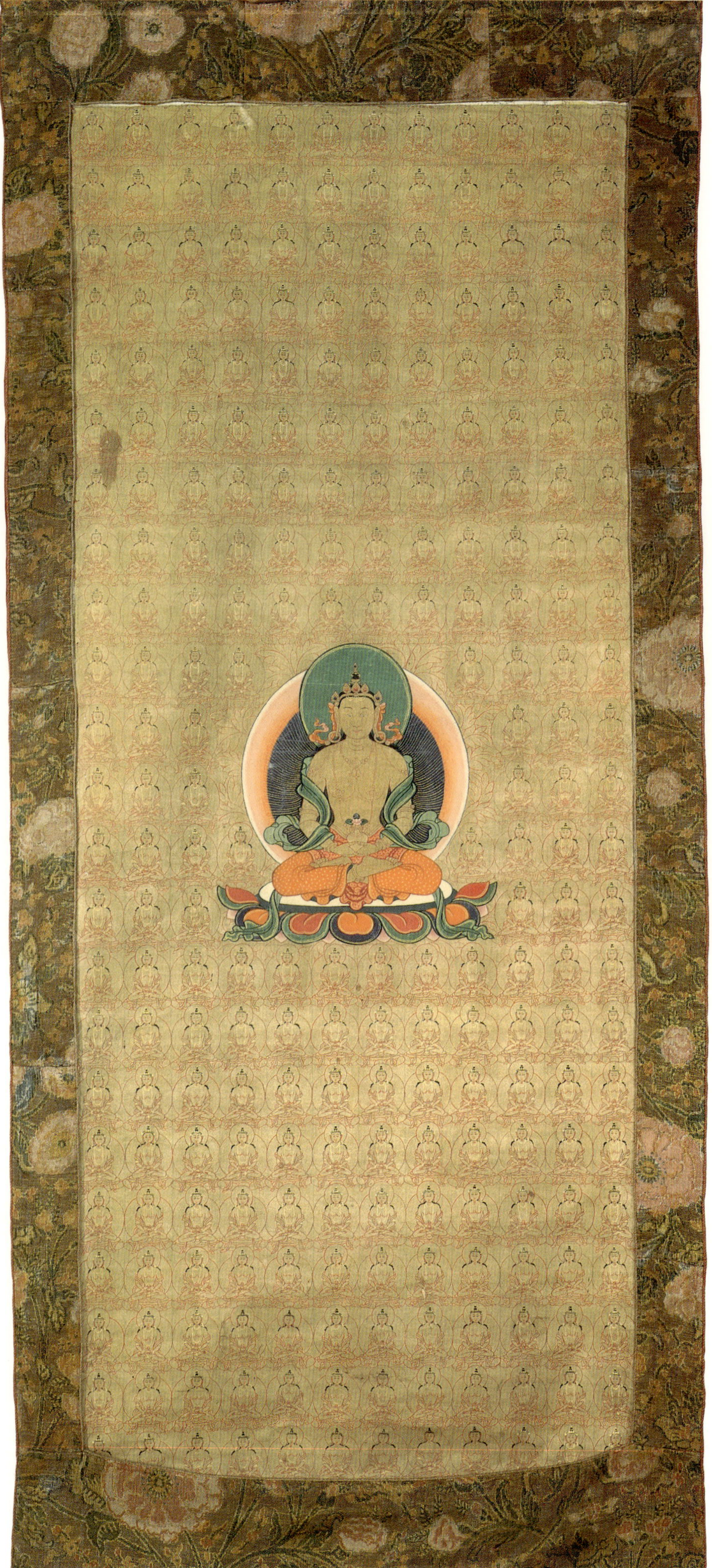

108

The large central figure of Amitāyus is fully painted. His complexion is golden, and he sits in the meditating posture on the white pericarp of a lotus, symbolizing the moon. The petals of the lotus are alternately painted red and orange within green borders. The Buddha's garment is bright orange, and he has a green scarf. His jewelry and tiara indicate that he is portrayed here in his *sambhogakāya* (body-of-enjoyment) form. In his lap rests the vase of immortality. His head is surrounded by a green halo and his body by an effulgent aureole of blue, orange, and white.

The same basic iconography is repeated for all his clones except that they are delineated only in red. The multiple miniature images are lightly drawn and serve as a background design to set off the brightly colored central figure. The drawing is so subtle and uniform that the design appears to be a printed pattern. The shape of the *thanka* is unusual in being exceptionally high in proportion to its width. It is mounted in its original Chinese brocade enframement. For a similar tall and narrow *gser-thang* painting in red with Vajrasattva and Tārā, see Lauf 1976, pl. 57.

109

Terrifying Deity

EASTERN TIBET, KAGYU ORDER, EIGHTEENTH CENTURY

WITH SILK SURROUND: 51 × 29½ IN. (129.5 × 74.9 CM)

This beautiful red-and-gold *thanka* depicts a terrifying deity whose exact identification remains unknown. His form is close to that of Yamāri, but the attributes are different. His right hand brandishes an ele-

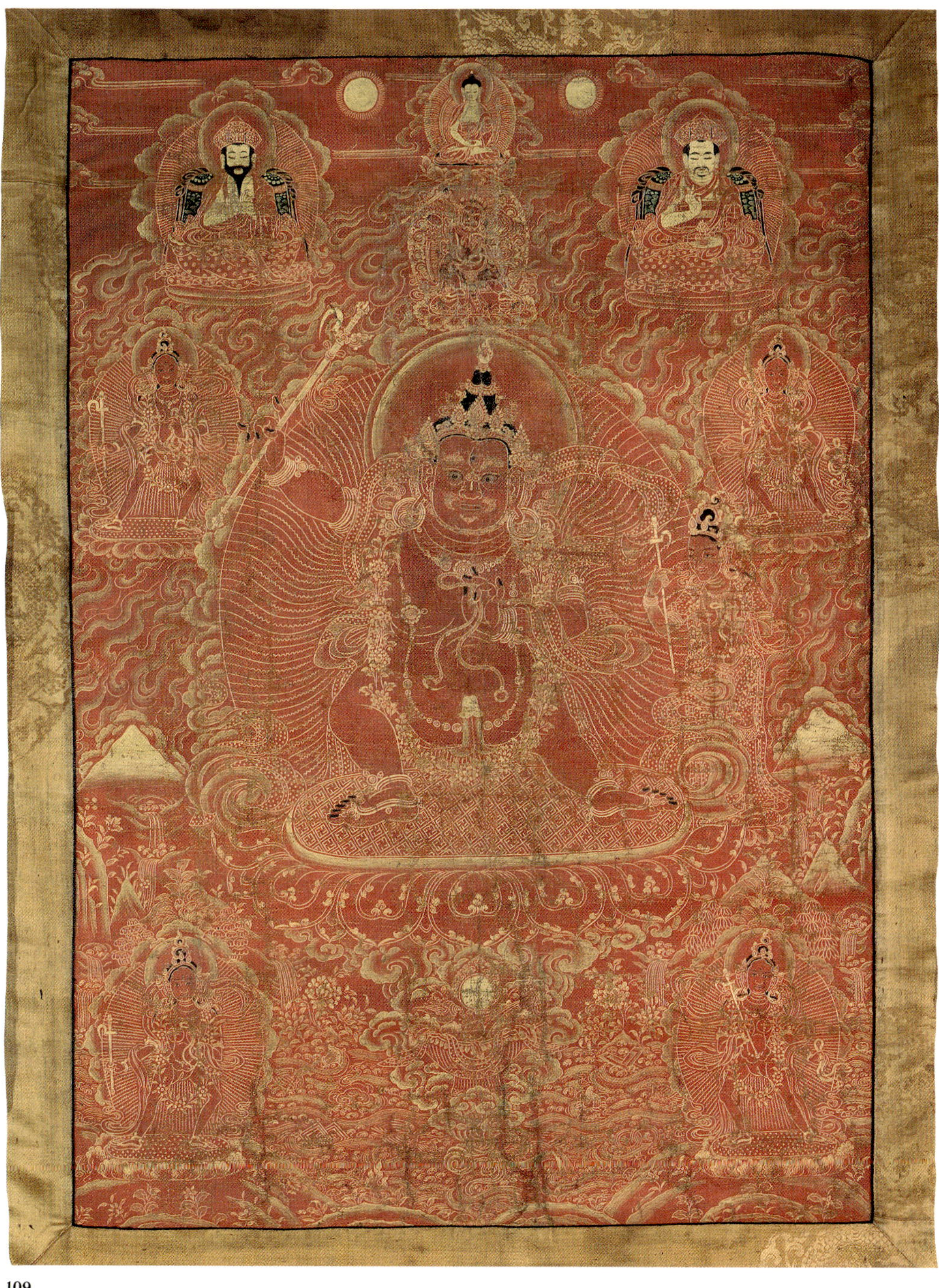

109

phant goad, while his left holds a rope as does Achala. Moreover, like Vajrabhairava (see no. 72) he has an erect penis. Another distinctive feature is the garland of flowers. Immediately to his left stands a goddess fully dressed in the Chinese manner and holding the same attributes. A smaller effigy of him is placed immediately above the main one. At the summit is a golden Buddha flanked by the sun and moon. On either side are two monks of the Kagyu order. Four identical naked goddesses, each holding an elephant goad in her right hand, make up the retinue of this unidentified deity. Although there is no buffalo, very likely the principal figure represents a form of Yama as Dharmarāja (or Chögyal).

Apart from the solar and lunar symbols, the sky is indicated by stylized representations of clouds. In the middle field rages a storm of fire. The lower section has hills and mountains with golden peaks, some vegetation, and an ocean or body of water in the middle in which a mirror can be recognized as an offering.

Other than gold, black is the only color used for the beard, hair, and throne backs of the two monks. In fact the latter almost look like epaulets on their shoulders. Fine brushwork and delicate drawing characterize the *thanka*.

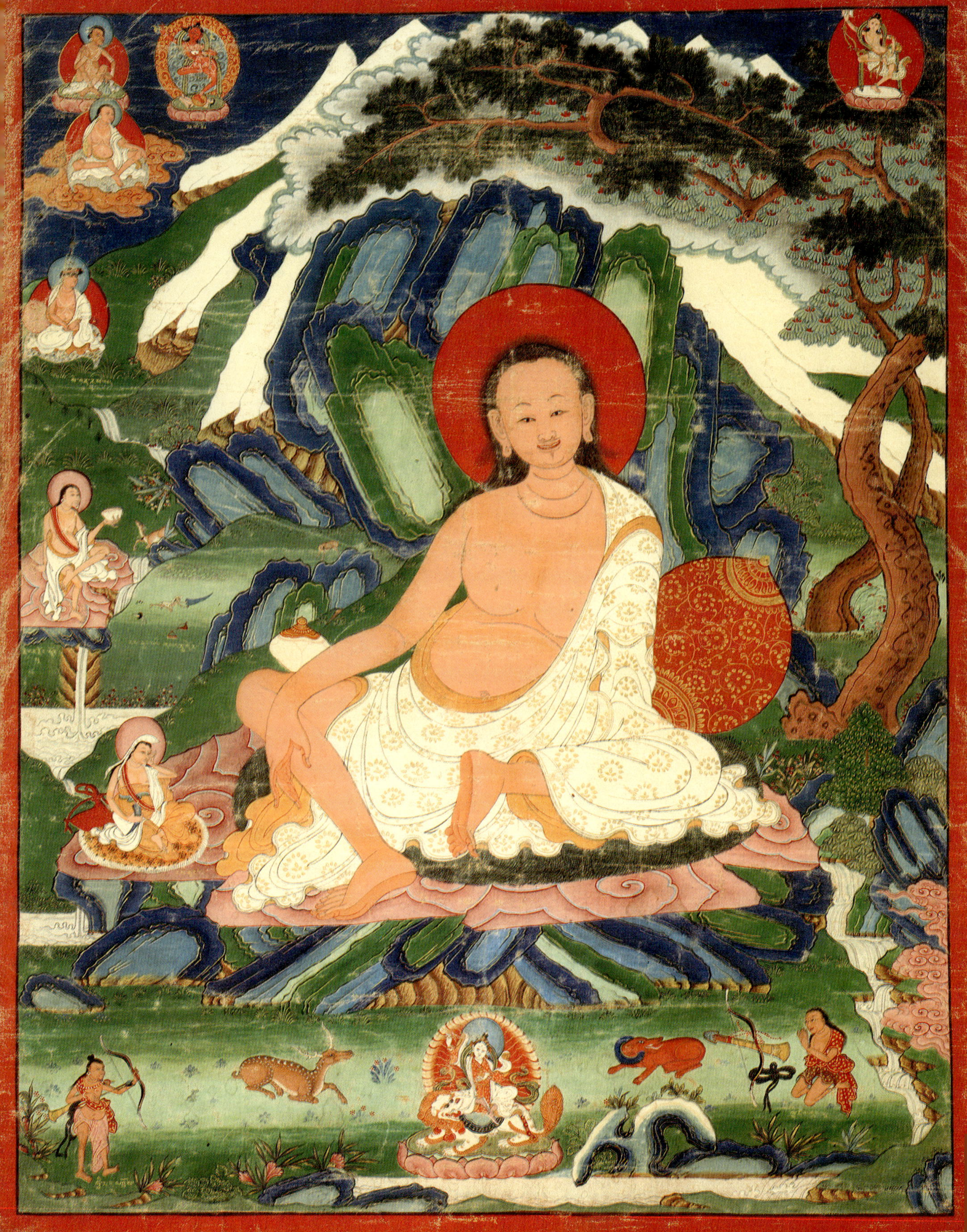

110

Milarepa in a Landscape

CENTRAL OR EASTERN TIBET, KAGYU ORDER, EIGHTEENTH CENTURY

24 × 21 IN. (61 × 53.3 CM)

This radiantly colorful *thanka* comes from a series of idealized representations belonging to the Kagyu order. According to Lauf (1976A, pp. 116–17), they can be specifically associated with the Talung monastery north of Lhasa, as several of the teachers portrayed belonged to that monastery. Talung belonged to the Kagyu order and was founded by Tashipal in 1180. The series obviously represents the Kagyu lineage associated with Talung. A comparison with the bronze image of Milarepa in the Zimmerman Collection (no. 68) makes the iconographic differences between the two representations clear. Here Milarepa does not cup his ear but lets his right hand hang over his thigh. He is seated on rocks with a rocky escarpment rising behind him. Branches of two pine trees form a canopy overhead. Beyond rise high mountains with snow-covered peaks.

Tiny inscriptions in gold help us identify all the figures represented on the *thanka*. These include (counterclockwise from upper left) the red Vajravārāhī and Phadampa or Dampa Sange, a great Indian tantric teacher who lived in the eleventh century, followed by four of Milarepa's disciples (see Appendix 2). At the bottom center is Tashi Tseringma, the goddess of auspicious long life, and at the upper right corner is Macig, one of the disciples of Phadampa and the most famous female mystic of Tibet.

Interesting as these idealized portraits are, even more fascinating are the two narrative scenes from the life of the poet-saint. In the middle left, above and to the right of the waterfall, is the scene in which Milarepa reduced himself in size to enter a yak horn to humble Rachungpa, who became one of his chief disciples. In fact the figure closest to Milarepa and seated on an animal skin is Rachungpa. The other story is depicted along the bottom in greater detail. Once when Milarepa was living in a secluded mountain retreat, a deer came before him chased by a hunter and his dog. The saint calmed the panting deer with a song. This had the same effect on the hunter and his canine friend. The converted hunter became Cirarepa, another famous disciple of Milarepa. At the left the hunter is seen taking aim at Milarepa, and on the right he throws down his arms and falls to his knees to salute the saint.

Whether rendered at Talung or somewhere in the Minyag district of eastern Tibet, as has been suggested by Beguin (1977, nos. 273–75; see Pal 1990A, no. P27), visually it remains a fine example of the rich landscape style that is so distinctly Tibetan.

111

Mandala of Symbols

CENTRAL TIBET, CA. 1800

24 × 18½ IN. (61 × 47 CM)

Neither the identification nor the symbolic significance of this expressive mandala is known. It appears to be represented within the flayed skin of a white figure seated on his haunches in a sea of pink fluids. The space immediately around the mandala is painted red, no doubt to indicate blood. The figure seems to be very much alive, flashing his teeth through his open mouth. The index fingers of both his hands point upward. The outer circle is filled with wavy, swirling forms in red and orange. This circle is accommodated within a blue isosceles triangle, along the bottom of which rests a bow with the string pointing up. At the summit, along the edge of the outer circle, is a second, smaller bow resting on its string. Beyond the triangle are leaping tongues of stylized flames in beige and gray against black.

The boundary wall of the mandala palace is densely packed with white bones, skulls, and skeletal fragments. The next surrounding wall is adorned with what appear to be entrails. Outside each gateway is an identical naked white male flanked by two other motifs, who are different in each case. At the top they are a rampant lion and a dog, but in the three other directions they appear to be flayed animal skins. The square courtyard is divided into four triangular segments and painted yellow, white, red, and green, as is usual in mandalas. Over this is the circle filled with stylized patterns in orange and red that may represent fluid or fire. Within is a triangle pointing upward and enclosing a smaller triangle pointing downward. The space between the two triangles is filled with a broad wavy pattern in mauve. The smaller triangle contains a festooned trident and another object within a skull cup against a black background.

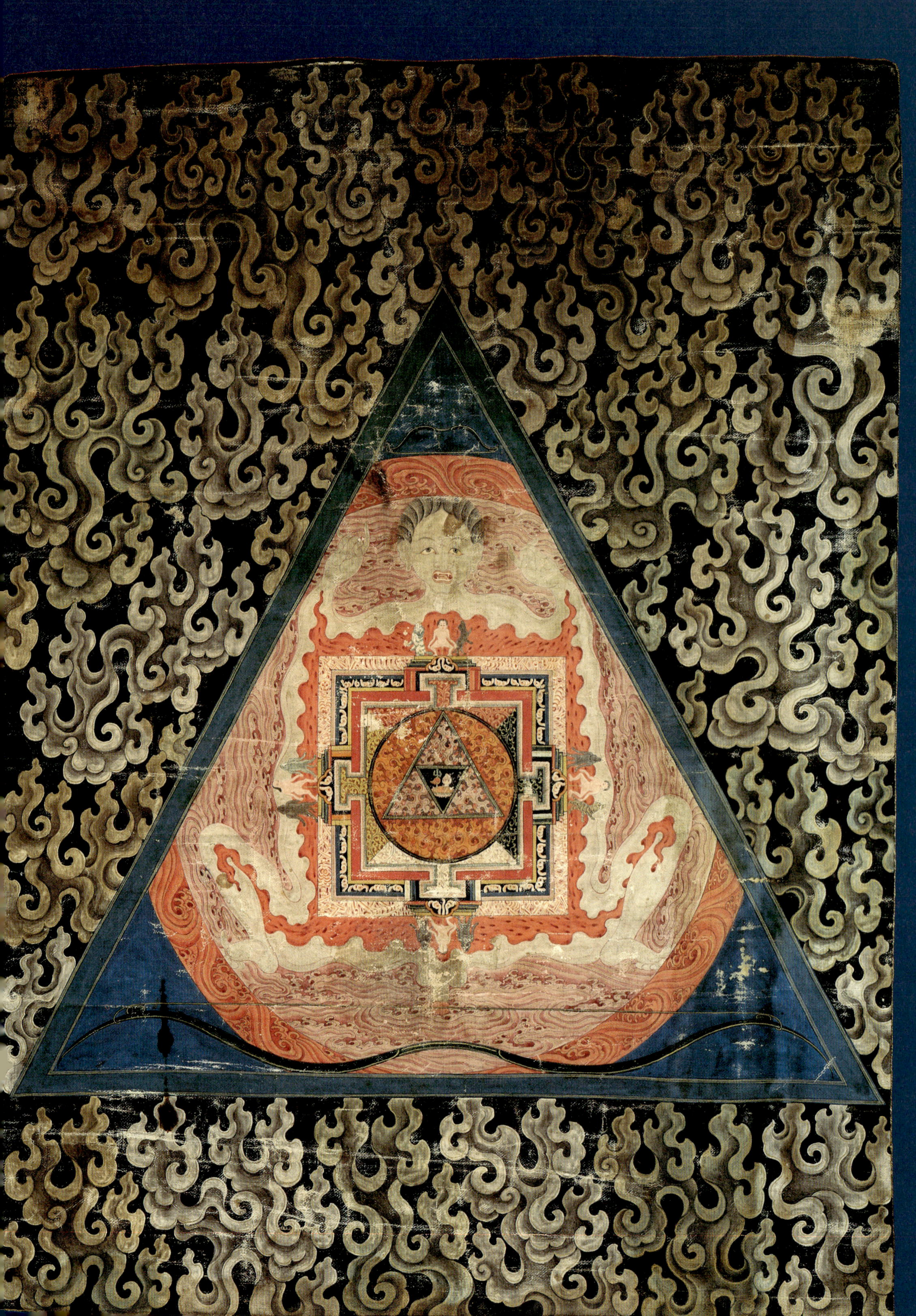

It is clear that the *thanka* literally and graphically demonstrates the interiorization of the mandala within the adept's body. However, nothing is known of the empowerment, the ritual, or the deity associated with the mandala. Whatever its symbolic significance, the form is visually compelling both for its highly imaginative composition and for the harmonious juxtaposition of the various shapes and patterns.

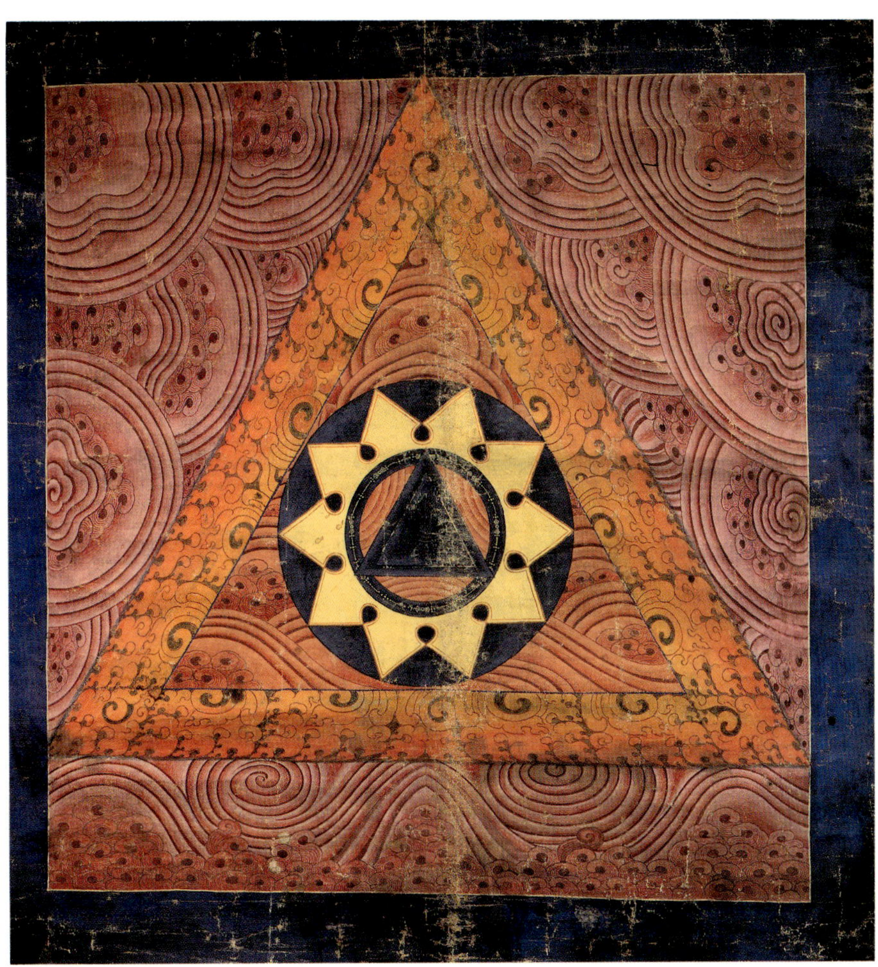

112

112

Mandala of Symbols

CENTRAL TIBET, CA. 1800

24½ × 23½ IN. (62.2 × 59.7 CM)

Unlike the other mandala with symbols in the Zimmerman Collection (no. 111), this example is square and nonfigurative. It is iconographically less complex but no less striking visually. The unknown artist has created an arresting abstract composition by brilliantly combining swelling convex forms with severely linear and angular geometric forms. Indeed the representation is so powerful that even to one uninitiated in Buddhist praxis the painting appears to be a source of cosmic energy.

Because of its square shape, the mandala can be viewed with the triangle pointing either upward or downward. Either way it may have something to do with the concept of Dharmodaya, usually shown as a triangle within a mandala. According to Wayman (1973, pp. 88–91), Dharmodaya is the "fecund source of all the natures of the world." A text cited by Wayman describes the triangular Dharmodaya as follows:

> In all the directional angles, the fire heap keeps on; within that, the diamond enclosure has the nature of the outer wall of the world (*mahācakravāla*) which is thick and compact. . . . The sort of *vajra* may be either five-pronged, three-pronged or a *viśva-vajra* (crossed thunderbolt); and if painted, is to be made accordingly. Our scholar holds that the circular line which encloses the *vajra* and the *padma* [lotus] symbolizes Dharmodaya.

In the center of this mandala is a blue triangle (see no. 111), within which is a faintly visible upright thunderbolt. The triangle is enclosed by a blue circle, the intervening space being filled with red and orange curved lines. The circle is surrounded by a yellow ten-pointed star, each point shaped like an arrowhead or the prong of a thunderbolt. This geometrical form may also represent a lotus. In any event the ten points probably symbolize the ten directions, thereby reiterating the cosmic symbolism of the mandala. The yellow star is placed within a blue circle enclosed in a triangle filled with stylized fluid motifs in pink and mauve. Then follows a triangular border with the conventional orange flame motif (the fire heap?). This triangle is surrounded by swelling shapes in two shades of purple that may symbolize a cosmic ocean.

It is also possible that both this and the preceding mandala (no. 112) had something to do with the initiation ceremonies in rites of the *Bardo*. Initiation cards with similar mandalas are used in *Bardo* rituals (see Lauf 1977, pl. 3).

113

Wheel of Life

EASTERN TIBET, CA. 1800

54 × 42 IN. (137.2 × 106.7 CM)

Of all the themes that one encounters in Tibetan painting, the wheel of life is one of the most distinctive. Although the conceptual basis goes back to ancient Buddhist teachings in India, the representation itself is quintessentially Tibetan. There is no evidence that such representations were familiar in India, even though the Tibetan title for such paintings, *srid-pa'i 'khor-lo,* is a translation of the Sanskrit *bhavachakra,* meaning both "wheel of life" and "existence." In Tibet the wheel of life may be painted directly on the wall of a monastery in a prominent place or on a *thanka* such as this hung for everyone to see. It is particularly important for the lay devotee to see it, as the paintings depict the six realms of existence from which one must be liberated and thereby freed from the chain of rebirth.

The Zimmerman wheel-of-life *thanka* is exceptionally interesting not only because of its subtle, almost pastel tones but also because of the clear delineation of its didactic and detailed content. Usually, such paintings are rather gaudy and less delicately rendered. The giant wheel caught in the grip of the red lord of death is represented here against a gentle landscape of snowy mountains, cascading waterfalls, and cotton-ball clouds floating in a light blue sky. A large white moon at the left and the standing figure of the Buddha Śākyamuni at the right share the firmament with the clouds.

Another important feature of this *thanka* is the plethora of gold inscriptions that identify the various scenes. Along the bottom is a long and interesting dedicatory inscription (see Appendix 2). Remaining anonymous, the donor wishes the light emanating from the painting to remove "the darkness of delusion for [all] living beings."

Along the outer circle of the wheel are the twelve oblong vignettes representing the twelve-fold causal nexus (*pratityasamudpāda*)—such as ignorance, consciousness, name, and form—that characterizes the phenomenal world, or *saṃsāra*. The wheel itself is cut like a pie into six uneven slices. These represent the six realms or worlds in which a sentient being can be reborn. At the top and bottom are the two largest segments representing the heavens of the gods and hells, respectively. The four narrower segments depict the realms of the titans (*asura*), tormented spirits (*preta*), humans, and animals. The circle in the center, common to all six worlds, encloses the symbols of the three poisons that cause the sorrowful cycle of rebirth. The poisons—desire, hatred, and ignorance—are symbolized by the rooster, the serpent, and the pig, respectively (see Lauf 1976, pp. 140–43).

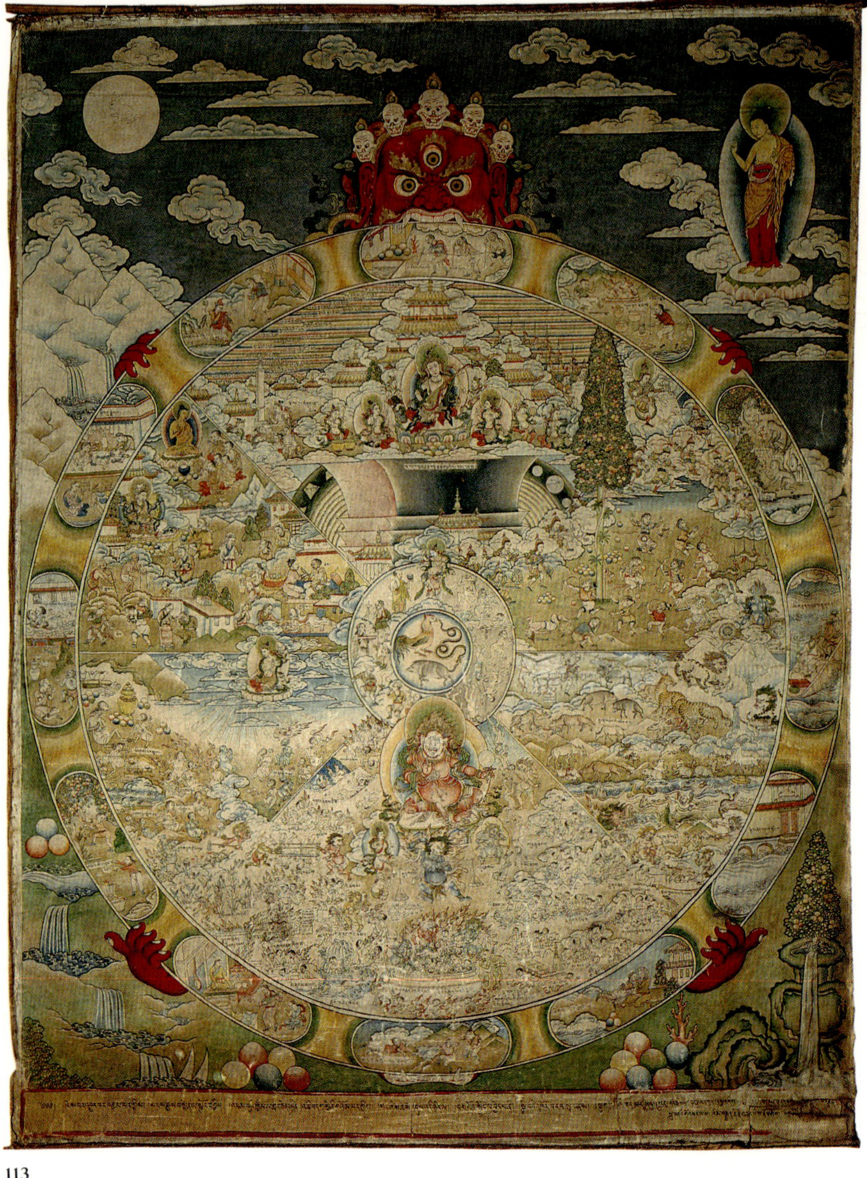

113

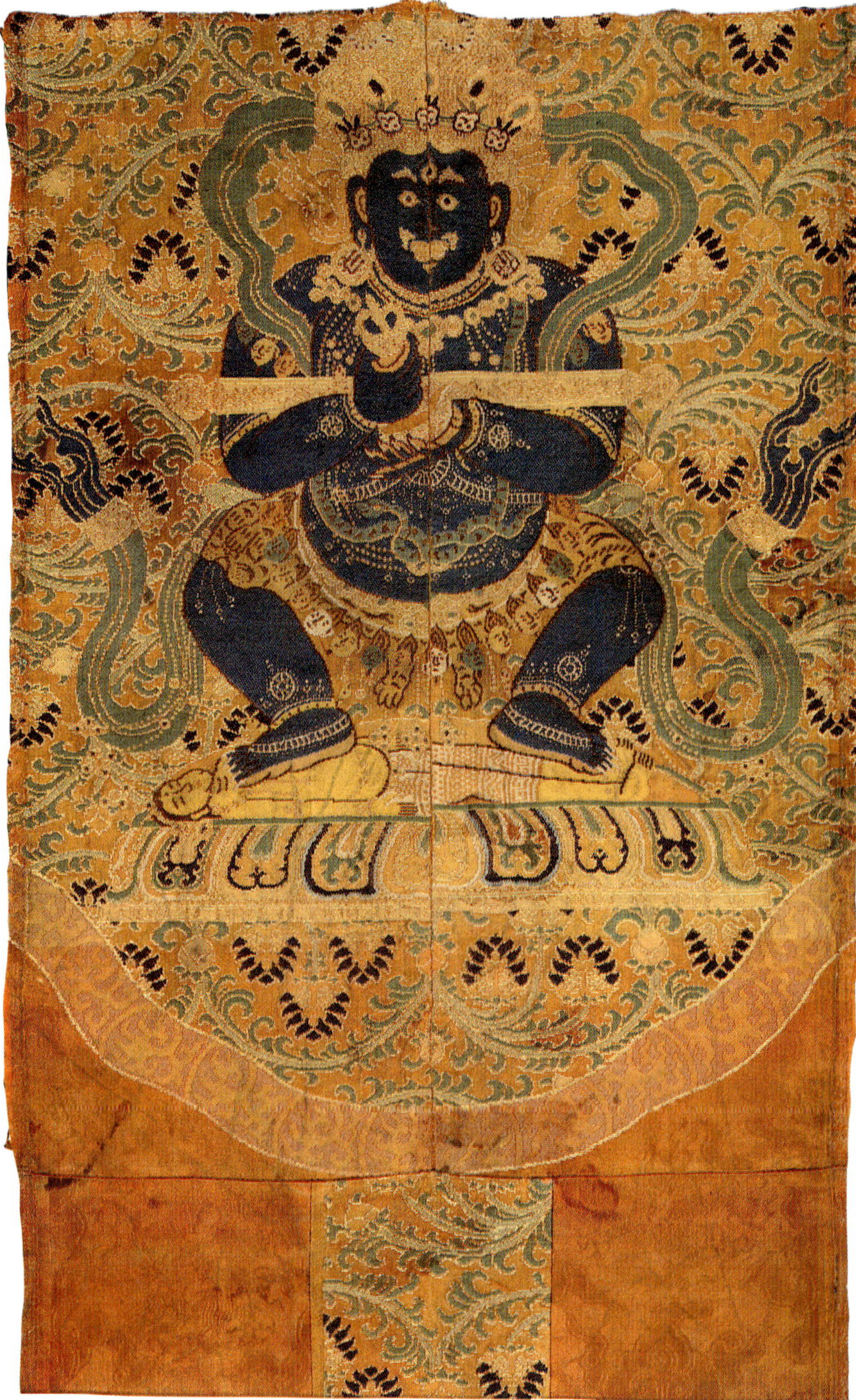

114

114

Mahākāla as Protector of the Tent

CHINA, AFTER TIBETAN ORIGINAL, FOURTEENTH–FIFTEENTH CENTURY

SILK AND GILT BROCADE

22¼ × 11½ IN. (56.5 × 29.2 CM)

The ponderous Mahākāla squats characteristically on a supine corpse. He holds a chopper and a skull cup, and his magic staff lies across his arms. Skulls adorn his flaming hair, and bone ornaments are at chest, stomach, arms, wrists, knees, and ankles. His fierce nature is further conveyed by the chain of severed heads, the tiger skin at his hips, and the snake entwined around his torso. This form of Mahākāla, known as Protector of the Tent, is frequently encountered in paintings and sketchbooks datable to the fifteenth century. Derived ultimately from India, he became one of the most important protector deities in Tibet. He was particularly popular with the Sakyapas, who introduced his cult to China during their close association with the Mongol court in the thirteenth century. Closely comparable to this image in fabric is a fine Sakyapa *thanka* in the Zimmerman Collection (no. 93).

It was doubtless such images of Mahākāla which were available as models for the brocade factories of Beijing (the upside-down skulls in the crown are the copyist's only mistake). The Zimmerman textile is obviously a fragment of a larger piece. This fragment has been cut down at the top and sides and pieced at the bottom from sections of the polychrome lotus scroll and damask fields that form the background of the image. The scalloped vine-scroll band below the figure may indicate that the original brocade was formed of lappets, perhaps each enclosing a different deity, in a horizontal row (Beguin et al. 1977, no. 295). The center seam, joining the two halves of Mahākāla's body, retains both selvedges and indicates the original manner of constructing the banner. Probably in Tibet, the banner was cut and resewn into its present vertical format. V.R.

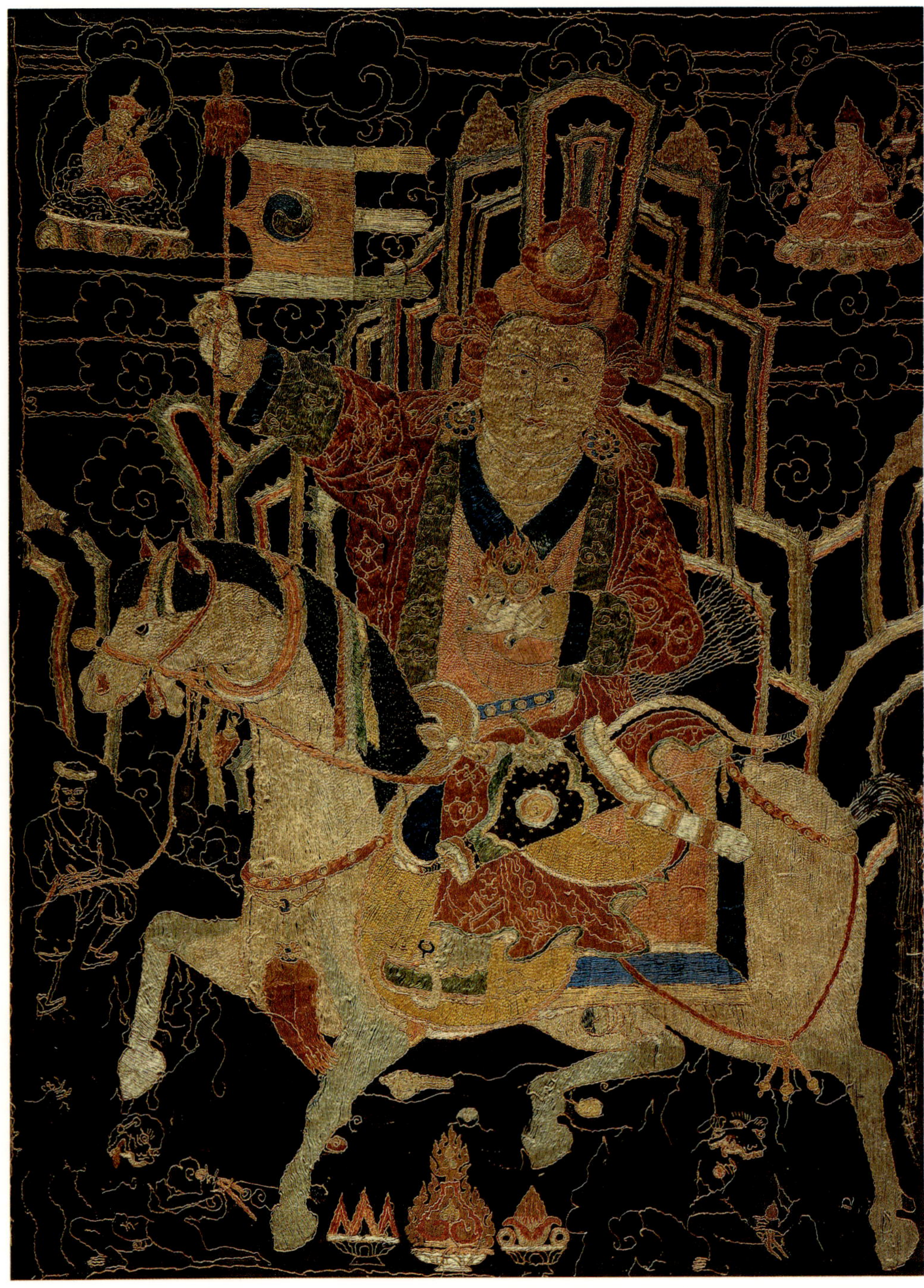

115

115

The Guardian Deity Tshangpa Karpo

MONGOLIA (?), SIXTEENTH–SEVENTEENTH CENTURY (?)

SILK, GOLD, AND PEACOCK-FEATHER EMBROIDERY ON SATIN

26½ × 20¼ IN. (67.3 × 51.4 CM)

The powerful central figure in this banner is a "white Tshangpa" form of Pehar (Pe har), an important Tibetan guardian deity. Distinguished by a conch shell in his turban, he rides a white horse. He carries a bowl filled with jewels and a banner; his sword, bow, and arrows are attached at his waist. Although Tshangpa can be shown in cuirass and armor, here he wears the loose voluminous robes and turban of the ancient Tibetan kings. In a cloud-filled sky are shown Padmasambhava (see no. 60) at the upper left and Tsongkhapa at the upper right. A sharply faceted mountain edged in rainbow-colored threads frames the central figure. An attendant holds the horse's neck rope at the lower left. Below, a central group of jewel and *torma* (*gtor ma;* ritual butter-and-flour "sculpture") offerings is well defined, but only a few threads remain from the fierce protectors at the sides, Yama and Begtse.

The somewhat awkward style of the central figure and of the embroidery suggests a provenance outside both Tibet and China. The silk floss used to form the body of the horse and Tshangpa's face, for example, is very wavy and irregular. Like the gold-foil-wrapped thread used for outlining, the floss is tacked down to the deep brown satin. Peacock feathers spun into thread, used here for the arrows, horse's mane and tail, and even the attendant's hair, are found on both Chinese imperial silks and Tibetan ritual textiles. The style of the banner and the hat and garment of the attendant point to Mongolia, where Tshangpa was particularly popular (Tsultem 1986, figs. 34, 82).

Pehar and his emanations are guardians of Samye, the first Buddhist monastery in Tibet. With Begtse they came to be alternate protectors of the Dalai Lamas in the seventeenth century. Tsongkhapa and the Gelukpa order he founded had special prestige in Mongolia, especially by the sixteenth century, when the Third Dalai Lama traveled there to meet Altan Khan. The Mongols may also have had an early affinity for Tshangpa and the more ferocious Setab (bSe'i Khrab) form of Pehar because of their association with Central Asian and Tibetan mythic traditions such as the *Gesar* legends. These idiosyncratic protective deities were incorporated into Buddhism as that religion spread across Tibet and, eventually, Mongolia. Tshangpa can also be translated as "Brahma," the Hindu deity incorporated as a guardian into Tibetan Buddhism (Nebesky-Wojkowitz 1956, pp. 145–53). V.R.

116

Bodhisattva Avalokiteshvara

CHINA, CA. 1780

SILK AND SILVER METAL CORD ON SILK

29½ × 20 IN. (74.9 × 50.8 CM)

The eleven-headed, thousand-armed form of the Bodhisattva of Compassion is here rendered in satin-stitched polychrome silk thread. The once bright blues, reds, and greens have faded to soft ivory and pale tones, and the couched silver-wrapped cord that forms the extraordinarily fine outlining and details has blackened. Avalokiteshvara's heads are framed in a multilobed halo; his body nimbus is obscured by the fanlike spread of his thousand arms. He stands on a lotus flower that grows out of a blue pool at the bottom of the *thanka,* flanked by two seated Tibetan lamas in a setting of trees and hills. A swirl of ivory clouds forms a pyramid behind Avalokiteshvara. Above this, in a cloud-filled deep blue sky, is a ceremonial umbrella flanked by seated images of the five Mystic Buddhas and the Buddha Śākyamuni. Every inch of the *thanka*'s surface is covered with embroidery, so that the silk ground cloth is visible only from the back.

This subject seems to have been popular in Beijing; two other identical examples are known, both with Chinese imperial dates, one of 1778 (New York, Metropolitan Museum of Art) and another of 1783 (London, Victoria and Albert Museum; Lowry 1973, no. 22). The embroidery style is completely Chinese, but the iconographic form and subsidiary figures are of Tibetan origin. V.R.

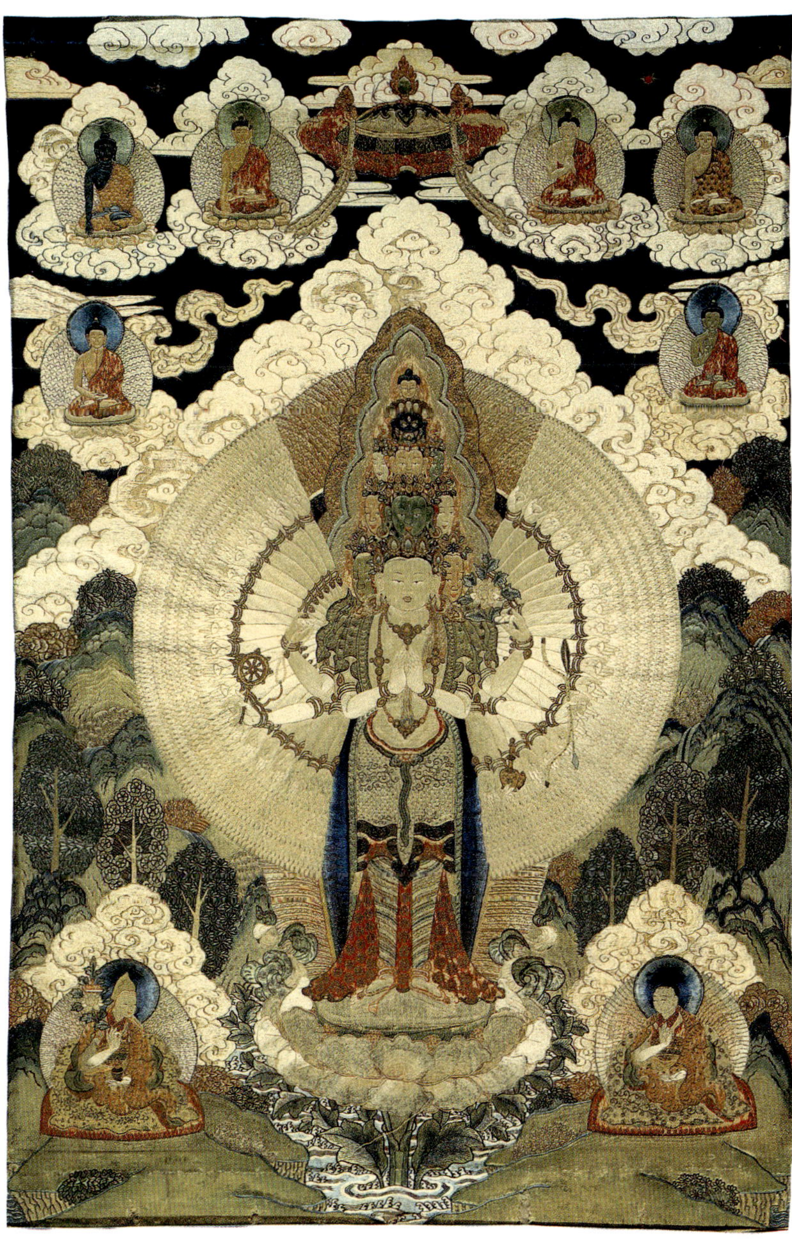

116

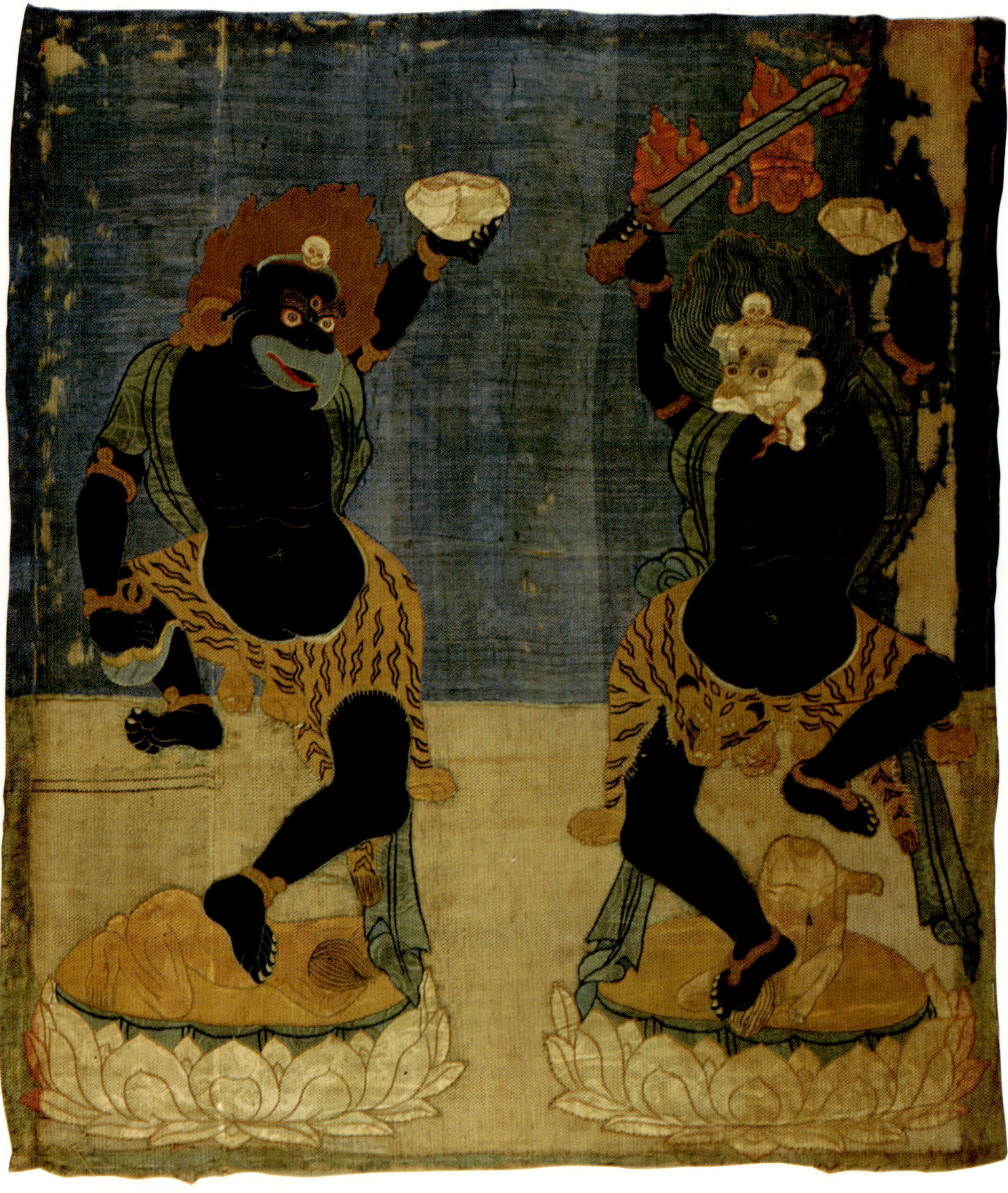

117

117

Pair of Animal-Headed Ḍākinīs

EIGHTEENTH CENTURY

APPLIQUÉD SILK AND SILK DAMASKS WITH EMBROIDERED DETAILS

30 × 26½ IN. (76.2 × 67.3 CM)

Gleeful dancing figures with animal heads and macabre accoutrements are commonly found in Tibetan paintings as attendants to protector deities or even historical figures. They are forms of *ḍākinīs*. The *ḍākinīs'* fierce nature is expressed here by their tiger-skin loincloths, skull diadems, and ritual implements (chopper, skull cups, sword). Both dance on crouched, naked human figures. The hooked beak of the bird's head and the fangs and flamelike tongue of the lion's head are also fearsome. Upraised hair, swirling scarves, and gold brocade jewelry complete the decorative scheme.

This textile appears to be a fragment of a bigger piece. It may have formed part of a longer horizontal series or the lower segment of a much larger central image. The rough cotton-cloth backing would have been appropriate for a large banner meant for outdoor display. Fine silks of pale and dark blue and buff are sewn to the backing to form the "sky" and main elements of the figures. The green silk of the lower ground area has almost completely disappeared, revealing the coarse cotton. The now-white lotus bases are formed of silk damask that originally was pink and red. Such fading from exposure to sunlight supports the theory that this was part of a banner for processions or outdoor use. An unusual technical feature of this appliqué is that silk floss stitches were used for all outlining and details. The usual Tibetan outlining is formed of cord couched down to the silks (see no. 118). The use of stitching here may indicate a particular workshop or region as yet unidentified. V.R.

118

The Goddess Kurukullā

NINETEENTH CENTURY

APPLIQUÉD SATINS, BROCADES, AND DAMASKS WITH SILK-WRAPPED HORSEHAIR CORDING, AND EMBROIDERED AND PAINTED DETAILS

56 × 47 IN. (142.2 × 119.4 CM)

An emanation of Tārā (see nos. 14, 89), Kurukullā is the goddess of love. Her ornaments and ritual weapons express her passionate nature. Her red body is adorned with bone and gold jewels, swirling scarves, and a tiger skin. She also wears a garland of severed heads and a skull crown over her flaming hair; she dances on three writhing human bodies. The bow, arrow, goad, and noose that are her weapons are here formed of flowers. Her halo and body nimbus are made of brilliant gilt brocades.

Below the blue damask sky (pieced with newer silks) is a mountain-and-lake landscape filled with gems and offerings. Three protector deities are arrayed across the bottom. From the left they are Tshangpa (?) (see no. 115), dressed as a king but wearing the headdress of a bodhisattva, carrying a lance with a banner and a bowl of gems, and riding a tan horse; a six-armed form of Mahākāla wearing fierce garments and brandishing weapons; and Setab, flame-engulfed, wearing armor and bow, carrying a lasso and lance, and riding a blue horse. This *thanka* is a brilliant example of the exuberance and complexity of Tibetan appliqué. The juxtaposition of brightly colored brocades and damasks, three-dimensional overlap, and cording threatens to overwhelm the viewer. Yet the appliqué master was in control of his forms, and the energy of the figures is not lost in decorative flourishes.

V.R.

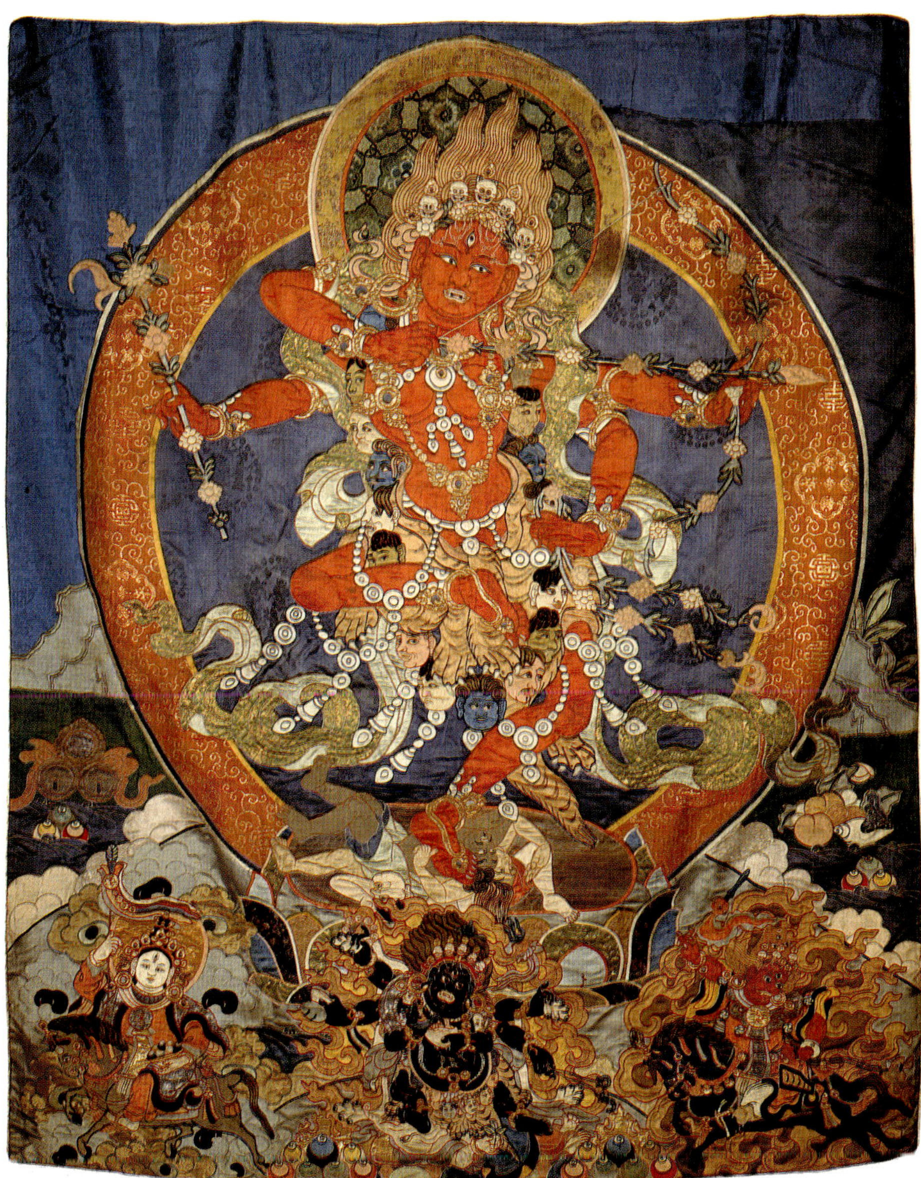

118

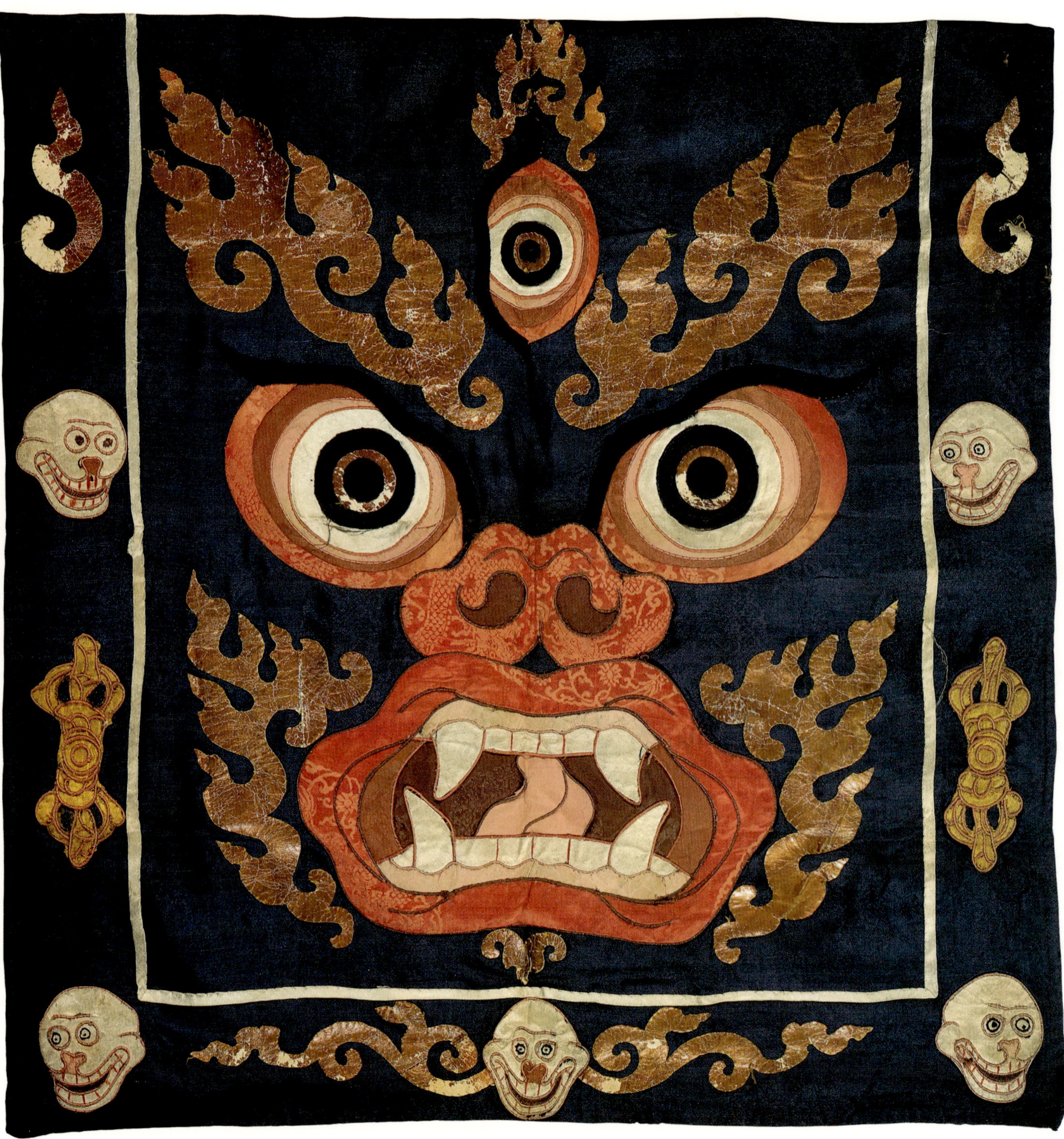

119

119

Dancer's Apron

NINETEENTH CENTURY

APPLIQUÉD SATINS, DAMASKS, AND LEATHER WITH SILK-WRAPPED HORSEHAIR CORDING

27 × 26 IN. (68.6 × 66 CM)

In the *cham* (*'chams*) dances performed for New Year celebrations and other religious holidays, monks wear elaborate costumes and masks, personifying deities and protectors. Aprons such as this are worn for protector roles. The ferocious face is that of Yama, Lord of Death, with his third eye, flaming brows and whiskers, and fangs, and is similar to that of Bhairava (see no. 22). Grinning skulls and the ritual scepter (*dorje*) decorate the sides and bottom. The apron originally had silk fringe across the lower edge and a waist sash across the top.

The appliqué technique used here is typical of Tibet, with brilliantly colored satins and damasks, lacquered leather, and silk-wrapped horsehair cording for outlines. V.R.

Appendix 1

NEWARI AND SANSKRIT INSCRIPTIONS

Ian Alsop

I would like to thank Kashinath Tamot and Dhanavajra Vajracharya, Kathmandu, for their help in deciphering and interpreting details of several of the inscriptions in this appendix. The successful interpretation of the inscription on number 10 is particularly due to their enthusiastic help. The spellings of the names of months and other astronomical phenomena mentioned in the inscriptions, as well as occasional caste names, have been left as is in the transliterations and corrected in the translations.

Brackets [ ] signify characters implied but not found in the inscription, while parentheses ( ) signify difficult-to-read or obliterated characters. An x represents a single difficult-to-read or obliterated character. Ellipses . . . represent a difficult-to-read or obliterated section.

10 GOD VISHNU ON GARUḌA

Inscription on base

Transliteration and many translation details by Dhanavajra Vajracharya and Kashinath Tamot.

Transliteration

1. samvatsare śatatame caturvviṃśatikā[dhike]; caitākhyāsita dvādaśyaṃ śaśiputradine

2. śubhe. śrī mahodayadevasya rājye ne(pā)la mandale; śrī ji(cco)dgesu viṣaye vidva-

3. tsādhujanānvite. kośaṃpradadyādgaruḍadhvajāya śraddhānvitaḥ śrī ḷpanāma dhe-

4. ya; anena punyena bhavantu lokā bhuktitvamuktitva phalaiḥ sametā.

Translation

On Wednesday, the twelfth of the dark half of Chaitra in the year 124 [A.D. 1004], during the reign of the great Udayadeva, in nobly inhabited Jichchodgesu district of the Nepāla mandala, the devout Śrī Ḷipa gave (this) covering [*kośa*] to Garuḍadhvaja. By this merit may enjoyment and emancipation result together for (all) people.

Comment

The location of "Jichchodgesu district" is unknown. The name "Lipa" is a correction of previous readings. Garuḍadhvaja is an epithet of Vishṇu.

27 WATERPOT

Inscription around foot

Transliteration

svasti. śrī 3 svaṣṭadevatā pritina, śrī 2 jaya jitāmitramalla devana, śrī 2 jaya ugra malla devana duṃtā, samvat 795 phāguṇa vadi 6 śubha.

Translation

Hail; on the sixth of the dark half of Phālguna, in the year 795 [February–March 1675], (this pot) was donated in honor of (their) tutelary deity by Śrī 2 Jaya Jitāmitramalla Deva and Śrī 2 Jaya Ugramalla Deva. May it be good.

Comments

Jitāmitramalla was king of Bhaktapur. His younger brother Ugramalla was a close associate who is often mentioned in his inscriptions.

28 IDEALIZED PORTRAIT

Inscription around base

Transliteration

samvat 818 āśuni śudi 7 śrī 3 pamapāni rokeśvarasake śrī vajrācāje muniyā nāmana dutā. śubha.

Translation

On the seventh of the bright half of Āśvina, in the year 818 [September–October 1698], (this) was donated in honor of Śrī 3 Padmapāṇi Lokeśvara in the name of Śrī Muni Vajrāchārya. Let it be good.

Comments

The inscription does not mention a locality.

29 PORTRAIT OF BHARAMAYĪ

Inscription around base

Transliteration

1. saṃ 882 māggaśira śukla pakṣa catudasi

2. thva kunhu śrī 3 kuradevatā āgmaju prītina podeyā bharama-

3. yīna sva ikṣāna thao sārika daya-

4. kā dio pyā 3 duntā juro śubhamagra bhavatu sarvvadā kāraṃ.

Translation

On the fourteenth of the bright half of Mārgaśirṣa, in the year 882 [November–December 1761], Bharamayī of Pode, of her own volition, donated this statue of herself with three lamps in honor of her lineage deity. May it be auspicious for all time.

Comments

It is very unusual to find a donor lamp donated by a living person.

In almost all cases, lamps like this one were donated by the family after the death of the person mentioned in the inscription. This inscription explicitly recognizes the unusual nature of the donation by emphasizing that Bharamayī donated an image "of herself" (*thao sārika*) "of her own volition" (*sva iksāna*). Pode may be Bode, a village near Thimi in the Kathmandu Valley.

30 **COMMEMORATIVE *CHAITYA***

Inscription around base

Transliteration

1. śubha saṃmvat 1003 mti poṣa kṛṣṇa paṃcami ṣunhu nakeba-
2. hilisa conamha raṃgikāra sinārāṃ satajiva dipaṃgata juyāo-
3. namha māma bhathakuṃ thao bābā bhimaratha kriyā yāta, sāya (ye?)
4. va siṃ, dhana suṃdhara, harṣanarasiṃ, rakṣminarasiṃ prabhiti-
5. yā dharmma citta utpati juyāo dhātuyā uṣṇiṣa caitya
6. dayakā jura śubha.

Translation

On the fifth of the dark half of Pauṣa in the year 1003 [December 1882], Sinārāṃ Raṃgikāra of Nake Bahil performed the *Bhīmaratha* ceremony in honor of his own father and deceased mother Bhathakuṃ, who lived a hundred years (?): Sāyavasiṃ, Dhana Suṃdhara, Harshanarasiṃ, Rakshminarasiṃ, and others, being inspired by piety, had made (this) metal *ushṇīsha* (for Ushṇishavījayā) *chaitya,* may it be good.

Comments

The inscription is full of errors and odd usages, and it is difficult to ascertain the exact relationship of all the people mentioned in it. "Raṃgikāra" is likely "Rañjitkīra," a Newari caste of cloth dyers. Kashinath Tamot points out that there is a community of Rañjitkāras near Nakabahil in Kathmandu.

33 **MANDALA OF THE SUN-GOD SŪRYA**

Inscription on upper portion of reverse

Transliteration

. . . saṃvat 4xx . . . śukle pacamyāti . . . śvare . . . (citrakāra?) kitaharasa li(khi)taṃ śubha.

Translation

On the fifth of the bright half of . . . , in the year 4xx [fourteenth century] . . . painted by Kitaharasa (Chitrakāra?). May it be good.

Comments

The painting has been restored and backed against a thin Plexiglas sheet with some sort of wax treatment. Unfortunately, the wax adhesive is quite cloudy, and it is difficult to decipher the inscription. If this wax were removed, the inscription would be considerably clearer. The "4" of the date is quite clear and thus would suggest a fourteenth-century date for the painting.

34 **GODDESS VASUDHĀRĀ AND COMPANIONS**

Inscription on reverse

Transliteration

saṃvat 523 bhārda . . . kunhu śrī (phākoṃ?)jusya patisthā yāṅā śubha.

Translation

In the year 523 [1403], in the month of Bhādra . . . on this day (this *paubhā*) was consecrated by Śrī Phākoṃju (?).

35 **MANDALA OF THE MOON GOD**

Inscription along bottom

Transliteration

saṃvat 57(6?) . . . kasa(na?) pratipadāyā ti. . . . śukra vāsare rājādhirājaparama. . . . śrīśu . . .

Translation

On the first of the . . . , a Friday, in the year 576 [?; 1456?], (during the reign of) the kings of kings, lord . . .

Comments

The inscription is badly worn and very difficult to read. Unfortunately, the king's name is not visible, as this would allow us to date the painting quite effectively. A previous reading of the inscription translates the date as A.D. 1426, interpreting the original as 546 rather than 576 (Pal 1978, fig. 81); as this disagreement suggests, the middle character is unclear.

36 **MYRIAD *CHAITYAS* WITH USHṆĪSHAVIJAYĀ**

Inscription at bottom of frame

Transliteration

oṃ sreyo(stu?) saṃvat 63x bhādrapada śukla pratipadyāyātithau utraphālaguna nakṣatre sādha jo x x x śrī jasarāja ā(cā?rya?)nā(ya?) x jasa śrī x x śi (ddha?vha) nāyakajuva(tva) pramukha nedhramuni samuha . . . bharipani samuha x śrī patibhala(ḍa?)tvaṃ . . .

Translation

On the first of the bright half of Bhādra, during the Uttaraphalgunī lunar asterism, during the sadhu yoga, in the year 63x (August–September 1510–19), this *paubhā* (was consecrated; the donors being) Śrī jasarāja, etc., (along with their) womenfolk . . .

Comments

The first character of the date is clear, but it is one that can easily be confused between 5 and 6. A previous publication reads it as 5, resulting in a date of 1416 (Pal 1978, p. 75). However, I would lean toward a 6. As a reference we may consult a manuscript in this exhibition, the *Graha Śānti Vidhi* (no. 43), which uses a similar character for 6.

40 **ICONOGRAPHIC SKETCHBOOK**

The sketchbook contains various deities, including most of the tantric divinities popular among Newar Buddhists. One side of the book is made up of drawings, while the other side includes text referring to the measurements of various deities. About halfway through the reverse side, above a drawing of a *chaitya,* is found this remark:

Transliteration

1. rekhakaḥ śrī siṃkomaguḍi vajrācārya

2. śrī harṣasenana sikṣārtha ratnasiṃha hetu nimitārthana harṣa senana

3. reṣayet dattaṃ. śubha.

Translation

Written by Vajrāchārya, Śrī Harshasena of Siṃkomaguḍi, for the sake of studying for Ratnasiṃha, for whom it was written and given by Harshasena. May it be good.

Comments

There is no date. "Siṃkomaguḍi" probably refers to the neighborhood of Kathmandu now known as Sikamugaḥ. The writing referred to is most likely the text giving the measurements of deities, rather than the drawings, which probably were made by Ratnasiṃha.

This manuscript has a number of other interesting aspects. Beside a drawing of the Buddha we find several recipes for metal alloys, which are often found in casters' handbooks. A figure of Mahāsamvara, a deity rarely found outside the Newari Buddhist tradition, is depicted. In two cases drawings are labeled with Tibetan names transliterated in Newari characters: these are "demajoka" (Tibetan: bDe mchog; Saṃvara) and "dhvaljāphakmu" (rdo rje phag mo; Vajravārāhī). These notes clearly indicate that the artist worked for Tibetan patrons. Either the drawings were made in Tibet and labeled when they were drawn, or, perhaps more likely, the artist was an itinerant who, when working in Tibet, scribbled the names under the deities so that he could recognize the Tibetan nomenclature.

43 **MEDICO-ASTROLOGICAL TREATISE**

This manuscript is a typical Newar astrological/medical text. It is an incomplete *Graha Śānti Vidhi,* detailing how to avoid the malefic influences or demons (*graha*) that attack children at certain stages of life. The stages are computed by days, months, and years. Thus one *graha* will be particularly dangerous during the second day, second month, or second year of life. There is no inclusive colophon and no date, but each *graha* has a cursory colophon such as that for number 2 (*sunanda*) below, *iti rākshaśa graha śānti vidhi*. The manuscript mentions an unusual number of *grahas* (most have only twelve), and whereas the individual *vidhis* on one side each take up a single page, on the other there are two pages for each *vidhi*.

Below are the names of each *graha,* followed by its number as found in the text (in parentheses). The names often relate to the faces or heads of the figures in the paintings.

Side 1

(one page per illustration)

yakṣa graha (5); rākṣaśa graha (6); mahiṣā (7); kurkuṭa (8); saṃkha kuṭaka (9); mipilikā (10); aśva (11); mayura (12); nāga (13); vyāghra (14); deva (15); kumāra (16); vetāla (17); revatī (18); bhūta (19); mukhamaṇḍikā (20).

Following the *Graha Śānti Vidhi* on the first side is a divination chart containing sixteen vowel characters laid out in a grid, named in the text as the *ṣoḍaśākṣarachakra,* the *chakra* of sixteen characters. A marker—such as a grain of rice—is thrown onto the grid, and one's question is answered according to the fortune associated by the text with the character on which the grain falls.

Side 2

(two pages per illustration; several of the illustrations have captions that are often difficult to make out; where legible, these have been given in parentheses)

sunanda (2); putanā (vyāghra) (3); mukhamaṇḍikā graha, sṛgāla rūpaṃ (sṛgāla) (4); viḍāla (mā(?ju)laxx) (5); sakunī [caption illegible, no number]; suskarevatī (śu(ska?mka)moga); [no colophon] (kasti); [no colophon] (gṛddha); muṃṇca [caption illegible].

45 **TWO FOLIOS FROM AN ICONOGRAPHICAL SKETCHBOOK**

These pages are inscribed with various notes, usually including the name of the deity depicted, abbreviations referring either to implements or weapons held in the hands, the mudrās, and the colors of faces or various parts of the body. These include *to* for *toyu* (Newari word for "white"); *kā* for *kāla* (Sanskrit word for "black"); *pī* or *pi* for *pīta* (Sanskrit word for "yellow"); *ra* for *rakta* (Sanskrit word for "red"); *ni* or *nī* for *nīla* (Sanskrit word for "blue"); *ku* for *kunkumam* (Sanskrit word for "saffron" or "gold-colored"); *dhu* for *dhūma* (Sanskrit word for "smoke," hence "smoke-colored").

1. śrī 3 vāgeśvari.

A diagram with weapons drawn in, including the notation *vara* for *varadamudrā,* and *abha-* for *abhayamudrā*; underneath, somewhat damaged, śrī pachi ānnāya.

Reverse: drawing of a bird identified as *gīdha* for *gṛdhra* (Sanskrit: vulture).

2. śrī 3 guru bhairava, with colors noted, and one mudrā noted as *tajani* for *tarjanīmudrā*. The vehicle is noted as *śava* (Sanskrit: corpse).

Reverse: śrī 3 vagarāmukhi [for Vagalāmukhī, one of the Daśamahāvidyā goddesses].

51 **NARRATIVE SCROLL**

Each section of the inscription appears under a narrative scene. Each transliteration is followed here by the corresponding translation.

1. Introductory *śloka*: xxx kamekaṃ ga x x ntmekaṃ x rtavya

rapaṃ jagadādipija x x x x x x x x dāvadanti x śabhusunu saguṇaṃ bhajāmiḥ.

1.1. thana śrī rukmāgadarājā saṃndhyāvarī rāṇi sabhā dayakāva ekādasiyā bākhana ṅeṅāo bijyāka.

Here King Rukmāṅgada and Queen Sandhyāvari, calling together the court, listen to the story of the *Ekādaśivrata*.

1.2. thana maṃntrī koṭavārana nāya hāṅāva ekādasī vrata danakeyāta nvāhārakayaku prajāpanisena ṅeṅāo harṣamāna yāṅāo cona.

Here the ministers and the courtiers, sending out drummers, proclaim the observance of the *Ekādaśivrata* while the people listen joyously.

1.3. thana rukmāgada rājā saṃndhyāvarī rāṇi putra dharmmāgada aga prajāpanisyana ekādasi vatra yāka vatra puṇyana nārāyana theṃ ṅaṅāo vaikuṇṭha oṃ.

Here King Rukmāṅgada and Queen Sandhyāvari, along with their son Dharmāṅgada, as the result of the merit of the *Ekādaśivrata* performed by (them and) the populace, ascend to Vaikuṇṭha like Nārāyaṇa.

1.4. thana jamarājāyāke citragvapina dhāra ova jamapuri ova madayāo laṃsa ujāla juo.

Here Chitragvapi (for Chitragupta), having gone to meet Yamarājā in Yamapuri and not finding him there, remains desolate on the road.

1.5. thana jamarājana nārada . . .

Here Yamarājā (has a conversation with?) Nārada . . .

2.1. thana brahmā sāvṛttī coṅa thāsa nāradao jamarājāo brahmāyāke bimati yāta ora.

Here in the place where Brahmā and Sāvitrī are staying, Nārada and Yamarājā go to supplicate Brahmā.

2.2. thana brahmāna thao mhutuna mohanī pikāo.

Here Brahmā materializes Mohani out of his own mouth.

2.3. thana nārada jamarājā.

Here are Nārada and Yamarājā (watching Brahmā).

2.4. thana rukmāgadarājāna putra dharmmādgada rājā sāla; thana rukmādgada.

Here King Rukmāṅgada proclaims his son Dharmāṅgada king.

2.5. thana sikāra bijyāyayāta sala pikāo.

Here a horse is taken out (for the king) to go hunting.

2.6. thana maṃdala parvvata śiyake dhaka bijyāka.

Here (the king) goes to find Maṃdala Mountain.

2.7. thana ahalayāka dhu chamha carā chamha nānā jaṃtuka rāka.

Here the hunters bag a tiger, a deer, and numerous animals.

2.8. thana maṃdala parvvatasa mohanī khaṅāo murchā juo.

Here on Maṃdala Mountain, (the king), seeing Mohani, faints.

2.9. thana rchā (for murchā) laṅāo che boṅa yane dhaka dhāo.

Here the king, recovering from his faint, tells (Mohani) that he will take her home.

3.1. thana mohanīna satya phona rukmāgadana bio.

Here Mohani begs a pledge, and Rukmāṅgada gives it.

3.2. thana nāradana rukmāgadarājāo mohanīo honaku.

Here Nārada joins (in marriage) Rukmāṅgada and Mohanī.

3.3. thana rukmāgada mohanī ovaṃ.

Here Rukmāṅgada and Mohanī go (to the horse).

3.4. thana mutghaḷ salana nhuyāo coṅa rukmāgadana mutghuḷ khaṅāo mut juyāoṃ.

Here the horse is trampling a mongoose (?); when the king sees the mongoose (?), it (is transubstantiated; disappears?).

3.5. thana rukmāgadarājāo mohonīo che ona.

Here King Rukmāṅgada and Mohanī go home.

3.6. thana chesa rānīyāke rukmāgadana mohanī laolhāka.

Here, at home, Rukmāṅgada hands Mohanī over to the queen.

3.7. thana rukmāgada mohanī coṅa thāsa putra dharmmāgana (for gadana) vata lolamanarā dhaka dhā ova; thana mohanīna vrata tolati dhaka tamacāsya gaṅa.

Here son Dharmāṅgada comes to where Rukmāṅgada and Mohanī are staying and says, "Have you forgotten the *vrata*?" Mohanī replies angrily, "Abandon the *vrata*."

3.8. thana dharmmāgadana satya gathe phutake ji syāṅāo mola bio dhaka dhāla.

Here Dharmāṅgada says, "How can the truth be (so) destroyed? Kill me and give (her) my head."

3.9. thana rukmāgadana satyayā nīmittina kāya syāka saṃdhyāvalīna mohanīyāta mola bio.

Here Rukmāṅgada, for the sake of the truth, kills his son, and (Queen) Saṃdhyavalī gives the head to Mohanī.

3.10. thana deoduta oyāva bimānasa thava vaikuṇṭha yaṅa.

Here the messengers of the gods come and, (putting them) in a flying chariot, bring them to Vaikuṇṭha.

3.11. thana mohanī vajrabhāṃ jula. śubha.

Here Mohanī becomes *vajrabhāṃ* (? is united with Vishṇu).

Comments

This *bilaṃpau* is much shorter than most paintings of this type. The incidents described appear to be but the highlights of the *Ekādaśivrata kathā;* a longer *bilaṃpau* would give a longer, more coherent version of the story.

Appendix 2

TIBETAN INSCRIPTIONS

Heather Stoddard

47 TWO FOLIOS FROM AN ARTIST'S MODEL BOOK

1. (Left page) Seated Buddha Maitreya, iconometric lines, and color key: *nga; tha; cam; ma;* (right page) standing Buddha Maitreya with vases on either side, color key: *mi; ser; nga; ka; nga*.
2. (Left page) Avalokiteshvara with eleven faces and a thousand hands.

The numerous inscriptions on this page are written in two different scripts, perhaps at different times, as artist's jottings. The main figure is identified as *Thugs.rje.chen.po* (The Great Lord of Compassion). Inscriptions on either side give lists of the main attributes held by the divinity in his right and left hands. For example:

Right: jewel, noose, sword, crystal, goad, lotus, sun, wheel.

Left: cloud, conch shell, rosary, hook, bell, palace, etc. Color codes are given as isolated letters or syllables in different sections: *ma; tha; mar; ser; kar*. Other surrounding notations suggest the placement of other divinities on a planned *thanka*. For example, the names of the five Tathāgata are written above, and below at the right are mentioned *thub.pa drug* (six *munis*).

(Right page) 'Phags.skyes Lho.cho.(phyogs) Viruḍhaka, [the King of the] south (holding a sword). Yul.'khor.'srung Shar.cho.(phyogs) Dhṛitarāshṭra, [the King of the] east (holding a lute).

60 TEACHER PADMASAMBHAVA

Inscription on back of base

Na.mo gu.ru Padma.yi // slob.dpon chen.po Padma 'Byung.nas.kyis / sku.'dra 'thong.pas dngos.bgrub dtsol.ba 'di // mi.dbang sa.skyong Kun.dga' rGyal.po yis(?).Sangs.rgyas stan.dar stan.'dzin ku(?).rim.dang // chab.srid mnga'.'bangs 'tha(?). nas.rgyas.phyir.dang //Khyed.par.sha.yab.yum.la.s "og.thug.gongs.rdzogs.pa'i.phyir / lhag.bsam dag.pa'i thug.gong.'e.ma.tshar / kra.shis.par. shog.gcig.

Salutations to the Lotus Guru! This statue of Padmasambhava, the Great Master of Studies, which bestows "magic" power when seen, was made for Kunga Gyalpo, Ruler and Lord of Men, so that the teaching of the Buddha shall spread and be upheld and so that ritual prayers may be said for the ruler, and so that his political dominion might grow, and more especially for the sake of his own [literally, fleshly] father and mother that they may perfectly realize their intentions. How astonishing the power of pure and sincere intentions! May all be auspicious!!

61 MONK CHAMPA PHUNTSHOK

Inscription on front of base

Kun.mkhyen Byams.pa Phun.tshogs / la.phyags.btshol / dge'o krashis.

Salutations to the omniscient Champa Phuntshok.[1] Virtue. Good Fortune.

Inscription on back of base

Kyid.grong nas.thams.cad.mkhyen. pa.rje.gnas.ba'i. nang.rten.yin / chos.mdzad rGyal.mtshan bZang.po'i.dad. pa'i.bzhengs.

This is a dharma support from Kyirong of the omniscient Lord Nepa (?). It was made through the faith of the dharma practitioner Gyaltshen Zangpo.

73 ARHAT BAKULA

Inscription on back of cushion

gyas lnga Ba.ku.la.

Fifth right Bakula.

80 FOUR BUDDHIST DEITIES

1. Four-armed white Avalokitśvara, holding a rosary and a white lotus

Inscription on front

Thugs.rje.chen.po.lagso.

This is the great Lord of Compassion, Mahakaruṇā.

Inscriptions on back

Ye dharma hetu prabha . . . Om maṇi padme hum.

"Buddhist credo" in Sanskrit transliterated in archaic Tibetan *dbu.med* script, followed by mantra of Avalokiteśvara.

2. Chakrasamvara in *yab-yum* embrace, blue with red and white faces, six arms, holding an elephant skin

Inscriptions on back

Mantras in *dbu.can* script; *Ye dharma* "Buddhist credo" in archaic *dbu.med* script.

3. Ushṇishachakravartin in *yab-yum* embrace, yellow with white and blue faces, holding wheel and sword in left hand, jewel (?) and white lotus in right hand

Inscription on front
Bla.ma'i.thugs.dam.
tsug.tor.'khor.lo.sgyur.ba.lagso.

This, Ushṇishachakravartin, is the tutelary deity of the lama.

Inscriptions on back
Mantras in *dbu.can* script; *Ye dharma* "Buddhist credo" in archaic *dbu.med*.

4. Vajravārāhī

Inscriptions on front
(Left) Bla.ma'i.thugs.dam

The tutelary deity of the lama.

(Right) rJe.btsun.ma
phag.mo.lags.so

This is the venerable (Vajra)varahi.

Inscriptions on back
Om Ah Hum; mantras in archaic *dbu.med* script.

84 **FOUR MANDALAS**

The *thanka* is identified by an inscription at the top as
rDo.rje phreng.ba'i ras.bris bdun.pa'o
The seventh *thanka* of the *Vajrāvalī*.

At the bottom (?) is a dedication,
dPal.ldan bla.ma dam.pa Sa.bzang 'Phags.pa'i thugs kyi dgongs.pa yongs.su.rdzogs. par.gyur.cig
May the glorious holy lama Sazang Phakpa's wishes be perfectly realized.

The two lamas in the middle are identified as Grags.pa rGyal.mtshan (Drakpa Gyaltsen) and Shes.rab rGyal.mtshan (Sherab Gyaltsen).

Sazang Phakpa, to whom a series of *Vajrāvalī* mandalas is dedicated, is no doubt the translator Sa.bzang 'Phags.pa gZhon.nu Blo.gros rGyal.mtshan (Ma.ti pan.chen), one of Tsongkhapa's teachers, who translated the *Samuchchaya* from Sanskrit into Tibetan together with the Indian pandit Mañjuśrī of Vikramaśīlā (Roerich 1949, p. 1045). Drakpa Gyaltsen was probably also a translator, known as Yarlung Lotsawa, who received the *Vajrāvalī* initiation from Bhumisri, the great pandit of Kashmir (ibid., pp. 1047–48, 1050). Sherab Gyaltsen is perhaps Gung.thang rab.'byams.pa Shes.rab rGyal.mtshan, who is fourth down in the lineage from Drakpa Gyaltsen for the mystical trance "Knowledge that reveals all" (*gCig.shes Kun.grol*); Drakpa Gyaltsen obtained it from the great venerable Man.lung.pa (*ibid*., p. 1050). But Sherab Gyaltsen might also be the "great all-knowing" Dolpowa Sherab Gyaltsen of the Jonangpa school (1292–1361) who took Mati panchen's (= Sazang Phakpa's) revised translation of the *Kalachakra* (done in 1334) and composed an abridged version, etc. (*ibid*., pp. 776–77).

The three persons mentioned in the inscriptions are closely linked through teachings. If the last is Gungthang Sherab Gyaltsen, who was contemporary with Gö Lotsawa Zhonupel ('Gos lo.tsa.ba gZhon.nu.dpal) (1392–1481), author of *The Blue Annals* (*ibid*.), then this series of *Vajrāvalī* mandalas would date to the second half of the fifteenth century at the earliest. However, if he is Dolpowa Sherab Gyaltsen, then perhaps the dating might be earlier.

Two other *thankas* from the same series are known in the West, one in a private collection and another recently published in *Art ésotérique de l'Himalaya: La donation Lionel Fournier* (Beguin 1990A, pl.32). Both have Buddha figures in the center of the four mandalas, one with Amitābha and the other with Vajradhara (?). In Beguin (ibid.), the inscription has been hastily read and the mention of the name 'Phags.pa taken as perhaps referring to 'Phags.pa Blo.gros rGyal.mtshan (1235–1280), imperial preceptor to Kublai Khan. The above-detailed reading, the specific title *Sa.bzang 'Phags.pa,* and the later date of the series (given as the end of fifteenth century in Beguin 1990A, pl. 32) go against this identification. See Rhie and Thurman, pl. 73, for further discussion concerning this series.

85 **MAṆḌALA OF RAKTAYAMĀRI**

Byang.phug.pa bla.ma dam.pa mkhas.btsun Kun.dga' Legs.pa'i thugs.dam la bzhengs.pa.yin.

[This *thanka*] was made as the precious possession of the holy lama of Changphuk, the learned, venerable Kunga Legpa.[2]

87 **SAKYAPA LINEAGE**

One of the main lamas may be identified in the inscription at the foot of the painting as rGyal.mtshan dPal.byor bZang.po (Gyaltsen Peljor Zangpo). All the names of the other figures are written in gold, and a proper historical study of the lineage represented will no doubt reveal the date of the painting.[3]

92 **MAHĀKĀLA IN THE FORM OF A BRAHMAN**

1. . . . ms.mkhan dam.can Pu.tra.chen. . . . la.na.mo.

Salutations to . . . the protecting deity, the Great Putra.

2.1. Buddha with hands in *dharmachakramudra*.

2.2. Sa.skya.pa chen.po Kun.dga' sNying.po

The Great Sakyapa Kunga Nyingpo [1092–1158].

2.3. sLob.dpon . . . ?

The master of studies . . .

3.1. Bla.chen . . . Rin.po.che bSod.nams rTse.mo.

The great lama Sonam Tsemo [1142–1182].

3.2. Se lotsawa 'Jam.dbyang Kun.dga'i bSod.rnams.

The translator Se Jamyang Kunga Sonam.

3.3. Chos.rje dGa'.ldan.pa Kun.bsod.

The Lord of the Dharma Gadenpa Kuns [Kunga Sonam?; first half of fourteenth century? (Roerich 1949, p. 775)].

4.1. bTsun.pa rin.po.che Grags.pa rGyal.mtshan.

The venerable precious Drakpa Gyaltsen [1147–1206].

4.2. . . . g.'chang.chos.kyi.rgyal.po. 'Jam.dbyangs. ngag.gi. kun.dga'.rin.chen .bkra.shis. grags.pa.rgyal.mtshan. dpal.bzang.po

The King of the Dharma Jamyang Ngak gi Kunga Rinchen Tashi Drakpa Gyaltsen Pelzangpo [Kuntrepa, thirty-second abbot of Sa.skya, b. 1349].

5. rGyal.'byor dam.can dgra.lha.nag.po.la.ra.ta.chen.po. brgyad.gyi . . .

6. mGon.po 'beng.

Panjara Mahākāla.

7. Chos.'khor.yongs.kyis.srog. shing.nag.po.la.snang. srid.lha(?).srin.sde. brgyad.yi.skor.ba.

Mahākāla with his entourage of eight demons.

8. (A demon?) holding the sun and moon.

9. Dam.can Bya.ta.nag.po.

10. sKyes.pa.

The hero.

11. 'Kha.'gro Srin.mo Chen.mo.

The great demoness ḍākinī.

12. Bur.med.

(demoness).

13. 'Jam.dbyangs dPal.grags.pa Blo.gros rGyal.mtshan dPal.bzang.po.

(With four monks and offerings) [first half of fifteenth century? (Roerich 1949, p. 548)].

14. dKar.mo Nyi.zla la.na.mo.

(Holding sun and moon offerings, the white goddess of the sun and moon).

15. bDud.kyi.rgyal.po.

The king of demons.

16. dGra.bcom.

The arhat.

99 BUDDHA ŚĀKYAMUNI WITH JĀTAKA TALES

Standing Buddha surrounded by eight monks and two bodhisattvas, Chinese inscription, bottom center

Da Ming Wanli nian zhi.

Made in the reign of Wanli of the great Ming dynasty [1573–1619].

Tibetan inscriptions

1. sTag.mo krems nas . . .

The story of the hungry tigress [*Avadāna* 95 in Tucci 1949, p. 528].

2. 'Dod.dgu'i.char.pod.pa(?) Utpala spyan.mchag.slar.rgyas. tshan.

(Scene with an elephant and a horse.)

3. Ko.sa'i.rgyal.po gyur.tshe.myu.gu.yi.brgya. byin.phun.tshogs.

When he became the king of Kosala . . .

4. lDog.par.ma.nus . . .

Not being able to repel . . .

5. Mig.sde.ldan.pa'i. nor.ba'i.phul.gyur. . . . mdangs.ldan. rtsa.rtsam.zhig /

6. rGyal.sras.ri.bong.zol.bston. mkhas.pa.lam.rgom.bkris.pas.

When the prince . . . was hungry and thirsty on the road. . . .

7. dKa'.thub.nags.su.shing.la. snying.bcos.dag.'chi.ba'i. rta.gan.bskrun.pa.slong.bo. la nyin.gsum.bar.du.byon. yang.cung. zad.tsam. g.yo.med.byin.ba.rtson. A.ga.sta.khyed.rgyal.

When performing austerities in the forest, and . . . came three days running, but without the slightest movement he. . . .

8. mNga'.ris byams.pa'i.rtobs. kyis.skyongs.mdzad.tshe / srin.po'i.rgyal.po sKyed.byed gnod.byin.lta.nyid sku'i.sha.khrag.'dod.dgur . . . 'dud.

When he was protecting his country through compassion . . . the king of demons . . . ?

9. rGyal.po Thams.sgrol.tshe. bzhon.pa'i.mchog rab.dkar.glong.chen. bu dang chung.ma.sogs. bdog.pa yongs.btang brgya.byin thabs.mkhas.kyis. rgyal.srid chos.bzhin.skyed.phyor.

When he was the king Thams.cad.sgrol. . . . the excellent young man and the white elephant . . .

10. bKa'.'khris rin.chen.'bar.sreg . . . ?

(Image of a man carrying a stone; a horse with jewels.)

The scenes are numbered in Tibetan from one to ten in a clockwise direction starting at the top right of the painting, with Tibetan inscriptions written in an abbreviated style that is difficult to decipher. Moreover, they do not follow the usual series of tales from the *Jātakamālā* or the *Avadānamala* (taken, for example, from the *dPag.bsam 'khri.shing*, using the xylographic blocks from sNar.thang as a basis for the paintings), and—except for the first one—the scenes remain difficult to identify.[4] Perhaps the images follow another version that was current in earlier times or in the Far East, since the painting bears a Ming-dynasty inscription and may have been made in an imperial workshop in China.

100 GOLDEN BUDDHA

With two attendant bodhisattvas, a *bKa'.brgyud* lama making offerings at the bottom left corner, and a group of monks or arhats in the bottom middle section.

Inscription at bottom left, below a seated monk figure (no doubt the donor, Lobzang Dondrup).

Thub.pa'i dbang.po la.na.mo // sku.'dun.kyis.sgrubs // Blob.bzang Don.'grub kyis.'dis / mkhas.rnams gyis.(b)zod. s(g)sol / dge'o.dag.

Salutations to the Buddha, Lord of Munis. (This statue) was ordered to be made by the lama. (If there is any error) in this (creation and dedication of the *thanka*) by Lobzang Dondrup, may scholars be patient! May there be virtue! May all be purified!

101 BUDDHA ŚĀKYAMUNI WITH JĀTAKA TALES

Scenes from the jātakas, numbered seventy-one through eighty (counterclockwise from the top left corner).

Inscriptions

71. rGyal.po 'Od.ldan.

King Oden.

72. Rigs.mthon bram.ze.

The brahman of high family.

73. rGyal.po.pa.

Gyelpopa.

74. rGyal.sbyin.

75. Rabs.mdzad glang.po.

(Hastaka? *Avadāna* 49 in Tucci 1949, p. 489?).

76. 'Char.ka.

The disciple Charka?

77. rGyal.po Nor.can.

(Dhanika? *Avadāna* 90 in Tucci 1949, p. 524.)

78. Bram.ze zla.dgar.

The brahman Candra?

79. rGyal.po Nam.kha.

King Namkha.

80. rGyal.po dPal.gyis.sde.

King Srisena, who gave away his wife (*Avadāna* 2 in Tucci 1949, p. 442).

110 MILAREPA IN A LANDSCAPE

One of a series of Karma Kagyu portraits. At least fifteen are known to have existed,[5] the central *thanka* being of Vajradhara. Around Milarepa are scattered several of his main disciples and two famous scenes from the *Hundred Thousand Songs*.

Inscriptions identifying figures and scenes

1. Phag.mo.

(Vajra)varahi.

2. Dam.pa (Pha.dam.pa Sangs.rgyas).

Phadampa Sangye, who taught the *gcod* ritual.

3. Zhi.ba.'od (ras.pa).

The Cotton-Clad Zhiwa'ö, disciple of Milarepa.

4. Se.ban.ras.pa.

The Cotton-Clad Seben of Dodrak (rDo.brag), disciple of Milarepa.

5. rJe Ngan.rdzong ston.pa Byang.chub.rGyal.po.

The teacher, lord of Ngendzong, Changchub Gyelpo of Chimlung ('Chims.lung), one of Milarepa's disciples.

6. Ras.chung.pa'i.g.yag.ru.kor.

Illustrates the chapter on Milarepa entering the yak horn to calm Rechung's pride (Chang 1977, chap. 38, p. 421).

7. Ras.chung.pa.

One of Milarepa's two foremost disciples, Rachungpa of Gungthang (1084–1161).

Nos. 8, 9, 11, and 12 illustrate the chapter on the hunter Khyirawa Gonpo Dorje (Khyi.ra.wa mGon.po rDo.rje) (Chang 1977, chap. 26, p. 275).

8. Khyi.ra.ba.'khros.

The angry hunter.

9. The deer.

10. (Bottom middle) bKra.shis Tshe.ring.ma.

The goddess of auspicious long life

11. The dog.

12. Khyi.ra.ba.gus.pa.

The hunter offers his respects to Milarepa.

13. Lab.kyi.sgron.me.

The Tibetan yogini Machik Labkyi Dronme (Ma.gcig.lab.kyi.sgron.me), disciple of Phadampa (see no. 2).

Inscriptions on back

Mi.la.g.yon.gnyis.pa.

Mila, second left center.

Lantsa inscription, probably mantras and prayers.

113 WHEEL OF LIFE

Inscription at foot of painting

Nges.par.'byung.bar brtsam.par.gyis / Sangs.rgyas bsten la sbyor.ba gyis / 'dam.bu'i khyim la glang.chen bzhin/ 'chi.bdag sde ni gzhom.par.gyis // gang zhig chos 'dul 'di nyid la / bag yod spyod.pa byed.pa ni/ skye.ba'i 'khor.lo rab spang nas/ sdug.bsngal zad.par.byed.pa.'gyur / / 'di bris dag.ba'i rnam dkar.'od snang.gis / gro..?rgyar rmongs.pa'i mun.sa? rab.bas . . . ?dam.brgyud sku bzhi'i go.'phang lam / rim brgyud rdo.rje.'chang gi sa thob shog / bkra.shis . . .

Set about renouncing the world
with disgust!
Take up the teaching of the
Buddha!
Like an elephant in a house of
reeds
Vanquish the troops of Yama!
Those who take up this religious
discipline
And practice it modestly
Will avoid the cycle of existence
And extinguish suffering.
May the pure white shining light
of this painting
Clear away the darkness of delusion for . . . living beings!
May they attain, step by step,
Along the path of the four
bodies (of Tathāgatas?)
The place of Vajradhara! Good
fortune!

Inscriptions

The twelve-fold causal nexus *pratityasamutpada*:

1. ma.rig.pa long.ba'i long.ba khrid.pa.

Ignorance. The blind leading the blind.

2. 'dus.byas rdza.mkhan 'khor.lo 'dra.ba.

Elemental impulses (*samskara*). Like the potter's wheel.

3. rnam.shes spre'u shing la mdzeg 'dra.

Consciousness. Like a monkey climbing a tree.

4. ming.gzugs snyan.pa gru zhug.pa.

Name and form, personality. A boat on its way.

5. skye mched khang.pa stong.pa

The six sense organs. An empty house.

6. reg.pa 'o.ba byed.pa.

Contact. Kissing.

7. tshor.ba mig la 'da' phog.pa.

Sensation. An arrow pierces the eye.

8. sred.pa chang thung dang klu.gar.

Desire. Drinking beer, singing, and dancing.

9. len.pa shing 'bras len.pa.

Grasping. Taking fruit from a tree.

10. srid.pa khrig.pas chos.su spyod.pa.

Becoming. Through coitus, being in the phenomenal world.

11. skye.ba bu skyes.pa.

Birth. A child is born.

12. rga shi rgas.po ro khur.ba.

Old age and death. Carrying the corpse of an old man.

The Six Realms of Rebirth:

13. The realm of the gods.

13A. Lha.gnas 33 rGya.byin lha'i khang bzang dam pa.

The thirty-three realms of the gods. The holy temple of rGya byin, keeper of the eastern direction.

13B. rGya.chen bzhi'i lha.gnas.

The realm of the four great kings, the Lokapalas.

13C. Byang sGra mi snyan.

The northern continent, Uttarakuru.

13D. Shar Lus 'phags.pa.

The eastern continent, Videha.

14. The realm of the titans or nongods: Lha.ma.yin gyi dbang.po Tha.zang.ris dBang po Tha.zang.ris (the king of the Asura).

15. The human realm: old age, birth, death, sickness.

16. The animal realm: slaughtering, beasts of burden, killing each other.

17. The realm of tormented spirits: Yi dag nang sgrib can (Pretas with interior obscurity).

18. The hells.

At the top of the hell scene is a red Yama holding a mirror. Below him are the *Lha'i.bu dkar.po* (the white son of the gods) and *bDud nag.po* (the black demon).

18A. Hot hells.

18B. Cold hells.

18C. Vajra hell.

18D. At the bottom right of the hell scene is depicted the suffering of those who commit "the sin of destroying or trading in the supports of the dharma" (Buddhist statues, paintings, books, and stūpas): *sKu gsung thugs rtan gshig.pa dang nyo.tshong byed.pa'i nyes.rmigs.*

They are being crushed and burnt under the weight of books and stūpas!

NOTES

1. Thirteenth–fourteenth century. See Essen and Thingo 1989, vol. 2, p. 284, no. 20. Byams.Pa Phun.tshogs is twentieth in one of the bKa'.brgyud.pa lineages, after rGod.tshang.ras.pa (1189–1258). See Beguin 1977, no. 157, for a very similar, though more sophisticated, bronze statue of rGod.tshang.ras.pa from the Newark Museum.

2. This is not the famous "Mad" yogi saint, 'Brug.pa Kun.legs (1455–1570), whose full name is Kun.dga' Legs.pa. The epithets "learned, venerable" go against this identification, and the name indicating his place of origin or one of his habitual residences, Byang.phug.pa, does not appear in the index of names in R. A. Stein's translation of his life, *Vie et chants de 'Brug.pa Kun.legs, les Yogin* (Paris, G. T. Maison Neuvea et Larose, 1972). See Rhie and Thurman 1991, no. 75, for more on Kun.dga' Legs.pa.

3. This translator did not work on this painting at the time of reading the inscriptions. Compare a similar painting dating to the end of the fifteenth century, in D. P. Jackson, "Identification of Teachers in Paintings of Sa.sky.pa Lineages" in *Indo-Tibetan Studies,* edited by T. Skorupski (Tring, U.K., The Institute of Buddha Studies, 1990), pp. 129–44, pl. 1.

4. See Tucci 1949, pp. 437–536. The translated indications are very tentative.

5. Others are in the Ford Collection, the Los Angeles County Museum of Art, and the Newark Museum.

Bibliography

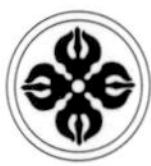

Allen, M. 1973. "Buddhism without Monks: The Vajrayana Religion of the Newars of Kathmandu Valley." *South Asia, Journal of South Asian Studies,* no. 3: 1–14.

Alsop, I. 1984. "Five Dated Medieval Nepalese Metal Sculptures." *Artibus Asiae* 45, nos. 2–3: 207–22.

———. 1984A. "Problems in Dating Nepalese Metal Sculpture: Three Images of Visnu." *Contributions to Nepalese Studies* 12, no. 1: 23–49.

———. 1986. "Repoussé in Nepal." *Orientations* 17, no. 17 (July): 14–27.

———. 1990. "Phagpa Lokesvara of the Potala." *Orientations* 21, no. 4 (April): 51–61.

Alsop, I., and J. Charlton. 1973. "Image Casting in Oku Bahal." *Contributions to Nepalese Studies* 1, no. 1: 22–49.

Bangdel, L. S. 1982. *The Early Sculptures of Nepal.* New Delhi: Bikash Publishing House.

———. 1987. *Nepal: Zweitausendfünfhundert Jahre Nepalische Kunst.* Leipzig: Veb E. A. Seeman Verlag.

Bartholomew, T. T. 1980. "Guardians of Tibetan Buddhism." *Apollo* 112, no. 222: 94–100.

———. 1987. "Tibetan Thangkas Relating to the Abbots of Ngor and Shalu in the Asian Art Museum of San Francisco." *Orientations* 18, no. 2 (February): 20–35.

Batchelor, S. 1987. *The Tibet Guide.* London: Wisdom Publications.

Bechert, H., and R. Gombrich, eds. 1984. *The World of Buddhism.* New York: Facts on File Publications.

Beguin, G. 1980. *Past Lives of the Buddha.* Paris: Editions Siaky.

———. 1981. *Les mandala himâlayens du Musée Guimet.* Paris: Réunion des Musées Nationaux.

———. 1984. "A propos d'une tiare d'officiant bouddhique." *La revue du Louvre et des Musées de France,* no. 3 (June): 176–83.

———. 1987. *Les Arts du Nepal et du Tibet.* Paris: Desclée de Brouwer.

———. 1989. *Terreur et Magie: Dieux farouches du Musée Guimet.* Brussels: Musées Royaux d'Art et d'Histoire.

———. 1990. *Miniatures et rouleaux enluminés du Nepal et du Tibet.* Geneva: Ed. de Crémille.

———. 1990A. *Art ésotérique de l'Himâlaya: La donation Lionel Fournier.* Paris: Réunion des Musées Nationaux.

Beguin, G., et al. 1977. *Dieux et démons de l'Himâlaya: Art du Bouddhisme lamaïque.* Paris: Réunion des Musées Nationaux.

Beyer, S. 1978. *The Cult of Tara.* Berkeley and Los Angeles: University of California Press.

Bhattacharyya, B. 1958. *The Indian Buddhist Iconography.* 2d rev. ed. Calcutta: Firma K. L. Mukhopadhyay.

Bhattacharyya, D. C. 1974. *Tantric Buddhist Iconographic Sources.* Delhi: Munshiram Manoharlal.

———. 1978. *Studies in Buddhist Iconography.* Delhi: Manohar Book Service.

Bhattasali, N. K. 1929. *Iconography of the Buddhist and Brahmanical Sculptures in the Dacca Museum.* Dacca: Rai S. N. Bhadra Bahadur.

Blom, M. L. B. 1989. *Depicted Deities: Painters' Model Books in Nepal.* Groningen: E. Forsten.

Chandra, L. 1986. *Buddhist Iconography of Tibet.* 2 vols. Kyoto: Rinsen.

Chang, G. C. C. 1977. *The Hundred Thousand Songs of Milarepa.* 2 vols. Boulder: Shambhala.

Clark, W. E. 1965. *Two Lamaistic Pantheons.* Cambridge, Mass.: Harvard University Press.

Copeland, C. 1980. *Tankas from the Koelz Collection.* Ann Arbor: University of Michigan, Museum of Anthropology.

Das, S. C. 1965. *Indian Pandits in the Land of Snow.* Calcutta: Firma K. L. Mukhopadhyay.

Essen, G., and T. T. Thingo. 1989. *Die Götter des Himalaya.* 2 vols. Munich: Prestel-Verlag.

Evans-Wentz, W. Y. 1951. *Tibet's Great Yogi Milarepa.* 2d ed. London: Oxford University Press.

Fisher, R. 1974. *Mystics and Mandalas.* Redlands, California: University of Redlands, Tom and Ann Peppers Art Gallery.

Getty, A. 1962. *The Gods of Northern Buddhism.* Tokyo: Charles E. Tuttle.

Goepper, R., B. Poncar-Lutterbeck, and J. Poncar. 1984. *Alchi.* Cologne: DuMont Buchverlag.

Gordon, A. K. 1959. *The Iconography of Tibetan Lamaism.* Rutland, Vermont: Charles E. Tuttle.

Govinda, L. G. 1979. *Tibet in Pictures.* 2 vols. Berkeley: Dharma Publishing.

Gulick, R. H. van. 1935. *Hayagriva: The Mantrayanic Aspect of Horse-Cult in China and Japan.* Leiden: E. J. Brill.

Guy, J. 1982. *Palm-Leaf and Paper.* Melbourne: National Gallery of Victoria.

Gyatsho, S. 1983. *Tibetan Mandalas: The Ngor Collection.* Tokyo: Kodansha.

Hackin, J., et al. 1932. *Asiatic Mythology.* London: George G. Harrar and Co.

Hatt, R. T. 1980. "A Thirteenth-Century Tibetan Reliquary." *Artibus Asiae* 42, nos. 2–3: 145–220.

Henss, M. 1981. *Tibet: Die Kulturdenkmäler.* Zurich: Atlantis.

Huntington, J. C. 1972. "Gu-ge Bris: A Stylistic Amalgam." In Pal, ed. *Aspects of Indian Art.* Leiden: E. J. Brill.

Huntington, S. L., and J. C. Huntington. 1990. *Leaves from the Bodhi Tree.* Dayton: The Dayton Art Institute.

Jackson, D. P., and J. A. Jackson. 1984. *Tibetan Thangka Painting: Methods and Materials.* London: Serindia Publications.

Karmay, H. 1975. *Early Sino-Tibetan Art.* Warminster, England: Aris and Phillips.

Karmay, S. G. 1988. *Secret Visions of the Fifth Dalai Lama.* London: Serindia Publications.

Kramrisch, S. 1933. "Nepalese Paintings." *Journal of the Indian Society of Oriental Art,* vol. I, no. 2: 129–47.

———. 1964. *The Art of Nepal.* New York: Asia Society.

Lama, G. 1985. *Principles of Tibetan Art.* 2d ed. Antwerp: Karma Sonam Gyantso Ling.

Lauf, D. I. 1976. *Tibetan Sacred Art.* Berkeley: Shambhala.

———. 1976A. *Secret Revelations of Tibetan Thankas.* Freiburg: Aurum Verlag.

———. 1977. *Secret Doctrines of the Tibetan Books of the Dead.* Boulder: Shambhala.

Lessing, F. D., and A. Wayman. 1968. *Mkhas grub rje's Fundamentals of the Buddhist Tantras.* The Hague: Mouton and Co.

Lo Bue, R. 1985. "The Newar Artists of the Nepal Valley: An Historical Account of Their Activities in Neighboring Areas with Particular References to Tibet—1." *Oriental Art,* n.s. 31, no. 3: 262–73.

———. 1985–86. "The Artists of the Nepal Valley—2." *Oriental Art,* n.s. 31, no. 4: 409–20.

Lowry, J. 1973. *Tibetan Art.* London: Victoria and Albert Museum.

———. 1977. "A Fifteenth-Century Sketchbook (Preliminary Study)." In A. Macdonald and Y. Imaeda, eds. *Essais sur l'art du Tibet.* Paris: Librairie d'Amérique et d'Orient.

Macdonald, A., and A. V. Stahl. 1979. *Newar Art.* Warminster, England: Aris and Phillips.

Mallman, M.-T. de. 1975. *Introduction à l'iconographie du tantrisme bouddhique.* Paris: Andrien-Maissoneuve.

Nebsky-Wojkowitz, de R. 1956. *Oracles and Demons of Tibet.* 'S-Gravenhage: Mouton and Co.

Olschak, B., and G. T. Wangyal. 1973. *Mystic Art of Ancient Tibet.* New York: McGraw-Hill.

Olson, E. 1974. *Tantric Buddhist Art.* New York: China House Gallery.

Pal, P. 1966. "The Iconography of Amoghapasa Lokesvara." Pt. 1. *Oriental Art,* n.s. 12, no. 4: 234–39. Pt. 2, n.s. 13, no. 1: 20–28.

———. 1967. *Two Buddhist Paintings from Nepal.* Amsterdam: Museum van Aziatische Kunst.

———. 1969. *The Art of Tibet.* New York: The Asia Society.

———. 1970. *Vaisnava Iconology in Nepal: A Study of Art and Religion.* Calcutta: Asiatic Society.

———. 1974. *The Arts of Nepal.* 2 vols. Vol. 1, *Sculpture.* Leiden: E. J. Brill.

———. 1974A. "Bronzes of Nepal." *Arts of Asia* 4, no. 5: 31–37.

———. 1974B. "The Zimmerman Collection of Nepali Art." *Arts of Asia* 4, no. 5: 44–50.

———. 1974C. *Buddhist Art in Licchavi Nepal.* Bombay: Marg Publications.

———. 1975. *Nepal: Where the Gods Are Young.* New York: Asia Society.

———. 1977. "The Bhimaratha Rite and Nepali Art." *Oriental Art* 23, no. 2: 176–89.

———. 1978. *The Arts of Nepal.* 2 vols. Vol. 2, *Painting.* Leiden: E. J. Brill.

———. 1981. *Hindu Religion and Iconology.* Los Angeles: Vichitra Press.

———. 1984. *Tibetan Painting: A Study of Tibetan Thankas Eleventh to Nineteenth Centuries.* Basel: Ravi Kumar.

———. 1985. *Art of Nepal.* Los Angeles: Los Angeles County Museum of Art.

———. 1987. "Tibetan Religious Paintings in the Virginia Museum of Fine Arts, I." *Arts in Virginia* 27, nos. 1–3: 44–65.

———. 1988. "Tibetan Religious Paintings in the Virginia Museum of Fine Arts, II." *Arts in Virginia* 28, nos. 2–3: 6–33.

———. 1990. "Arhats and Mahasiddhas in Himalayan Art." *Arts of Asia* 20, no. 1: 66–78.

———. 1990A. *Art of Tibet.* Expanded ed. Los Angeles: Los Angeles County Museum of Art.

Pal, P., and D. C. Bhattacharyya. 1969. *The Astral Divinities of Nepal.* Varanasi: Prithivi Prakashan.

Pal, P., and H. Tseng. N.d. *Lamaist Art: The Aesthetics of Harmony.* Boston: Museum of Fine Arts.

Pal, P., and L. Fournier. 1982. *A Buddhist Paradise: The Murals of Alchi.* Basel: Ravi Kumar.

Pal, P., and J. Meech-Pekarik. 1988. *Buddhist Book Illumination.* New York: Ravi Kumno.

Pathak, S. K., ed. 1986. *The Album of the Tibetan Art Collections.* Patna: K. P. Jayaswal Research Institute.

Paul, R. A. 1982. *The Tibetan Symbolic World.* Chicago: The University of Chicago Press.

Pritzker, T. J. 1989. "The Wall Paintings of Tabo." *Orientations* 20, no. 2: 38–47.

Reedy, C. L. 1986. "A Buddha within a Buddha: Two Medieval Himalayan Statues." *Arts of Asia* 16, no. 2: 94–103.

———. 1987. "Tibetan Art as an Expression of North Indian Buddhism." In D. Shimkhada, ed. *Himalayas at a Crossroads: Portrait of a Changing World.* Pasadena: Pacific Asia Museum.

———. 1991. "The Opening of Consecrated Tibetan Bronzes with Interior Contents: Scholarly, Conservation, and Ethical Considerations." *Journal of the American Institute for Conservation* 30, no. 1 (Spring): 13–34.

Reynolds, V. 1978. *Tibet: A Lost World.* New York: The American Federation of Arts.

———. 1986. "The Zimmerman Family Collection." In P. Pal, ed. *American Collectors of Asian Art.* Bombay: Marg Publications.

Reynolds, V., A. Heller, and J. Gyatso. 1986. *Catalogue of the Newark Museum Tibetan Collection, III, Sculpture and Painting.* Newark: The Newark Museum.

Rhie, M. M. 1985. "The Buddhist Art of Tibet." *Arts of Asia* 15, no. 1 (January): 82–95.

Rhie, M. M., and R. Thurman. 1984. *From the Lands of the Snows.* Amherst, Massachusetts: Mead Art Museum.

———. 1991. *Wisdom and Compassion: The Sacred Art of Tibet.* New York: Harry N. Abrams.

Roerich, G., ed. and trans. 1949–53. *The Blue Annals.* Calcutta: Royal Asiatic Society of Bengal.

———, ed. and trans. 1976. *The Blue Annals.* Delhi: Motilal Banarsidass.

Ruegg, D. S. 1966. *The Life of Bu Ston Rin Po Che.* Rome: Istituto Italiano per il Medio ed Estremo Oriente.

Schmid, T. 1958. *The Eighty-five Mahasiddhas.* Stockholm: Statenz Etnografiska Museum.

Schroeder, U. von. 1981. *Indo-Tibetan Bronzes.* Hong Kong: Visual Dharma Publications.

Singer, J. C. 1986. "An Early Painting from Tibet." *Orientations* 17, no. 7 (July): 41–45.

Slusser, M. S. 1976. "On the Antiquity of Nepalese Metalcraft." *Archives of Asian Art* 39: 80–95.

———. 1982. *Nepal Mandala: A Cultural Study of the Kathmandu Valley.* 2 vols. Princeton: Princeton University Press.

Snellgrove, D. 1959. *The Hevajra Tantra.* 2 pts. London: Oxford University Press.

———. 1987. *Indo-Tibetan Buddhism.* 2 vols. Boston: Shambhala.

Snellgrove, D., and H. E. Richardson. 1968. *A Cultural History of Tibet.* New York: Praeger.

Snellgrove, D., and T. Skorupski. 1980. *The Cultural Heritage of Ladakh.* 2 vols. Warminster, England: Aris and Phillips.

Stein, R. A. 1972. *Tibetan Civilization.* Stanford: Stanford University Press.

Tsong-ka-pa. 1977. *Tantra in Tibet.* Ed. and trans. J. Hopkins. London: Allen and Unwin.

Tsultem, N. 1986. *Development of the Mongolian National Style Painting "Mongol Zureg" in Brief.* Ulan-Bator: State Publishing House.

Tucci, G. 1949. *Tibetan Painted Scrolls.* 3 vols. Rome: Libreria dello Stato.

———. 1959. "A Tibetan Classification of Buddhist Images According to Their Style." *Artibus Asiae* 22: 179–87.

———. 1973. *The Theory and Practice of the Mandala, with Special Reference to the Modern Psychology of the Subconscious.* Trans. A. H. Broderick. New York: Samuel Weiser.

———. 1973A. *Transhimalaya archaeologia mundi.* Geneva: Nagel Publishers.

———. 1980. *The Religions of Tibet.* Trans. G. Samuel. Bombay: Allied.

———. 1988–89. *Indo-Tibetica.* 4 vols. Ed. L. Chandra. Trans. U. M. Vesci. New Delhi: Aditya Prakashav.

Vitali, R. 1990. *Early Temples of Central Tibet.* London: Serindia Press.

Waldschmidt, E., and R. Waldschmidt. 1969. *Nepal: Art Treasures from the Himalayas.* Calcutta: Oxford and IBH Publishing Co.

Wayman, A. 1973. *The Buddhist Tantras.* New York: Samuel Weiser.

———. 1977. *Yoga of the Guhyasamajatantra.* Delhi: Motilal Banarsidass.

Weyer, H. and J. C. Aschoff. 1987. *Tsaparang Tibets Grosses Geheimnis.* Freiburg: Eulen Verlag.

Whitfeld, R. 1983. *The Art of Central Asia.* 2 vols. Tokyo: Kodansha.

Woodroffe, J. 1975. *Sakti and Sakta.* Madras: Ganesh and Co.

Zimmer, H. 1984. *Artistic Form and Yoga in the Sacred Images of India.* Trans. G. Chapple and J. B. Lawson. Princeton: Princeton University Press.

Zwalf, W. 1981. *Heritage of Tibet.* London: The British Museum.

———, ed. 1985. *Buddhism: Art and Faith.* London: The British Museum.

Index

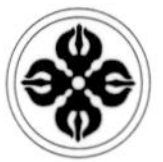

Page numbers in italics *refer to illustrations.*

Photograph Credits

Aida and Robert Mates: nos. 2–8, 11–15, 18, 20, 21, 23–25, 27–52, 56, 57a, 59–63, 68–84, 86–92, 94–103, 105–119
Otto E. Nelson: nos. 1, 9, 10, 16, 17, 19, 22, 26, 53–55, 57b, 58, 60, 64, 66
John Bigelow Taylor: nos. 58, 65, 67, 85, 93, 104